MASTER VISUALLY®

by Rob Tidrow

Visual®

Microsoft®

Windows Vista™

Master VISUALLY Microsoft® Windows Vista™

Published by
Wiley Publishing, Inc.
111 River Street
Hoboken, NJ 07030-5774

Published simultaneously in Canada

Library of Congress Control Number: 2006939468

ISBN: 978-0-470-04577-0

Manufactured in the United States of America

10 9 8 7 6 5 4 3 2 1

Trademark Acknowledgments

Wiley, the Wiley Publishing logo, Visual, the Visual logo, Master VISUALLY, Read Less - Learn More and related trade dress are trademarks or registered trademarks of John Wiley & Sons, Inc. and/or its affiliates. Windows Vista is a trademark of Microsoft Corporation in the U.S. and/or other countries. All other trademarks are the property of their respective owners. Wiley Publishing, Inc. is not associated with any product or vendor mentioned in this book.

Contact Us

For general information on our other products and services please contact our Customer Care Department within the U.S. at 800-762-2974, outside the U.S. at 317-572-3993 or fax 317-572-4002.

For technical support please visit www.wiley.com/techsupport.

Wiley Publishing, Inc.

U.S. Sales

Contact Wiley
at (800) 762-2974 or
fax (317) 572-4002.

Praise for Visual Books...

"If you have to see it to believe it, this is the book for you!"

—PC World

"A master tutorial/reference — from the leaders in visual learning!"

—Infoworld

"A publishing concept whose time has come!"

—The Globe and Mail

"Just wanted to say THANK YOU to your company for providing books which make learning fast, easy, and exciting! I learn visually so your books have helped me greatly — from Windows instruction to Web development. Best wishes for continued success."

—Angela J. Barker (Springfield, MO)

"I have over the last 10–15 years purchased thousands of dollars worth of computer books but find your books the most easily read, best set out, and most helpful and easily understood books on software and computers I have ever read. Please keep up the good work."

—John Gatt (Adamstown Heights, Australia)

"You're marvelous! I am greatly in your debt."

—Patrick Baird (Lacey, WA)

"I am an avid fan of your Visual books. If I need to learn anything, I just buy one of your books and learn the topic in no time. Wonders! I have even trained my friends to give me Visual books as gifts."

—Illona Bergstrom (Aventura, FL)

"I have quite a few of your Visual books and have been very pleased with all of them. I love the way the lessons are presented!"

—Mary Jane Newman (Yorba Linda, CA)

"Like a lot of other people, I understand things best when I see them visually. Your books really make learning easy and life more fun."

—John T. Frey (Cadillac, MI)

"Your Visual books have been a great help to me. I now have a number of your books and they are all great. My friends always ask to borrow my Visual books — trouble is, I always have to ask for them back!"

—John Robson
(Brampton, Ontario, Canada)

"I write to extend my thanks and appreciation for your books. They are clear, easy to follow, and straight to the point. Keep up the good work! I bought several of your books and they are just right! No regrets! I will always buy your books because they are the best."

—Seward Kollie (Dakar, Senegal)

"What fantastic teaching books you have produced! Congratulations to you and your staff."

—Bruno Tonon (Melbourne, Australia)

"Thank you for the wonderful books you produce. It wasn't until I was an adult that I discovered how I learn — visually. Although a few publishers claim to present the materially visually, nothing compares to Visual books. I love the simple layout. Everything is easy to follow. I can just grab a book and use it at my computer, lesson by lesson. And I understand the material! You really know the way I think and learn. Thanks so much!"

—Stacey Han (Avondale, AZ)

"The Greatest. This whole series is the best computer-learning tool of any kind I've ever seen."

—Joe Orr (Brooklyn, NY)

Credits

About the Author

Rob Tidrow is a freelance writer and consultant for Tidrow Communications, Inc., a firm specializing in content creation and delivery. Rob has authored or co-authored over 30 books on a wide variety of computer and technical topics, including Microsoft Windows Vista, Wireless Networking technologies, Microsoft Windows XP, Microsoft Outlook 2003, Windows 2003 Server, and Microsoft Internet Information Server. His most current work is *Teach Yourself Visually Wireless Networking*. He lives in Centerville, Indiana with his wife Tammy and their two sons, Adam and Wesley. You can reach him robtidrow@yahoo.com.

Author's Acknowledgments

I wish to thank the following people for their outstanding commitment to excellence on this book: Jody Lefevere, acquisitions editor; Jenny Watson, acquisitions editor, Jade Williams, project editor; Carole McClendon, literary agent; and the production crew. I would also like to thank my wife, Tammy, and my sons Adam and Wesley, for continuing to give me encouragement and motivation to finish. —**Rob Tidrow**

PART I — Setting Up Windows Vista

1) Preparing for Installation
2) Installing Windows Vista
3) Customizing and Updating Windows Vista

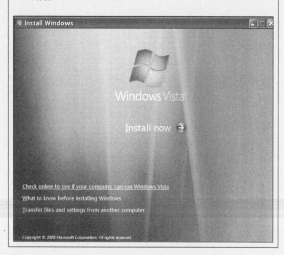

PART II — Managing the Desktop Environment

4) Using the Windows Vista Interface
5) Customizing the Desktop
6) Managing Users
7) Managing Files and Folders
8) Managing Security

PART III — Mastering Multimedia with Windows Vista

9) Managing Your Music with Windows Media Player 11
10) Working with Multimedia Hardware
11) Creating Digital Content with Windows Vista
12) Enjoying Digital Entertainment with Media Center

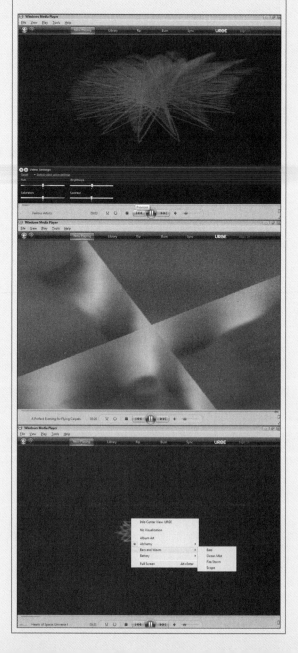

WHAT'S INSIDE

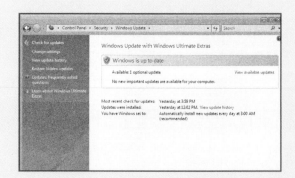

TABLE OF CONTENTS

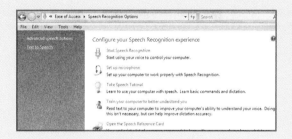

⑤ Customizing the Desktop

⑥ Managing Users

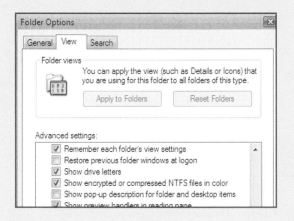

PART III

Mastering Multimedia with Windows Vista

9 Managing Your Music with Windows Media Player 11

TABLE OF CONTENTS

PART IV

Using Windows Vista Productivity Features

TABLE OF CONTENTS

PART VI   Managing the Hardware Environment

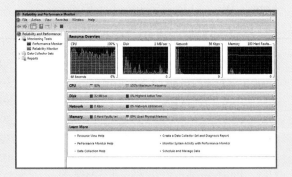

TABLE OF CONTENTS

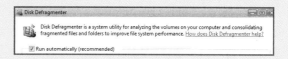

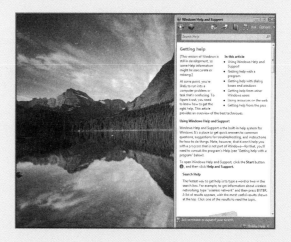

How to Use this Master VISUALLY Book

Do you look at the pictures in a book or newspaper before anything else on a page? Would you rather see an image than read how to do something? Search no further. This book is for you. Opening *Master VISUALLY Microsoft Windows Vista* allows you to read less and learn more about the Windows Vista system.

Who Needs This Book

This book is for a reader who has never used this particular technology or software application. Windows novices can also find full coverage of many basic Windows tasks in *Teach Yourself VISUALLY Windows Vista*. It is also for more computer literate individuals who want to expand their knowledge of the different features that Windows Vista has to offer.

Book Organization

Master VISUALLY Microsoft Windows Vista has 25 chapters and is divided into six parts.

Part I – Setting Up Windows Vista

Chapter 1 introduces Microsoft Windows Vista and helps prepare you for installing or upgrading to Microsoft's desktop operating system.

Chapter 2 walks through the different ways you can install Windows Vista and provides some tools to help with troubleshooting if problems arise in the future.

Chapter 3 goes "under the hood" and shows you how to control the fundamental ways that Windows functions on your desktop.

Part II – Managing the Desktop Environment

Chapters 4 and 5 explain the many ways to maneuver through the Windows Vista interface, how to use the new Vista Explorers, how to use the new Flip 3D and Live Taskbar features, and how to customize the desktop.

Chapter 6 covers how to add, configure, and customize user accounts in Windows Vista.

Chapter 7 shows you how to use Windows Vista's advanced file system to share, compress, encrypt, and customize folders and file properties.

Chapter 8 includes information on the updated and advanced Windows Security Center, Windows Firewall, Windows Defender, antivirus software, and more.

Part III – Mastering Multimedia with Windows Vista

In Chapter 9, you find out how to take advantage of Windows Vista's multimedia features, including how to rip, play, and burn music tracks, and how to configure Vista for external digital devices such as scanners and cameras.

Chapter 10 details how to use your multimedia hardware, such as your CD and DVD burners, portable media devices, and scanners, with Windows Vista.

In Chapter 11, you are shown how to create and edit digital content—photos and videos—using Windows Vista's new photo software, Windows Photo Gallery.

One of the most impressive features of Windows Vista is its inclusion of the improved Media Center. This feature enables Vista to control all your media devices in one location. Chapter 12 shows how to use Media Center to handle your music, television, DVD, and other devices.

Part IV Using Windows Vista Productivity Features

Chapter 13 shows you how to use Windows Mail, the updated e-mail application that was named Outlook Express in previous Windows releases.

To help you get a grasp on you schedules, Chapter 14 provides information on the new Windows Calendar tool. You learn how to set appointments, send e-mail invitations to meetings, set alarms, publish your calendar as an iCalendar, and more.

Chapter 15 is all about Microsoft Fax and Scanning, the new fax and scanning tool provided with Microsoft Vista.

Part V – Networking with Windows Vista

Chapter 16 details how you can connect to networks — local area networks, wide area networks, wireless networks, and the Internet — as well as use the Sync Center to keep your information in sync.

With Chapter 17, you learn how to use Internet Explorer 7, the updated Web browser available with Windows Vista, including how to use tabs, subscribe to and read BSS feeds, and use the Phishing Filter.

You can use Chapter 18 to take advantage of network services, including sharing printers, using Remote Desktop and Remote Assistance, and how to troubleshoot network errors.

If you want to set up a Web site on your Windows Vista computer, Chapter 19 covers Internet Information Service and its accessories — FTP server, SMTP server, and configuring your default page settings.

Chapter 20 shows how to use Windows Vista on a Windows Server 2003 domain.

Part VI – Managing the Hardware Environment

Chapter 21 explains how to perform essential tasks relating to your computer's hardware environment, such as scheduling maintenance tasks and monitoring performance.

Chapter 22 shows you how to work with hard drives installed on Windows Vista computers, including create new disk partitions and setting disk quotas.

Chapter 23 describes how to perform the most frequent tasks related to portable computers, such as working with wireless networks, configuring power management settings, and working with VPNs.

Chapter 24 describes several basic ways to optimize your PC's performance.

Chapter 25 closes with ways to troubleshoot Windows Vista, including why and how to run in Safe Mode in case Windows does not boot correctly, and how to restore Windows Vista.

HOW TO USE THIS BOOK

Chapter Organization

This book consists of sections, all listed in the book's table of contents. A *section* is a set of steps that show you how to complete a specific computer task.

Each section, usually contained on two facing pages, has an introduction to the task at hand, a set of full-color screen shots and steps that walk you through the task, and a set of tips. This format allows you to quickly look at a topic of interest and learn it instantly.

Chapters group together three or more sections with a common theme. A chapter may also contain pages that give you the background information needed to understand the sections in a chapter.

What You Need to Use This Book

To perform the tasks in this book, you need a computer with these specific requirements.

Windows Vista Ultimate Edition, Windows Vista Home Basic, Home Premium, or Business Editions.

- 512 MB RAM
- PC with 800 MHz 32-bit (x86) or 64-bit (x64) CPU
- 15 GB of available hard disk space
- CD or DVD drive
- Keyboard and pointing device such as a mouse
- SuperVGA display capable of a resolution of 800x600 or greater
- Internet connectivity strongly recommended

The Conventions in This Book

A number of typographic and layout styles have been used throughout *Master VISUALLY Microsoft Windows Vista* to distinguish different types of information.

Using the Mouse

This book uses the following conventions to describe the actions you perform when using the mouse:

Click

Press your left mouse button once. You generally click your mouse on something to select something on the screen.

Double-click

Press your left mouse button twice. Double-clicking something on the computer screen generally opens whatever item you have double-clicked.

Right-click

Press your right mouse button. When you right-click anything on the computer screen, the program displays a shortcut menu containing commands specific to the selected item.

Click and Drag, and Release the Mouse

Move your mouse pointer and hover it over an item on the screen. Press and hold down the left mouse button. Now, move the mouse to where you want to place the item and then release the button. You use this method to move an item from one area of the computer screen to another.

Bold

Bold type represents the names of commands and options with which you interact. Bold type also indicates text and numbers that you must type into a dialog box or window.

Italics

Italic words introduce a new term and are followed by a definition.

Numbered Steps

You must perform the instructions in numbered steps in order to successfully complete a section and achieve the final results.

Bulleted Steps

These steps point out various optional features. You do not have to perform these steps; they simply give additional information about a feature.

Indented Text

Indented text tells you what the program does in response to you following a numbered step. For example, if you click a certain menu command, a dialog box may appear, or a window may open. Indented text may also tell you what the final result is when you follow a set of numbered steps.

Notes

Notes give additional information. They may describe special conditions that may occur during an operation. They may warn you of a situation that you want to avoid, for example, the loss of data. A note may also cross reference a related area of the book. A cross reference may guide you to another chapter, or another section within the current chapter.

Icons and Buttons

Icons and buttons are graphical representations within the text. They show you exactly what you need to click to perform a step.

 You can easily identify the tips in any section by looking for the Master It icon. Master It offer additional information, including tips, hints, and tricks. You can use the Master It information to go beyond what you have learn learned in the steps.

Disclaimer

In order to get this information to you in a timely manner, this book was based on a pre-release version of Microsoft Vista/Microsoft Office 2007. There may be some minor changes between the screenshots in this book and what you see on your desktop. As always, Microsoft has the final word on how programs look and function; if you have any questions or see any discrepancies, consult the online help for further information about the software.

3 Customizing and Updating Windows Vista

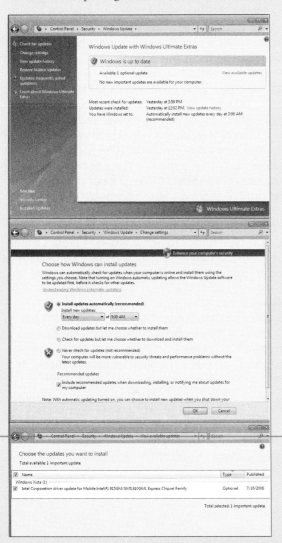

Differences Between Vista Editions

Microsoft Windows Vista is a desktop operating system designed for both home and professional use. It comes in several different versions, including Home Basic, Home Premium, Ultimate, Business, and Enterprise.

Windows Vista Ultimate includes all the best business, mobile, and entertainment features of the other versions of Windows Vista. It brings together many of the consumer features found in earlier versions of Windows, such as Windows XP and Windows Me, and business features found in Windows 2002, and merges them into a single, flexible, and powerful desktop operating system.

Searching and Encrypted Files

Ultimate includes better support for networking, file searching, and managing folders. It provides an outstanding environment for those users who use their laptops both at work and at home. Improved features include enhanced security from Windows BitLocker Drive Encryption technology. BitLocker helps secure all files on a computer, including system files, so data is protected if the computer is stolen or lost. The Windows Search tool provides improved indexing and searching features to help locate files and folders on your computer. Because all your files are indexed, Windows Search does not have to look through your entire hard disk to locate files and folders. This makes searching very fast. Search results are returned almost as soon as you start your search. After you run a search, you can save searches to a file so you can use them later.

Improved Collaboration

Windows Vista includes Windows Meeting Space. Meeting Space provides users with the capability to communicate between computers in real time in "virtual" meetings. Users can edit documents simultaneously, write notes to each other, share a program on the desktop, share files, and perform other tasks. Meeting Space can be used whenever two or more computers can connect with each other over a network, including a wireless one. Windows Vista also includes a link to download the new Windows Live Messenger program, which enables you to communicate over the Internet using Internet chat.

Enhanced Entertainment Support

The Home Premium and Ultimate editions include Windows Media Center. Windows Media Center provides tools and features that help users get the most out of their entertainment experiences. With Media Center, you can use Windows to search your system for media files — music, pictures, and videos — to play back music, show picture slide shows, and play back video files stored on your computer and other entertainment devices. By adding a TV tuner card or USB device to your computer, you can view television shows through your computer and display them on your computer monitor, a TV, or projector. Media Center also, enables you to record television shows, pause and rewind live TV, and play back recorded shows. Media Center also makes it easy to burn DVDs or CDs of your stored music, video, and picture files.

Remote Desktop

Remote desktop support enables you to access Windows Vista remotely from another Windows computer, so you can control your computer and work with all your data and applications while away from your home or office. The Windows Vista Home Basic and Home Premium editions enable you to set up your computer only as a client computer so others can access your computer with Remote Desktop. However, with the Vista Business, Enterprise, and Ultimate editions, you can set up your computer as a client and a host so you can access other clients.

Improved Network Integration

The Vista Home Basic and Home Premium editions leave out one of the single biggest features found in the Business, Enterprise, and Ultimate editions: the capability to participate in a Windows Server domain. Active Directory support is not included, so features such as Group Policy, centralized administration, roaming user profiles, and access control to files, folders, and applications is not available. Although most homes probably do not have an Active Directory network installed for casual or home use, small office/home office (SOHO) environments or small businesses all the way up to multinational corporations may want to install Active Directory because of the degree of control and reduced maintenance costs it provides.

Enhanced Security Features

Windows Vista includes the Security Center interface that enables users to manage their security and virus protection applications in one spot. You can set up the Windows Firewall, configure Automatic Updating settings, check out your malware protection programs, and configure other security settings. These include antivirus and spyware protection programs. These other settings include Internet security settings and user account control. All versions of Windows Vista include the Security Center tool. In addition to these security features, the new Internet Explorer 7 Web browser can block pop-up ads and warn you when you are visiting a site that has been reported as a phishing site. *Phishing sites* are Web sites that appear to be legitimate sites but are actually designed to trick you into providing your personal and confidential information. You also can report sites to the Microsoft Anti-Phishing site that you suspect may be phishing sites.

Web Services

The Home editions lack the capability to run scaled-down Web Services. The Business, Enterprise, and Ultimate editions can be set up to support a Web server, a File Transfer Protocol (FTP) server, and a Telnet server. These services support a maximum of ten connections, so it is not recommended that they be used for significant Web traffic. However, for users testing and developing Web Services for later deployment on the Internet, the Ultimate Edition is excellent for creating and refining basic Web Services.

Built-In Software

Windows Vista has several new programs, including Windows Calendar, Windows Mail, Windows Slideshow, Windows Photo Gallery, Windows Speech Recognition, Network Projection, Windows Fax and Scan, Windows Sidebar, Windows DVD Maker, and new premium games. Windows Vista also has upgraded and improved bundled programs you get with Windows, including Windows Movie Maker 6, Internet Explorer 7, Windows Paint, and Windows Media Player 11. Some of these programs, such as Windows Mail —replacing Microsoft Outlook Express — Windows Sidebar, and Windows Calendar are available in all editions. However, to get all of them, you will need to purchase Windows Ultimate.

Integrated Versions

As Windows has grown in popularity, niche versions of it have been created to support specific hardware configurations. In the past, Microsoft manufactured Windows Media Center Edition and Tablet PC Edition, as separate installed operating systems. Now Windows Vista integrates those features into the Windows Vista Home Premium, Windows Vista Business, Windows Vista Enterprise, and Windows Vista Ultimate versions. Another feature of Windows Vista is that you do not have to obtain separate installation discs for the version of Windows Vista you want to install. All versions come on the same DVD. You purchase a license for the version you want to install, type in the authentication key for that version, and Windows installs the version you paid for. If you decide later to upgrade to a different version, such as from Windows Vista Home Premium to Windows Vista Ultimate, simply purchase a license for that version and re-run the installation program, selecting the upgraded version.

Collect System Information

Microsoft has made great advances in making installation and configuration simpler for end users and system administrators alike. For the most part, the process can be done with little to no intervention. With the Windows Vista Upgrade Advisor, you can see if your computer is capable of running Windows Vista. The Windows Vista Upgrade Advisor can be run by visiting the Get Ready Web site at www.microsoft.com/windowsvista/upgradeadvisor/default.mspx and clicking the Windows Vista Upgrade Advisor RC link. For instance, you may want to run the Advisor prior to purchasing Windows Vista to ensure your current computer meets the system requirements for installing Vista. For more information, see the "Use the Upgrade Advisor" section.

However, there is still no substitute for knowing the details of what hardware, firmware, and connectivity are being configured on the system. Windows asks for some of this information not only during different phases of configuration, but also if there are problems with installing new hardware, software, or driver updates; having this information at hand goes a long way in helping to solve such problems.

If you plan to do a number of installations, or have several computers at home that you maintain, you should collect the necessary information for each computer and keep it in a safe place where it can be referred to when needed, such as in a notebook or on a CD-ROM with the necessary drivers.

Use the SysInfo Utility

If you are running Windows XP, you can print much of the necessary information with the SysInfo utility. Click Start, All Programs, Accessories, System Tools, and then System Information. After the window has refreshed, click File and then Print to print a list of the hardware components, driver information, and other useful details. The report is exhaustive and may take several pages to report. If you do not want to print the report, you can export the report as a text file and view it on screen. If you do this, you may want to save the file to a removable disk or network drive so you can view the report on a different computer if your computer fails to start after Windows Vista installs. This will help with troubleshooting installation problems, for instance. To export a file in SysInfo, choose the File menu and then click Export. Type a name for the report in the Export As dialog box. Click Save. The file is saved as .txt text file.

Hardware Model Numbers

If you purchased a computer from a hardware vendor, make sure you have a list of the model numbers for all the components in your system: motherboard, video card, hard drives, CD or DVD drive, and network card. You will need this information if you have to find and install updated device drivers for your system, or if there are known incompatibilities between some of the devices. In some cases, the only way to find out the particular model number of a component is to open the computer case and look at the component in question.

Firmware Versions

Some hardware devices have device-specific codes embedded in them, called *firmware*. Firmware enables features and functions so that operating systems can make the best use of the hardware. Devices that often have firmware are motherboards (basic input/output system, or BIOS), CD or DVD drives, network cards, and routers. Sometimes video cards have firmware as well. Check with each device's manufacturer to see if updated firmware is available for your device. *Caution:* You can completely disable hardware if you flash it with the wrong firmware, such as the wrong BIOS for your motherboard. Follow the manufacturer's instructions exactly, or have a computer professional help you.

Device Drivers

Device drivers are hardware-specific code used by the operating system so that it can interact with, manage, and control its functions. Windows Vista ships with device drivers for a large number of hardware devices on the market, and new ones are sometimes made available on the Windows Update site. See Chapter 3 for information on the Windows Update service. You should check with the device manufacturer to see if new drivers have been made available since Windows Vista's publication. The Internet offers another source for updated device drivers. By using search engines, such as Google, Yahoo, and Live Search, you can type in the make and model of your hardware device and search for sites that include links to download updated drivers. Some sites, such as DriverGuide.Com, specialize in helping users find updated device drivers. DriverGuide.Com provides thousands of links to different device drivers, as well as a forum area where users post messages and questions about problems and concerns they have with specific hardware devices. When you find a driver you are looking for, you simply download it to your computer and install it.

File System Type

If you are performing an upgrade from an earlier version of Windows, find out the file system type in use: File Allocation Table (FAT), FAT32, or New Technology File System (NTFS). The first two of these are more likely found on Windows 9x or Windows Me machines, whereas NTFS is more likely found on Windows XP, NT, or Windows 2000 machines. The file system type is relevant. Vista uses NTFS so your disk drives must support that file system type. In most cases, especially with drives that have capacities large enough to support Windows Vista (over 40GB), your system will support NTFS. You will also want to make sure that any file-system utilities that are installed on your computer, such as Symantec's Norton Utilities, are supported by Windows Vista. If the version of the file system utility you have running on your computer is not Windows Vista compatible, you should uninstall it before installing Windows Vista. If you leave it installed, you may encounter problems with Windows Vista, or Windows Vista may not install at all.

Internet Settings

Internet connectivity is perhaps the single most important function of any computer today. Whether you are connected to the Internet through a cable modem, an independent Internet service provider (ISP), or your company's service provider, you should have the necessary connection information so that you can set up your new computer properly. This information may already be available on your computer, or you may need to get it from your system administrator. On existing Windows systems, you can find this information by choosing Control Panel and then Network Connections. Right-click a connection and choose Properties. The Properties dialog box for that network connection appears. Gather information from the Internet Protocol (TCP/IP) item on the General tab by double-clicking it. Many times the IP address is obtained automatically, which will be specified on the TCP/IP Properties dialog box. However, if a specific IP address is given, write it down in case you need to input it later during Windows Vista setup.

Use the Upgrade Advisor

The Upgrade Advisor is one of the most useful tools available to anyone upgrading an older version of Windows to Windows Vista. The Upgrade Advisor takes an inventory of system hardware, software, and device drivers; compares the existing system against a component database; and presents a report of its findings. It lets you know if your system needs a hardware upgrade to meet minimum system requirements for Windows Vista or if your hardware is on the Windows Hardware Compatibility List (WHCL). This way you approach an upgrade forewarned and forearmed, able to correct any potential pitfalls or shortcomings before installation.

Although the Upgrade Advisor does not guarantee it will find all known problems or system incompatibilities, it does help you avoid ones that have previously been reported to Microsoft and will provide suggestions on how to avoid the problems, for example, install more memory, obtain upgraded device drivers, or make more room on a hard drive.

You can run the Upgrade Advisor on Windows XP-based systems; however, you must have an Internet connection to use it.

Use the Upgrade Advisor

① Connect to the Internet.

② Insert the Windows Vista CD.

The Install Windows screen appears.

Note: You can also browse to the CD drive and click Setup to launch the CD.

③ Click the Check compatibility online option.

Internet Explorer opens with the Windows Vista Upgrade Advisor Web page.

④ Click the Windows Vista Upgrade Advisor link.

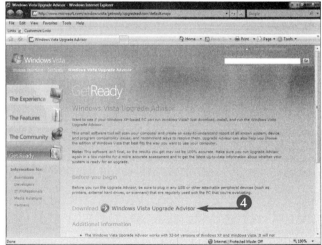

The File Download - Security Warning window appears.

5 Click Run.

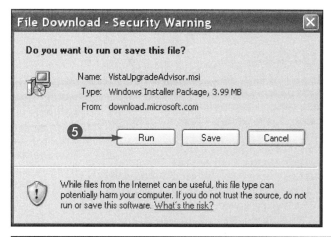

The Upgrade Advisor downloads to your computer.

6 Click Run.

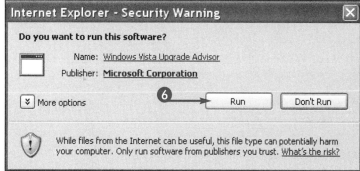

What is the difference between the minimum and recommended system requirements for Windows Vista?

▼ Microsoft uses the term *minimum* for the bare-bones system configuration needed to run an operating system. However, even though you can install Windows Vista on a minimum configuration, system performance is barely tolerable, especially if you run any applications that take significant amounts of memory or processing power. The "recommended" system configuration should be considered the bare minimum for minimally tolerable performance. Most blocking issues reported by the Upgrade Advisor are based on the minimum hardware requirements, not the recommended ones.

Should I upgrade from the recommended system requirements?

▼ To install the basics for Windows Vista, you will need a computer that has an 800 MHz processor, 512MB of RAM, and a hard drive with a capacity of at least 20GB. The hard drive also must have at least 15GB free to install Vista. For advanced features, however, you may need a computer with more memory and faster processor speeds than the basic minium. Finally, to take advantage of Vista's high-end graphics capabilities, you need a graphics card that is compatible with DirectX 9, uses the Windows Display Driver Model (WDDM) driver, and has a minimum of 64MB of video RAM.

continued

Use the Upgrade Advisor
(Continued)

The Upgrade Advisor generates two types of errors: blocking errors and incompatibility warnings. *Blocking errors* are ones that prevent you from running the installation program at all, such as insufficient disk space or RAM. *Incompatibility warnings* are generated either for hardware that may need additional files marked with the red Do Not Enter symbol or for software that does not support Windows Vista marked with the yellow warning triangle. The incompatibility warnings do not stop the upgrade process, but the hardware and software may not function properly, or at all, after the upgrade.

The Upgrade Advisor bases its findings on the WHCL. The warnings do not mean that your existing hardware or software will not work, only that there are known problems that have been reported to Microsoft, or that the particular hardware and software has not been tested by Microsoft. In any event, you should check the hardware and software manufacturers' Web sites to see if known problems exist, or if updated components are available.

The Welcome to the Microsoft Windows Vista Advisor Setup Wizard screen appears.

7 Click Next.

The License Agreement screen appears.

8 Click the I Agree option (○ changes to ◉).

9 Click Next.

The Select Installation Folder screen appears.

⑩ Click Next.

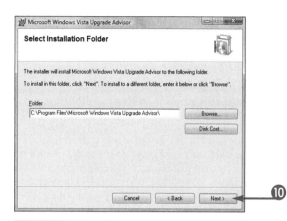

The Confirm Installation screen appears.

⑪ Click Next.

The Upgrade Advisor installs on your computer.

Does the Upgrade Compatibility Wizard work with all versions of Windows?

▼ The Wizard does not work with Windows 95 or Windows NT 3.5x. You need to upgrade Windows 95 to Windows 98 or later, and upgrade Windows NT 3.5x to Windows NT 4.0 or later. If you are running those earlier versions, upgrading your hardware and performing a new install may be easier than upgrading your operating system.

What if I want to check compatibility before I buy Windows Vista?

▼ You can still use the Upgrade Advisor, but you will have to locate it manually through your Web browser. You can download the Advisor at www.microsoft.com/windowsvista/getready/upgradeadvisor/default.mspx and then run it on your computer.

I have a laptop, and Upgrade Advisor recommends upgrading my hardware. Can I do this?

▼ For some hardware devices, you can upgrade a laptop just like any other computer. For example, if the Upgrade Advisor recommends that additional memory be installed in your laptop, you can do this by purchasing memory cards for your type of laptop. Similarly, most laptops can have their hard drives upgraded or CD-ROM drives swapped out for DVD drives. One hardware upgrade you cannot do on most laptops is upgrade the graphics card. To do this, you need to contact the manufacturer and inquire if your laptop can have a different graphics card inserted.

continued

Use the Upgrade Advisor
(Continued)

The Upgrade Advisor helps you determine the edition of Windows that is best suited for your computing needs. For instance, if you use your computer strictly for home use and do not connect to a company computer over the telephone or Internet, you may just want to purchase Windows Vista Home Basic. However, if you need to connect your computer to a company-wide network and you need the most advanced data security tools offered for Windows, the best route might be to go with Windows Vista Enterprise or Windows Vista Ultimate.

Other factors to consider when upgrading your computer include the multimedia devices you plan to use, your wireless networking needs, network backups, Windows Media Center needs, and the like. In addition, if you plan to create your own DVDs and you want to use Windows DVD Maker, you will need to purchase Windows Vista Home Premium or Windows Vista Ultimate.

Use the Upgrade Advisor (continued)

The Installation Complete screen appears.

⑫ Click Close.

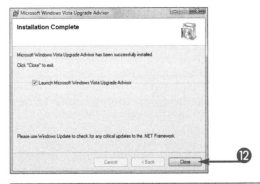

The Welcome to Windows Vista Upgrade Advisor Web page appears.

⑬ Click Start Scan.

The Scanning System page of the Upgrade Advisor appears.

When the scan finishes, the Scan complete page appears.

⑭ Click the See Details button. (☐ changes to ☑).

The Your computer can run Windows Vista screen appears.

⑮ Click the Close box.

The Upgrade Advisor window closes.

What does the Upgrade Advisor check?

▼ The Upgrade Advisor checks your system for incompatibilities and lists common tasks that you may use with your computer to help you figure out which edition of Windows you should purchase. It creates a summary report, showing you problems or potential problems that may occur. When the Upgrade Advisor finishes, you can view information about your system, including System Requirements, Devices, and Programs. To read information about these topics, click the corresponding See Details button at the bottom of the Your Computer Can Run Windows Vista page. For example, if you click the See Details button in the System Requirements section, you are shown a report about any issues about the hardware on your computer.

What if the Upgrade Advisor suggests an edition of Windows that is not powerful enough for what I need?

▼ If the Upgrade Advisor suggests an edition lower than what you think you need, you will probably need to upgrade your hardware to meet the basic requirements of that edition. For example, you want to purchase Windows Vista Ultimate but the Advisor suggests Windows Vista Home Basic. If you plan to purchase the Enterprise or Ultimate editions of Vista, check the most current system requirements for those editions and make sure your system meets or exceeds those requirements. The latest requirements can be found at www.microsoft.com/windowsvista/getready/upgradeadvisor/faq.mspx.

Transfer Files and Settings

If you are performing a new install rather than an upgrade, you can use another wizard to transfer existing files and settings to Windows Vista. The time-saving Windows Easy Transfer restores personal desktop settings and menu options that you set up previously in other versions of Windows, including user accounts, programs, Internet Explorer security settings, bookmarks, and cookies.

Before running the Windows Easy Transfer wizard, you should perform some maintenance on your existing system. Run the Disk Cleanup utility to remove temporary files and Internet Explorer cached files; this reduces the number of files to be transferred.

You should also be connected to a network share or have a CD or DVD burner available, because you probably cannot fit all the necessary files onto a floppy disk. You can save the files to a different partition on the same hard drive if you are not deleting or reformatting it during the install process. You can also install the settings directly across a network to the new computer. Make sure you have the necessary shares and permissions set up before you do so.

Transfer Files and Settings

① Close all programs.

② Insert the Windows Vista CD.

The Install Windows screen appears.

Note: You can also browse to the DVD drive and click Setup to launch the DVD.

③ Click Transfer files and settings from another computer.

The Welcome to Windows Easy Transfer screen appears.

④ Click Next.

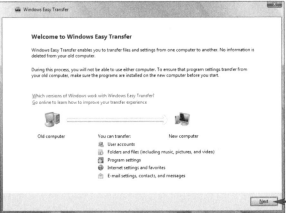

The Which computer are you using now
screen appears.

⑤ Click My old computer.

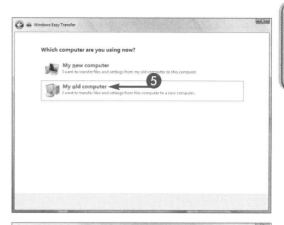

The Choose how to transfer files and settings
to your new computer screen appears.

⑥ Click a transfer method to specify how you
want Windows Easy Transfer to transfer your
files and settings to the new computer.

Can I use the Windows Easy Transfer wizard to keep my settings in a dual-boot environment?	**Does the Windows Easy Transfer wizard transfer any special folders I have set up on my computer?**	**I ran the Windows Easy Transfer wizard, but when I log in to the new computer I do not see the files anywhere. Why is this?**
▼ Yes. You can transfer the necessary settings to the new Windows Vista installation if you have installed Windows Vista to a different partition. Otherwise, you run the risk of overwriting settings in the shared partition. See Chapter 2 for more information on installation methods and caveats.	▼ The Windows Easy Transfer wizard packages up any files and folders that you add to it during the transfer process, but it does not always create special folders or paths on the new computer. If you have a special share that you want to transfer, re-create the share on the new computer before you run the wizard.	▼ When you import the files and folders to the new system, you must be logged in as the same user. If there are Active Directory policies preventing you from logging in at more than one computer at a time, you need to save the files to an intermediate share first.

continued

Transfer Files and Settings
(Continued)

The Windows Easy Transfer moves a large number of files and settings by default. It can also be used to move additional files and folders that you can select when you run the program. You can point the program at any folder and move its contents, or you can select files by file type and have those moved to the new system.

Moving only settings does not take up much space. Moving files, especially if you have selected additional files and folders, takes up much more space. Plan on anywhere from 5MB to 5GB of space needed on the target system — more if you choose to move movie, multimedia, or music files such as MP3s.

Although the program is good about packing up settings, keep a few caveats for the target system in mind. First, the program moves only settings, not entire applications. Second, the specific application should be installed on the target system first, before the settings are imported. Third, the program supports only some third-party applications or may support only later versions. An updated list of supported applications can be found at http://support.microsoft.com/default.aspx?scid=kb;en-us;304903.

Transfer Files and Settings *(continued)*

The Choose how to transfer files and settings over a network screen appears.

7 Click Copy to and from a network location to specify that Windows Easy Transfer is to copy files to a shared network location.

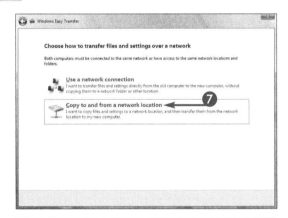

The Choose a network location screen appears.

8 Type the network location where you want to store your files.

- You can click Browse to find a network location where you want to store your files.

9 Click Next.

Note: *If the Windows Security Alert appears, click Unblock.*

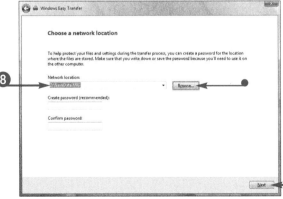

The What do you want to transfer to your new computer screen appears.

⑩ Click All user accounts, files, and settings to specify that you want Windows Easy Transfer to save those files to transfer.

The Review selected files and settings screen appears.

⑪ Click Transfer for Windows Easy Transfer to save your files and settings to the network location.

The You're ready to transfer files and settings to your new computer screen appears.

⑫ Click Close to close the Windows Easy Transfer wizard.

The Windows desktop appears.

What information is migrated by the Windows Easy Transfer wizard?

▼ The Windows Easy Transfer wizard is designed to transfer settings for Windows, some Windows applications, and user files. The default settings include the following.

Default Settings	Description
Hardware settings	Mouse, keyboard, regional settings, network, dial-up, and printer driver settings
Desktop settings	Wallpaper, colors, screen saver, menu and taskbar options, and folder and audio settings
Software settings	Internet Explorer bookmarks and cookies, Microsoft Office settings, Outlook and Outlook Express settings, mail folders and address books, and some third-party application settings
Files and folders	Desktop, My Documents, My Pictures, My Favorites, shared desktop, and fonts

How long does the Windows Easy Transfer wizard take to finish?

▼ That depends on how many files you selected to transfer and the speed of your computer. If you store a number of large files, such as pictures, music files, and videos on your computer, Windows Easy Transfer can take several hours to complete. However, if you have just a handful of documents, saved e-mail, and similar files, you can expect Windows Easy Transfer to finish within a few minutes.

Restore Files and Settings

After you have collected your files and settings from the source computer, you can import and install them onto the target computer running Windows Vista. Only Windows Vista natively ships Windows Easy Transfer as part of the operating system, giving you easy access to the Windows Easy Transfer wizard for any new installations you may be creating. Windows XP, SP2 did include the Files and Settings Transfer Wizard, the predecessor to the Windows Easy Transfer wizard.

Windows Easy Transfer contains a safety valve: If you are running the Windows Easy Transfer wizard from Windows Vista, it gives you the opportunity to create a

Windows Easy Transfer wizard Disk that you can run on the source machine without requiring the Windows Vista install disk. This shortcut is extremely handy and gives you the ability to create another tool for your support toolbox so that you do not have to carry around the Windows Vista install disk, which is worth its weight in gold.

The following task assumes you have already run the Windows Easy Transfer wizard to collect settings on the source computer. If you have not, see the "Transfer Files and Settings" section for more information.

Restore Files and Settings

① Start the Windows Easy Transfer program on your new computer.

The Welcome to Windows Easy Transfer screen appears.

② Click Next.

The Do you want to start a new transfer or continue one in progress screen appears.

③ Click Start a new transfer to indicate you are ready to transfer files to this computer.

The Which computer are you using now screen appears.

④ Click My new computer to indicate that you are at your new computer.

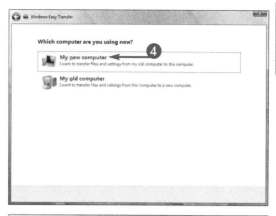

The Do you have an Easy Transfer Cable screen appears.

⑤ Click No, show me more options to indicate you want to use a network to transfer files.

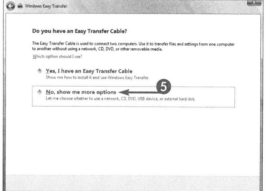

I have several users I need to migrate to new computers. Should I use Windows Easy Transfer for all of them?

▼ Windows Easy Transfer is an ideal tool if you have only a few users that you need to migrate to Windows Vista, such as in a home or a small office or home office (SOHO) environment. If you are using Active Directory, there may be easier ways to migrate users. See Chapter 10 for information on working with Active Directory.

Why do I get a Security Alert when I try to run the Windows Easy Transfer Wizard?

▼ Windows Vista includes a Security Console that detects unauthorized attempts to access your computer or its files from across the network. You can temporarily bypass the system security to allow Windows Easy Transfer to complete the transfer process. After your files and settings are transferred, Windows reapplies the system security on your computer.

Why did my game, or other application, not migrate over?

▼ Most Windows applications modify the Registry in ways not detected by the wizard. Your best bet is to capture any saved game files — or other data files — reinstall the application, and then migrate the files to your new system.

continued

Restore Files and Settings

(Continued)

When you start the files and settings restore process, you have to specify if your old computer has the Windows Easy Transfer program installed on it. If you have a different version of the Windows Easy Transfer program on your old computer, such as the Files and Settings Transfer Wizard that came with Windows XP, SP2, you must update it to the current one. That is why Windows Vista includes the program on the Install Windows dialog box.

If you do not have Windows Easy Transfer on your old computer, you can use the Windows Vista Installation disc, but you can also create copies of the program onto different media and then install Windows Easy Transfer on your old computer. For instance, you can create a CD or DVD of the program if you have a CD or DVD burner on your new computer — most new computers have at least a CD-R or CD-RW drive for burning CDs. Alternatively, you can use a USB flash drive to make a copy of the Easy Windows Transfer program. Plug in the device, copy the program over to the USB drive, insert the USB drive into your old computer, and install the program from there.

Restore Files and Settings *(continued)*

The Is Windows Easy Transfer installed on your old computer screen appears.

6 Click Yes, I installed it to indicate that the old computer has Windows Easy Transfer installed.

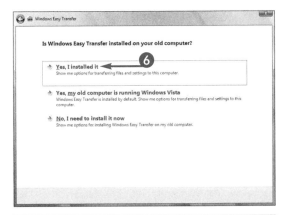

The Are your computers connected to a network screen appears.

7 Click Yes, I'll transfer files and settings over the network to indicate that you want to transfer files from a network drive.

Note: *If a message appears indicating that your firewall is blocking network access, click Yes.*

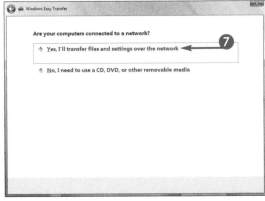

PART I

The Do you have a Windows Easy Transfer key screen appears.

⑧ Click Yes, I have a key to indicate that you have a key.

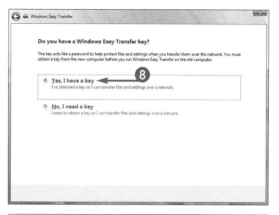

The Windows Easy Transfer key from the other computer appears in the Type Your Windows Easy Transfer key box.

⑨ Click Next.

Your files transfer.

I am trying to run the Windows Easy Transfer program on Windows Me. Why will it not appear?

▼ Windows Vista assumes that you have Windows XP on your computer, not an earlier version. Therefore when you attempt to run the Install Windows program on non-XP machines, you will error out. Since Windows Easy Transfer is part of the Windows Vista Install Windows package, you will not be able to use the Windows Easy Transfer program on older versions of Windows either. It is not recommended that you copy settings from older versions of Windows to Windows Vista.

Do I have to use Windows Easy Transfer?

▼ No, in fact if you want to transfer files to your new computer, and not settings, your best bet is to copy the files you want to move to your new computer onto removable media. Then when you get Windows Vista installed, insert or connect the removable media to your new computer and copy your files to your new hard drive. Examples of removable media include external hard drives, flash drives, CD-R, and DVD-R.

Introduction to Installation Types

Installing Windows Vista involves more than just clicking a Setup icon in Windows XP, Service Pack 2. In most cases, you will want to run the Check compatibility online feature that is discussed in Chapter 1, "Preparing for Installation." When you use that tool, and your computer passes the compatibility requirements, you can be assured your computer will be able to install and run Windows Vista without much of a problem. Of course, each computer setup is unique, so you may experience some problems with the devices and applications you install on your system if they are not 100 percent Windows Vista compatible.

Depending on the type of installation you choose, you can bring additional functionality to your existing computer. The different types of installations available reflect the different needs of users: Install on a brand-new computer, upgrade an older version of Windows, dual-boot between versions of Windows, install computers across a network, and script the installation so that it takes place automatically, without user intervention.

Full or Upgrade

The type of installation you choose—full or upgrade—largely depends on if your current operating system allows an upgrade to Windows Vista. Currently only Windows XP allows the upgrade path to Windows Vista. If you use a different operating system, such as Windows 98, you will have to install Windows Vista using the full install method. What this does is remove everything from your hard drive (your hard drive is reformatted during the install process) and install Windows Vista in a "clean" environment. Of course, when finished you must reinstall all programs that were on the computer prior to the install process, and copy all your personal files (such as word processing documents, photographs, spreadsheets, and the like) back to your computer. Before you even start the installation process you will have to copy any files you want to preserve over to a removal disc (such as a CD or DVD) so you can replace them once Windows Vista is up and running.

Installation Methods

Your choice of installation method may depend on what your role is. If you are a home user, you are most likely to use an upgrade installation. If you are a small office/home office (SOHO) or networking professional supporting many computers, you may use all these methods for varying reasons. You also may want to use the Windows Automated Installation Kit (WAIK), as described in the "Using the Windows Automated Installation Kit (WAIK)" section.

In all cases, Microsoft has made it fairly easy for you to get Windows Vista up and running, no matter how you plan to install it. For the most part, these installation types vary only in the first steps. After the system has booted into graphical mode, the rest of the installation takes place normally.

New Installation

A new installation is performed on *bare metal,* a hard drive with no other operating system on it. You use this installation most often when you want to wipe out everything and start over, or when you have backed up your previous operating system's contents and data files and want to learn about Windows Vista from the ground up. If you choose this path, you need to reinstall your applications, such as Microsoft Office 2007, before you can use them again. See Chapter 1 for information about transferring your files and settings from an existing installation to a new installation.

Upgrade Installation

An upgrade installation is used when you want to install Windows Vista on top of an earlier version of Windows, such as Windows XP. An upgrade preserves your existing applications and settings so that you can be productive more quickly than you can with a new installation. This installation is frequently used by people who purchase an upgrade version of Windows Vista at a retail or an online store, which costs much less than a full install version. Compatibility can be an issue, so see Chapter 1 for information on running the Upgrade Advisor prior to starting your upgrade.

Other Installation Methods

You can use other methods to install Windows Vista onto a computer, including cloning (using either Microsoft's Sysprep utility available at http://oem.microsoft.com/script/sites/public/sysprep.htm or a commercial program like Norton Ghost) and Remote Installation Services (RIS). Both methods are more likely to be used in larger enterprises, though they can also be used in SOHO environments. Although these methods are not covered in this book, you can find out more information in both the online help files and the release notes for Windows Vista, as well as at the Microsoft Web site.

Using the Windows Automated Installation Kit (WAIK)

If you are in charge of installing Windows Vista to multiple new computers in your business or organization, consider using the Windows Automated Installation Kit (WAIK). The Windows Automated Installation Kit allows you to automate the process of setting up Windows Vista so you can install Windows Vista on several computers without requiring your input during the installation process. When you use the WAIK, you do not, for instance, have to select the Install Now button on the first screen of the Install Windows dialog box. Other user prompts, such as inputting the Windows activation key, setting the time zone, and specifying the type of network the computer connects to, are not presented during the installation process when the Windows Automated Installation Kit is employed.

Recommended for Ten or More Computers

The Windows Automated Installation Kit is designed for information technology (IT), original equipment manufactures (OEM), and corporate network departments. Users with fewer than ten computers may find setting up the Windows Automated Installation Kit and testing it is not worth the trouble (that is, it is easier just to install Windows Vista manually on the ten computers). However, for those departments or businesses that expect to install Windows Vista on ten or more computers, or have plans to install to an entire department or division, the Windows Automated Installation Kit makes the install process easy after creating the initial Windows Vista Image using the Windows System Image Manager (Windows SIM).

The process for using the Windows Automated Installation Kit involves four basic steps. First, create an answer file by using Windows SIM. Second, use the Windows Vista DVD and the answer file you created in the first step to build a master installation. Third, create an image of the master installation using ImageX and the Windows Presinstallation Environment (Windows PE) technologies. Finally, deploy the master installation across a network to each computer using Windows PE and ImageX.

To learn more about the Windows Automated Installation Kit, go to www.microsoft.com/technet/windowsvista/library/88f80cb7-d44f-47f7-a10d-e23dd53bc3fa.mspx.

Install Windows Vista: New Installation

Performing a new installation is one of the best ways to learn the fundamentals of how Windows Vista is set up for your computer. A new installation wipes everything clean, starts fresh, and lets you configure Windows Vista to conform to your environment. After you have run through a new installation a few times, you may want to examine scripting your installation so that user intervention is not required.

In some cases, you may not be able to perform a new installation on your computer. For example, most systems from major computer manufacturers ship with *restore DVDs* that contain an image of your operating system and applications that were preselected and preinstalled by the manufacturer. This may not always be what you want, especially if the applications are incompatible with the ones you want to install. Your only solution is to go buy a retail copy of Windows Vista and install it — but be warned that if you do this, you may void your customer-support agreement with your manufacturer.

Install Windows Vista: New Installation

① Insert your Windows Vista DVD and reboot the computer.

The text-mode setup program launches.

The Install Windows window appears.

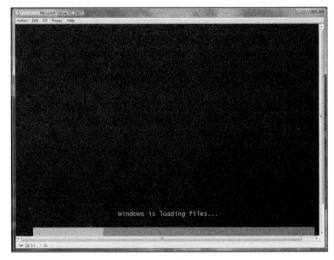

② Click the Language to install down-arrow and select a language.

③ Click the Time and currency format down-arrow and select the time and currency.

④ Click the Keyboard or input method down-arrow and select the keyboard language.

⑤ Click Next to continue.

The Install now window appears.

⑥ Click Install now.

The Type your product key for activation window appears.

⑦ Type in the 25-digit Windows Vista serial number, found on either your DVD jewel case or a separate license with a license sticker on it.

Note: *You may work for a company that has a site license for Windows Vista; if so, use the site license key instead.*

⑧ Click Next to continue.

I use the Dvorak keyboard. Can I install options for it during setup?

▼ Yes, during the installation process, you use the first window that the Install Windows program displays for setting keyboard options. Click the Keyboard or Input Method drop-down list. Three options for the Dvorak keyboard appear toward the bottom of the list: United States-Dvorak, United States-Dvorak for Left Hand, and United States-Dvorak for Right Hand. Click your keyboard type and click Next to continue with the setup process.

Why does my computer not boot from a DVD?

▼ Your motherboard's basic input/output system (BIOS) has been set to boot from a hard drive, or your BIOS does not support booting from DVD (actually, the setting usually appears as CD or CD\DVD), which was common in pre-1998 hardware. Go into your BIOS, usually by pressing the Delete or F1 key during boot time, and change the boot order. Visit your motherboard manufacturer's Web site for information on changing the BIOS or flashing a new version. *Caution:* You can render your computer unbootable if you use the wrong BIOS version, so follow all cautions and instructions from your manufacturer exactly.

continued

Install Windows Vista:
New Installation *(Continued)*

A new installation will take you anywhere from one to several hours, depending on the speed of your computer, the number of hard drives and amount of drive space you have, and whether you sit by and babysit the computer, ready to click Next or fill in parameters when asked. If you have not done so, you should collect information about your hardware as detailed in Chapter 1. You should also have your Internet connection information handy so you can connect to the Internet during setup.

If you do not currently have an Internet service provider (ISP), Windows Vista provides you with the means of using dial-up connectivity to reach one. You cannot automatically connect to a broadband provider; to do that, you must contact a provider ahead of time, install the necessary hardware, and set up your broadband account. However, if your broadband connection was working fine prior to installing Windows Vista, the setup program usually finds it and sets up the Internet connection automatically. If you bought a new system from a hardware vendor, it may come preinstalled with software to connect to the more popular dial-up services, such as AOL, among others. You should shop around to see if there are better deals from ISPs in your area.

Install Windows Vista: New Installation *(continued)*

The Windows Vista license agreement window appears.

9 Click I accept the license terms
(☐ changes to ☑).

10 Click Next to continue.

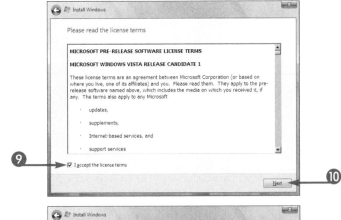

The Which type of installation do you want? screen appears.

● Upgrade is not available when you perform a full install.

11 Click Custom (advanced).

The Where do you want to install Windows? window appears.

⑫ Select a drive.

● Click here to see advanced drive options, such as formatting and partitioning disks.

⑬ Click Next to continue.

The Installing Windows window appears.

● You can view the progress of each part of the installation process.

Depending on the speed of your system, the install process can take a long time (several hours, in some cases).

After the installation, Windows Vista has to shut down and reboot your computer. Let it do this. Upon restart, do *not* select to boot from the DVD. Let the Windows Vista install process continue.

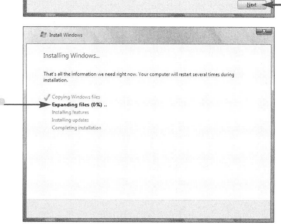

Should I use my entire hard drive as a single partition?

▼ On step 12, you can click the Drive options (advanced) link to set up partitions (which requires you to format your hard disks first). Most admins will tell you that creating two partitions — one for your operating systems and applications, and one for your data and user files — is a good idea. Backing up user data when it resides on only one partition is easier. However, if you are using dynamic disks for all your drives, this is not possible. In that case, you should either have an automated backup in place for your data, or save your user files out to a drive on a network server.

Can I change Windows Vista to a different language?

▼ When you initially start Windows Vista setup, select a language other than English from the Language to install drop-down list. The Regional and Language Options change only some aspects of Windows Vista, such as the date, time, and currency formats, as well as the kinds of input devices that are different depending on the country. If you need a different language for your version of Windows Vista, you must purchase that language version from a Microsoft partner (go to http://partner.microsoft.com/global for more information). For example, if you need the Japenese version of Windows Vista, purchase the Windows Vista Japenese Edition. The Regional and Language Options settings will not change the language version you are installing.

continued

Install Windows Vista: New Installation *(Continued)*

Windows Product Activation (WPA) is used to signal whether software piracy is taking place, such as a single retail copy of Windows Vista being installed on an entire department's PCs.

WPA does this by creating a hash using the license key and certain identifying characteristics of your hardware, like processor and hard-drive size. It sends this hash back to Microsoft, though no personally identifying information is sent. You can have up to three installations on different hardware configurations, such as when you install a new hard

drive or increase the amount of RAM. If you exceed the number of activations, your computer will not let you log in until you contact Microsoft to reset the activation information in its database.

Without WPA, your installation will function for 30 days and then refuse to let you log in. If you are at a business that has a site license, product activation is not required and you will not see the WPA screen.

Product activation differs from product registration: The latter is not required, and when you register you provide personal information to Microsoft.

Install Windows Vista: New Installation *(continued)*

Windows Vista displays a window showing that it is preparing to start for the first time.

Windows may need to shut down and restart again. If so, again, let it continue without interrupting it.

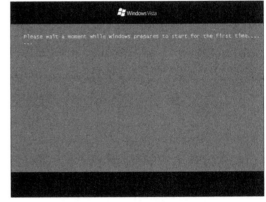

● At some point the Completing installation option on the Install Windows window highlights, showing you the installation is getting nearer to the end.

When the Choose a user name and picture screen appears, you must continue interacting with the setup process.

⑭ Type a user name.

⑮ Type a password.

A password is not required.

⑯ Retype the password.

⑰ Type a password hint.

⑱ Click to select a picture for the user account.

⑲ Click Next to continue.

The Type a computer name and choose a desktop background window appears.

⑳ Type a name for your computer.

Note: The computer name should be different from a user's name.

㉑ Click a background.

㉒ Click Next to continue.

The Help protect Windows automatically window appears.

You can click here to turn off automatic updates (not recommended).

㉓ Click Use recommended settings.

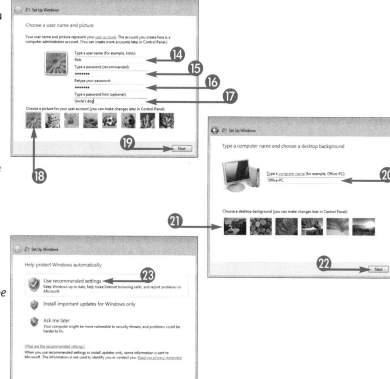

How long can computer names be?

▼ You can have a computer name up to 63 characters. However, if you are running older versions of Windows on your network, those versions recognize only names up to 15 characters.

Why is it not recommended to turn off automatic updates?

▼ With the automatic update feature turned on, Windows Vista periodically downloads and installs important updates to the Windows system. Some of these updates include security updates, which can help keep your computer free of malicious software and unwanted applications running on your computer.

Can I select which components I want to install during setup, like games?

▼ Unlike previous consumer versions of Windows (except for Windows XP), Windows Vista does not let you pick and choose which programs and features are installed during the Install Windows process. This makes the installation process go more quickly and simply for new users but does not provide the flexibility a system administrator needs. If you need to be more selective about which programs to install, you can investigate the User State Migration Tool 3.0, found on the Windows Vista DVD. It enables you to be granular about which programs and services are installed.

Install Windows Vista: New Installation *(Continued)*

The setup process asks you if you want to join a workgroup or domain. The difference between the two revolves around the centralized authentication, access, and security a Microsoft Windows domain controller provides. If you are not running a version of Windows Server on your network, then workgroups are appropriate for your setup.

In order to join a domain, you must have a domain controller running on your network, and you need the name and password of an account with rights to add

a computer to a domain. Most commonly this is someone who is a member of the Domain Admins account, but it can be any group that has been given rights to join computers to a domain.

If your computer cannot find the domain server, either because you specified an incorrect domain or because you lack the rights to join the computer to a domain, setup asks if you want to try joining a domain later. See Chapter 20 for information on joining a domain.

Install Windows Vista: New Installation *(continued)*

The Review your time and date settings window appears.

24 Make any adjustments to the date and time, including your time zone and whether daylight saving time is observed.

25 Click Next to continue.

The Select your computer's current location window appears.

26 Click Home, Work, or Public location.

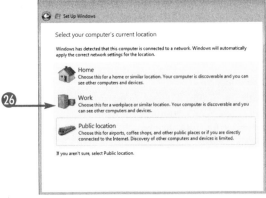

The Thank you screen appears.

㉗ Click Start.

Windows Vista appears to stall for a few moments, and then it starts.

The Windows Vista Welcome screen appears.

㉘ Type your password.

㉙ Press Enter or click the arrow button.

Windows prepares your desktop for the first time. This may take some time depending on the speed of your computer.

Windows displays the Welcome Center.

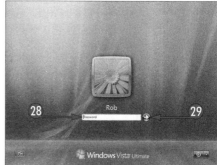

Why does Windows Vista ask where my computer will be?

▼ This is to help set up your network and Internet connections. The primary difference is whether you need hard-coded connection information (direct connection) or use Dynamic Host Configuration Protocol, or DHCP (LAN), to gain access to the Internet. If you are a home or an office worker, your network will be private, so the connections will be easier to locate. If you use a public setting, such as an Internet café or library, the connections will be public and may be more difficult for Windows Vista to set up (due to access restrictions and passwords). If in doubt, choose the home or office setting.

What should I do if my power goes out in the middle of the installation process?

▼ Keep everything the way it was when the power went off. Get your power back up, start your computer, and wait and see. The setup may pick up where it was and finish without a problem. However, if the setup program does not come back on, or some weird things are going on during the install, consider restarting the install. Click the Close button on the Install Windows window and click that you want to quit without finishing the installation. Eject your DVD, shut down, and restart your computer. Reinsert your DVD and then restart the computer again.

Install Windows Vista: Upgrade Installation

An upgrade installation occurs when you move Windows XP, Service Pack 2 to Windows Vista. See Chapter 1 for information on checking upgrade compatibility and obtaining any necessary updates so that Windows can install smoothly. Back up your data files to removable media or to a network drive so you can restore them in case the upgrade does not go smoothly.

Plug in and turn on any hardware you want to use with your new installation, such as scanners, Personal Digital Assistants (PDAs), printers, or Universal Serial

Bus (USB) hard drives. Last, turn off antivirus software and shut down all background applications such as file-sharing utilities or PDA synchronization utilities. You can also run the Files and Settings Transfer Wizard (which is named Windows Easy Transfer in Windows Vista) to capture your changes to the desktop and vital settings and files. This acts as a safety net in case some settings do not transfer cleanly. See Chapter 1 for information on this wizard.

You can perform an upgrade with either the retail or the upgrade version of Windows as long as you start the upgrade within Windows XP.

Install Windows Vista: Upgrade Installation

① Boot your computer and start Windows XP.

② Insert the Windows Vista DVD in your computer.

The Install Windows screen appears.

Note: *You can browse to the DVD and click Setup.exe if the Install Windows screen does not automatically start.*

③ Click Install now.

The Get important updates for installation window appears.

④ Click Do not get the latest updates for installation.

● You can click here to connect to the Windows Vista Web site and download updates to the installation.

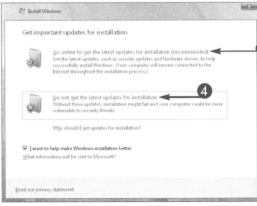

PART I

The Type your product key for activation window appears.

⑤ Type in the 25-digit Windows Vista serial number, found on either your CD jewel case or a separate license with a license sticker on it.

Note: You may work for a company that has a site license for Windows Vista; if so, use the site license key instead.

⑥ Click Next to continue.

The Windows Vista license agreement window appears.

⑦ Click I accept the license terms (☐ changes to ☑).

⑧ Click Next to continue.

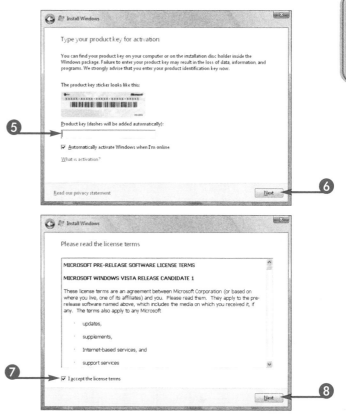

Will all my older software work under Windows Vista?

▼ It depends on which operating system the program was originally written for. If it was written for Windows XP, Service Pack 2, it is likely that Windows Vista has the necessary software support. Older applications that may have run on Windows 2000 or Windows 98, such as DOS games or applications that wrote directly to the video card, may not natively run on Windows Vista. You need to create a custom environment for those applications. See Chapter 3 for information on application compatibility.

Can I convert my partition format without performing a new install?

▼ Yes. You *must* convert a pre-existing File Allocation Table32 (FAT32) partition to New Technology File System (NTFS) during the upgrade. In fact, Windows Vista does it automatically unless you choose the Disk options (advanced) link. Unlike Windows XP, Windows Vista does not give you the option of using FAT32 or NTFS. You must use the NTFS file system under Windows Vista.

continued

Install Windows Vista:
Upgrade Installation *(Continued)*

I f your previous experiences with computers used older operating systems, such as those termed "consumer editions" of Windows, such as Windows 98 or Windows Me, note that you are now moving to a true 32-bit operating system and gaining the protection of an enterprise-grade kernel and memory manager. Earlier versions had 16-bit components that were used throughout the product, including the core parts of the operating system, and this caused problems with hardware and applications that tried to write directly to hardware. This resulted in hard locks or sudden reboots.

With Windows Vista, the kernel and memory manager are written so that applications cannot write directly to hardware, but must go through managers that keep track of application access and memory management. Hard locks and crashes are drastically reduced and uptime is increased. When you install certified device drivers written specifically for Windows Vista, you ensure that those devices will not bring your work or your desktop to a screeching halt.

If you are migrating to Windows Vista from a workstation version of Windows NT or Windows 2000, you are gaining improved performance, reliability, and a much-improved interface that makes your work more streamlined and seamless.

Install Windows Vista: Upgrade Installation *(continued)*

The Which type of installation do you want? screen appears.

9 Click Upgrade.

A system compatibility report displays any hardware that you will need to update (new device drivers, usually) after you install Windows Vista.

Note: *A copy of the report will be saved to your desktop upon finishing the Windows Vista setup process.*

10 Click Next to continue.

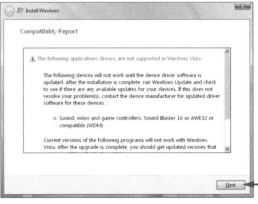

The Upgrading Windows window appears.

● You can view the progress of each part of the installation process.

Note: Depending on the speed of your system, the install process can take a long time (several hours, in some cases).

After the installation, Windows Vista has to shut down and reboot your computer. Let it do this. Upon restart, do *not* select to boot from the DVD. Let the Windows Vista install process continue.

Setup continues in graphical mode.

The Help protect Windows automatically window appears.

⑪ Click Use recommended settings.

Note: The rest of the setup proceeds as shown in the section "Install Windows Vista: New Installation." See step 24 in that section.

Windows Vista uses your username and password (if any) from your Windows XP installation.

After I upgrade my operating system, can I remove Windows Vista?

▼ No, because Windows Vista uses a different boot loader than previous versions of Windows. Instead of the Boot.ini file used in Windows XP and Windows Server 2003, for example, Windows Vista uses the Boot Configuratin Data (BCD) store. The recommended practice from Microsoft is that you reinstall Windows XP, Service Pack 2 edition if you want to return to Windows XP. At the time of this writing, Windows Vista did not have an option for reverting to an earlier operating system (Windows XP).

Can I upgrade from an earlier server version of Windows to Windows Vista?

▼ No. The Windows Vista setup program does not enable you to upgrade over a server version of Windows. You must boot to the DVD . This is done to preserve the domain, security, and services information that is available only to server editions of Windows. If for some reason you want to upgrade, your choices are either to perform a new installation in the same partition, which reformats your hard drives causing you to lose all your server information, or to perform a dual-boot installation to a different partition.

Launch and Use
Safe Mode

All versions of the Windows operating system have stripped-down versions that users can launch to help troubleshoot a system. This is preferable to wiping the hard drive, reinstalling the operating system and applications, and then copying the relevant data files back onto the user's desktop.

Safe Mode is a bare-bones graphical environment that can be started with or without network support, with or without a graphical user interface (GUI), or started in Video Graphics Array (VGA) mode. By not installing these various drivers, which tend to cause the most

problems with any computer installation, a system administrator can remove the troublesome drivers and back down to a version of stable drivers instead.

Safe Mode often is the only way to uninstall drivers. Some services are still functional in Safe Mode, though if you choose to boot without network drivers, many network-based services are not available. For that reason, if you need to boot into Safe Mode, it helps to have various device drivers and troubleshooting utilities available on a CD so you can use them on the standalone system.

Launch and Use Safe Mode

1 Reboot your computer.

2 Press and hold F8 while the computer reboots.

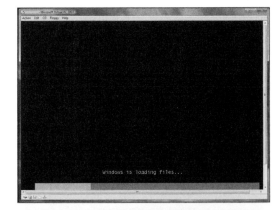

The Windows Advanced Boot Options menu appears.

3 Press the arrow keys to highlight the mode you want to use.

For this example, select Safe Mode with Command Prompt.

4 Press Enter.

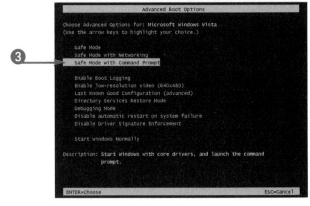

Windows restarts in the appropriate mode.

5 Log on to Windows.

Note: *You need to use the local administrator account, or an account of someone with local administrator rights.*

Windows starts in Safe Mode.

What are the different modes available in Safe Mode?

▼ There are five general categories for Safe Mode that you can use:

Safe Modes

Mode	Description
Safe Mode	Restarts Windows without networking or other common services. By starting with minimal services, you can add services one by one to determine which are misbehaving.
Safe Mode with Networking	Adds network services and Active Directory connectivity to Safe Mode.
Safe Mode with Command Prompt	Restarts Windows at a command prompt.
Enable VGA Mode	Starts Windows using a generic VGA driver, providing 640 × 480 × 16 color display.
Last Known Good Configuration	Restores your previous boot settings that successfully started Windows. Note that this does not necessarily restore a working copy of Windows, just one that managed to get to the desktop.

Customize Windows Startup with MSCONFIG

When Windows Vista boots, it starts a number of services and applications so that the Windows environment is configured for optimal use. These may or may not actually be needed; many of them are enabled "out of the box," while others are added by applications or device managers you install.

Microsoft provides a program called MSCONFIG that lets you determine which services and applications run at startup. You can see which programs are starting, find out where they reside on your system, and enable or disable them by clicking a check box. This makes it easy for you to determine if a particular service or application is needed and lets you edit the configuration files involved without risking a syntax error.

You can also control these programs using the Services Manager and RegEdit or RegEdt32, which provide more granular control and options to restore deleted or modified registry keys. (See Chapter 11 for more information on these applications.) However, if you are experimenting with the boot time and application startup, MSCONFIG is easier to use than the other applications.

1. Click Start.
2. Click All Programs.

3. Click Accessories.
4. Click Run.

The Run dialog box appears.

⑤ Type **msconfig** in the Open text box.

⑥ Click OK.

The System Configuration utility dialog box, also know as MSCONFIG, appears.

● You can click Diagnostic startup to load with only a minimum of drivers and services available (○ changes to ◉).

Note: When you reboot, the list of loaded services and applications can be viewed again in MSCONFIG.

⑦ Click the Startup tab.

The Startup items appear.

● Click next to an applet to choose whether it loads on the next reboot (☐ changes to ☑).

● The Command heading shows from where the applet or application was launched.

How do I tell which applet is associated with which program?

▼ MSCONFIG usually gives you the path to where an applet originates. By looking at the path, you can usually tell the application to which it belongs. For example, ccApp.exe belongs to Norton AntiVirus.

Why are SYSTEM.INI and WIN.INI listed on my system? I thought they were only for 16-bit Windows?

▼ These files have been present in both 16- and 32-bit Windows for backwards compatibility and for applications that run in the Program Compatibilty evironment. If you have custom applications that have trouble running, you can debug the drivers by not loading them in these files at startup. See the "Configure Application Compatibility" section.

Can I edit the BOOT.INI file manually?

▼ It depends on what you want to accomplish. If all you want to do is change the boot order or add some command-line options, you are better off using MSCONFIG to make the necessary changes. If you want to add paths for a new kernel (such as booting into a Linux partition), you will need to use Notepad or some other text editor to make the changes. The disk and drive syntax is tricky, so you should check TechNet or any Microsoft FAQs on how to modify BOOT.INI.

Configure Automatic Windows Updates

Windows Update is the Windows service that provides bug fixes, patches, service packs, and optional features that you can install on Windows and other Microsoft products. This enables you to keep your system up-to-date, helping defend against hacker attempts and rogue programs that can corrupt or steal data from your computer.

Windows Update can still be reached from the Start menu, but you can also start it through the Control Panel.

For most users, setting Windows Update to download and install new code is the easiest way to keep computers up-to-date. In larger organizations, it is

better to use the Microsoft Windows Server Update Services because it gives you time to test the code for compatibility before rolling it out to the rest of the organization.

You can still manually check for available updates, or disable Windows Updates if you prefer to have more control over what your PC does in the background. To do this, you use the Change Settings link on the Windows Update window. Then click Never check for updates (not recommended) and click OK to save your settings. To manually check the updates, open the Windows Update window and click the Check for updates button.

Configure Automatic Windows Updates

① Click Start.

② Click Control Panel.

The Control Panel window appears.

③ Click Check for updates.

The Windows Update window appears.

Note: *You can also launch the Windows Update tool by clicking Start, clicking All Programs, and then clicking Windows Update.*

④ Click Change settings.

The Change settings window appears.

⑤ Click to select which option to use for downloading and installing updates (○ changes to ◉).

⑥ Click OK to apply your selections.

⑦ Click the View available updates link, which updates your system needs.

The View available updates window appears.

⑧ Click a checkbox next to an update (☐ changes to ☑).

⑨ Click Install to install the update.

Is there a way to roll back software that gets installed using Windows Update?

▼ If you know the name or Knowledge Base number of the software, you often will find the updates listed in the Add or Remove Programs section of the Windows Control Panel and can remove it from there. You can also go to the Windows Update window and click View update history to get a listing of what has been successfully installed and what failed to install. Or at the left side of the Control Panel, click View update history. You will see a list of the specific names of the updates and their status.

Why can I not uninstall a particular update?

▼ There are some updates that cannot be uninstalled. These are most often specific security updates or updates to core system services. For example, updates to Windows Media Player 11 cannot be uninstalled after you update it on your system. This is because the updates are integral components to Windows Media Player. Windows Update will tell you prior to installation if that is the case, and you may wish to test the update before rolling it out to the rest of your organization. The best way to test an update is to have a dedicated computer that you use just for testing. After you test the install, you will need to rebuild the computer by re-installing Windows Vista as a new install.

Add, Remove, and Change Windows Components

You can add, remove, and change the components that are available to Windows and other applications. These run the gamut from games, such as Chess Titans and Inkball, to services such as Internet Information Server (IIS) or Microsoft Message Queue Server, which are not available in the Windows Home editions. Unlike previous versions of Windows, however, Windows Vista does not provide you with options for turning off Windows applets, such as Calculator, WordPad, Paint, and NotePad. These applets are installed automatically and remain on your system.

Some components, such as additional mouse pointers, are just for fun or enhance the things you can do with

Windows. Others, like IIS, are meant for heavier-duty use or more extensive use of Windows than as an ordinary desktop PC.

Because many of these components and services are really meant for development usage, not production, there are limits on what you can do with some of them. For example, the version of IIS that ships with Windows Vista has a limit to the number of concurrent users who can connect to the server. So while you can run a Web server on your desktop, it is more for development efforts than for actually serving content on the Internet.

Add, Remove, and Change Windows Components

① Click Start.

② Click Control Panel.

The Control Panel opens.

③ Click Programs.

The Programs window appears.

④ Click Turn on or off Windows features.

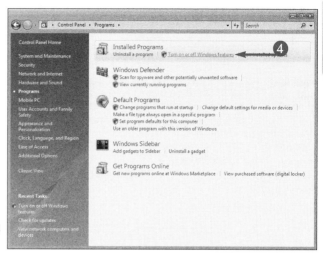

The Windows Features dialog box appears.

⑤ Scroll through the list to find the components you want to add or remove.

⑥ Click the plus sign (+) to get a list of subcomponents that can be added or removed.

⑦ Click a component to turn a feature on (☑) or to turn a feature off (☐).

⑧ Click OK.

Windows adds or removes the selected component.

Note: Depending on the component, you may need to reboot your system.

What does the Programs and Features item in the Control Panel do?

▼ You can use the Programs and Features item to view the Uninstall or change a program window. This window displays a list of all the programs installed on your computer, as well as modifying the installation settings. You can, for example, click a program in the list and then click Repair to run any repair utilities that the program provides. You also can uinstall programs using this window. Finally, you can click the Change button to display a window for changing options installed for a particular program.

How do I remove components of a program that I have installed?

▼ Some programs, such as Microsoft Office, provide ways to install all or part of the entire program while you are initially installing the program. After the program is installed, you can use the Installed Programs window to view and change these installations. Click Control Panel, click Programs, and then click Uninstall a Program. The Uninstall or change a program window appears. Select the program to change and then click Uninstall. A window displays with options for changing the installation for the program. The window that displays varies depending on the program you change.

Configure Windows Ultimate Extras

When you install the Windows Vista Ultimate Edition, you get access to the Windows Ultimate Extras. Ultimate Extras are programs, helpful documents, services, and other items that help you expand the usage of Windows Vista. For example, you can download tutorials that help you learn about securing your computer against malicious users.

When you use the Ultimate Extras feature in Vista, you connect via the Internet to the Ultimate Extras Web site, which is part of the Windows Update Web site.

Here you can find a list of downloads you can install on your computer. In fact, you can search for Ultimate Extras using the Windows Update service. When an item is available that you want to install, you just download and install it like any other update.

Some of the types of items that Windows Ultimate Extras provide include updates to desktop components, such as background and images, new programs that Windows Vista Ultimate users can download and install, and documents that will help Ultimate users get the most out of their computer system.

Configure Windows Ultimate Extras

① Click Start.

② Click All Programs.

③ Click Extras and Upgrades.

④ Click Windows Ultimate Extras.

The Windows Update with Windows Ultimate Extras window appears.

5 Click Check for updates.

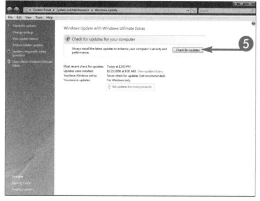

Windows checks the Windows Ultimate Extras Web site for any extras that are available and downloads them to your computer.

Can I see a list of Windows Ultimate Extras?

▼ Microsoft has a Web page designed to showcase the Windows Ultimate Extras that are available. At the time of this writing, the Web page is at www.microsoft. com/windowsvista. As the Windows Ultimate Extras Web site grows, the Web site address may change. To find the most current site, use the Windows Ultimate Extras program icon. Click Start, click All Programs, click Extras and Updates, and finally click Windows Ultimate Extras. Click Learn about Windows Ultimate Extras in the task pane. Click For more information about Windows Ultimate Extras services and software offers, visit the Windows Ultimate Extras website.

Are there ways to contribute to the Windows Ultimate Extras Web site?

▼ To find out more about the Windows Ultimate Extras Web site and if Microsoft will enable users and developers to contribute to the site, visit the Microsoft Vista Web site at www.microsoft.com/ vista. Also, consider purchasing a subscription to the Microsoft Developer Network (MSDN), which provides developers with updated programming tools and information. Through the MSDN subscription, you will be able to obtain information about contributing to the Windows Ultimate Extras site. Visit http://msdn.microsoft.com for more information on MSDN subscriptions.

Configure Application Compatibility

With Windows 2000, Microsoft removed support for older DOS and 16-bit Windows applications found in Windows 9x and Windows Me. This code, though well written, enabled applications to write directly to hardware, causing hard locks, system-level crashes, and the infamous "blue screen of death." Removing the code dramatically reduced the number of crashes but also made backwards compatibility trickier, especially for businesses that relied on legacy applications or for gamers with several years of older games they wanted to play.

However, with Window XP (and now with Windows Vista) Microsoft included *compatibility mode*, a set of software services and database information that provides limited emulation for older applications. For example, some Windows 16-bit applications query for the OS version and will not run if the version is less than that needed. Compatibility mode provides the necessary information to the application, allowing it to run. This includes re-creating registry structures and other OS-specific variables.

You can invoke compatibility mode using a wizard, or by creating a custom icon that points to your application and modifying its properties. With the Program Compatibility Wizard you can configure which operating system the program executes correctly (such as Windows XP), a program's optimal display settings, and if the program should run with administrator privileges.

Configure Application Compatibility

① Click Start.

② Click Control Panel.

The Control Panel window appears.

③ Click Programs.

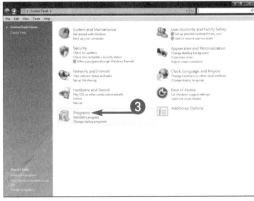

The Programs window appears.

④ Click Use an older program with this version of Windows.

The Program Compatibility Wizard appears.

⑤ Click Next to continue.

Can I use compatibility mode to run operating system or hardware-management applications?

▼ Compatibility mode attempts to re-create operating system and environment variables from older versions of Windows. If you try to run an application that directly manages hardware or the operating system using compatibility mode, you stand an excellent chance of corrupting your system and making it unbootable. Applications that fall into this category include antivirus, disk defragmentation, registry cleanup, and rescue utilities such as Symantec's Norton Utilities.

Can I configure compatibility mode without using the wizard?

▼ Yes, you can set compatibility for any application without using the wizard. Right-click an executable or a shorcut that launches it and then click Properties. Click the Compatibility tab to show the compatibility mode options on a single dialog box page, make the necessary selections, and then click OK. Clicking the executable or the shortcut launches your application using the compatibility mode settings.

continued

Configure Application Compatibility *(Continued)*

If you want to run MS-DOS applications on Windows Vista, your course of action is a little trickier. You can run applications in the standard command-line virtual machine, CMD.EXE. Or you can run your application in a DOS emulation environment, COMMAND.COM. Both are managed by NT Virtual DOS Machine (NTVDM), which sets environment variables needed by a program when you run it.

Environment variables can be set two ways: by modifying or creating custom AUTOEXEC.NT and CONFIG.NT files that are run when the virtual machine starts, or by creating a custom PIF (Program Information File) file that creates specific environments for the application in question. You can find the AUTOEXEC and CONFIG files in the <%windir%>\system32 directory. If you were comfortable modifying their analogues in DOS, you can do the same in Windows Vista.

PIF files are kept in <%windir%>\PIF, a hidden system folder. You can make your own folder by copying COMMAND.COM to the folder, right-clicking it, and then clicking the Compatibility tab.

All things being equal, it is better to use PIF files. However, because they do not give you as much flexibility, you may need to use AUTOEXEC.NT and CONFIG.NT instead.

Configure Application Compatibility *(continued)*

⑥ Click the program that you would like to run with the compatibility settings option (○ changes to ◉).

⑦ Click Next to continue.

⑧ Scroll through the list to find the program you want to configure.

⑨ Select the program.

⑩ Click Next to continue.

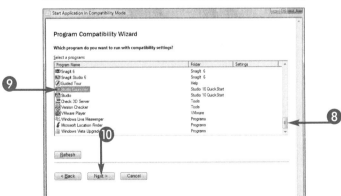

⓫ Click the operating system compatibility mode
(○ changes to ◉).

⓬ Click Next to continue.

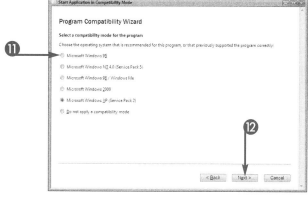

⓭ Select optional display modes for your
application (☐ changes to ☑).

⓮ Click Next to continue.

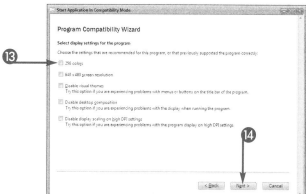

I have configured everything, but my MS-DOS application runs too fast. Can I slow it down?

▼ Very old MS-DOS applications relied on the CPU clock speed to determine how fast the application ran. Even if you configure the environment correctly, there is no easy way with Windows Vista to slow down the emulation environment. Your best bet is to download a third-party "slowdown" applet that you can run prior to launching your older application. This can provide some relief for impossibly fast applications. However, this is not guaranteed, and the environment may not be stable, so use slowdown applications at your own risk.

I do not want to spend my time playing with settings. Is there an easier way to create a compatible environment?

▼ Microsoft offers an advanced set of applications intended for system administrators, called the Application Compatibility Toolkit. Its core application is the Compatibility Administrator, which contains a number of fixes and settings for many applications. They are settings that have worked in other environments and may work in yours. You can download the toolkit at http://msdn.microsoft.com/library/default.asp?url=/downloads/list/appcomp.asp.

continued

Configure Application Compatibility *(Continued)*

One of the settings you can modify with the Application Compatibility Wizard is display settings for the program. Some older programs, such as games, graphics programs, and hardware-testing programs, work best at a specific display setting. For example, some games run only under a display setting of 640 × 480. Usually, newer computers running Windows Vista have the display setting configured for 1026 × 768 or higher. Instead of manually switching to the lower setting each time you want to run the game, use the Application Compatibility Wizard to set the display setting to 640 × 480.

Another display setting you can configure with the Application Compatibility Wizard is the one disabling visual themes. Visual themes are graphics and text features that Windows Vista applies to menus, buttons, title bars, and other features of Windows that programs display. If you notice that a program has problems displaying menus and buttons when you run them in Windows Vista, click the Disable visual themes option on the Select display settings for the program portion of the Application Compatibility Wizard. Windows Vista will turn off visual themes when you run that program.

Configure Application Compatibility *(continued)*

⑮ Select if you want to run this program as an administrator (☐ changes to ☑).

⑯ Click Next to continue.

The Test your compatibility settings window appears.

⑰ Click Next to test the compatibility settings.

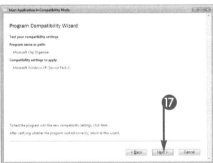

If the wizard detects a compatibility problem with the program, the This program has known compatibility issues window appears.

⑱ Click Check for solutions online to continue.

A window appears prompting you that the program has compatibility issues.

⑲ Click Check online for a solution.

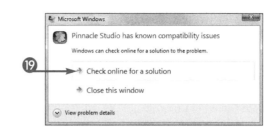

The Problem Reports and Solutions window appears.

⑳ Click OK to continue.

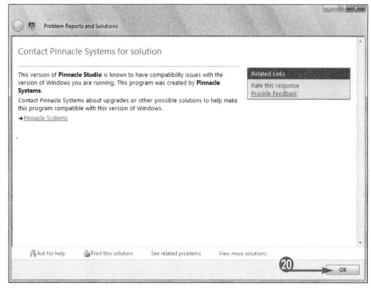

Can I see the compatibility issues of a program before I check for solutions?

▼ Yes, after the Application Compatibility Wizard runs a test and finds problems, click Check for solutions online. When the next window appears, which again tells you that the program has known compatibility issues, click View problem details at the bottom of the window. The window expands to show you a description of the problem, and the Problem signature list. This list shows problem information, such as the Problem Event Name and Problem Signature.

What if my program does not have a solution that runs under Windows Vista?

▼ You can still try running the program under Windows Vista. In some cases, you may not notice any execution problems. In other cases, the program may not run at all. For the latter case, contact the manufacturer of the affected program and ask if they plan to release updates for the program to run under Windows Vista. If so, they should provide a link you can use to download the updates or provide information on where you can obtain the updates.

continued

Configure Application
Compatibility *(Continued)*

When you test an application for compatibility with the Program Compatibility Wizard, Windows Vista may be able to find solutions for any known compatibility programs. If the Program Compatibility Wizard finds a solution, it includes links to it on the Problem Reports and Solutions window. Click a link to learn more about the compatibility issue and how to correct it.

In some cases, the Problem Reports and Solutions window displays a generic message, such as "Contact Pinnacle Systems for solution," or some similar message. If this is the case for your program, click the link provided on the Problem Reports and Solutions

window. Usually this link takes you to the home page of the manufacturer, not to a solutions page. However, once you are at the manufacturer's home page, look for a link to troubleshooting information, support documents, frequently asked questions, or similar links. Click that link to look for more information about known compatibility issues with Windows Vista.

The Program Compatibility Wizard also lets you send information back to Microsoft to provide feedback to the Online Crash Analysis Web site. See the "Report Compatibility Feedback to Microsoft" section for more information.

Configure Application Compatibility *(continued)*

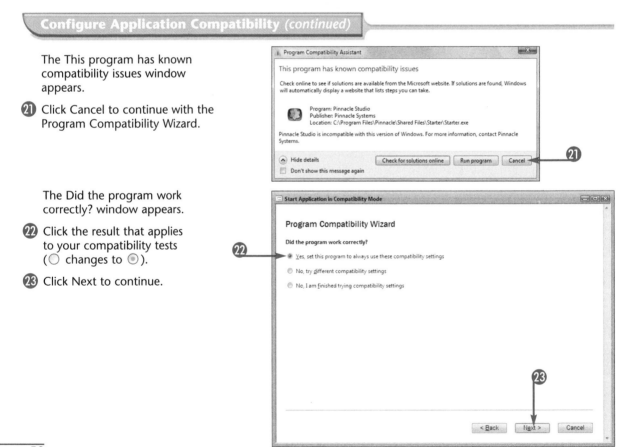

The This program has known compatibility issues window appears.

㉑ Click Cancel to continue with the Program Compatibility Wizard.

The Did the program work correctly? window appears.

㉒ Click the result that applies to your compatibility tests (○ changes to ◉).

㉓ Click Next to continue.

A window appears asking you if you want to send your custom configuration to Microsoft.

㉔ Click No (○ changes to ◉) to specify that you do not want to send the information to Microsoft.

㉕ Click Next to continue.

The Completing the Program Compatibility Wizard screen appears.

㉖ Click Finish.

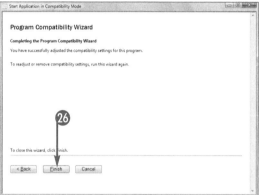

Can I print the solution that the Program Compatibility Wizard displays?

▼ Yes, you can do so when you display the Program Reports and Solutions window during the Program Compatibility Wizard (refer to step 19). Click Print this solution to display the Print dialog box. Click a printer in the Select Printer area of the General tab. Finally, click Print. Windows Vista prints the solution that displays on the Program Reports and Solutions window. After you print the solution, the Print dialog box disappears from the screen.

What if the solution does not work?

▼ If the Program Compatibility Wizard provides a solution and that solution does not work, click View more solutions on the Program Reports and Solutions window during the Program Compatibility Wizard (see step 19). The Solve problems on your computer window appears. Any known solutions for the compatability issue appear in the Solutions to install area of this window. Click a solution to learn more about it. If additional solutions are not available, the words "No solutions" appear in the Solutions to install area.

Report Compatibility Feedback to Microsoft

In an attempt to improve how Windows Vista operates with the myriad of programs available today, Microsoft gives users the chance to provide feedback while using the Program Compatibility Wizard.

To provide feedback, you must work through the steps in the "Configure Application Compatibility" section. Complete steps 1 to 19. When you have finished these steps, you see a link called Provide Feedback. Click it. Windows Vista displays Internet Explorer and connects you to the Microsoft Online Crash Analysis Web page.

On this page, you can select choices to rate how well the reporting system worked, how well the solution worked to solve your issue, and if the information was easy to understand. You also can add your own comments about the reporting system, with up to 1,000 characters, in the Additional comments area.

When you finish filling out the Microsoft Online Crash Analysis survey, click the Submit button to send your feedback to the Microsoft Online Analysis Web site. You do not have to provide personal information, such as your e-mail address, when you provide feedback.

Report Compatibility Feedback to Microsoft

① Perform steps **1** to **19** in the "Configure Application Compatibility" section.

The Problem Reports and Solutions window appears.

② Click Provide Feedback.

The Microsoft Online Crash Analysis Web page appears.

③ Use the drop-down menus and the radio buttons to select answers to the survey questions.

④ Move the scroll bar down to view the survey information at the bottom of the Web page.

5 Continue selecting answers to the survey form.

6 Click inside the Additional comments area.

7 Type additional comments.

8 When you have finished, click the Submit button.

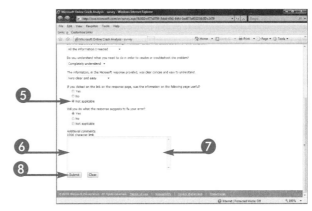

The Thank you for taking the time to provide your feedback window appears.

9 Click Close Window.

The Internet Explorer browser window closes.

Will Microsoft analize the crash results I report?

▼ Yes, in fact if you are an information technology (IT) worker, you may want to use the Microsoft Online Crash Analysis Web site (https://oca.microsoft.com) to help solve problems with programs and hardware device drivers you may be having when you are using Windows Vista. To do this, you must have a Microsoft Passport account (go to www.passport. com to sign up for one). Go to https:// oca.microsoft.com/en/secure/status.aspx and click Sign In. Type your e-mail address and password and click Sign In. The Error Reports page appears, which shows records of all your error reports and analysis. Click a record for more information.

Are there other ways I can obtain solutions to compatibilty issues?

▼ Yes, you can use the Microsoft Knowledge Base Web site. Open Internet Explorer and go to http://support.microsoft.com. In the Search Support (KB) box, type a keyword or phrase describing the application issue. Press Enter or click the right arrow next to the Search Support (KB) box. Microsoft returns links to Knowledge Base articles related to the issue you are experiencing. For more information on using the Knowledge Base, see "Search the Microsoft Support Knowledge Base" section in Chapter 25.

Disable Startup Programs

When you start up Windows Vista, more than just the operating system starts. You may notice that after you have been using Windows Vista for several days or weeks, and have been adding programs to your system, your computer takes a little longer to start up. This is because some of the programs you have installed probably have added programs or applets (small programs) to the startup sequence when you start Windows. Each item takes time to load every time you start Windows.

You can manage the programs that start up with Windows Vista by opening the Software Explorer. The

Software Explorer is a part of the Windows Defender application, which scans your computer for malicious and unwanted software.

On the Software Explorer window, you can modify how your startup programs behave. You can remove, disable, or enable a startup program. When you remove a startup program, you simply remove its listing from the programs that start when Windows Vista starts. You do not remove the program from Windows (that is, you do not uninstall it). You can leave a program on the list of startup programs, but instruct it to not start by disabling it.

① Click Start.

② Click Control Panel.

The Control Panel window appears.

③ Click Change startup programs.

The Software Explorer window of the Windows Defender program appears.

④ Click a program you want to disable.

⑤ Click Disable to disable the program.

The Windows Defender dialog box appears.

⑥ Click Yes.

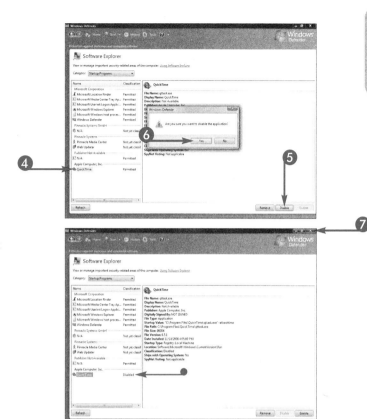

● Windows Defender classifies the program as Disabled so it does not start the next time you start Windows Vista.

⑦ Click Close.

The Software Explorer window closes.

Why does Windows Defender keep track of my startup programs?

▼ Because many programs designed to wreak havoc on your compter do so after you shut down and restart Windows. Upon startup, these programs execute and perform actions programmed by the author of that application. For instance, a typical action that some unwanted software performs is changing a user's Internet Explorer home page. It does this by modifying the home page address on the General tab of the Internet Options dialog box. Windows Defender is responsible for scannig startup programs and issuing warnings about malicious software it finds there.

Can I still add programs to the Startup folder?

▼ Yes, the Startup folder is still available. That folder has been part of Windows since the Windows 95 release. By copying programs to that folder, users can specify which programs start when Windows Vista does. To see which programs are in that folder, click the Start menu, click All Programs, and, finally, click Startup. Because Windows Vista is designed to use Windows Defender to manage startup programs, however, you may not see any programs in the Startup folder unless you add them there manually. Instead, the startup programs appear on the Software Explorer window.

7 — Managing Files and Folders

8 — Managing Security

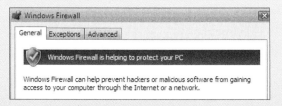

Get to Know the Windows Vista Desktop

You can save time in the long run by spending a few moments familiarizing yourself with the Windows Vista desktop. If you have used an earlier version, you will see mostly similarities and a few differences. When you first log in to Windows Vista, a Welcome Center window appears showing you information about your computer and icons that will help you get started setting up and using Windows Vista.

The screen here shows the Windows Vista desktop with its default settings. The Windows Vista desktop is designed to be highly customizable to suit your individual needs. Consequently, your PC's desktop may have a different background picture (or no picture), or it may have additional icons. You can learn about some of the additional icons and features available, as well as how to customize your desktop, in Chapter 5.

A Computer Icon
Double-click the Computer icon to browse your computer's disks and network locations.

B Recycle Bin
Drag files to the Recycle Bin to delete them or retrieve them later.

C Network Icon
Double-click the Network icon to view network drives and resources.

D Internet Explorer Icon
Double-click the Internet Explorer icon to browse the Web.

E Start Menu
Click Start to launch programs, change settings, or get help.

H Display Clock
Move your mouse over the clock to display the day and date.

G Hidden Icons
Click here to display hidden icons.

F Taskbar
View open files and click to switch between them.

Get to Know the Windows Vista Start Menu

By clicking the Start button, you can display the Windows Vista Start menu. From the Start menu you can launch programs, change settings, access Help, open your documents, view your pictures, and play your music or videos.

The Start menu is also where you find the commands to log off, shut down, and restart your computer. The screen here shows a sample Start menu. Yours may be slightly different.

Ⓐ User Name

Name of the user currently logged in at this PC.

Ⓑ Folders

Open folders containing your documents, pictures, music, and games.

Ⓒ Search

Search for files, folders, or other computers on a network.

Ⓓ Recent Items

Choose from a list of recently used files.

Ⓔ Computer

Access the files, folders, and settings on your PC.

Ⓕ Network

Access the files, folders, and resources on your network.

Ⓖ Connections

Choose to connect to a network.

Ⓗ Control Panel

Adjust the settings on your PC.

Ⓘ Default Programs

Choose the default programs that Windows uses.

Ⓙ Help and Support

Get help or technical support.

Ⓝ Start Search

Start a search for files, folders, network resources, or Web pages.

Ⓜ All Programs

A complete list of installed programs.

Ⓛ Programs

Commonly and most recently used programs.

Ⓚ Icons

Lock, put to sleep, shut down, or change users.

Learn About the New Vista Explorers

Windows Vista introduces new Explorers, which provide users with access to files, folders, drives, and network resources. The new Explorers have a new look to match many of the new graphics features introduced in Vista.

The new Explorers include several features that were not part of previous Windows versions:

The navigation pane has a new search tool called Instant Search available on it. The Command Bar includes commands and tools that are most appropriate for the file, folder, or object you are viewing. Live Icons are thumbnail views of documents, photos, videos, and other items you store on your computer. The screen here shows a sample Explorer window. Yours may be slightly different.

Ⓐ Navigation Buttons

Navigate to previously viewed folders or drives.

Ⓑ Address Bar

View your current location and path.

Ⓒ Navigation Pane

Helps you access common folders.

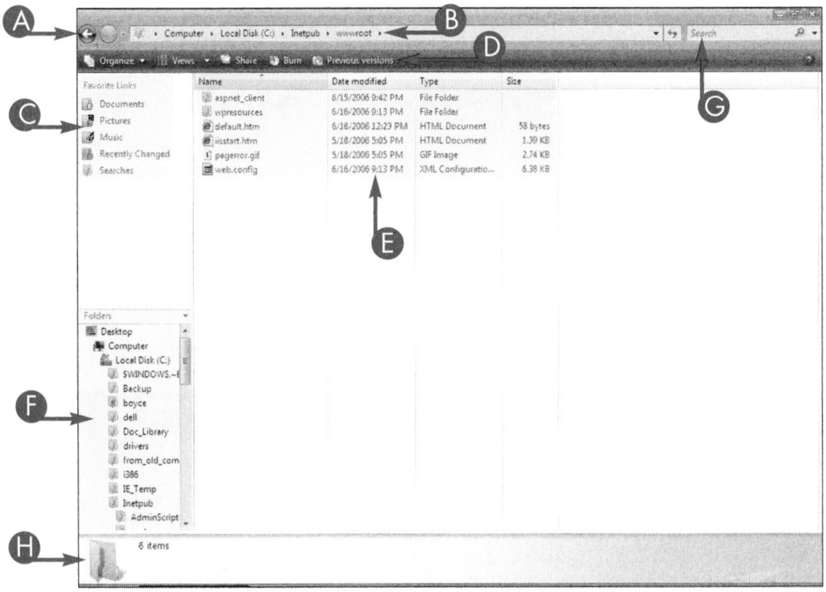

Ⓓ Command Bar

Commands you can perform on selected files or folders.

Ⓔ Files and Folders

List of files and folders stored on your drive.

Ⓗ Preview Pane

Showing property information about each file or folder.

Ⓖ Search Box

Finding files based on names, dates, keywords, and other information.

Ⓕ Folders Pane

Enables you to view folders and subfolders stored on your drives.

Learn About the Control Panel

The Control Panel is the area you use to access most of Windows Vista's configuration tools. To change security settings, for instance, you use the Security item in the Control Panel to launch the Security Center tool.

Windows Vista introduces a new Control Panel window. Instead of using icons to represent each program or configuration tool you launch, Windows Vista's Control Panel organizes tools into categories. Under each category are two or three links to common tasks that take you directly to a configuration tool.

You can click a category to view individual tools within that category. For example, when you click the System and Maintenance category in the Control Panel, you see a number of additional tools, including the Welcome Center, Backup and Restore Center, System, and Power Options.

You access the Control Panel by clicking the Start menu and then clicking Control Panel on the right side of the Start menu.

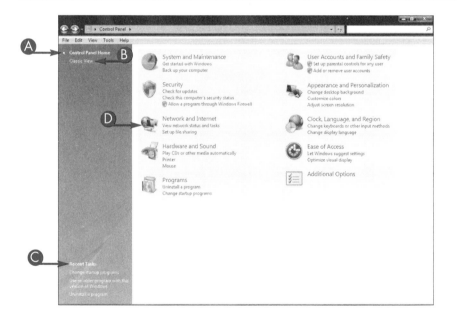

A **Task Pane**

Displays common tasks you can perform.

B **Classic View Link**

Link to display the Control Panel using the icon view that was common in Windows XP.

C **Recent Tasks**

Displays the most recent tasks you perfomed in the Control Panel.

D **Control Panel Categories**

Categories of configuration tools.

Switch Between Open Windows

Windows Vista is a multitasking operating system. This means you can have more than one program running simultaneously. In fact, you can have as many applications and windows open as your system processor, memory, and graphics adapter can handle. Some computers are powerful enough to enable users to run five or more programs at once.

For example, you could have Internet Explorer open to browse the Internet; open Windows Mail to download, view, and send e-mail messages; start Microsoft Office Word 2007 to compose a word-processing document;

display a spreadsheet in Microsoft Office Excel 20007; and open Windows Calendar to check your daily schedule. All of these programs can run at the same time, granted your computer has the power to run them.

After you have these programs running, you need to switch between them. Windows includes a few ways you can switch between open application windows. One of the most common ways to switch between windows is to click a taskbar button on the taskbar. Another way is to use the Windows Flip, or Alt+Tab, procedure.

① Using the Start menu, open at least three different programs.

Some examples include Internet Explorer, Windows Calendar, and Windows Photo Gallery.

② Click a minimized application window on the taskbar to switch programs.

Windows Vista displays the program window for the program you clicked.

③ Press and hold the Alt key.

④ Press the Tab key.

The Flip window appears.

⑤ While continuing to hold the Alt key, press the Tab key until the window you want to switch to is highlighted.

⑥ Release the Tab and Alt keys.

Windows Vista displays the program window for the program you selected.

Can I switch to an application that is not running?

▼ No, you cannot do that using the methods shown in this section Instead you must launch the application by choosing it from the Start menu, double-clicking a shortcut to the program on the desktop, clicking a program shortcut on a taskbar toolbar (such as the Quick Launch toolbar), double-clicking a program file from Windows Explorer (program files end with a .exe file name), or executing a program using the Run command. You can learn more about the Run command from the "Launch Programs with the Run Command" section, in this chapter.

When I use Alt+Tab, what happens when I reach the last program on the Windows Flip window?

▼ Simply keep pressing the Tab key to continue cycling through the open program windows. Sometimes when you use the Alt+Tab method you accidentally go past the window to which you want to switch. There are no penalties for missing your choice the first time (or even the twentieth time!). Simply continue Alt+Tabbing until you come back to the window you want. Then release the Alt+Tab keys. Likewise if you choose a window but want to switch to another one before doing any work in that window, that's OK. Press Alt+Tab to make another choice.

Use the Live Taskbar

With Windows Vista, you can have more than one program running at a time. You can, for example, have a word processor, database, Web browser, and graphics program going all at once. To make it easy to switch between these programs, you can use the taskbar, which displays at the bottom of the Windows desktop. In Windows Vista, you can extend the capabilities of the taskbar by using the Live Taskbar. With the Live Taskbar, a small thumbnail image of each window appears when you hover the mouse pointer over a taskbar button.

To use the Live Taskbar, your computer must be able to run the Windows Aero interface. To use Aero, your computer must meet certain hardware requirements, including a 1-GHz or higher processor, 1-GB or more of random access memory (RAM), and a video card that has at least 128MB of on-board memory. Then, to switch to the Aero interface, see the "Change Display Settings" section in Chapter 5.

The Live Taskbar thumbnail provides you with a view of the open document, picture, spreadsheet, or other type of file before you switch to it, enabling you to know exactly which window you are switching to.

Use the Live Taskbar

① Using the Start menu, open at least three different programs.

② Hover the mouse pointer over a taskbar button.

A Live Taskbar thumbnail appears.

③ Click the Live Taskbar thumbnail to select it.

Windows Vista displays the selected window.

Use Windows Flip 3D

Windows Vista enables you to switch between open applications by using the Windows Flip — press Alt+Tab on the keyboard. This is nothing new to the Windows operating system. However, with Windows Vista you can use the new Windows Flip 3D feature.

With the Windows Flip 3D feature, you are shown your open windows as windows layer diagonally across the desktop. You can cycle through the windows to pick which one you want to work on.

Like the Live Taskbar feature, Windows Flip 3D requires that your computer run the Aero interface.

Read the "Use the Live Taskbar" section to learn more about the Aero interface hardware requirements.

To use Windows Flip 3D, you use the Windows Key, which is part of most Windows-compatible keyboards. It is the key to the left and right of the spacebar, usually just to the left of the Alt key. Press and hold down the Windows Key and then press Tab. When you display open windows using Windows Flip 3D, you can select an item using the mouse, the Enter key, or simply release the Windows Key+Tab combination when your choice is at the front of the Flip 3D list.

Use Windows Flip 3D

① Using the Start menu, open at least three different programs.

② Press and hold the Windows Key.

③ Press Tab.

● Windows Vista displays the open windows in the Flip 3D list arrangement.

④ Press Tab to cycle through the windows.

⑤ Release Tab.

● Windows Vista displays the window at the front of the Flip 3D list.

Adjust Mouse Controls

Y ou can adjust your mouse settings to meet your needs and to fit your work style in Windows Vista: You can switch the functions of the left and right mouse buttons (for those who are left-handed), adjust the speed of double-clicking to match your personal comfort level, and turn on ClickLock (which lets you drag something without holding down the left mouse button — this can be especially handy if you are trying to perform this operation with a touchpad on a laptop computer).

You can also adjust the mouse pointer. You can adjust the speed of the pointer, enhance its precision, and use the Snap To feature to have the pointer automatically move to the default button in a dialog box. You can also change settings related to the pointer's visibility: You can display pointer trails that leave a trace of the path the pointer has traveled across the desktop so that it is easier to follow (especially useful on large monitors working with graphics or large spreadsheets), make the pointer appear or disappear while you are typing, and show the pointer location when you press the Ctrl key.

Adjust Mouse Controls

1 Click Start.

2 Click Control Panel.

The Control Panel window appears.

3 Click Mouse.

The Mouse Properties dialog box appears.

4 Click to switch the order of the mouse buttons (☐ changes to ☑).

5 Drag the slider and then double-click the folder icon to adjust the double-clicking speed.

6 Click to enable ClickLock (☐ changes to ☑).

7 Click the Pointer Options tab.

The Pointer Options tab appears.

8 Drag the slider to adjust the speed of the pointer relative to mouse movements.

9 Click to enable the Snap To feature (☐ changes to ☑).

10 Click to display pointer trails (☐ changes to ☑) and then adjust the speed with the slider control.

11 Click to show the location of the pointer when you press the Ctrl key (☐ changes to ☑).

12 Click the Wheel tab.

The Wheel tab appears where you can adjust the speed of your mouse wheel.

13 Click here to set one screen at a time when you move the mouse's scrolling wheel.

14 Click OK to save your changes.

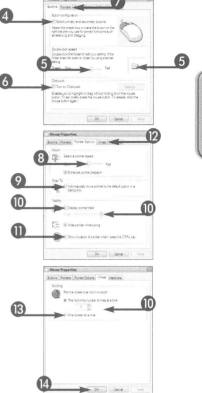

I have trouble finding the pointer on screen. How can I make it more visible when it is not moving?

▼ Pointers can be hard to see, especially on large monitors with lots of white space. From the Pointer Options tab of the Mouse Properties dialog box, click the Show location of pointer when I press the Ctrl key option. Click Apply to save your changes. Click OK to close the Mouse Properties dialog box. With the Show location of pointer when I press the Ctrl key option enabled, an animated feature zeroes in on your pointer when you press the Ctrl key.

My mouse often does not react when I double-click it. How do I get the mouse to recognize my double-click?

▼ Everyone double-clicks at a different speed. Fortunately, this setting can be easily adjusted. From the Buttons tab of the Mouse Properties dialog box, move the slider to a slower or faster setting depending on your needs. Then click the sample folder to the right of the slider to see if it opens when you double-click. Keep adjusting the slider until the rate is just the way you like it.

Save Time with the Right Mouse Button

You can save time in your work with Windows Vista simply by taking advantage of the secondary mouse button. This is usually the right mouse button (unless you switched the position of the two buttons — see the earlier section "Adjust Mouse Controls" for more details). By right-clicking (if you switched the buttons, substitute left-click in all these instructions), you access the short list of most likely operations in any given context in Windows Vista. Make a habit of right-clicking any icons or desktop areas to see whether the task you want to perform is in the list that pops up when you right-click.

Right-clicking the desktop brings up options to arrange the icons, create a new file, paste a file or shortcut, or change the Display properties. Right-clicking the Toolbar enables you to change settings related to the Toolbar. Right-clicking the Recycle Bin gives you a quick way to empty or open the Recycle Bin, and so on. Take a moment to right-click the various desktop elements; you will see many time-saving shortcuts. (Do not worry about experimenting with right-clicking once — it always brings up a menu; it never executes a command.)

Save Time with the Right Mouse Button

Note: *This is just one example of how using the right mouse button can save time. You could also accomplish this task via the Control Panel, but it would take more steps.*

① Right-click an unoccupied area of the desktop.

A menu appears with several frequently used options.

② Position your mouse pointer over View.

● A submenu appears with tasks relating to ordering icons on your desktop.

③ Position the mouse pointer over New.

A submenu appears with a choice of applications from which you may create a new file, as well as options to create a new folder or shortcut.

④ Scroll down the menu and click Personalize.

The Personalization window appears.

● You can click a Personalization tool to change its settings, such as clicking Desktop Background to change your background image.

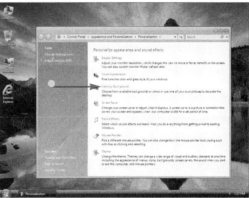

Is there a quick way to change my Internet settings?

▼ Yes. Right-click the Internet Explorer icon on the desktop and click Properties from the menu that appears. The Internet Options dialog box appears. Here you can change several options for browsing the Internet, including your default home page, your security settings, and Internet connection options.

If I have many application windows open, is there a quick way to minimize them all so just the desktop appears?

▼ Yes. Right-click the taskbar and click Show the Desktop. All open windows are minimized to buttons on the taskbar, and your desktop is clear. You can also click the Show desktop icon on the Quick Launch toolbar if it is showing.

Is there a quick way to change my date and time settings?

▼ Yes. Right-click the time in the lower right corner of the taskbar and click Adjust Date/Time from the menu that appears. The Date and Time dialog box appears. Click the Date and Time tab (if it is not already selected) and click the Change date and time button. The Date and Time Settings dialog box appears. In the Date area, select today's date. Under the clock icon, click in the hour, minute, or second field and change the time to the correct time. Click OK to close the Date and Time Settings dialog box. Click OK to close the Date and Time dialog box.

Use Search Features

Windows Vista includes an expanded and powerful search feature. You can use the search tool to locate files and folders a number of ways. Windows Vista provides the Search box on every folder view, such as when you are viewing the Computer folder, Windows Explorer, or an Open or Save window.

Another Search tool provided with Windows Vista is the Search box, located directly above the Start icon and below the All Programs link on the Start menu. This Search box is designed to help you find system-wide and even Internet-wide items. For example, if you are looking for a program installed on your computer, you can type its name (such as Word) in the Search box. Press Enter and Windows locates and starts that program.

Another way you can use Search in Windows Vista is to use the Search folder. The Search folder is designed for those times when you are not sure where an item may be (on a local disk, Internet site, or network disk) or when you want to locate a file or folder using more advanced searching techniques.

① Click Start.

② Click Search.

The Search platform appears.

③ Type a search word or phrase in the Search box.

④ To narrow your search to a type of file, click a button next to Show results for.

⑤ Click the magnifying glass icon or press Enter to start the search.

The Search folder shows a list of files, documents, and other items returned. This example shows search results for a keyword located in e-mails.

6 To view an item in the Search window, double-click it.

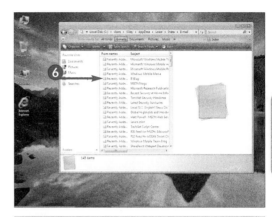

● The item or file displays in the application to which it is associated. Here the application is Microsoft Office Outlooks displaying a Web feed, an RSS feed.

Is there a way I can speed up searches?

▼ Yes. Make sure the Windows Vista Indexing service is turned on. By default, Windows Vista has it turned on when you install Windows Vista or upgrade to it from Windows XP. The Indexing service keeps a dynamic "database" of your files, folders, and other items so that searching in the future is faster. The Indexing service keeps track of items that you add, modify, and remove. To modify how Indexing works, open Control Panel, click System and Maintenace, and click Indexing Options. Click the Modify button and change settings as necessary.

When I open the Indexing Options window, the top of the window says Windows Searching service is not running. How can I turn it on?

▼ Open the System and Maintenance Control Panel option, click Administrative Tools, and then double-click Services to displays the Services window. Double-click Windows Search to display the Windows Search Properties dialog box. Select Automatic from the Startup type drop-down list and click Apply. Click the Start button to turn on the service and then click OK. Click the Close button on the Services window to close it. It may take several hours for the index to rebuild. Any searches you do after the index rebuilds fully may take longer than normal.

Make Use of Speech Recognition

If you have speech recognition software installed on your computer and a high-quality microphone, you can adjust your microphone and train your speech recognition software in Windows Vista. Starting with Office XP, Microsoft began shipping speech recognition capabilities such as voice commands and dictation with its Office product suite. For more information on text to speech, see the section "Make Use of Text to Speech."

You may also have specialized speech recognition software. If your computer has Microsoft Office XP (or later) or other speech-recognition software, use the related tools in the Windows Vista Control Panel

to make the best use of speech recognition capabilities. After you have set up speech recognition, you can also use it with Windows Vista accessories such as Notepad.

For speech recognition to function reliably, it is critical that you have a quiet work environment, a good (preferably headset) microphone, that you take the time to adjust your microphone sound levels, and that you train the speech engine to recognize your personal speech profile. While dictation may never be perfect, using voice commands can work surprisingly well if you take the time to adjust the settings and train your computer to understand you.

Make Use of Speech Recognition

Note: *Before you get started, make sure that your work environment is quiet, your microphone is attached, and your sound is on (not muted).*

① In the Control Panel window, click Ease of Access

The Ease of Access window opens.

② Click Speech Recognition Options.

The Speech Recognition window appears.

● You can click here to start Speech Recognition if you have previously configured it for your voice and hardware.

● You can click here to learn how best to use your computer for speech recognition.

● You can click here to train your computer for your voice.

③ Click here to set up your computer's microphone.

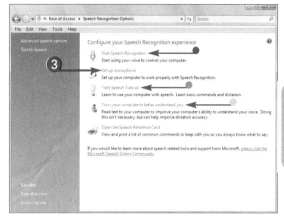

The Microphone Setup Wizard appears. You can use this wizard to set up your computer's microphone for speech recognition.

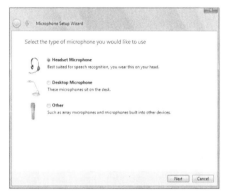

How do I get the best performance out of my speech recognition?

▼ Train your profile by reading the samples provided. Each takes about 10 to 15 minutes, although you may pause during any training session and take a break. The more samples the software has to work with, the greater the accuracy of the speech recognition software.

Try to speak clearly and at an even volume level. Make sure that you are at the right distance from your microphone. The Microphone Setup Wizard (click the Set-up Microphone link) and profile training screens provide other tips as you go along.

How can I improve the accuracy of the dictation?

▼ If you are noticing that the dictation is keeping up with your speed of talking but frequently making incorrect word choices (such as "the felt second" instead of "the Phelps account"), go to the Speech Recognition tab of the Text to Speech Properties dialog box and click Settings. In the User Settings area, select the Allow computer to review your documents and mail to improve speech recognition accuracy option. This option lets the Speech Recognition tool keep track of words and phrases you commonly use in documents in order to improve the accuracy of the speech recognition.

Make Use of
Text to Speech

I f you have text-to-speech software installed on your computer, you can select a computerized voice and adjust your speaker volume and talk speed settings in Windows Vista. Starting with Office XP, Microsoft began shipping text-to-speech and speech recognition capabilities with its Office product suite. (Note: Speech recognition is covered in the section "Make Use of Speech Recognition.") You may also have specialized text-to-speech software. If your computer has Office XP (or later) or other text-to-speech software, use the related tools in the Windows Vista Control Panel to adjust text-to-speech capabilities.

For optimal text to speech, make sure you have a good set of headphones or external speakers and a sound environment that enables you to hear the computerized voice clearly. From the Text to Speech tab in the Speech Properties dialog box you can select a preferred voice (the number of voices varies based on what speech-enabled software is installed on your computer), usually allowing you to choose between a male and female voice. Computerized text to speech works quite well for certain applications, such as reading documents and e-mail.

Make Use of Text to Speech

Note: *Before you get started, make sure that your work environment is quiet, your headphones or speakers are attached, and your sound is on (not muted).*

① In the Control Panel window, click Ease of Access.

The Ease of Access window opens.

② Click Speech Recognition Options.

The Speech Recognition window appears.

③ Click Text to Speech.

The Speech Properties dialog box appears, with the Text To Speech tab open.

④ Click the Voice selection down-arrow and select a voice.

⑤ Click Preview Voice to hear a sample of the voice you chose.

The computerized voice you selected says the sample sentence, highlighting each word as it is said.

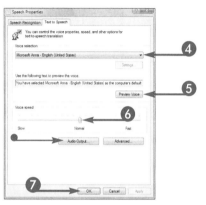

⑥ Drag the slider to quicken or slow the speed of speech.

- Click Audio Output to change audio output devices or adjust volume.

⑦ Click OK to save the voice sample.

I am having difficulty understanding the computerized voice. What can I do?

▼ You can try several things: On the Text to Speech tab of the Speech Properties dialog box of the Control Panel, try moving the slider to slow the voice speed. Try clicking Audio Output to display the Playback tab of the Sound dialog box. Click the speaker or headphone device you are using from the Select a playback device below option to modify its settings area. Click the Properties button to display the Speakers Properties dialog box. On the Levels tab, adjust the volume to a higher level. Also, on the General tab, make sure the Jack Information setting is correct for your system.

After I configure Speech Recognition, it always displays on the desktop when I start Windows. Can I shut this off?

▼ Yes. By default after you set up Speech Recognition, Windows Vista automatically starts it each time you start Windows. To shut it off, right-click the Speech Recognition tool and click Options. On the submenu that appears, click to deselect the Run at startup option. Right-click the Speech Recognition tool again and click the Exit command on the menu that appears. When Windows starts the next time, Speech Recognition does not start.

Activate Ease of Access Features

If you or someone you know is deaf, hard of hearing, blind, or has impaired vision or limited mobility, you can improve access to Windows Vista using the Ease of Access features, reached from the Control Panel.

For the deaf and hard of hearing, the Sounds feature directs programs that use sound cues to give visual cues, such as displayed text or icons. The Sentry gives visual warnings with blinking and flashing to take the place of sounds intended to get your attention.

For the blind, the Narrator reads aloud text elements on the screen in Windows and other applications. For the sight-impaired, the Magnifier is provided to enlarge the active area of the screen, and options exist to increase the size of screen fonts and provide a higher contrast display.

For those with impaired mobility, FilterKeys, MouseKeys, On-Screen Keyboard, and ToggleKeys allow for easier user input. These features were designed to provide basic accessibility to the largest amount of users.

Activate Ease of Access Features

① In the Control Panel window, click Ease of Access.

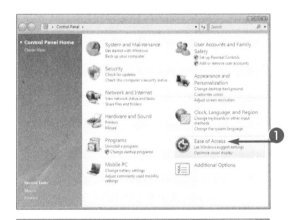

The Ease of Access window appears.

② Click Ease of Access Center.

The Ease of Access Center appears.

- You can click Start Magnifier to greatly enlarge the currently active area of the screen as if under a magnifying glass.

- You can click Start On-Screen Keyboard to use the mouse on-screen to point to keys as an alternative to typing on the computer's physical keyboard.

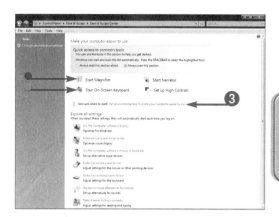

3 Click the Get recommendations to make your computer easier to use option to have Windows help you set up Ease of Access options for your needs.

The Get recommendations to make your computer easier to use wizard opens.

4 Click Next to proceed through the Wizard's steps.

5 Follow the instructions and answer the questions to let Windows Vista guide you through the set up of those Ease of Access options that are right for you, until you reach the final screen on which you click Finish.

I want to have visual alerts only when there is a system sound. How do I do that?

▼ From the Control Panel, click Ease of Access and then click Ease of Access Center on the next screen. The Ease of Access Center window appears. Click the Use text or visual alternatives for sounds link to display the Use text or visual alternatives for sounds window. Click Turn on visual notifications for sounds (Sound Sentry). Click Save.

Where can I go for more help with accessibility?

▼ These features were designed to provide basic accessibility to the largest amount of users. Those with special needs can visit www.microsoft.com/enable for more tools and information.

I have difficulty using the mouse. Are there Ease of Access tools I can use?

▼ Yes, on the Ease of Access Center window, click the Make the mouse easier to use link. The Make the mouse easier to use window appears. In the Mouse Pointers area, click a color and size option that best suits your needs. For example, you may want to use the Large Black pointer or the Large Inverting pointer if you have difficulty seeing the pointer on the screen. Also, consider using Mouse Keys by clicking the Turn on Mouse Keys option. Mouse Keys enables you to control the mouse using the numerica keypad on your computer's keyboard. Click Save to save your changes.

Launch Programs with the Run Command

You can use the Run command to quickly launch a program by typing in the name of the executable file. This feature is particularly convenient if you are running a system administrative or diagnostic tool and do not want to go through several levels of menus to get to the program you need.

Some users who make frequent use of batch files, such as network administrators and programmers, or those familiar with Unix and MS-DOS who still prefer a command-line interface for some tasks, will find this feature helpful.

It is not necessary to know the exact file name of the executable to use this feature, however. The Browse button enables you to explore folders graphically as well. The drop-down list also keeps track of the last few entries you made while using this feature. If you are performing a task often, find your previous entry in the list to save time. The example here shows you how to quickly bring up the MS-DOS style command line.

Launch Programs with the Run Command

① Click Start.

② Click All Programs.

③ Click Accessories.

④ Click Run.

The Run dialog box appears.

⑤ Type **cmd** in the Open field.

- You can click here to select from a list of previous entries.

⑥ Click OK.

- You can click Browse to explore folders to find the program or file you want to launch.

The program launches. In this example, the Windows Vista command prompt appears.

⑦ Type **exit**.

⑧ Press Enter or click the Close button to close the command prompt.

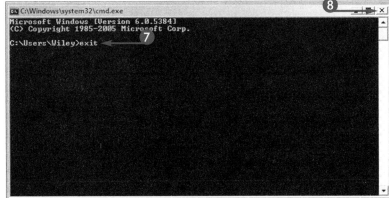

PART II

Can I add Run to the Start menu, like it was in Windows XP?

▼ Yes. Right-click the Start button and then click Properties. The Taskbar and Start Menu Properties dialog box appears. Select the Start Menu tab and click the Customize button next to the Start Menu option. The Customize Start Menu dialog box appears. In the list of items to add to the Start menu, scroll down the list to the Run command and click it. Click OK to close the Customize Start Menu dialog box. Click OK to close the Taskbar and Start Menu Properties dialog box. Click the Start button to see the Run command on the right side of the menu below the Help and Support item. Click it to start the Run command.

How do I launch a program from somewhere other than my hard drive?

▼ Type the assigned drive letter, followed by a colon and a backslash (:\). For example, to run a program called setup.exe located on a CD-ROM in the CD-ROM drive E, type **e:\setup.exe** in the Open field of the Run command and then click OK.

Can I get to a Web site this way?

▼ Yes. Type the Internet address (URL) in the Open field. For example, to reach the Microsoft home page, type **www.microsoft.com** in the Open field and then click OK.

Change Display Settings

You can adjust your display settings in Windows Vista according to your needs. If you have a large monitor, you may have chosen it so that you can view lots of detailed information. If so, you may want a different set of settings than if you chose a large monitor because you wanted everything to be larger and more readable on-screen. The PC's video adapter sends signals to draw the images on your display. The tiny dots that make up these images are referred to as *pixels*. By selecting the size of these pixels, you can adjust the relative size and sharpness of the images on your screen.

You can also select the number of colors Windows Vista displays on your screen. For example, you may want to ensure that you have the most accurate color representation when working with photos, or you may want to choose to display fewer colors in order to gain speed or to play a game designed to use fewer colors. You can make these adjustments from the Settings tab of the Display Properties dialog box.

Change Display Settings

1 Right-click the desktop.

A menu appears.

2 Click Personalize.

The Personalization area of the Control Panel appears.

3 Click Display Settings.

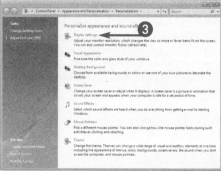

The Display Settings dialog box appears.

● Display shows which display screen is attached and which video adapter is installed.

● Click Identify Monitors to have Windows specify the number (1 or 2) for each monitor, if you have two monitors attached.

● Click Advanced Settings to make other display adjustments.

④ Drag the Resolution slider from Low toward High to increase the resolution.

Screen resolution controls the dimensions of the pixels that are used to draw your display screen.

○ In the preview window you can see the relative size of the desktop elements change.

⑤ Click the Colors drop-down list to select another quality, such as Medium (16 bit).

⑥ Click Apply.

Your screen redraws again with the new settings.

The Display Settings window appears, asking if the display change is OK. If not, the display setting reverts to the previous setting in 15 seconds.

⑦ Click Yes.

⑧ Click OK to save your new screen settings.

A window appears.

Note: *To change back to your original settings, change the screen resolution and color quality back to your previous settings and click OK.*

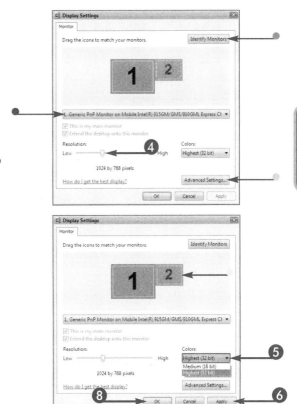

I increased my screen resolution, but now I cannot see Start or the taskbar. How do I get them back?

▼ Windows Vista enables you to set a higher screen resolution, even if your monitor cannot physically display a screen of those dimensions. A frame within a larger, "virtual" display is what you are actually seeing. To move this frame to the part of the "virtual" display you want to see, such as the taskbar, drag your mouse pointer to the corresponding edge of the display. The desktop scrolls until you see the part of the display that you need. If you do not like this effect, simply adjust your screen resolution to a setting that fits entirely on your display.

My display is showing only a few colors, and the display is of poor resolution. How can I correct this problem?

▼ In the Display Settings dialog box, make sure that your screen resolution is 800 × 600 pixels or higher. Next, click the Colors drop-down list and then click the last selection available; it is always the highest color quality available to display with your video adapter (graphics card) and monitor. If this does not fix the problem or if the highest available color quality is very low (8 bit), you may have a problem with your video adapter or monitor. Click How do I get the best display? and follow the procedures to diagnose the problem and find a solution.

Choose Windows Themes

Windows *themes* are a collection of graphic elements and sounds that enable you to customize your desktop around a central subject. You can also change settings and create your own theme. Windows Vista has a default theme and a legacy theme called Windows Classic.

You can select a theme and change icons, sounds, screen savers, backgrounds, mouse pointers, and so on and then click Save As and give your theme a new name. In this way you can have several themes, one for work and one for play, and name them

accordingly. By default Windows Vista stores your saved themes in the Documents folder under your user account.

You can view themes in the sample window and then switch back to your current theme by clicking My Current Theme, or back to the default Windows Vista theme. If, after sampling different themes, you decide to change yours, when you click OK your desktop fades to gray and Windows Vista displays a Please Wait pop-up window for several seconds. This is normal; Windows Vista is making changes and redrawing your screen.

Choose Windows Themes

1 Right-click the desktop.

A menu appears.

2 Click Personalize.

The Personalization area of the Control Panel appears.

3 Click Theme.

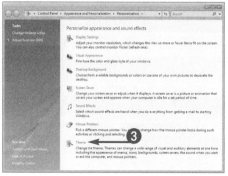

The Theme Settings dialog box appears.

● If you want to save your current theme and revert to it later, be sure to click Save As and give your current theme a name so that you can quickly return to it later.

④ Click the Theme down-arrow and select a theme, for example, Windows Classic.

● You can click Delete to delete a selected theme.

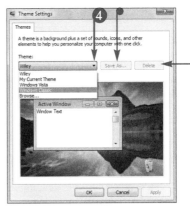

● The selected theme appears in the Sample window.

● You can click Apply to change the theme but keep the Theme Settings dialog box open.

⑤ Click OK to change the theme and close the dialog box.

The new theme is now installed.

Note: To return to your previous theme, follow the same steps and choose your previous theme from the list.

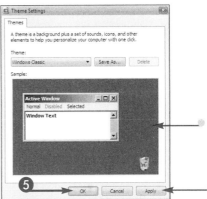

Do I have to keep the same icons and other settings of the theme I select?

▼ No. You can make any modifications to individual desktop settings that you want. The theme then appears in the Theme drop-down list with the theme name followed by *(Modified)*, indicating that you have made changes to the theme. And if you like the changes you make to a stock theme, do not forget to save it. Any time you make a change to a desktop component and you want to make sure it is part your theme, remember to come back to the Theme Settings dialog box, click the Save As button to display the Save As dialog box, type your theme name in the File Name box, and click Save. Click Yes when prompted if you want to replace the theme file.

Do the changes I make affect other users of this PC?

▼ No, each user has his or her own theme selection. When you log on as a new user, that new user's theme appears in Windows Vista. If another user wants to use your settings, you can copy the .theme file to a shared folder on the computer. For example, create a folder on the C:\ drive called Themes. Then copy your .theme file to that folder. When the next person logs on, instruct them to open the Theme Settings dialog box, click the Theme drop-down list, click Browse, navigate to the C:\Themes folder, and click the .theme file you placed there. Click Open and then click OK to apply the theme.

Switch to Large Windows Fonts and Icons

You can use larger fonts and enlarge the icons in Windows Vista. This is especially useful if you are using a large monitor with a high screen resolution. You may be able to fit everything onto the display, but the text and icons appear relatively small and difficult to read in such a situation. Changing these settings is also useful if your eyesight requires larger text and icons to work with Windows Vista comfortably.

You can accomplish these changes most readily by using the Appearance Settings dialog box. From here you can make changes not only to the size of the

fonts but also to the style of windows and buttons — choosing between Windows Vista or Windows Classic — and you can choose the Windows Vista color scheme. Clicking Effects takes you to a dialog box that controls the size of icons. It also enables you to control how menus appear on the screen, how font edges are smoothed — Standard or ClearType — whether to show a window's contents while dragging it, and whether to hide or display underlined letters for keyboard navigation.

Switch to Large Windows Fonts and Icons

① Right-click the desktop.

② Click Personalize on the menu that appears.

The Personalization area of the Control Panel opens.

③ Click Adjust font size (DPI) in the left pane.

The DPI Scaling dialog box appears.

④ Click the Larger scale (120 DPI) – make text more readable option (○ changes to ◉).

- A note appears at the bottom of the dialog box indicating that the font change will take place after you restart Window Vista.

⑤ Click OK.

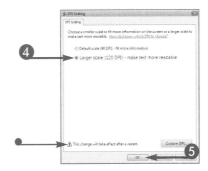

The You must restart your computer to apply these changes window appears.

⑥ Click Restart Now.

Windows shuts down, restarts, and displays fonts in a larger size. Note the increased font size of the Start menu items.

PART II

Can I make the fonts display even larger?

▼ Yes. In the DPI Scaling dialog box, click the Custom DPI button. You can choose a new DPI setting, such as 200%, based on the normal font size setting. Bear in mind that using extra large fonts often means that only part of a list of menu options appears on the screen, and you may need to scroll down to view all the options in a menu in such a case.

How do I know which is the best display settings for my monitor?

▼ You can choose several differnet font size and screen resolutions until you like what you see. As you change the settings, open different applications you plan to use every day so you see how well they look on your screen. Of course, the larger the physical size of the monitor, the higher the screen resolution you can use. With a 19-inch monitor, for example, you can use the 1280 × 1024 resolution and smaller fonts.

My display looks wavy and when I play video it looks choppy. What should I do?

▼ Let's assume that your monitor and display card work fine. If they do not, consider purchasing new ones. Otherwise, to help improve your display performance, limit the number of applications you run at the same time. For every application running and window displayed, more system resources are used, thereby reducing your display quality. Also reduce the resolution of your monitor, such as from 1152 × 864 to 1024 × 768.

Change the Look of Windows and Menus

Y ou can make custom refinements to the appearance of windows and menus by clicking Advanced on the Appearance Settings dialog box. From the Advanced Appearance dialog box, you can change the look — font, color, and size — of many desktop user interface elements, such as the desktop, menu title bars, text, and buttons. Windows Vista attempts to standardize some of these attributes, so some are only customizable with Windows Classic menus.

You can select the item on the desktop whose appearance you want to modify either by selecting it from the Item drop-down list or by clicking the

corresponding item on the preview window in the Advanced Appearance dialog box. If you select a non-text item, you can choose a different size and/or color, or two colors if applicable. If the item contains text, such as the Active Title Bar, you can also choose the font, font size, and any font attributes — bold or italic. If you decide to change the font, experiment with several to find one that appears readable to you on-screen; fonts that are pleasing to the eye on paper are sometimes hard to read on-screen.

Change the Look of Windows and Menus

① Right-click the desktop and click Personalize from the menu that appears to open the Personalization area of the Control Panel.

② Click Windows Color and Appearance.

The Appearance Settings dialog box appears.

③ Click Windows Classic style in the Colors scheme list.

Note: *Some changes work only with Windows Classic style, so this style has been selected for this example.*

④ Click Advanced.

The Advanced Appearance dialog box appears.

- The preview window shows how changes you make will affect the appearance of Windows.

5 Click Active Window in the preview window to select the Active Title Bar.

- Active Title Bar appears in the Item drop-down list.

- The font for the selected item appears in the Font drop-down list.

6 Click a font attribute.

- The text in the preview windows is bold in this example.

7 Click Color 1 to open a color palette.

8 Click a new color.

The new color appears in the left side of the menu bar.

9 Click OK to close the Advanced Appearance dialog box.

10 Click OK to close the Appearance Settings dialog box.

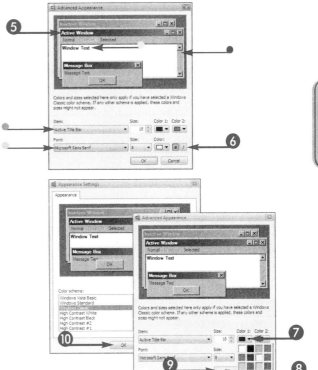

After making a number of changes, is there a way I can save these settings?

▼ Yes. After you have saved your settings by clicking OK to close the Appearance Settings dialog box, click Theme in the Personalization area of the Control Panel and select My Current Theme from the Theme drop-down list. Click Save As, assign your current settings a name, and then click OK. If you are already using a custom theme, select Save As, select the theme name from the File name drop-down list, and click Save. Click Yes when prompted to replace the theme. Click OK. For more details on themes, see the section "Choose Windows Themes," earlier in this chapter.

I changed the color of the menu bars and the font, but when I saved the changes, only the font changed. What happened?

▼ Unless you changed windows and buttons to Windows Classic style on the Appearance Settings dialog box before clicking Advanced, only some of your changes will be made, even though they appear on the preview window. You can either choose from one of the three color schemes of Windows Vista Basic style or change to Windows Classic style to have your color changes take effect.

Clean Up the Desktop

Desktop icons provide a quick way to access many of your programs, important documents, Windows tools, and more. Over time, however, users tend to put every kind of icon on their desktop — they should really set up shortcuts to folders in which they can store individual documents or files — making it difficult to find anything. You can take advantage of a handy Windows Vista feature to help you clean up your desktop when it becomes too cluttered with old or unused shortcuts. This feature is especially useful if you have many programs, because most commercial software creates a shortcut on your

desktop automatically during installation. You may also have a work style that entails creating shortcuts to frequently accessed files, folders, or Web sites that you need less as time goes by.

The Show Desktop Icons feature lets you show or hide all your desktop icons. When you hide the desktop icons, Windows does not delete them; the icons simply just do not show up. Windows hides shortcut icons to documents, programs, and other objects. It also hides icons that it creates, such as the Recycle Bin and Internet Explorer icons.

Clean Up the Desktop

① Right-click the desktop.

Note: You will notice the desktop includes several icons.

A menu appears.

② Click View.

A submenu appears.

A check mark appears next to the Show Desktop Icons command to indicate that it is currently activated.

③ Click Show Desktop Icons to deactivate this setting.

The icons disappear from the desktop.

④ To turn on the icons, right-click the desktop.

⑤ Click View.

⑥ Click Show Desktop Icons.

Can I remove just one or two icons from the desktop and not turn off all of them?

▼ Yes. To remove an icon, drag and drop it to the Recycle Bin or right-click it and choose Delete. When asked if you want to remove the icon or send the shortcut to the Recycle Bin, click Yes. When you remove a shortcut icon, remember that this does not delete the program or the document to which it is associated. It simply removes the shortcut link to it. However, some icons on your desktop may not be shortcuts. If you have saved any files to the Desktop folder, those files are not shortcuts; they are the real thing. When you delete them, they are put in the Recycle Bin. The quick way to tell if an icon is a shortcut is to look for a curved arrow on the lower left side of the icon.

Can I show other icons on the desktop, such as Control Panel?

▼ Yes. Right-click the desktop, choose Personalization, and click Change desktop icons from the Tasks pane of the Control Panel window. The Desktop Icons Settings dialog box appears. On the Desktop tab, click those items that you want to show up on your desktop. You can select Computer, User's Files, Network, Recycle Bin, and Control Panel. While you are adding these icons, you can change the icon's picture too. Click an icon in the preview window and click the Change Icon button to open the Change Icon dialog box. Click a differnet icon picture and click OK. Click OK to save your settings.

Select a Screen Saver

S creen savers were first introduced to keep monitors from being damaged by users leaving their computers idle for long periods of time. On-screen characters would actually etch an image on the display monitor, permanently damaging the monitor. Now screen savers are used for decoration and a way to secure a computer while the user is away from their desk.

You can choose from a number of screen savers in Windows Vista that replace your current desktop display when it is not in use. The screen saver can be a slide show viewer, a marquee for your company, an interesting graphic animation, or simply a blank screen. There is a preview that enables you to view each screen saver. You can also set the number of minutes that must pass without a keystroke or mouse movement before the screen saver starts. If you have Windows Vista Ultimate or if you chose to use a password with Windows Vista Basic, you also have the option of protecting your computer with a password when the screen saver is activated.

You can make changes and select screen savers on the Screen Saver Settings dialog box. If you have additional screen savers installed on your computer, they are also accessible from that location.

Select a Screen Saver

① Right-click the desktop and click Personalization to open the Personalization area of the Control Panel.

② Click Screen Saver.

The Screen Saver Settings dialog box appears.

③ Click the Screen saver down arrow and select a screen saver.

● You can type a number (1 to 9999) here to select the number of minutes Windows Vista waits with no user input before launching the screen saver.

● Click here for a full screen preview of the screen saver.

● Click here to adjust power settings related to having your monitor idle.

④ Click Settings.

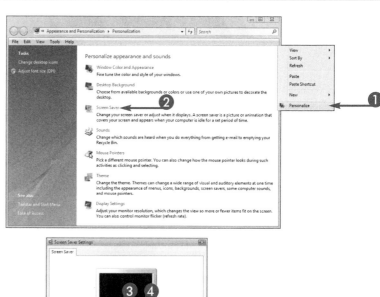

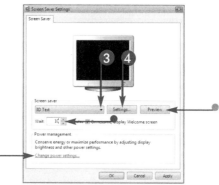

The settings screen for the selected screen saver appears, for example, 3D Text.

5 Type your text here.

6 Click OK.

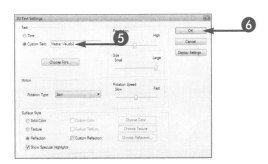

The Screen Saver Settings dialog box appears again. Click Preview to see the full screen preview shown here. Moving your mouse or pressing any key takes you back to the Screen Saver tab, where you can click OK to confirm the selection or Cancel to exit without saving your changes.

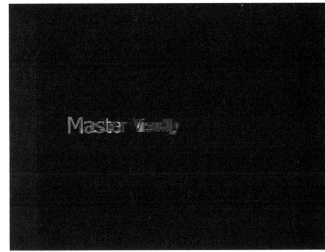

How do I show my photos in a slideshow?

▼ Select Photos from the Screen saver drop-down list in the Screen Saver Settings dialog box. Click Settings to make changes to how often the pictures are swapped, to transition effects, and so on. Also, you will need to click Use pictures and video from and click Browse to open the Browse For Folder dialog box. Click the folder in which you have your photos stored. By default this folder is your Pictures folder stored in your user account folder, such as C:\Users\Bill Smith\Pictures. Click OK to return to the Photos Screen Saver Settings dialog box. Click Save to save your settings and then click OK to close the Screen Saver Settings dialog box.

I have selected a screen saver, but it displays for a few minutes, and then my monitor goes blank. What is happening?

▼ It is likely that you have your screen saver set to display after a certain number of minutes, and your PC's power management features are also set to turn off your monitor after a certain number of minutes to conserve power. On the Screen Saver Settings dialog box, click Change power settings to display the Select a power plan window. Click the Change plan settings link that is beneath the power plan you are using, such as Balanced. This displays the Change settings for the plan window. From the Turn off the display drop-down list, select a longer time period, such as 30 minutes. Click Save changes.

Change Items on the Start Menu

The Windows Vista Start menu provides access to almost everything on your computer. You can start programs from it, open the Control Panel to access configuration tools, get assistance from the Help and Support button, and access your network settings.

You can choose which items display on the Start menu in Windows Vista. If you make no changes, Windows Vista uses its own guidelines and rules to learn which programs you use most often, and adapts to your work habits to some extent. However, you probably know right at the outset which items you want to have readily available and which items are more of a distraction.

To customize the Start menu, you can right-click the Start menu and select Properties. This brings up the Start Menu tab of the Taskbar and Start Menu Properties dialog box. At this point you can choose between Windows Vista and Classic Start menu styles and then click Customize. This section assumes Vista style. The Customize Start Menu dialog box gives you some basic settings. You can, for example, change the number of programs to list those you have most recently used. You can also choose whether to display a browser or e-mail program permanently and, if so, which one.

Change Items on the Start Menu

① Right-click the Start menu.

A menu appears.

② Click Properties.

The Start Menu tab of the Taskbar and Start Menu Properties dialog box appears.

● You can select to revert to Windows Classic style start menu and customization.

③ Click Customize.

The Customize Start Menu dialog box appears.

④ Click options on how you want links, icons, and menus to appear on the Start menu.

⑤ Type the number of programs to show on the Start menu.

⑥ Click to deselect the Internet or E-mail option so they do not appear on your Start menu (☐ changes to ☑).

⑦ Click OK to close the Customize Start Menu dialog box.

⑧ Click OK to close the Properties dialog box.

⑨ Click Start to show the changes.

The Internet browser no longer appears on the permanent list.

● The Computer folder shows as a menu.

● Up to six of the last used items are now displayed. Your screen may show fewer if you have used less than eight programs.

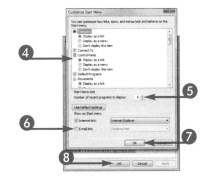

I want to keep a particular program on my permanent list, but it is not my e-mail or Internet program. How can I do this?

▼ From the Start menu, find the program you want to have on your permanent list. It can be on the temporary list of most recent programs or in the set of menus found when you click All Programs. Right-click the program. In the menu that appears, click Pin to Start menu. The program icon is added to the top of the Start menu and stays there until you remove it. You can remove it at any time by right-clicking the program's icon again and clicking Unpin from Start menu.

Can I remove one item from my recently used program list without clearing the entire list?

▼ Yes. Click the Start menu and right-click the item's icon in the recently used area, below the divider line of programs that pinned to the Start menu. From the menu that appears, click Remove from this list. Windows Vista removes the icon from the recently used area of the Start menu. This only removes the program from the list and does not uninstall or delete the program from your PC.

Hide or Show Notifications on the Taskbar

You can control how and when icons for notifications are displayed on the taskbar in Windows Vista. You may find that the number of helper applications running on your PC that display on the taskbar is very large. Antivirus software, printer software, sound software, and any software designed to work with specialized hardware tend to have icons for notifications that appear on the taskbar. For this reason, Windows Vista has a feature that enables you to hide icons for all of these applications while they are inactive as the default setting, or to individually set them to always show, always hide, or hide when inactive.

You can change these individual settings by right-clicking the taskbar, clicking Properties, clicking the Notification Area tab, and clicking Customize in the Properties dialog box. Each notification is listed by Icon, as it appears when you pause with your mouse over the icon, and Behavior, whether it is set to hide when inactive, always hide, or always show. By clicking the Behavior setting next to the notification you want to change, you can select one of the other two remaining settings from a drop-down list. You can also choose behavior for items that appeared in the past, so the behavior applies to them when they occur again in the future.

Hide or Show Notifications on the Taskbar

① Right-click the taskbar.

A menu appears.

② Click Properties.

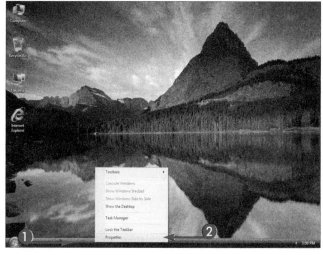

The Taskbar tab of the Taskbar and Start Menu Properties dialog box appears.

③ Click the Notification Area tab.

④ Click Customize.

96

The Customize Icons dialog box appears.

5 Click here and select the setting in the Behavior list for a notification, for example, Show.

● You can click here to restore notifications to their default settings.

6 Click OK to close the Customize Notifications dialog box.

7 Click OK to close the Properties dialog box.

● The Office 2007 Side Note icon displays, even when not in use.

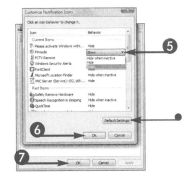

I can open the Customize Icons dialog box, but it does not allow me to make changes to the settings. Why not?

▼ You must have administrator privileges for your PC to make changes to these settings. If you would like to make changes to notifications, log on as network administrator or contact your network administrator.

How can I quickly view the hidden icons?

▼ Click the show hidden icons button to display any icons for hidden but currently running items. Click the hide button to hide them again.

Can I remove an icon from the notification area?

▼ Yes, to do this right-click the item you want to delete on the notification area. A menu appears. Click Exit, Quit, Close, or a similar command. The command that appears depends on the application. If prompted, confirm that you want to exit the program. In some cases, you may not be able to remove the icon from the notification area using the right-click procedure. Instead, open the application's Options or Preferences dialog box, or similar type of dialog box, and deselect any option specifying that the program should appear on the notification area or task tray.

Enable and Add Items to Quick Launch

You can use the Quick Launch feature to launch your most frequently used items with a single click on the taskbar. To do this, you must enable the Quick Launch toolbar. When you have enabled it, a set of icons appears just to the right of Start. You can add items to the Quick Launch toolbar by dragging them from the Start menu. You can also change the order in which they appear by simply dragging them to the left or right. If your taskbar is locked, only three items appear on the taskbar. If you choose to have more than three with the taskbar locked, you must first click the double chevrons to see the remaining Quick Launch items.

You can add not only programs but also individual folders, files, Web links, or other Windows Vista desktop items, such as the Control Panel or My Computer. To remove an item, drag it to the Recycle Bin. This removes it from only the Quick Launch toolbar; it does not delete the item from your PC.

The Show desktop icon on the Quick Launch toolbar enables you to quickly minimize all open windows so that you can see the desktop.

Enable and Add Items to Quick Launch

① Right-click the taskbar.

② Click Toolbars.

③ Click Quick Launch.

● The Quick Launch icons now appear to the right of Start.

④ Click Start.

5 Right-click the item from the Start menu, for example, Windows Photo Gallery.

6 Click Add to Quick Launch.

● The item's icon now appears in the Quick Launch section of the taskbar.

You can pause with the mouse pointer over the icon to see the name of the item, or click to launch the item.

7 Click here to see additional Quick Launch items.

● A menu showing one or more additional Quick Launch items appears.

Can I add an item to the Quick Launch toolbar even if that item is not on the Start menu?

▼ Yes, to do this locate the item you want to add to the Quick Launch toolbar. For example, some users add shortcuts to documents or spreadsheets they often update. This enables them to quickly open them without displaying the desktop, Start menu, or a subfolder. Once you locate the item, click and hold down the right-mouse button over the item. Drag to the Quick Launch toolbar and release the right-mouse button. A menu appears. Click Create Shortcut(s) Here. Windows Vista adds a shortcut to the item on the Quick Launch toolbar.

Is there a way to minimize all my open applications so that I see a clear desktop with one click?

▼ Yes. If you enabled Quick Launch, one of the default items, Shows Desktop, performs this function. Just click this icon once; all of your open applications are minimized as buttons on the taskbar, and the desktop is clear.

Can I change the icon or description for the item in Quick Launch?

▼ Yes, in most cases. Right-click the icon on the Quick Launch section of the taskbar and then click Properties. To add or change the description, edit or add something to the Comments field. To change the icon, click Change Icon and browse visually through a list of Microsoft stock icons or select one of your own.

Create Your Own Toolbar

If you want to have ready access to a folder that you use all the time, but you want to keep your desktop clear, you can create your own toolbar that takes you to a shortcut, file, Web address, or folder. And you can create a folder that groups together any collection of items — such as shortcuts, files, or Web links — that are accessible by one click on the taskbar. You can also use this feature for an entire drive or storage device, if you so choose.

To create a new toolbar, right-click the taskbar, click Toolbars, and then click New Toolbar and select a folder, file, or other item from the lists. You can also create a new folder here by clicking the New Folder button on the New Toolbar – Choose a folder dialog box. If you click Make New Folder, be sure to select New Folder and rename it accordingly, or it will remain New Folder. When you are finished, click Select Folder, and the name of your new toolbar appears at the right side of the taskbar near the notification and clock area. Click the double chevron to the immediate right of your toolbar name to launch the toolbar.

Create Your Own Toolbar

① Right-click the taskbar.

A menu appears.

② Click Toolbars.

③ Click New Toolbar.

The New Toolbar – Choose a folder dialog box appears.

④ Click a folder.

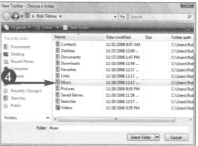

⑤ Click Select Folder.

The new toolbar appears on the taskbar.

⑥ Click the double chevron to launch the toolbar menu.

⑦ Click the double chevron again to close the toolbar menu.

How do I remove a toolbar?

▼ Right-click the taskbar and click Toolbars. Any toolbars that currently appear have a check mark next to them. Click the toolbar you want to remove. If it is a predefined toolbar such as Quick Launch or Links, it remains on the list but does not have a check mark next to it and does not appear on the taskbar. If the toolbar is one you created, it is removed from the menu, and you need to create it again later if you change your mind. Use the New Toolbar command as shown in the "Create Your Own Toolbar" section.

Can I open my custom toolbar as a window instead of a menu?

▼ Yes. To open it as a window, right-click the name of the custom toolbar and then click Open Folder to open it in a standard Windows Vista folder window. To open it as a menu, click or right-click the double chevron.

Is there a way to enlarge the toolbar icons on the taskbar?

▼ Yes, you can use the Large Icons command to make the toolbars larger. To do this, right-click the taskbar toolbar and click View. A menu appears with the choices Large Icons and Small Icons. Click Large Icons. The icons on the toolbar increase in size to make them easier to see and select.

Enable Windows Sidebar

Windows Vista includes Windows Sidebar, which is a vertical bar that resides on the side of the screen. It includes Windows gadgets, or small programs, to help you keep important information on your desktop. For example, you can display Web feeds that constantly show up-to-date information downloaded from the Internet. These Web feeds use a technology called RSS (Really Simple Syndication) to stream information to your desktop.

When you set up Sidebar, you can determine which gadgets to display, in which order they appear, and how often dynamic information, such as Web feeds, is updated. Another customization choice is how Sidebar appears. For instance, you can display it so it is always on top of your open applications or hide it when you display an application window. Finally, you can detach a gadget from Sidebar and place it on your desktop. See the section "Use Vista Gadgets" for more information on gadgets.

Enable Windows Sidebar

① Click Start.

② Click All Programs.

Note: *After you click All Programs, the name changes to Back.*

③ Click Accessories.

④ Click Windows Sidebar.

Sidebar appears on the right side of the desktop. The gadgets displayed on your desktop may be different from the ones shown here.

⑤ Click the plus sign (+) at the top of Sidebar.

The Gadget Gallery window appears.

⑥ Double-click a gadget that you want to add to Sidebar.

- You can click here to see additional gadgets. Then double-click the gadgets to add them to your sidebar.

⑦ Click the Close box to close the Gadget Gallery window.

- If you were not able to see the gadget you double-clicked added to Sidebar during step 6, you should be able to see it now.

⑧ To remove a gadget from Sidebar, hover the mouse over the gadget until the gadget controls appear.

⑨ Click the Close box.

When I choose Windows Sidebar, nothing appears on my screen. What should I do?

▼ Look at the Notification area of the taskbar. There will be a blue icon called Windows Sidebar there. You may have started Sidebar in the past at some point and turned it off. Click the Windows Sidebar icon and click Show Sidebar.

Can I move Sidebar to the left side of the screen?

▼ Yes. Any icons you have displayed on that side of the desktop will be covered by Sidebar. You will need to move them to the right side or someplace else on the desktop and then right-click an open area of Sidebar and click Properties. The Windows Sidebar Properties dialog box appears. Click Left under Display Sidebar on this side of screen. Click OK. The Sidebar switches to the left side.

How can I get Sidebar to show when Windows starts?

▼ Right-click an open area of Sidebar and click Properties. The Windows Sidebar Properties dialog box appears. Click the Start Sidebar when Windows starts option. Click OK. The next time you start Windows Vista, Windows Sidebar will start as well. If you are using any gadgets that execute long scripts or gather information from the Web, you may notice that your start-up process will get longer as Sidebar starts each gadget.

Use Vista Gadgets

Vista gadgets are small programs that appear on the Windows Sidebar. Some common gadgets include Calculator, Clock, Recycle Bin, Notes, and Feed Watcher.

To see which gadgets are on your computer, use the Gadget Gallery. The Gadget Gallery lets you view each gadget, add it to your Sidebar, read a short description of the gadget, and uninstall it from Sidebar. The Gadget Gallery also provides a link so you can connect to the Microsoft Windows Vista Gadgets

for Windows Sidebar Web page and download new gadgets. You should visit this site periodically for new or updated gadgets.

There are too many gadgets to review each one here, so the following demonstrates how to use one of the most popular gadgets, the Feed Viewer. This gadget shows RSS (Really Simple Syndication) feeds from the Internet, so you will need to have an Internet connection to follow along.

Use Vista Gadgets

① Add the Feed Viewer to the Sidebar.

Note: *To add the Feed Viewer to the Sidebar, see the "Enable Vista Sidebar" section.*

② Right-click the Feed Viewer and click Settings.

The Feed Viewer setting dialog box opens.

③ Click here to select a Microsoft RSS feed.

The Internet Explorer Team Blog feed is selected in this example.

④ Click OK.

The Feed Viewer gadget shows the title of the feed you selected. As Windows Vista receives RSS feeds from the Internet Explorer Team Blog, you can see the title of the feed.

⑤ To expand the gadget window to see more feeds, hover the mouse at the bottom of the gadget and click the check mark.

The gadget expands to show more RSS feed titles.

⑥ Click an RSS article to read.

Internet Explorer appears, attaches to the Internet, and displays the article you selected.

When I try to select an RSS feed from the Feed Viewer setting dialog box, I do not have additional feeds. How do I get these?

▼ You must subscribe to an RSS feed. To do this, open Internet Explorer and visit the site that has the feed. Click the Feeds button on Internet Explorer to see the names of the RSS feeds on that page. Select a feed and click the Add/Subscribe button. Type a name for the feed and select the folder in which you want to store the feed data. Click Add.

What types of gadgets are available on the Web?

▼ Just about anything you want! Many developers have submitted their gadgets to the Gadgets for Windows Sidebar Web site. The Web site categorizes the gadgets to make them easy to find. Categories include All Categories, Fun and games, Tools and utilities, and Lifestyle. Some of the ones available at the time of this writing included gadgets for the Google search site, Xbox video game system, Microsoft Outlook, and Media Player. Some of the names of the gadgets that you can download and use on your Sidebar include iTunes Gadget, Remote Desktop Gadget, Google-bar, Xbox Gamertag, Ping Gadget, and Phone Notify.

Add a User Account

You can add user accounts to Windows Vista to enable multiple users to share the same computer. By default, Windows Vista creates a default administrator for your computer. Unless you specify one during setup, a password is not created for the computer. This computer boots straight into Windows. Because you should password-protect your computer in a multi-user environment, you can create a password for the default administrator user, or, better yet, create a second user for your computer. You also can create additional users in case others need to use your computer. Each user can have different environmental setups, including different desktop icons, individualized wallpaper settings, unique printer setups, and so on.

The easiest way to create additional users is through the User Accounts and Family Safety program in the Control Panel. With User Accounts and Family Safety, you can add user accounts, modify accounts, and even delete accounts.

User accounts can be set as Standard or Administrator. Standard users are allowed to use programs and can make a few system changes (such as wallpaper and themes changes). Administrators have full authority over Windows and can add and remove programs.

Add a User Account

1 Click Start.

2 Click Control Panel.

The Control Panel appears.

3 Click the Add or remove user accounts link under the User Accounts and Family Safety heading.

PART II

The Manage Accounts window appears.

④ Click Create a new account.

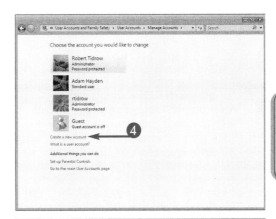

The Create New Account window appears.

⑤ Type a name for the new user account.

⑥ Click an option to choose whether you want the account to be a Standard user or an Administrator account (○ changes to a ◉).

⑦ Click Create Account.

Windows creates a new user account, and the User Account window appears.

Note: *See the next section, "Modify User Accounts" for more on the User Account window.*

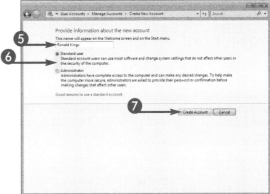

Can I create user accounts from a server?

▼ Yes. When you connect to a Windows domain controller, such as to a Windows 2003 Server network, the domain controller stores authorized domain user accounts. When you log in to the domain, you use a username and password for the domain, which in turn authorizes you to work in the Windows Vista computer.

Can more than one user account be an administrator?

▼ Yes. However, you should have only one Administrator account per computer. You can assign additional users as administrators if you feel that they are responsible enough to make system-wide changes, such as installing programs, and to have access to all files (including system and hidden files).

Can non-administrators make user accounts?

▼ No, Windows does not allow Standard users to create new user accounts. This way only those deemed an adminstrator can make critical system changes. For example, if any user could create new user accounts, a malicious user (even one from the Internet) could create an Administrator account and then access all your files and settings.

Modify User Accounts

Y ou can modify user accounts with the User Accounts and Family Safety feature. One modification is to add a password for the user. Other modifications you can make include changing the user account name, changing the Welcome screen picture associated with the user account, modifying the account type, and deleting the account. The changes you make using the User Accounts and Family Safety feature are changes that affect the user account and account type, not how Windows is set up or behaves.

Other settings for each user account are saved while the user works inside Windows. For example, when a

user logs in and makes changes to the Windows wallpaper, that wallpaper setting is saved for that user. Similarly, each user can set up a collection of desktop icons and shortcuts to suit his or her work habits. When the user logs out and logs back in later, those same icons are available for that user.

To make change to a user account, you must log on as the user you plan to modify, or log on with an administrator account. This eliminates the chances that a non-administrator will delete another user's account information.

Modify User Accounts

Change the Account Name

① Click Start.

② Click Control Panel.

The Control Panel appears.

③ Click User Accounts and Family Safety.

The User Accounts and Family Safety window appears.

④ Click User Accounts.

The User Accounts window appears with a list of changes you can make to your account.

⑤ To change the account name, click Change your name.

Why does Windows show a Guest account when I click the Manage another account link?

▼ The Guest account is automatically created when Windows is installed. Users not set up on your computer can log in using it. This account includes only basic authorizations, such as permission to start Windows and use programs available to all users. Password-protected files, Windows settings, and protected folders are not accessible to Guest accounts.

How do users switch from one user to another?

▼ The current user must log off for another user to use the computer. To do this, click Start and then click Log Off. Click the user account name, type a password (if required), and press Enter.

Is the Guest account enabled automatically during installation?

▼ No, by default, Windows does not enable the Guest account. You must select it in the Manage Accounts window. (Click Manage another user from the User Accounts window and then click the Turn On button on the Turn on Guest Account window.) Later, you can go back and turn off the account if you want to disable it. Microsoft recommends that you leave the Guest account disabled unless you change its default password. This way, unauthorized users cannot access your computer using the default Guest account username and password.

continued

Modify User Accounts
(Continued)

You can change the name of an account. Changing the name is handy if you have a user who no longer needs to use your computer, but you want to keep all the settings associated with that user. Or the original user may be leaving altogether. In that case, another user can use the same setup. Simply change the user account name to that of the new person.

Password-protecting your Windows machine is a good practice to thwart others from accessing or destroying your files. In fact, some companies require that all users have passwords to access company computers.

When you create a password, use one that is difficult to guess (do not use last names, common nicknames, or children's names) and at least six characters in length. Some companies require passwords to include a combination of uppercase and lowercase letters as well as numbers.

The picture associated with a user account can be changed to one that closely matches the personality of the user. For example, a person who likes sports can choose a sports-themed picture. If one of the default pictures does not work, choose a different one using the Browse for more pictures link.

Modify User Accounts *(continued)*

The next screen, asking you for a new name for the account, appears.

⑥ Type a new name for the account.

⑦ Click Change Name.

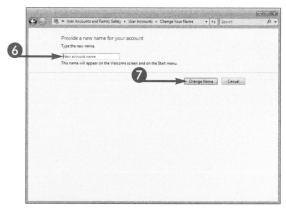

Change the Account Password

Windows saves the new account name, and the User Accounts screen reappears.

⑧ To change the password, click Change your password.

The Change Your Password screen appears.

9 Type your current password.

10 Type a new password.

11 Type the new password again to confirm the password.

12 Type a password hint.

13 Click Change password.

Windows saves the new password.

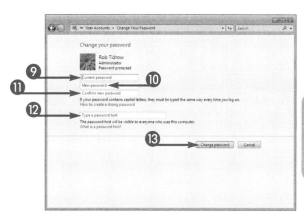

Change the Account Picture

1 Repeat steps **1** to **5** on the previous page, selecting the Change your picture link in the Make changes to your user account window.

2 Click a picture.

3 Click Change Picture.

Windows saves the new account picture.

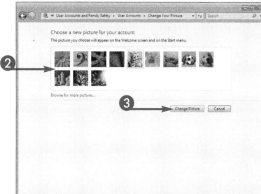

Why does a screen appear every time I try to install a program?

▼ Windows Vista includes a new security feature called User Account Control (UAC). It is designed for more control over who (which user account) can access critical system resources, such as those to install programs, change system settings, and delete user accounts.

▼ By default, UAC is turned on, so when you install a program, you are presented with a screen asking if you are sure you want to continue with the installation. If you are logged on as an administrator, you simply have to click the Continue button. If, however, you are logged on as a Standard user, you must enter a valid adminstrator user name and password to continue.

When I delete a user, are the user's files removed as well?

▼ Files stored in a user's Documents folder can be saved or deleted when you delete an account. You must specify which you want to do. If you want to maintain those files, click Keep Files. Click Delete Files to delete files in the Documents folder. Some files, such as Internet favorites, desktop settings, and e-mail messages, cannot be saved.

Change Group Membership

Windows lets you join users to groups using Local Users and Groups. It is a Windows security feature that lets you assign users to groups that have specific rights and permissions granted to them. For example, a user can be part of the Administrator group that grants that user full rights to the Windows environment.

On the other hand, a user can be added as a member of the Users group (called *Standard* in the User Accounts window). This group prevents users from changing system settings, installing programs, and adding new printers.

Administrators and limited types of users are available when you set up a user. Additional built-in groups, available only through Local Users and Groups, include Backup Operators, Cryptographic Operators, Distributed COM Users, Network Configuration Operators, Performance Monitor Users, Power Users, Remote Desktop Users, and Debugger Users. You also can create your own groups and add users to them.

To work with Local Users and Groups, use the Computer Management program.

Change Group Membership

① Right-click the Computer icon on the desktop.

A shortcut menu appears.

② Click Manage.

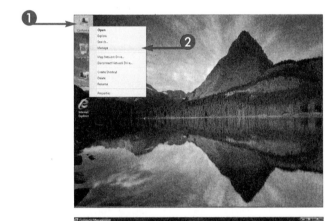

The Computer Management window appears.

③ Click here to see all System Tools folders.

④ Click here to see all Local Users and Groups folders.

⑤ Click Users.

⑥ Double-click a username.

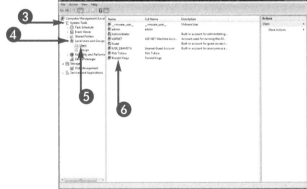

The Properties dialog box for the user appears.

7 Click the Member Of tab.

● This area displays groups to which the user belongs.

8 Click Add.

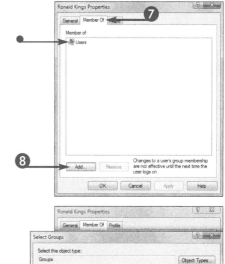

The Select Groups dialog box appears.

9 Type the name of a group here.

For this example, Power Users is the group.

10 Click OK to close the Select Groups dialog box.

11 Click OK to confirm your changes in the Properties dialog box.

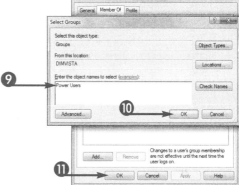

Do I have to use the Local Users and Groups feature?	I belong to a domain at work. Should I be changing my Local Users and Groups settings?	I am using Windows Vista Home Edition. Why can I not see the Local Users and Groups information?
▼ You do not have to assign a user to a group beyond what you set up when you created the user. You should, however, consider using Local Users and Groups if you need to enforce tighter security on your users.	▼ Anytime you change something locally, remember that it could change how your computer works on the network. That said, check with your network administrator before changing you Local Users and Groups settings.	▼ Local Users and Groups is not available on Windows Vista Home Edition. Because Local Users and Groups security features are considered mainly business related (rather than needed in a home environment), only Windows Vista Professional, Windows 2000 Professional, and member servers in a domain include it.

Create a Password Reset Disk

With the Password Reset Disk, you can create a new password that lets you access your computer. Windows Vista is a very secure operating system. If you forget your logon password, you cannot bypass the setup screen to access your files. For this reason, Windows lets you create a Password Reset disk that enables you to recover your Windows settings if you forget your password.

There are two primary considerations to keep in mind about the Password Reset disk. First, this is a preventative task. You must do it within Windows; that is, you cannot wait until after you forget your password and can no longer access Windows. So perform this task now so that you will have the disk ready if you ever need it.

Second, the disk can let anyone reset your password and have access to your user account. For this reason, make the disk and then keep it in a secure location.

Create a Password Reset Disk

1 In the User Accounts window, click Create a password reset disk in the left pane.

Note: Follow steps 1 to 4 in the "Modify User Accounts" section to access the User Accounts window.

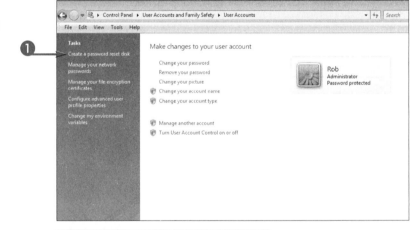

The Welcome to the Forgotten Password Wizard window appears.

2 Click Next to continue.

The Create a Password Reset Disk window appears, telling you to insert a blank floppy disk into drive A.

③ Insert a blank floppy disk into drive A.

④ Click here and select a drive on which to create a password key disk.

⑤ Click Next to continue.

⑥ Type the current user account password.

⑦ Click Next to continue.

The wizard creates your disk. When this is complete, a window appears.

⑧ Click Next to continue.

The Completing the Forgotten Password Wizard screen appears.

⑨ Click Finish in the last screen.

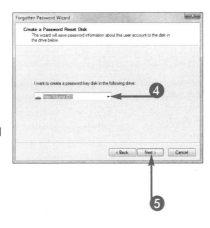

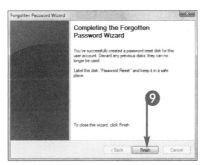

What is on the Password Reset disk?

▼ There is only one file on this disk. It is called userkey.psw and is an encrypted version of your password. Be sure to keep this disk in a safe place so other people cannot use it to break into your computer. Some organizations, in fact, require the Password Reset disk be stored in the company safe, accessible only by system administrators or executives.

Can I create a Password Reset disk for another user?

▼ No. You must be logged in as the user for which you are creating the Password Reset disk. This eliminates the possibility of a user resetting another user's password. If this happened, the user who reset the password could gain unrestricted access to another user's files and could block the original user from logging in to Windows. With this said, if another user happens to find your Password Reset disk (or USB drive that has your Password Reset file on it), he or she can gain access to your account without knowing your password. Read the section "Reset a Password with the Password Reset Disk" to see how easy it is to use the Password Reset disk.

Reset a Password with the Password Reset Disk

If you forget your password and have a Password Reset disk created (this includes having the Password Reset disk created on a USB flash drive), you can use it to change your password to a new password and then log on to Windows Vista.

At the Windows Vista Welcome screen, if you enter a password that is now the correct one, the Reset password link appears. Insert your Password Reset disk and then click the Reset password link. A window appears asking you to enter a new password and then confirm the password. Type a password hint in the place provided and then click Next. Windows Vista then resets your password to the new one so that you can gain access to your account. Unless you change it, your password remains as the one you just reset it to. See the section "Modify User Accounts" for more information.

You can use the Password Reset disk over and over because it maintains the last password you created when you used the disk. However, if you change your password using the Change Password feature in the User Accounts and Family Safety tools, you must create a new Password Reset disk.

Reset a Password with the Password Reset Disk

① Start your computer.

The Windows Vista user logon screen appears.

② Type a password.

③ Press Enter.

Windows starts if the password is correct. You do not have to use the Password Reset disk.

If the password is incorrect, a red X appears with text that reads "The user name or password is incorrect."

④ Click OK.

The Windows Vista user logon screen reappears.

⑤ Click the Reset password link.

The Password Reset Wizard appears.

⑥ Click Next.

The Insert the Password Reset
Disk window appears.

7 Insert your Password Reset disk.

8 Click Next.

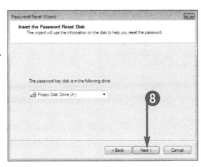

The Reset the User Account
Password window appears.

9 Type a new password.

10 Type the new password again.

11 Type a password hint.

12 Click Next.

13 Click Finish.

Windows Vista starts up.

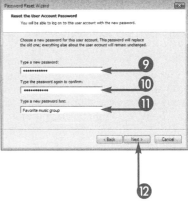

**My company does not allow me to make
a Password Reset disk. Why not?**

▼ Some organizations have very strict
security policies. For the most part, the the
Password Reset disk feature does not
provide adequate security for most of
these stricter policies. The reason is
because anyone who has the Password
Reset disk can use it. Of course, the disk
can be used only on the computer on
which it was created, and only for the
account that it was created for. However,
the disk does not know if the appropriate
person is using it, which could allow an
unauthorized user access to the account.

**Can I change my password in Windows
without affecting the Password Reset
disk?**

▼ No, if you change your Windows Vista
password in Windows, you must re-create
the Password Reset disk to update it with
the new password. Follow the steps in the
"Create a Password Reset Disk" section. At
step 5, you will be prompted that the disk
you insert, or the USB flash drive, already
has a password reset file on it. Click Yes to
overwrite the old file and to continue. For
more information on changing your
pasword, see the section "Modify User
Accounts."

Launch the Run as Administrator Command

The Run as Administrator command lets you start programs as a different user than you currently are logged in as. For example, you may be logged in as a Limited user, but you need to run a program that is configured only for administrators. The Run as Administrator command lets you log in as the administrator and run that program.

The Run as Administrator command lets you stay logged in as the current user and run the command without the hassle of shutting down all your applications, logging in as administrator (or any other

user for that matter), and then running the desired program. An example of a program that you may want to run as an administrator is the Group Policy Object Editor. Limited users are not authorized for access to the group policy settings.

The Run as Administrator command should be treated seriously if you are an administrator. Keep in mind that if you use the Run as Administrator command on a user's computer and encounter a virus, you could destroy all the accounts on the computer, including the Administrator account. This could render Windows and your data useless until you clean up the virus.

Launch the Run as Administrator Command

① Log on as a Standard user.

② Click Start.

③ Click All Programs.

Note: After you click All Programs, the name changes to Back.

④ Click Accessories.

⑤ Click Windows Explorer.

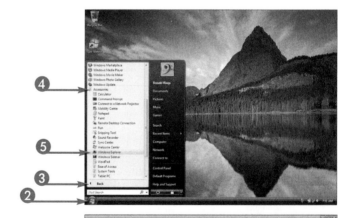

Windows Explorer appears.

⑥ Locate the program file you want to open as a different user and right-click the program name.

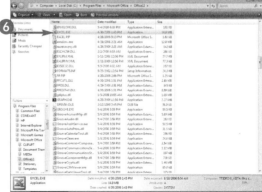

⑦ Click Run as administrator from the menu that appears.

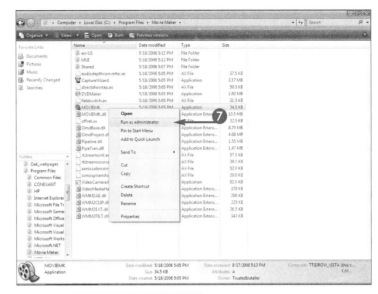

The Run As dialog box appears.

⑧ Click the option to specify a user.

⑨ Click here and select a user from the User name drop-down list.

⑩ Type the user's password in the Password box.

⑪ Click OK to run the program.

I do not know the administrator password. How can I run a program as that user?

▼ To use the Run As command, you must know the password for the user you want to run as.

I do not see the Run as Administrator command when I right-click a file. Is there another way to start it?

▼ The Run as Administrator command is installed by default now with Windows Vista. If you are having difficulty using it, be sure you are right-clicking an executable file and not a nonexecutable file. For example, the Run as Administrator command is not available if you right-click a document file (.doc). It is, however, available when you right-click a program file (.exe).

When I used the Run As Administrator command to run a program under a different user, the program did not run. Why not?

▼ More than likely the user you selected from the User name drop-down list in the Run As Administrator dialog box did not have sufficient rights to run the program. Check Local Users and Groups to see in which groups the user belongs. If the privileges are too restrictive, you may need to change the user to a different group, such as to the Power Users group. For more information, see the section "Change Group Membership."

Edit Group Policies

A group policy is a collection of settings that controls a user's Windows environment. System and computer administrators can use group policies to enable or disable access to various items available to a user. For example, a group policy can be set up to restrict users from accessing the Start menu.

Group policies can be applied to a single computer, group of computers, or all the computers on a Windows domain. Policies can be set for the entire computer, for local users, or both. One policy that a computer may have enabled is to disallow printers to be published. This means that a shared printer cannot be shown in the Active Directory of a Windows domain. By doing this, a network administrator can restrict other users on the network from "seeing" this printer and printing to it.

A policy that can be user-specific, for example, is one that removes access to the Microsoft Windows Vista Update site. Administrators can disable access to this site so that a user cannot download update software to his computer.

① Click Start.

② Click All Programs.

Note: After you click All Programs, the name changes to Back.

③ Click Accessories.

④ Click Run.

The Run dialog box appears.

⑤ Type gpedit.msc in the Open box.

⑥ Click OK.

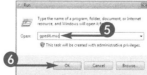

The Group Policy Object Editor appears.

● This area displays computer and user folders. To modify a setting, click the plus sign (+) next to a folder and then click a folder.

7 Click the arrow to the left of Administrative Templates.

8 Click Printers.

● This area displays subfolders and specific policy settings.

9 To edit a setting, double-click it.

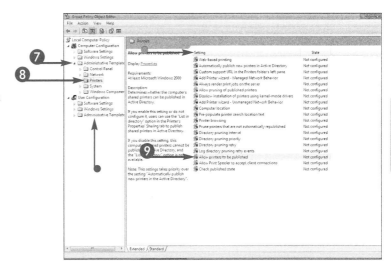

A Properties dialog box for the setting appears.

10 Click the Enabled option (○ changes to ◉).

11 Click Apply.

12 Click OK.

Why are group policies even available? They seem rather confusing to me.

▼ The main reason is that many power users and administrators want a way to configure advanced environmental settings without using the Windows Registry (the main Windows database). With the Group Policy Object Editor, administrators can create templates that they can then apply to multiple computers in an enterprise, a workgroup, or a domain.

Do I need to use group policies?

▼ No, but if you are part of a domain, you may be using them right now without knowing it. Your system administrator may have created a group policy template that your computer applied to your system when you loggged in to the network.

How can I find out more about the policies available in Windows Vista?

▼ There are a few resources on the Internet, including www.Microsoft.com, which provide documentation on the thousands of policies available. One way to learn which settings are available, however, is to open the Group Policy Object Editor and scan through the collection of policies. Most policies include a short description.

Configure Roaming Group Policies

One of the most useful ways to deploy group policies is to use them for roaming users. These are users who must log on to several different computers in an organization. For example, some organizations have conference rooms or training rooms with computers set up for demonstrations, training lessons, and similar tasks. With roaming group policies, a user can log on to those computers and be presented with his or her desktop setup and other Windows configurations. With roaming policies, a user's Windows environment can be copied to any computer the user logs on to, regardless of the location within the company.

To use roaming group policies, an organization must have a Windows domain and use Active Directory. The roaming policy (sometimes referred to as *roaming profiles* in previous Windows versions) is stored on the network server and then downloaded to the machine a user logs on to. Any changes a user makes to Windows settings are then saved to both the local copy and the network copy. This ensures that the profile is always the most current one for that user.

Mobile group policies can be used to assign user logon requirements, restrict folder access, or redirect a local folder to a network drive. A user's Documents or Pictures folder can be redirected.

Configure Roaming Group Policies

1. Right-click Computer.
2. Click Manage.

The Computer Management window appears.

3. Double-click System Tools.
4. Double-click Local Users and Groups.
5. Click Users.
6. In the right pane, double-click the user you want to configure.

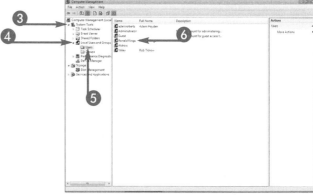

The Properties dialog box for that user appears.

7 Click the Profile tab.

8 Type the network path where the profile is stored. For example, the path may look like \\servername\folder\profile.

9 If the home folder for this user is on the network, click the Connect option (○ changes to ◉).

10 Click here and then select the network drive.

11 Type the path to the home folder.

12 Click OK.

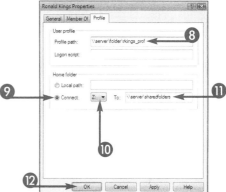

Can I use roaming group policies for mobile users?

▼ Yes. In fact, this is one way companies can help mobile users get up and running more quickly each time they visit the office. With mobile group policies, you can set up scripts, redirections, and software settings that laptop users can download each time they access the company network. A script is a file that has specific instructions that computers will execute during startup. For example, a script can tell a computer to look for updated software and how to install that software.

Sometimes a roaming profile is not available. How can I use a local one?

▼ Open the Control Panel and click System and Maintenance. Click System to open the System Properties dialog box. Click the Advanced System Settings link on the left side of the window and then click Settings under User Profiles. Select a profile to change, click Change Type, and then click Local profile from the Change Profile Type dialog box. Click OK and click OK again. Click OK to close the System Properties dialog box.

Turn on Parental Controls

For home users, a common problem parents have is monitoring how their children use the computer. With Windows Vista, parents can set several Parental Controls to manage it. To use Parental Controls, the parents must create a separate user account for their child. If they have several children who will be accessing the computer, parents should set up user accounts for each child. This way, if one of the children needs different access rights (such as if an older sibling is allowed to use the computer for longer time periods), parents can customize that one account, while leaving the other accounts alone.

With Parental Controls, you can restrict the Web sites that a user can access by limiting the user to specific ones. You also can specify if a user is allowed to download files from the Web.

You also can use time limits to control when users are allowed to log on to the computer. For example, you can specify that a user can log on only during the hours of 4:00 p.m. to 7:00 p.m. on Mondays, Wednesdays, and Fridays, but anytime on Saturdays and Sundays.

Turn on Parental Controls

1 Click Start.

2 Click Control Panel.

The Control Panel window appears.

3 Click Set up parental controls for any user.

The Choose a user and set up Parental
Controls window appears.

④ Click a user.

The Set up how *username* will use the
computer screen appears.

⑤ Click On, enforce current settings
(○ changes to ◉).

⑥ Click On, collect information about computer
usage (○ changes to ◉).

⑦ Click OK.

Can I use Parental Controls for other users, not just children?

▼ Yes, in fact if you have a small office or
area where multiple people need to access
the computer, you may consider setting up
a universal account visitors can use. Then
you can use Parental Controls to control
times the computer is used, apply Web
filters, and set other settings to control
what that account can do. For example,
create a new account and name it Visitor.
Create a password that you can give to
anybody who wants access with the Visitor
account. Do not use a password that you
use for other accounts. Then set up
Parental Controls for that account.

Can I specify that all users on a computer have Parental Controls set up?

▼ No, you must have at least one user set up
as the administrator or you will not be able
to modify any configuration settings on
your computer. However, you can set up
all other accounts to use Parental Controls,
although you must set up Parental
Controls for each account one at a time.
You cannot create a Parental Controls
"profile" on one account and then copy
those settings to other users.

Limit Web Site Access for Users

After you turn on Parental Controls for a user, you can specify that the user have Web restrictions enforced. Web restrictions enable you to block Web sites or Web site content you feel is inappropriate for a user. You can, for example, set up a permitted list of Web sites, called the *Allowed websites list*, that you deem appropriate for a user. In the Allowed websites list, you can enter Web sites that you know contain safe content for the user.

You also can create a list of Web sites that you want blocked, called the *Blocked websites list*. In this list you can add sites that you feel are simply not appropriate

for the user. These can range from sites that contain mature content, hate-related speech, weapons sites, and more. You can control the list that Parental Controls will block.

Parental Controls includes automatic Web blocking as well, based on restriction levels. High allows only content rated for children to display. Medium blocks content such as mature content, pornography, drugs, and other sites. You use None if you do not want Parental Controls to automatically block content. And Custom lets you pick the content categories to block automatically.

Limit Web Site Access for Users

① Click Start.

② Click Control Panel.

The Control Panel window appears.

③ Click Set up parental controls for any user.

The Choose a user and set up Parental
Controls window appears.

④ Click a user that has Parental Controls turned
on in the Choose a user and set up Parental
Controls window.

The Set up how *username* will use the
computer window appears.

⑤ Click Windows Vista Web Filter.

I turned on Parental Controls Web restrictions, but an adult site was not blocked. I thought Parental Controls caught all the sites?	If I choose a restriction level, can I still use the Allowed websites list or Blocked websites list?
▼ No, it does not. The Web filters you can set through Parental Controls catches many, but not all, sites you want blocked. You will still need to monitor your users' activities to ensure questionable material is not accessed. You might also want to purchase additional Web-filtering software to limit sites that users' can view. One of the most popular programs is CyberSitter, found at www.cybersitter.com. You can download a ten-day trial version from that site as well.	▼ Yes, the Allowed websites list and Blocked websites list are not mutually exclusive from the restriction levels, so you can use both a list and a level setting. For example, if you specify that a user be set up with the High Web restriction level but want to allow that user access to a specific site (say a health-oriented site), you can specify that site in the Allowed websites list. Further, if you want to specify a site that should never be allowed and you fear the High Web restriction level will not catch it, add it to the user's Blocked websites list.

continued

Limit Web Site Access for Users

(Continued)

Another issue you have to deal with when setting up Parental Controls Web Restrictions is whether to allow or block file downloads. Even if you block users from viewing certain Web sites, they still might be able to download objectionable material in files. Types of files that can be downloaded include videos, music files, animations, documents, and pictures. By blocking file downloads, you can specify that Parental Controls does not allow users to download files from the Web.

When you block file downloads, you also block unwanted software from entering the computer. This type of software usually is called *malware* (for

malicious software), *adware* (for advertisement software), or *spyware* (for software that reports on your Internet activity). Some sites your users connect to may have legitimate files that need to be downloaded to execute files or to view all of the site. For example, some sites require you to install ActiveX controls or Java programs before you can view content. If this software is blocked, parents can override the blocked file using an administrator password and allow the file to download. This does, of course, require that the parent be nearby to key in the password.

Limit Web Site Access for Users *(continued)*

The Which parts of the Internet can *username* visit? window appears.

⑥ Click Block some websites or content.

⑦ Click Edit the Allow and block list.

The Allow or Block specific websites window appears.

⑧ Type a Web site address you want to block.

⑨ Click Allow.

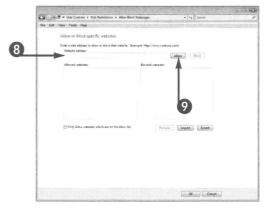

The Web site appears in the Allowed websites list.

⑩ Type a Web site address you want to block.

⑪ Click Block.

The Web site appears in the Blocked websites list.

⑫ Click OK to continue.

The Which parts of the Internet can *username* visit? window appears again.

⑬ Click High to set an automatic Web content filter (○ changes to ◉).

⑭ Click Block file downloads (☐ changes to ☑).

⑮ Click OK.

The Set up how *username* will use the computer window appears.

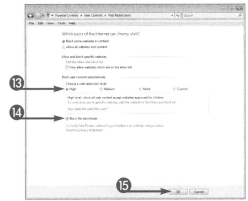

I want my son to have access only to a list of sites I create. Can I do that?

▼ Yes, on the Allow or Block specific websites window, fill in the Allowed websites list using the Website address box and Allow button. Then click the Only Allow websites which are on the allow list option. Click OK. Now, if your son attempts to navigate to a Web site that is not on the list, a message appears indicating the site is blocked. If you find a site should be taken off the list, select it and then click Remove.

Is there a way to enter a lot of sites in the Allowed and Blocked websites lists without typing them all in?

▼ Yes, you can import a list of Web sites using the Import button on the Allow or Block specific websites window. When you click the Import button, the Open dialog box appears. You can select files that are of the Web Allow Block Lists type. Click Open and then Yes to import the list. When you import this file, your existing list of blocked and allowed sites is replaced with this list. Instructions telling the Parental Controls tool which sites should appear on the Allow websites list and which sites should appear on the Blocked websites list are built in.

Limit Logon Times for Users

Windows Vista's Parental Controls tool includes a feature that enables you to set times when a user is allowed to log on to the computer. With the Time Restrictions feature in Parental Controls, you select the hours of each day when users can use the computer. A grid that includes each day of the week (Sunday to Saturday) and every hour (Midnight to 12) makes it easy to select those times you want to block or allow.

You can select only full hours; you cannot select parts of an hour. For example, you cannot specify that users are not allowed to log in on Mondays between

7:30 a.m. and 3:30 p.m., which are traditionally times that a child is at school or being transported to or from school. Instead, you can specify whole hour times, such as 8:00 a.m. to 3:00 p.m., or some such.

By default, the Time Restrictions grid is set to allow access all day, every day. In the grid, allowed times are represented by white squares. When you click a square, it changes to blue to indicate the time is blocked. You can click a blue square to turn it back to white, allowing the user access at that time.

Limit Logon Times for Users

① Click Start.

② Click Control Panel.

The Control Panel window appears.

③ Click Set up parental controls for any user.

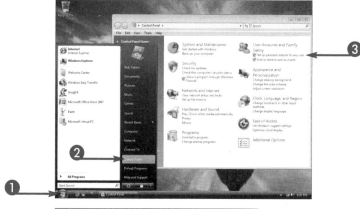

The Choose a user and set up Parental Controls window appears.

④ Click a user that has Parental Controls turned on in the Choose a user and set up Parental Controls window.

The Set up how *username* will use the computer window appears.

5 Click Time limits to set time restrictions for the user.

The Control when *username* will use the computer window appears.

6 Click the times box for each time period that you want to block.

The blocked times turn blue.

7 Click OK to save your settings.

The Set up how *username* will use the computer window reappears.

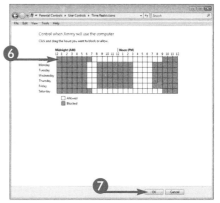

I set the Time Restrictions so my daughter can access the computer only after 4:00 p.m. Monday through Friday. Why can she still log on during those times?

▼ You may have to check some things in your computer settings to make sure you are blocking your daughter's access. First, log in as a user with administrator privileges. Check the time and date set on your computer in the tasktray. If it is not set correctly, double-click it and set the correct time and date. The Time Restrictions feature uses your computer's time and date to know when to block or allow user access.

What happens if my child is working and the end of the time comes?

▼ When the end of the block of time for the user arrives, Windows Vista automatically turns the screen black and then displays the Windows Vista logon screen. It will show all the users and the words "Logged on" will appear under the user whose time ran out. If the user attempts to log in again before the next allowed time block occurs, a message displays saying, "Your account has time restrictions that prevent you from logging on at this time. Please try again later."

Limit Games Users Can Play

Computers have become useful tools for getting work done. However, they also become excellent platforms for playing games. Many of these games involve plots, graphics, and action sequences that you may deem inappropriate for your children. The Entertainment Software Rating Board (ESRB) assigns ratings to games, or *interactive entertainment programs,* as they are known in the software industry. Using the ESRB ratings, Windows Vista's Parental Controls enables you to limit the types of games that a user can play on the computer.

The ESRB ranks games in six categories. The Early Childhood category (rated EC) includes games suitable for ages three and older. The Everyone (E) category includes games suited for ages six and older. For the Everyone 10+ (E10) category, games are rated for everyone ten and older.

The Teen category (T) includes games that are rated suitable for persons 13 and older. In the Mature (M) category are games that are rated for people 17 and older. Finally, the Adults Only (AO) category includes games suitable for adults only.

You can use the Game Restrictions feature of the Parental Controls tool to specify the ratings that are suitable for your user.

Limit Games Users Can Play

① Click Start.

② Click Control Panel.

The Control Panel window appears.

③ Click Set up parental controls for any user.

The Choose a user and set up Parental Controls window appears.

④ Click a user that has Parental Controls turned on in the Choose a user and set up Parental Controls window.

The Set up how *username* will use the
computer window appears.

5 Click Games to set game restrictions.

The Control which types of games *username*
can play window appears.

6 Click Set game ratings to specify the ratings
you will allow for this user.

**I think my son is using a different user
name to access Windows Vista and games
I have restricted. What should I do?**

▼ Start Windows and log in as a user with
administrator priveleges. Click Start, click
Control Panel, and then click Add or
Remove User Accounts. Look at the user
accounts. Is there one there that your son
may be using without your knowledge? If
so, ask your son if he is. If so, warn him that
you plan to delete the account and that he
needs to copy over any documents or files
he wants before you delete the account.
Then delete the account (or change the
password to one only you know).

**A game my daughter received does not
have a rating. Can she still play it?**

▼ Yes, she can if you did not specifically set
the option to block games that are not
rated. If you want to block all games that
are not rated (which may be a good idea if
you have younger users in your
household), click Games on the Set up
how *username* will use the computer
window and then click Set game ratings.
On the Control which types of games
username can play window, click Block
games with no rating. Click OK and then
click OK again.

continued

Limit Games Users Can Play
(Continued)

When you specify the types of games to allow or block, you have a whole range of items from which to choose. You can select to allow games that meet an ESRB rating or select multiple ratings. If a game is rated for a specific level, and that level includes content that you particularly do not want your children to experience, you can block games based on specific content types.

For example, you may have a teenage boy who you decide can play games that have a rating of Teen (T). In the Teen rating, games can have violent content, mild or strong language, and/or strong language. Let's

say you want to limit games in the Teen category that have strong language. Select the Teen rating, which by default selects the ratings below it (Early Childhood, Everyone, and Everyone 10+). Then select Strong Language from the Block these types of content list that appears at the bottom of the Control which types of games *username* can play window.

Now your son can play all Teen-rated games that do not include strong language. By default, if you do not select any ratings, every user can play all types of games, including Adults Only–rated games.

Limit Games Users Can Play *(continued)*

The second Control which types of games *username* can play window appears.

7 Click a rating to specify which ones are allowed (○ changes to ◉).

8 Scroll down the window to see other options.

9 Click additional types of content you want to block.

10 Click OK.

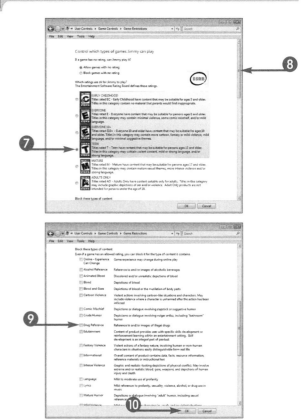

PART II

The first Control which types of games *username* can play window appears.

⑪ Click Block or Allow specific games.

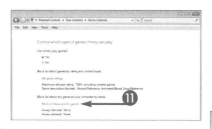

The Control specific games *username* can and can not play window appears.

⑫ Click Always Allow, Always Block, or keep it set to User Rating Setting to control if the user can play a specific game.

⑬ Click OK.

The Control which types of games *username* can play window appears.

⑭ Click OK.

The Set up how *username* will use the computer window appears.

I have an employee who sits and plays Spider Solitaire for hours. Can I limit how much time he plays it?

▼ No, Parental Controls does not limit how much time a program, such as a game, can run. You can block a game from being played while that user is logged in by setting up Parental Controls on that user, clicking Games on the Set up how *username* will use the computer, and then clicking Block or Allow specific games. Under the Always Block column, click Spider Solitaire (you may also want to block all the other games as well) and then click OK three times.

I have a game installed but Parental Controls does not list it. How can I block it?

▼ You will need to limit access to a specific program — that game program — to block it from being used. Sometimes Windows Vista does not list games in the Control specific games *username* can and can not play window if it (Vista) does not know it is a game. To learn how to block specific applications using Parental Controls, read the "Limit Program Access for Users" section.

Limit Program Access for Users

Not only can you limit which Web sites a user can visit, when a user can log in, and what games a user can play, you also can specify which programs installed on your computer a user can use. With Parental Controls, you can allow or block any program, including programs you install and ones installed by Windows Vista.

By default, all programs are allowed (except for any games you specify that cannot be played). With the Allow and block specific programs feature of Parental Controls, you see a list of all the programs Windows Vista finds on your computer. If there is a program you know is on your computer but is not listed, you can even specify it using the Browse feature.

You can block all programs (but why would a user need to use the computer if you do that?), one program, or many. To specify that you want to limit the programs a person can use, you click the *Username* can only use the programs I allow option. When you select this option, all programs are blocked. You then go through the list selecting those programs you want to allow. The quickest way to allow all programs but a few to run is to click the Check All button, and then deselect any programs you want to block.

Limit Program Access for Users

① Click Start.

② Click Control Panel.

The Control Panel window appears.

③ Click Set up parental controls for any user.

The Choose a user and set up Parental Controls window appears.

④ Click a user that has Parental Controls turned on in the Choose a user and set up Parental Controls window.

The Set up how *username* will use the computer window appears.

5 Click Allow or block specific programs.

The Which programs can *username* use? window appears.

6 Click *Username* can only use programs I allow to see a list of programs (○ changes to ◉).

A list of programs installed on your computer appears.

7 Click next to each program you want to allow the user to use.

8 Click OK to save your selections.

The Set up how *username* will use the computer window appears.

How do I know if Parental Controls are working?

▼ Log in as one of the users and attempt to use some of the features you disabled. For example, if you set Parental Controls to block all Web sites except those listed on the Allowed websites list, type in a Web address of a site not on the list. Internet Explorer should block the site from viewing. Also, attempt to log on to the account during one of the times you specified for the account not to work (such as during school hours or after-school chore times).

I blocked a program, but it does not block the entire program. Why not?

▼ Make sure that you removed a check mark next to the name of the program you want to block when using the Which programs can *username* use? window. If a check mark appears in a box next to a program name, it indicates that you are allowing that program to run. Also, make sure you cleared the box next to the correct program name. Some programs include multiple parts that perform different jobs when you run the program. For instance, if you want to block Adobe Reader from starting, make sure you clear the check box next to the AcroRd32.exe listing.

View Parental Control Activity Reports

A s a parent, you can use the Parental Controls feature to help you minimize the exposure your children have to objectionable and potentially harmful Web sites, games, and programs. Although you should supplement the protection that Parental Controls offers you by using other monitoring software and Web filters (such as Cybernanny), you can keep tabs on what users are attempting to access with Parental Controls activity reports.

Parental Controls activity reports are available to you (or any other administrator-level user on your computer). They provide individual reports for each user on the computer that has Parental Controls turned on. The reports for each user include seven

areas: Web Browsing, System, Applications, Gaming, E-mail, Instant Messaging, and Media.

You use the Activity Viewer to see a summary of users — only those set up as standard users appear. When you click a user's name, you can get one report showing all seven areas. You then can drill down to individual areas to see report details for each one.

The Parental Controls activity reports can help you keep an eye on what users are really doing.

To view activity reports for a user, the collect information about computer usage option must be selected for that user.

View Parental Control Activity Reports

① Click Start.

② Click Control Panel.

   The Control Panel window appears.

③ Click Set up parental controls for any user.

   The Choose a user and set up Parental Controls window appears.

④ Click a user that has Parental Controls turned on in the Choose a user and set up Parental Controls window.

The Set up how *username* will use the computer window appears.

⑤ Click View activity reports to open the Activity Viewer.

The Activity Viewer window appears.

⑥ Click the plus sign (+) next to the user's name to expand the listing.

⑦ Click the plus sign (+) next to Web Browsing.

⑧ Click Websites Visited to see which sites the user was able to view.

A list of all sites and times the sites were visited appears.

⑨ Click the Close box to close the report.

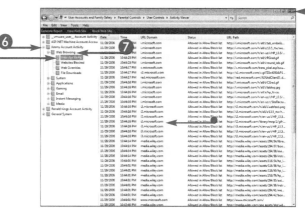

Can I print the Parental Controls activity report?

▼ Yes, but you need to first generate the report as a Web page. Then you can print the report as a Web page. To do this, click the Generate Report button on the Activity Viewer window. The Save As dialog box appears. Type a name for the report and click Save. Go to the folder in which you saved the report and double-click it. Internet Explorer appears with the report displayed in it. Click the File menu and then click Print. The Print dialog box appears. Click the Print button to send the report to your printer for a hard copy.

I would like to set up Windows Mail with Parental Controls. How can I do this?

▼ Currently, Windows Mail does not support the Parental Controls features. Similarly, Windows Messenger does not support the Parental Controls features yet. At some point, probably in the near future, Microsoft plans to introduce updates that will enable you to manage these programs using Parental Controls. Look for Parental Controls applications for e-mail and chat software from third-party software publishers as well.

Change Folder Views

Windows enables you to change the way you view your folders. You can choose to view folders as icons from small to extra large, tiles, or lists. Changes you make can apply to all the folders, some of the folders, such as subfolders, or the current folder.

To keep important Windows systems files and hidden files from view, you can hide them. You also can remove from view the file extension of files that Windows knows how to open, which keeps users from accidentally changing them.

Windows lets you see information about each file in the Preview Pane and show a snapshot view of the file in the Reading Pane. If you do not want to see this information, you have the option to turn off those views.

Another option for your folders is to have Windows display a pop-up description of each folder item. You can see these by moving your mouse over an item and pausing it there for a few seconds. Many refer to this as *hovering* the mouse.

Windows also lets you change how you share folders on a network. If you choose simple file sharing, you can set up shared folders so everyone in your workgroup can access your folders.

Change Folder Views

① Double-click Computer.

The Computer window appears.

② Click Organize.

③ Click Folder Options.

The Folder Options dialog box appears.

④ Click the View tab.

● This option has Windows search networks for shared printers.

● These options display or hide hidden files and folders.

● This option tells Windows to remember how your folder view is configured. It opens the same way the next time.

● This option uses the Sharing Wizard to help you set up file sharing.

⑤ Click OK to save any changes.

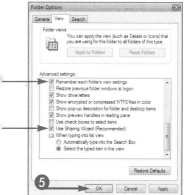

What is a file extension?

▼ Windows uses the three-character file extensions after a period to associate that file with installed applications. For example, Microsoft Office Excel 2007 worksheet files use an XLSX extension. When you click or double-click any file with an XLSX extension, Windows knows which application to start — Excel — for you to view the selected file.

Does Windows Vista prompt me if I change a file-name extension?

▼ Yes, when working in a file management program — Computer or Windows Explorer — be sure to change the file extension back to its proper extension. You can do this by answering No when prompted during a name change procedure that changing a file name can make the file unrecognizable by Windows Vista.

What happens if I change a file extension to a file?

▼ If you change a file-name extension, click Edit and then click Undo to return the file name back to its original name. If you change a file extension on the desktop, you will need to right-click the file name, choose Rename from the menu that appears, and then rename the file with the original file-name extension. Press Enter to complete the renaming procedure.

Customize Folder Details

When you view folders and files in Computer or Windows Explorer, the information that displays for each item is called the *details*. With Windows Vista, you can see a whole host of details, including name, type of file, modification date, and so on.

These details are shown in columns that you can click to sort folders and files. For example, if you want to sort files by type, click the Type column heading. Or, to see files sorted by size, click the Size column heading.

The detail columns that display depend on the folder template that is used to describe how a folder displays its contents. Folders set up as pictures, for example, display columns relating to photographs, such as Date Taken and Dimensions. Music Album folders, on the other hand, show Artists, Album Title, Year, # for track number, and Length.

Windows lets you change which column headings appear. You may, for example, want to see the author of a particular document. In Microsoft Excel, you can choose File and then Properties to see summary information about a workbook's author.

Customize Folder Details

① Open the folder whose folder detail you want to change.

② Click here and choose a view.

This example changes the view to Details, letting you see folder detail columns.

③ Right-click a column.

A list of column headings appears. Those selected include a check mark (☑) next to them.

④ Click a heading name to add it to your list of column headings (☐ changes to ☑).

⑤ To see additional column headings, click More.

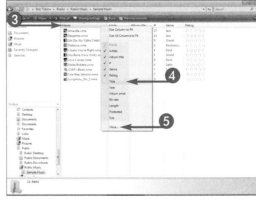

The Choose Details dialog box appears, letting you select several different column headings, such as Kinds, Copyright, Location, and so on.

- To rearrange the columns, select a column and click Move Up or Move Down.

⑥ Click OK to confirm your changes.

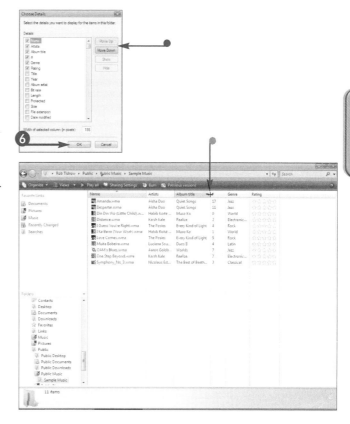

- To resize a column, click the line between two columns. A resize pointer appears. Drag to the right or left until the column is sized to your liking.

Can I remove or resize a column that I have added?

▼ Yes. Right-click a column and then click to uncheck the column name you want to remove (☑ changes to ☐). You also can display the Choose Details dialog box and clear a selection to remove the column. Or you can select a column name and then click Hide. Click OK to confirm your changes. You also can resize a column to make it larger. On the Choose Details dialog box, select the column you want to change and increase the width of the selected column (in pixels) to a larger number, such as 30. Click OK.

How do I sort folders and files in a column?

▼ To sort using a column as the sort criteria — such as by Name, Size, Type, and so on — click the column name. This sorts the folders and files in alphanumeric order, for example, A – Z. Click the column name again to reverse the sort, Z – A.

Can I rearrange folder detail columns?

▼ Yes. Select the column you want to move and hold down the left mouse button. Drag the column to the new location and drop it. A solid black line appears as you drag the column. This line shows where the column will be moved when you release the mouse button.

View Vista Explorers

Windows Vista includes new Explorers that help you view and manage your drives, files, and folders. An Explorer window appears when you open Computer, Windows Explorer, or any other folder on your desktop. You also can see Explorer windows when you open and save files in applications. For example, when you are working in Microsoft Office PowerPoint 2007 and you click File and then click Save As, the Save As dialog box appears. This is an Explorer window that gives you a specific view of your PowerPoint and related files. You can use the dialog box to save, rename, or delete a file.

The Explorer view also appears when you use the new Windows Contacts program. When you click the Contacts folder that resides in your User folder, Windows Vista displays contact information using the Explorer view. Column headings include Name, Date Modified, Type, Size, and so on.

With Vista, you can change the way the Explorer looks when you view files. For example, if you want to see a preview of your files when you open Windows Explorer and click a file, you can choose to display the Reading Pane.

① Double-click the Computer icon on your desktop.

The Computer window appears. This is one type of Vista Explorer.

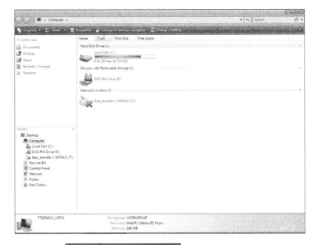

② Click Start.

③ Click All Programs.

Note: After you click All Programs, the name changes to Back.

④ Click Windows Movie Maker.

Windows Movie Maker starts.

5 Click File.

6 Click Open Project.

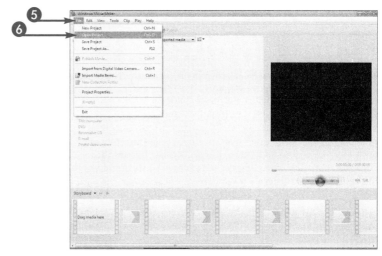

The Open Project window appears. This is another type of Vista Explorer.

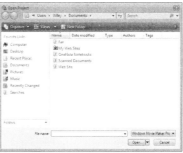

Why does the toolbar above the files and folders change?

▼ This toolbar is called the Tasks toolbar. It changes to reflect the types of tasks you can peform on the objects you display in the Explorer window. For example, if you display drives in Explorer, such as your hard drive, DVD drive, and network locations, the Tasks toolbar lets you do things like change or remove a program, change settings, and view properties. However, if you were to display a folder with pictures in it, such as the Pictures folder, you would see these tasks: Slide Show, Share, Burn, and Previous versions.

What happened to the Tasks Pane from Windows XP?

▼ The Tasks Pane, which used to reside on the left side of Windows Explorer and could be displayed in My Computer, has been replaced by the Tasks toolbar. In Windows Vista, some windows show similar types of links that used to be on the Tasks Pane. For example, as you navigate through Control Panel windows, links to related Control Panel applets appear in the left pane. This enables you to jump to these related areas without navigating back to the main Control Panel window.

Customize the Vista Explorers

Windows Vista enables you to modify the Vista Explorers to suit your working habits. For example, some users like to know everything they can about a file. These details are called *file properties*. The users will modify the Explorer window so that the Preview Pane, Reading Pane, and Navigation Pane appear. On the other hand, some users could care less about file properties. They just want to be able to find a file and open it, and they do not care if the file is a TIF file, for example, or that its dimensions are 1024 × 768.

Some of the items you can decide to turn on or off include the Search Pane, Preview Pane, Reading Pane, and Navigation Pane. As you show these layout options, your computer has to expend more processing power and use more memory. Probably the most taxing Explorer pane on your system resources is the Reading Pane. This pane shows a selected file inside the Explorer so you do not have to open the file in its related application. Depending on the file type and its size, your computer may slow down a great deal just to show this preview.

Customize the Vista Explorers

① Double-click the Computer icon on the desktop.

The Computer window appears.

② Open a folder in which you have some files, such as the Documents folder.

Files appear in the Working Pane of the Explorer window.

③ Click Organize.

④ Click Layout.

⑤ Click Search Pane.

- The Search Pane appears at the top of the Explorer window.

6 Click Organize.

7 Click Layout.

8 Click Reading Pane.

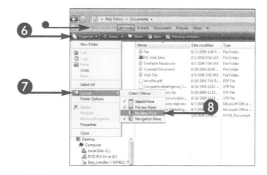

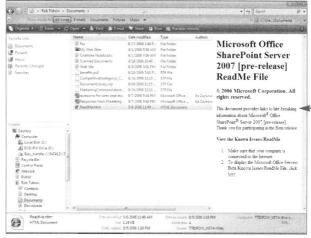

- The Reading Pane appears on the right side of the Explorer window. A sample view of the file appears in this pane.

PART II

What is the Navigation Pane?

▼ The Navigation Pane displays a hierarchical view of the desktop, computer, drives, and other items. To view the contents of these items, double-click them. Subfolders and files that appear in these drives and folders appear in the Working area. As its name implies, the Navigation Pane is probably the easiest way to navigate around your drives and folders. To see if you like having the pane displayed or not, turn it off by clicking Organize, Layout, and then Navigation Pane. Notice that the left pane disappears. To navigate from one drive to another, you have to use the Address bar at the top of the Explorer window.

What is the Preview Pane?

▼ The Preview Pane replaces the Status bar from earlier versions of Windows, such as in Windows XP or Windows Me. It shows property details about the item you select in the Working Pane. For example, when you select a document file that was created in Microsoft Office Word 2007, the Preview Pane displays the following types of information:

Name of the file

File type (.doc)

Modification date

Size

Title

Authors

Owner

Pages

Date created and date accessed

Change File Associations

A *file association* is information that tells Windows which program to launch when you double-click a file name. Windows knows which program to open based on the file's extension, usually it is a three- or four-character name to the right of the period in a file name. All files with the same extension are opened by the same program.

For example, Microsoft Office Word 2007 opens all files with the extension DOC if you have Microsoft Office installed on your computer. However, if you do not have Microsoft Office Word 2007 installed, Windows WordPad opens files with a DOC extension. If you want to change this so a different program opens DOC files, such as Corel WordPerfect, you can change the file association to that program.

File associations can change without manual modifications. After you install a new program, it may automatically change a file association so it is able to open that file. Sometimes programs prompt you first before changing your file associations. If so, read over the types of files changed before accepting the change.

If the program supports that file type, Windows lets you open a file with a different program on a file-by-file basis. This is handy if you want to open a file in Notepad, for example, that a spreadsheet program normally opens. In Notepad, you can view the raw data without any formatting applied.

Change File Associations

① Click Start.

The Start menu appears.

② Click Default Programs.

The Default Programs window appears.

③ Click Associate a file type or protocol with a program.

The Set Associations window appears. This window lists the file extensions and associated file types on your computer.

④ To change a file type association, click a file type.

⑤ Click Change program.

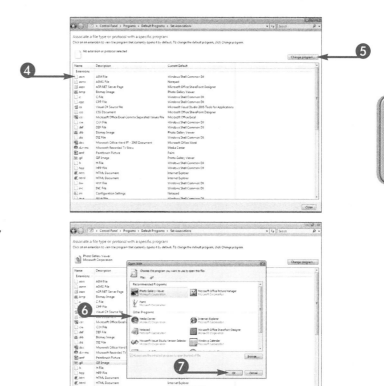

The Open With dialog box appears, displaying a list of programs installed on your computer.

⑥ Click the program you want to associate with the file type you selected in step 4.

⑦ Click OK to confirm the changes.

⑧ Click the Close button to close the Set Associations window.

Since I installed Mozilla Firefox, all the Web pages I saved to my hard drive are opened by Firefox. However, I want Internet Explorer to open Web pages that I double-click. Can I change this setting?

▼ Yes, to change the file association from Firefox to Internet Explorer, open the Set Associations window. In the Name column, click .htm. Click Change Program, and, in the Open With dialog box, click Internet Explorer and then click OK. Do the same with the .html file type. Click the Close button when you are finished to confirm your changes.

When I open the Set Associations window to change my file assocations, why does it take so long to show registered file types?

▼ Windows needs to find all the file types registered on your computer to display them on the Set Associations window. The more programs and files you have stored on your computer, the longer it takes to fill the Registered file types list. When the list is filled for the current Windows session, however, the Set Associations window is filled more quickly the next time you use it.

Add Files and Folders to the Start Menu

When you access the Windows Start menu, you are viewing a special Windows folder that contains files, folders, and links to your programs. There are also links to special Windows system folders and commands.

You can add files and folders to the Start menu if you are not satisfied with the ones that are there. For example, you may want to add a link to Mozilla Firefox at the top of the Start menu to quickly start Firefox each time. Or you can add a link to a folder or file directly to the Start menu to find what you need quickly.

When you install most programs, Windows automatically creates a shortcut to the program folder and other important program files. If the program does not create a shortcut during the install process, you can add one yourself later.

The Start menu on Windows Vista is much more sophisticated than the one on previous versions of Windows. For example, you have the option of highlighting newly installed programs, listing the most recently used programs, displaying the Control Panel applets as links or as a menu item, or showing or hiding the Favorites menu.

Add Files and Folders to the Start Menu

① Right-click Start.

② Click Properties from the menu that appears.

The Taskbar and Start Menu Properties dialog box appears.

③ Click Customize.

The Customize Start Menu dialog box appears.

● This area displays a list of items you can add to the Start menu. To add one, click it in the list.

④ Scroll down the list to choose additional options.

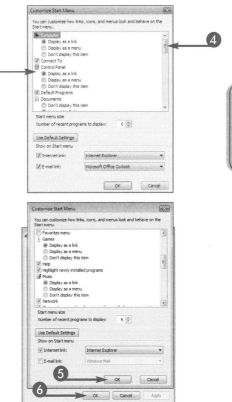

⑤ Click OK to confirm your changes.

⑥ Click OK to close the Taskbar and Start Menu Properties dialog box.

Is there a quick way to add and remove items to the Start menu?

▼ It depends on if you have drag-and-drop enabled on the Start menu. If so, all you have to do is drag the item to the Start menu and drop the item there. The item appears at the top of the Start menu.

To remove an item, open the Start menu and right-click the item you want to remove. A menu appears. Click Remove from this list if the item is in the left column of the Start menu. If the item is in the All Programs list, click Delete and then click Yes.

I dragged and dropped an item to the Start menu. Can I put it someplace else besides the top of the menu?

▼ Yes. Drag the item to the location you want it to appear and drop it. You cannot place the item on the right side of the Start menu, such as where the Control Panel and Network command options are. You can place an item only on the left side of the Start menu, or on the All Programs section.

How do I rename a folder or file I added to the Start menu?

▼ Click Start to display the Start menu. Right-click the file or folder you want to modify and click Rename. Type a new name and click OK.

Customize Folder Properties

Folders are like files or other objects in Windows in that they can have *properties*. Each folder has properties that you can customize. These properties include the type of folder template used, a folder picture to show you what file type is in the folder, and the icon used to illustrate the folder.

With a folder template, you can apply certain features to a folder based on the type of files you store in the folder. When you view the contents of the folder, the details Windows displays are based on the template you selected. For example, for folders containing music files from an album, a template named Music Album exists. It shows Artist name, Album Title, Year of the recording, Track number, and Length of each track.

Folders can be represented by pictures that you can view when using an icon view, such as Large Icons. They help you quickly identify the contents of folders when you view them in thumbnail view. By default, Windows uses the first four images in the folder as the folder picture. You can, however, change this picture to one more representative of the folder.

Customize a Folder Template

1 Right-click the folder whose template you want to change.

2 Click Properties.

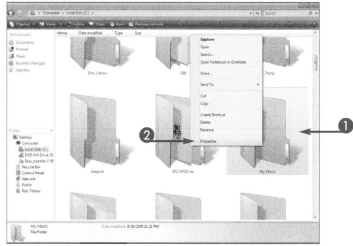

Customize a Folder Picture

The My Music Properties dialog box appears.

3 Click the Customize tab.

● This area displays the names of the folder templates.

4 To change the folder template, click here and select the template name.

● This area displays the folder picture assigned to the selected folder.

5 To change the folder picture, click Choose file.

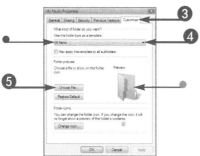

The Browse dialog box appears.

6 Click a picture you want to use as the folder picture.

7 Click Open to confirm your change.

Customize a Folder Icon

8 To change the icon, click Change Icon in the properties dialog box.

The Change Icon for my Music Properties dialog box appears.

9 Click an icon.

10 Click OK.

11 Click OK in the My Music Properties dialog box to confirm your changes.

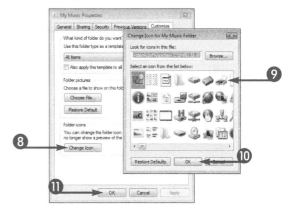

Do I have to use a folder template for all my folders?	Can I have subfolders use the same folder template as their root folder?	When I click Choose File, I do not see any pictures. How can I find them?
▼ No. By default Windows uses the All Items folder for your folders. The folder templates are just another way to customize your Windows environment to your needs. When you create a folder and save files to it, Windows attempts to guess the type of contents of a folder and apply the closest template choice to that folder. Windows uses file types and file extensions to guess the contents.	▼ Yes. When you apply a template to a folder, you also have the option of applying it to the folder's subfolders. Do this only if the subfolders contain the same type of folders as the main folder. Right-click a folder, click Properties, and then click the Customize tab. Click the option to also apply this template to all subfolders. Click OK.	▼ You may need to navigate to other folders to find a picture you want to use for your folder. To do this, click the Computer icon on the left pane of the Browse dialog box and navigate to a folder that contains pictures.

Share Files Using the Public Folder

Windows enables you to share files with other users when you are part of a network. The network can be a workgroup network, in which you are connected to a few other computers through a centralized hub or switch, often called *peer-to-peer networking*. It can also be a domain-based network, in which a centralized server controls directory services.

Windows Vista includes two main methods for sharing files: sharing files directly from folders on your computer, and sharing files from the Public folder on your computer.

When you share files directly from folders on you computer, you set up sharing for each folder that you want users to access. Setting up sharing involves specifying who can access the folder and what types of permissions you give those users.

To share files in the Public folder and its subfolders, copy or move files from other folders into the Public folder. Some of the Public folders' subfolders include Public Desktop, Public Documents, and Public Pictures.

Before setting up shared files on your system, you must have a network connection established. If you do not, read Chapter 16, "Networking and the Internet."

Share Files Using the Public Folder

① Open a folder and right-click a file to copy it to the Clipboard.

② Double-click Computer on your desktop.

The Computer window appears.

③ Double-click the Public folder.

The Public folder expands to show subfolders.

④ Double-click the Public Documents folder.

The Public Documents folder opens.

⑤ Right-click in an empty area of the files list pane.

⑥ Click Paste from the submenu that appears.

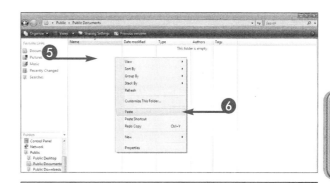

The file is pasted to the Public Documents folder, ready for other users to access it via the network.

What is a workgroup?

▼ A *workgroup* is a collection of computers on a network. For computers to share files and printers, they must all belong to the same workgroup. The default workgroup name is MSHOME; however, you can change this to one more suited to your working environment. For example, a workgroup in a marketing department might be named MARKETING.

Do I need to turn on file sharing for the Public folder on my computer?

▼ If your PC is part of a workgroup when you first install Windows Vista, Windows automatically sets up the Public folder for sharing on your computer.

Do I have to copy picture files into the Public Pictures folder, music files into the Public Music folder, and so on?

▼ No. Windows Vista creates these folders to help users organize the different types of files they might share with others. It really is a good idea to separate each type of file so that other users on the network can find them more easily.

Share Files Directly from Your Computer

Another way to share files in Windows Vista is by sharing them directly from your computer. This method lets you share any of your folders with others on your network. Keep in mind, however, you should choose only those folders that you want everyone else on the network to be able to access.

There are many reasons to share folders across a network. One reason is to let others have access to a shared document on which many people need to work, such as a marketing plan or sales budget. Another reason for shared folders is to allow others to quickly copy files, such as templates, programs, videos, and pictures, from one computer to the next.

Windows enables you to share entire drives, such as your C: drive, but this is not recommended. For security reasons, you do not want to give others this kind of access to your entire drive. A user could gain control over your system and delete vital system files, introduce harmful viruses, or access confidential documents.

Instead, select subfolders that contain documents and files to which others should have access. Then copy updated or new files to those shared folders.

Share Files Directly from Your Computer

① Double-click Computer.

② Double-click the C: drive, or your root drive letter.

The contents of the C: drive appear.

③ Right-click the folder you want to share.

④ Click Share from the menu that appears.

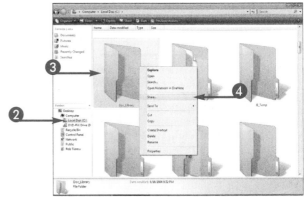

The File Sharing windows appears.

⑤ Click the down arrow and select the name of a user who you want to authorize to access this folder.

⑥ Click Add.

● The user's name appears in the Name list.

⑦ Repeat steps **5** and **6** to add other users as necessary.

⑧ Click Share to confirm your changes.

The Your Folder is shared window appears.

⑨ Click Done.

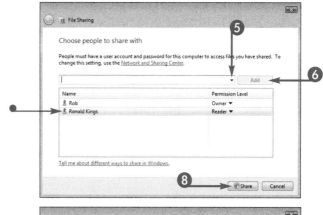

When I try to share a folder that belongs to another user on this computer, Windows does not let me. Why not?

▼ You cannot share folders that belong to another user account. To be able to do this you must have administrator privileges on that computer and specify that those folders can be shared with others. Otherwise, the owner of that user account must set up the folder to be shared. The same is true for your user account as well. Other users, unless they are administrators, cannot share your folders on the network. If you notice that your folders are being shared and you did not set up the share, contact your administrator and find out why.

A user has full access to my files. If he deletes the file, is the file sent to a Recycle Bin? If so, which one?

▼ No, the file is not sent to a Recycle Bin. As soon as the file is deleted, it is gone for good. The only way to regain the file is to copy it from another location — if you have it stored someplace else — or restore it from a backup. Windows requires that you manually set up backup services, so unless you specifically configured a backup for your sytem, you may not be able to retrieve the deleted file.

Create Compressed Folders

Nowadays folders can get fairly large. To reduce the amount of space they consume, they can be compressed. When you compress a folder, you shrink the contents of it without losing any information contained in the folder.

In some cases, you can save up to 90 percent of the original space the folder consumed. For systems with limited disk space, this is a handy tool to help save space.

When you are ready to use the folder again, you can uncompress it to its original size. Another reason to compress a folder is to transfer it to other users. You can compress a folder full of files you want to send to someone over the Internet. This reduces the bandwidth needed to send the file, and, in some cases, greatly speeds up delivery time.

You can also compress a folder full of files so they can fit on a removable disk, such as a Zip disk, compact disc, or other media storage device. Transport the files to another computer, copy them to that computer, and then uncompress them to their original size.

Create Compressed Folders

① Double-click Computer on your desktop.

The contents of the C: drive appear.

② Right-click the folder you want to compress.

③ Click Send To from the menu that appears.

④ Click Compressed (zipped) Folder in the submenu that appears.

The folder automatically begins compressing.

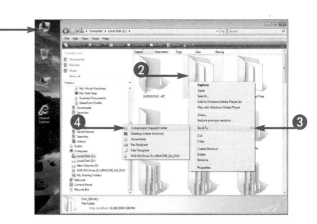

When it has finished compressing, Windows creates a folder using the original folder name with a .zip extension. Notice the icon for the folder includes a picture of a zipper.

⑤ Double-click the compressed folder.

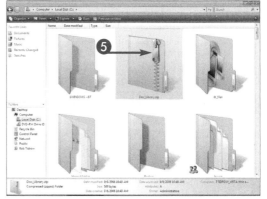

The contents of the compressed file appear.

⑥ To see the contents of a compressed folder, double-click it.

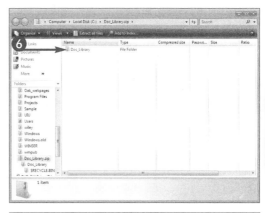

The contents of the folder within the compressed folder become visible.

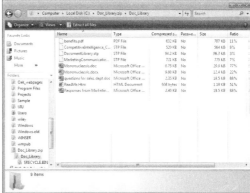

Can I still use other compression programs with Windows Vista?

▼ Yes. Programs such as WinZip and ZipToA are very nice programs to use when you want to compress files and folders. Many times these third-party compression programs include many more features than the built-in Windows compression tools, such as ones for uncompressing folders that are compressed using different algorithms than the one Windows uses.

I have a number of picture files saved on my computer. When I compress them, they do not get any smaller. Why not?

▼ Some picture formats, such as GIF and JPG/JPEG, are already compressed when you create them. Windows compression cannot reduce them any more. This is true of some video and most music formats. MPEG-7, for example, is a highly compressed format for music and video. Compressing folders that include these types of files does not decrease the amount of space they take on your disk.

After I create a compressed folder, is there a quick way to attach it to an e-mail message?

▼ A quick way is to right-click the compressed folder, click Send To, and then click Mail Recipient. A blank e-mail message window opens with the compressed folder attached to that message.

Encrypt
a Folder

Windows includes a feature that enables you to encrypt a folder and its contents. Encrypting a folder lets you add a layer of security to the folder so other users cannot modify or delete it.

Working with an encrypted folder or file is the same as working on one that is not encrypted. As long as you are the one who encrypted the folder — that is, the encryption was done while you were logged on under your user name — you should not have any problems using, editing, or even deleting the file.

One difference you see in Computer is that the encrypted folder names appear in a green font instead of the default black font.

Encrypted folders open for anyone, but their contents do not. When a user who is not the one who encrypted the folder tries to open an encrypted file, Windows displays an Access is denied screen.

When you encrypt a folder, you have the option of applying the encryption to all subfolders and files within those subfolders as well.

Encrypt a Folder

① **Double-click Computer on your desktop.**

The contents of the C: drive appear.

② **Right-click the folder you want to encrypt.**

③ **Click Properties from the menu that appears.**

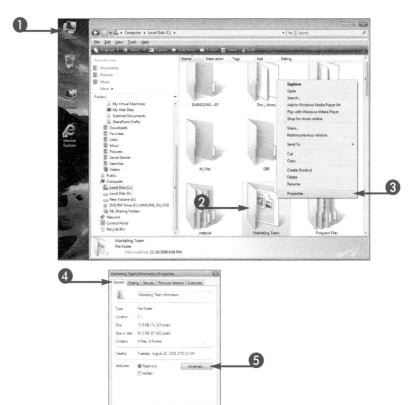

The Properties dialog box for that folder appears.

④ **Click the General tab.**

⑤ **Click Advanced.**

The Advanced Attributes dialog box appears.

6 Click the Encrypt contents to secure data option (☐ changes to ☑).

7 Click OK to close the Advanced Attributes dialog box.

8 Click Apply on the General tab.

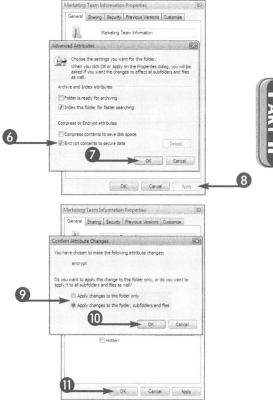

The Confirm Attribute Changes dialog box appears.

9 Click an option to encrypt the folder only, or to encrypt the folder, subfolders, and files (○ changes to ◉).

10 Click OK to confirm your changes.

11 Click OK on the General tab to close the Properties dialog box.

I have a folder that is compressed. I am trying to encrypt it, but Windows is not letting me. Why not?

▼ You should be able to encrypt a compressed folder that was compressed using Windows compressing. However, if the file was compressed with a different program, you may not be able to encrypt it.

There is a file on the system that does not open for me. Is there any way to turn off encryption?

▼ No. The only user who can disable encryption on a folder is the user who applied it in the first place. You can get around this if you are an administrator for the computer. You then have ample rights to unencrypt a file.

Another user deleted an encrypted folder I had on my computer. I thought you could not do this unless you encrypted the folder.

▼ Not true. You can move or delete an encrypted folder, even copy to a different computer, regardless of who created the encryption. The problem is that you cannot open the files within the folder unless you are the owner. The only way to ensure your files are not deleted is to use the Security tab in the properties dialog box and assign permissions and users to the folder.

Check Security at the Security Center

Windows Vista includes enhanced security features to help keep your PC secure. However, the security enhancements are effective only if they are turned on and set properly. Part of guaranteeing that your computer is secure is being able to see your security-related settings quickly. With Vista, you can monitor most of your security settings from a centralized location called the Windows Security Center. Here, you can enable and configure your firewall (whether Microsoft's or one from another vendor), enable Automatic Updates, monitor antivirus software and verify that it is working, and make changes to your security settings for your firewall and Internet options.

The Security Center is easily accessible from the Control Panel and has a shield icon that displays in the Notification Area of the taskbar when security-related notices appear. You can determine the nature of the security setting or issue by the color of the shield: Green means your PC is secure, yellow means that something warrants your attention, and red indicates a security breach or that unprotected data is present. Because antivirus software is not part of Windows Vista, Security Center only checks to verify that the antivirus software is working.

Check Security at the Security Center

1 Click Start.

2 Click Control Panel.

The Control Panel appears.

3 Click Check this computer's security status.

The Windows Security Center appears, indicating the status of the security essentials on your computer.

4️⃣ Click here to display more information about one of the security essentials.

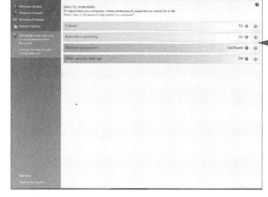

④

● A drop-down box appears with brief explanatory text and a link to information that is more detailed.

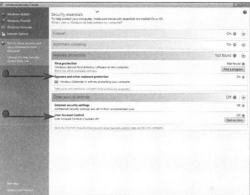

I do not have antivirus software installed, and the Security Center displays a red color shield. What can I do to protect my computer?	**Does antivirus software protect me from spyware?**

▼ Assuming you have a working Internet connection, you can download antivirus software from a trusted location and install it. Microsoft does not produce antivirus software per se but does offer links from www.microsoft.com/security/partners/ to trusted partners who provide such software, often with a free trial period from 90 days to a year. After you install the antivirus software, make sure that you keep it up-to-date, installing any updates from the software publisher. Also, make sure to get software that scans files in real time as they arrive on your computer, and make sure that feature is turned on.

▼ No. However, programs that fall into the category of "antispyware" can detect spyware — software that monitors your Internet browsing and collects information without your knowledge. Microsoft offers Windows Defender, antispyware software that is installed with Windows Vista. Currently Windows Defender is free, but there may be a subscription fee added to it at some point. See the section "Protect Windows with Windows Defender" for more information. Another antispyware program that you can use with Windows Vista is Adaware, found at www.lavasoft.com. Adaware is free for home users.

Manage Windows Firewall

With Windows Vista, you can control access to your computer from your network and the Internet using Windows Firewall. Windows Firewall monitors incoming network and Internet traffic and protects your PC from unauthorized access via the Internet. If you are in a corporate environment, your IT department may use a different firewall, in which case Windows Firewall is turned off. In a home-computing environment, you should always have Windows Firewall turned on unless you use another firewall, such as one antivirus software may provide.

The default setting with Windows Vista is to have Windows Firewall turned on for maximum protection. However, there are situations in which you want to allow a trusted source access to your machine, such as for interactive technical support or interactive gaming. For this reason, Windows Firewall allows exceptions, and you can elect to grant access to a specific program or service. Conversely, there are some situations in which security breaches are especially likely, such as while a user is browsing the Web in an airport over a wireless Internet connection. For such cases, there is an option that grants no exceptions to the Windows Firewall settings.

Manage Windows Firewall

① From the Windows Security Center, click Windows Firewall.

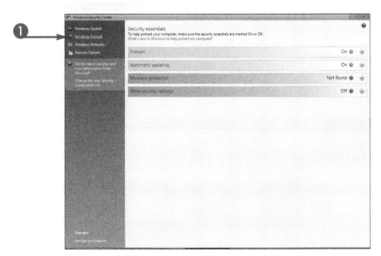

The Windows Firewall dialog box appears.

- Click the Block all programs option to allow no exceptions, including using a public WiFi hot spot to access the Internet (☐ changes to ☑).

- Click the Off option to turn off Windows Firewall (◉ changes to ○).

Note: *Use the Off option only when you have an alternative firewall in place.*

② Click the Exceptions tab.

The Exceptions tab of the
Windows Firewall dialog box
appears.

③ To unblock a program, click
one of the exceptions listed to
remove it from the exceptions
list (☐ changes to ☑).

④ Click OK.

⑤ Click the Close box to close
the Windows Security Center.

**The Security Center shows Windows
Firewall is turned off, but when I check
the security status with my antivirus
software, it says my firewall is turned
on. What is happening?**

▼ The Security Center in Windows Vista only
reports whether Windows Firewall is
running; it does not check on the status of
any other firewall, such as one provided
with antivirus software or with a hardware
device, such as a network router. If you are
using such a firewall, use the antivirus
software or the hardware-monitoring
software to check on your firewall status.
Also, if you are running multiple firewalls,
Microsoft recommends you turn off
Windows Firewall to eliminate possible
conflicts with the firewall programs.

**Is there any risk in allowing an exception
so that a program or service may get
through the firewall?**

▼ Yes. Exceptions essentially defeat the
purpose of a firewall. However, some
programs and services will not run when a
firewall is present. That is why exceptions
are needed. Every time you allow an
exception, you increase your security risk
to some degree. With each exception you
must weigh whether the program or
service is sufficiently trustworthy. It is a
good security practice to review the
exceptions periodically and remove any
that you no longer need.

Protect Windows with Windows Defender

One of the most common problems users have when using the Internet is infection by malicious software. This software is commonly referred to as *spyware* or *adware.* It usually disguises itself as a benign advertisement or system program, only to cause problems later. Sometimes the problems start right away — as soon as you encounter the software — other times the problem does not occur until after a given time or event, such as shutting down and restarting Windows.

Some of the most common problems users experience include slow connection speeds, pop-ups (Web pages that display automatically on your screen), downloads of unwanted Web pages, and overall system performance problems. In some cases, malicious software can render Windows and your PC virtually unusable until you clear out the offending software.

A way to combat malicious software is to enable the Windows Defender program. It watches and scans your system for thousands of possible adware and spyware programs. If Defender finds a problem, it attempts to remove it and clean up your system.

Protect Windows with Windows Defender

① From the Windows Security Center, click Windows Defender.

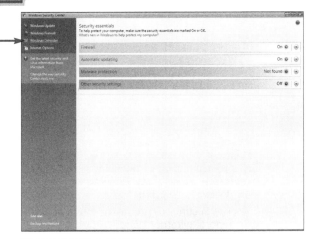

The Windows Defender window appears.

② Click Scan Now.

Windows Defender performs a scan of your system.

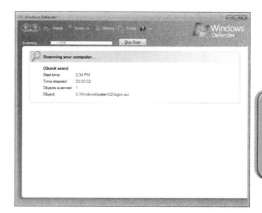

When finished, it displays a message that your system has been scanned.

If your system is running normally, Windows displays a message to that effect.

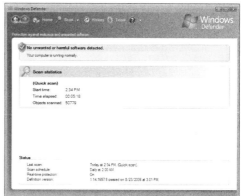

Do I have to run Windows Defender every day?

▼ No, you do not have to. However, it is a good idea to let it run every day if you use the Internet every day. Even if you think that you have not downloaded harmful spyware programs, you may have done so without your knowledge. They can sneak in with any Internet application (especially chat programs). Because Windows Defender may slow down your system some while it is running, schedule it to run when you are not using it, such as during a daily meeting time, coffee break, or lunchtime. To set a scan time, click Tools and then click Options. From the Time of day list, select the time you want Defender to run, such as 12:00 PM. Click Save.

Why does Windows Defender need to connect to the Internet?

▼ Microsoft designed Defender to combat the latest spyware (or malware) that you can download from the Internet. Every day new spyware programs are released on the Internet. To combat these programs, Windows Defender downloads updates from the Microsoft Web site to keep it up-to-date on the latest security problems. If you do not have a connection to the Internet, when Windows Defender is outdated, you will be instructed to connect to the Internet and allow Defender to download available updates.

Manage and Monitor Antivirus Software

With Windows Security Center in Windows Vista, you can quickly check to see whether your PC has any virus protection. While Microsoft addresses security breaches with periodic updates (see Chapter 3 for information on automatic updates), it does not produce antivirus software per se. What Microsoft has done, instead, is provide information about why you should have antivirus software, how it works, and links to where you can obtain it from trusted sources. In addition, Windows Security Center integrates with most

antivirus software so that if you have antivirus software installed, Windows Security Center can report whether it is turned on and up-to-date.

In the Security Center, if you have up-to-date antivirus software running on your PC, the Virus Protection section should show a green light. If antivirus software is not present, turned off, or undetected (some antivirus software is not integrated with the Security Center and will not be detected), a red bar and red light appear, along with a Recommendations button that directs you to how you can fix the problem.

Manage and Monitor Antivirus Software

Check for Virus Protection

1 Click Start.

2 Click Control Panel.

The Control Panel appears.

3 Click Check this computer's security status.

The Windows Security Center appears.

④ Click here to display more information about virus protection.

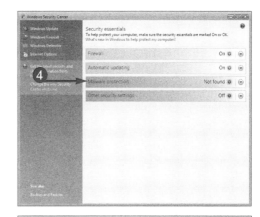

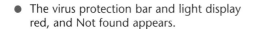

● The virus protection bar and light display red, and Not found appears.

How do I find out more about antivirus software?

▼ Click the Find a program button in the Malware protection area of the Windows Security Center. Windows Vista launches Internet Explorer and connects you to the Windows Vista Antivirus Providers Web site. On this site you can find links to manufacturer Web sites that distribute antivirus software. Some of the manufacturers offer trial versions of their software to enable you to try out a program before purchasing it. Usually these trials expire after 30 days, at which time you are encouraged to purchase the full version of the software or subscribe to a monthly or annual download service.

I installed antivirus software and scanned my system for viruses, but the Security Center says that virus protection is turned off, and the light is red. What should I do?

▼ This probably means that you have at some time performed a scan for viruses but do not have the antivirus software's real-time scanning turned on. If you do not have real-time scanning turned on, you should enable that feature. Another possibility is that the Windows Vista Security Center does not recognize your antivirus software. The Security Center is designed to help you *manage* the programs that protect your system, not actually protect your system. Because of this, some tools are just not recognized by the Security Center.

continued

Manage and Monitor
Antivirus Software *(Continued)*

Avast AntiVirus from is used in this example, but many other programs are available. See the section "Check Security at the Security Center," earlier in this chapter, for information on how to find antivirus software. With Avast AntiVirus (as well as most other antivirus products), an icon displays in the Notification Area of the taskbar showing the status of virus protection. To access the software, right-click the icon and select Start avast! Antivirus from the menu that appears.

After you have launched the antivirus application, you can perform several tasks. These differ slightly from

program to program, but conceptually, the three key operations are: installing virus definition updates (new viruses are continually being developed, so antivirus software providers need to send your program frequent updates of what to look for), scanning existing files, and dealing with any infected files the software might find (by quarantine, deletion, repair, and so on). Make sure that the automatic virus definition update feature (in this example, the feature is called iAVS Update) is turned on, and that you schedule regular system scans of all the files currently on your PC. This example shows you how to launch Avast AntiVirus and scan your system for viruses.

Manage and Monitor Antivirus Software *(continued)*

Scan for Viruses

1 Right-click the Avast AntiVirus icon.

2 Click Start avast! Antivirus.

The Avast AntiVirus dashboard window appears.

3 Click the Menu button to see a list of commands.

4 Click Start Scan to choose scanning choices.

5 Click here to select the area you want to scan for viruses.

6 Click here to scan your local disks for viruses.

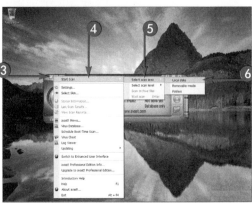

The Standard Scan window appears.

⑦ Click Start to start the scan process.

Avast AntiVirus scans your hard drive and reports scanning activities in the Status Information window.

I have heard about a new virus that is spreading. What can I do to protect my PC from it?

▼ First, go to the Control Panel to make sure that you have your Virus Protection and Automatic Updates turned on. If you are not using Automatic Updates, click the Get the latest security and virus information from Microsoft link and follow the instructions. Next, use the online update feature of your antivirus software to download the latest virus information. Perform a full system scan to ensure that you have not already received the virus. For information about e-mail viruses, see the section "Secure Microsoft Office Outlook and Windows Mail," later in this chapter.

I do not remember when I last scanned my computer for viruses. How do I find that out?

▼ Antivirus software keeps track of your virus scanning history. In the Norton AntiVirus software used in this example, this is called the Activity Log. To view the report of recent activity, click Reports and then click View Reports on the Activity Log section. You see a report of each activity and which user initiated the activity (if your PC has more than one user).

Add Logon Warning

If you are running Windows Vista Ultimate and have administrator privileges, you can add a logon warning or message whenever a user logs on to the system. Many corporate networks have a legal notice expressively notifying anyone who attempts to log on to their network that only those authorized to log on may do so. To add such a warning, you can launch the Security Settings snap-in to the Microsoft Management Console (MMC). Access to MMC snap-ins is not displayed on the All Programs menu by default. From the Customize Start Menu dialog box, you can elect to show System

Administrative Tools on the All Programs menu and the Start menu.

The Administrative Tools menu contains a list of MMC snap-ins such as Component Services, Computer Management, Data Sources (ODBC), Event Viewer, Local Security Policy, Performance, and Services. To make changes to security, such as adding a logon warning, select Local Security Policy. Note that you can adjust *local* security policies here. It is beyond the scope of this book to discuss network-wide security policies and their enforcement. Local Security Settings contains the Security Options section of Local Policies.

Add Logon Warning

① Click Start.

② Click Control Panel.

The Control Panel window appears.

③ Click System and Maintenance.

The System and Maintenance window appears.

④ Click Administrative Tools.

The Administrative Tools window appears.

⑤ Double-click Local Security Policy.

When I click Local Security Policy, it takes me directly to Security Options. Why is this different from the steps listed previously?

▼ That was the last place you were using the snap-in. MMC snap-ins keep track of how they were last used. For example, if you have been working with the security options and then close the snap-in, when you next open it, the security options are expanded. Likewise, if you have not yet used an option, it may be minimized; you can expand it by clicking the plus sign to access that option.

My computer already has a logon message. Can I remove or change the message that my network administrator has included?

▼ If you are working in a corporate network environment, such messages tend to be for the entire department or network and are not subject to modification by individual users. If your network does not use a logon message, you may still be able to add one locally (just for your computer). However, if there is already a network- or department-wide message, you cannot change or remove this message without the help of a network administrator.

continued

Add Logon
Warning *(Continued)*

Assuming you have local administrator privileges, you can make changes to the interactive logon security policies for your local system from the Local Security Settings MMC snap-in. To add a warning message that comes up in a window at logon time, click Interactive logon: Message text for users attempting to log on. You can then type a message regarding the authorized use of the system (or an appropriate logon notice). In order for the warning message or notice to pop up at logon, you need to add a message title. You can do this by clicking Interactive logon: Message title for users

attempting to log on. Type a brief message title (such as Warning or Legal Notice) in the text box. This appears in the title bar of the logon's warning message box.

The next time a user logs on to the system, immediately prior to the logon screen for user name and password, the user sees your text message box with the message title you assigned against a blank screen. In order to proceed to the logon screen, the user must click OK or press Enter to acknowledge reading the message.

Add Logon Warning *(continued)*

The Local Security Settings MMC snap-in appears.

6 Click the expand arrow next to Local Policies.

7 Click Security Options.

Scroll through the Policy list in the right pane.

8 Double-click Interactive logon: Message text for users attempting to log on.

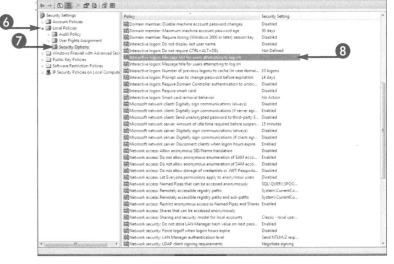

The Interactive logon: Message text for users attempting to log on Properties dialog box appears.

9 Type **Unauthorized use of this computer is strictly prohibited** in the text box (or your own text message).

10 Click OK.

⓫ Click Interactive logon: Message title for users attempting to log on.

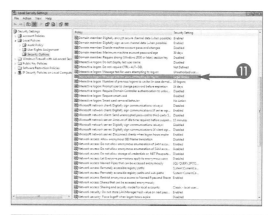

The corresponding Properties dialog box appears.

⓬ Type **Legal Notice** (or your own brief message title) in the text box.

⓭ Click OK to close the dialog box.

⓮ Click the Close box to close the Local Security Settings snap-in.

When a user next attempts to log on, the user sees the message title and text you entered.

Can a user avoid seeing this message when attempting to log on?

▼ No. The only user action possible, other than pressing Ctrl+Alt+Del or performing a hardware power-down or reset, is to view the screen and click OK or press Enter. If a reset occurs, however, it simply brings the user back to this screen. Many companies require these warning prompts to ensure users know that the information and data stored on the computer and on computers they can access (such as on a local area network) is private property or confidential (or both).

Can I modify the message title and text or remove it later?

▼ Yes. You can change the message title and text at any time, provided you have the necessary privileges. You must have adminstrator privileges to modify the Local Security Policy setting. This keeps unauthorized users from changing or removing the message. To remove the logon message, simply return to the Security Options settings in the Local Security Policy snap-in, double-click the logon messages you chose in the "Add Logon Warning" section in this chapter, and delete the message title and text. The next time you start Windows Vista, the logon warnings will not appear.

Install and Manage Digital Certificates

You can view and manage digital certificates in Windows Vista by adding the MMC Certificates snap-in. Certificates are a way to guarantee the authenticity of digital data to ensure what you are receiving and that the sender really is who the sender claims to be. Certificates use public key encryption to verify the identity of a person, service, program, Web site, or other entity electronically.

The Certificate Authority (CA) is a trusted entity that issues and verifies these certificates. The CA issues a public key for a person or other entity, and that

person or entity retains the corresponding private key. In this way, certificates can safely be widely distributed because the CA with a private key must verify them before they are authorized.

To add the Certificates snap-in, you can run MMC and add Certificates. This snap-in has several functions. You can manage certificates for your user account, a service, or a computer. However, you must add a separate instance of the Certificates snap-in for each of these tasks; for example, MMC does not allow you to switch between managing the certificates for your user account and managing the certificates for your PC.

① Click **Start**.

② Click **All Programs**.

Note: After you click All Programs, the name changes to Back.

③ Click **Accessories**.

④ Click **Run**.

⑤ Type **mmc.exe**.

⑥ Click **OK**.

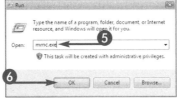

An MMC console window appears.

7 Click File.

8 Click Add/Remove Snap-in.

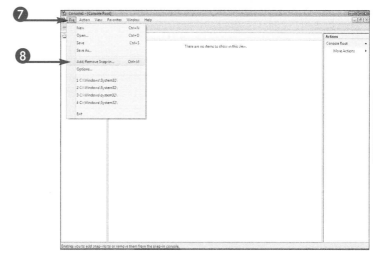

The Add or Remove Snap-ins dialog box appears.

9 Click Certificates.

10 Click Add.

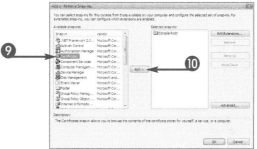

How do I obtain a personal digital certificate?

▼ If you have need for a personal digital certificate (for such things as verifying the authenticity of e-mail), you can obtain one from one of several certificate authorities via the Web. One way is to click Get a Digital ID on the Security tab of the Options dialog box from the Tools menu in Microsoft Office Outlook. This takes you to a Microsoft Web page with a list of partners who provide digital IDs (personal digital certificates), along with customer ratings for each one.

Is it necessary to install and use the Certificates MMC snap-in to have or use digital certificates?

▼ No. This snap-in simply enables you to monitor and manage your certificates. It is not required that you install the snap-in to use digital certificates. In fact, in many cases, users will not have access to the Certificates MMC if they have only Standard user privileges. Only users that are set up as Administrators are allowed to run the MMC application. If you are the only user on your computer, however, you have Administrator privileges.

continued

Install and Manage Digital Certificates *(Continued)*

Some of the most common uses for public key certificates are secure Web sites, which use the https protocol, and software program code. You can also use personal digital certificates to verify authenticity in sensitive e-mail correspondence, provided each person has an e-mail application (such as Microsoft Office Outlook or Windows Mail) that supports certificates.

When you have added the Certificates snap-in to the MMC console, you can click it to view the various categories of certificates: Personal, Trusted Root Certification Authorities, Enterprise Trust, Intermediate Certification Authorities, Active Directory User Object, Trusted Publishers, Untrusted Certificates, Third-Party

Root Certificate Authorities, and Trusted People. The certificates most relevant to individual PC users are the Personal category, which contains your own certificates for e-mail and Encrypting File System, or EFS, and Trusted Persons category, which contains certificates for verified e-mail correspondents.

Once you install and save the MMC Certificates snap-in, you can return to manage these certificates by running MMC, opening up the corresponding snap-in by typing **mmc.exe /s /path/filename.msc** in the Run command's text box, and clicking OK. You can review existing certificates, copy personal certificates to a file (if, for example, you need to move to another PC), or delete certificates.

Install and Manage Digital Certificates *(continued)*

The Certificates snap-in dialog box appears.

⑪ Click the type of account to manage certificates for; My user account, in this example (○ changes to ◉).

⑫ Click Finish.

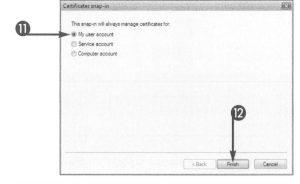

The Certificates snap-in now appears in the Selected snap-ins list.

⑬ Click OK.

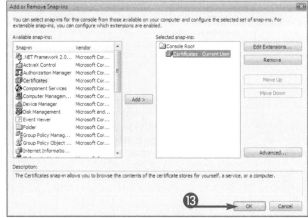

⑭ Double-click Certificates – Current User to display a list of certificate categories beneath the selection.

⑮ Double-click a certificate category folder (Trusted Root Certification Authorities, in this example).

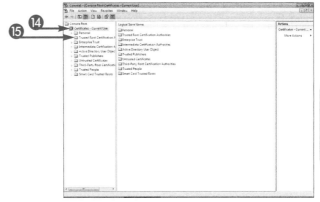

⑯ Double-click Certificates to view and manage certificates in this category.

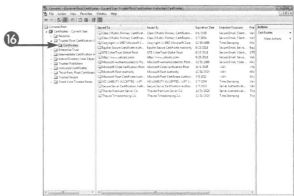

What if I want to save this snap-in view and work with it again?

▼ You can save the MMC view so you can return to it quicker and easier next time. To do this, when you exit MMC, you are prompted to save this file. Choose a name (such as Certificates) and save the file. That way, if you want to reopen the snap-in, you can either use the Run command and specify the file name (using the .msc extension) or you can simply type **mmc.exe** from the Run command, click File, and then click Open to select the file from a list. If you use the MMC tool often, consider creating a shortcut to it on your desktop.

How do I move my personal certificate from one computer to another?

▼ You can use the Certificates snap-in to do this. From the Certificates snap-in, locate the certificate in the Certificates folder of the Personal certificate category and double-click the certificate. Next click the Details tab and then click Copy to File. This takes you to the Certificate Export Wizard, which walks you through the steps of exporting a certificate. Click Next and pick a format to use. The standard format is DER encoded binary X.509. Click Next and specify a file name for the certificate. Click Next and then Click Finish.

Secure Microsoft Office Outlook and Windows Mail

Y ou can keep your Microsoft Office Outlook and Windows Mail e-mail more secure by setting the security options. Because Outlook and Windows Mail have a similar security options interface, the material covered here is for both, though it uses screens mostly from Windows Mail. To access the security features in Outlook or Windows Mail, launch the program and select the Security tab from the Options dialog box, accessible from the Tools menu. On the Security tab in Windows Mail, the first set of options addresses Virus Protection (Security Zones in Outlook). When you receive HTML messages,

you need protection from malicious scripts and other code. You can also elect to block images. This is useful, because sometimes malicious code can be hidden in image file formats.

Another level of security that you can add is a digital ID (or certificate). With a digital certificate, you can send your e-mail in an encrypted format and the recipient can verify that it has arrived unaltered. After you have put an address with a certificate in your Contacts list, that certificate is stored and you can communicate securely over e-mail.

Secure Microsoft Office Outlook and Windows Mail

Windows Mail Security Tab

1 After launching Windows Mail (or Outlook), click Tools.

2 Click Options.

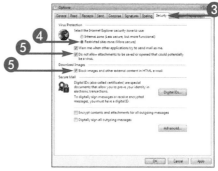

The Options dialog box appears.

3 Click the Security tab.

4 Click the Restricted sites zone (More secure) option (○ changes to ◉).

5 Make sure these options are selected (☑) for more security.

6 If you have a digital ID (certificate) and want to encrypt your outgoing e-mail, click here.

7 If you have a digital ID (certificate), click here to digitally sign your outgoing mail as authentic.

8 Click OK to save your changes.

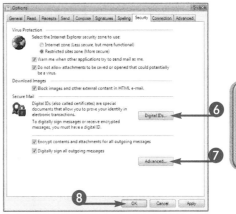

The Outlook Security Tab

1 Repeat steps **1** to **3** to access the Security tab.

2 To encrypt your outgoing e-mail, click this option (☐ changes to ☑).

3 To sign your outgoing mail digitally as authentic, click this option (☐ changes to ☑).

4 Click here and select Restricted sites for more security.

5 Click OK to save your changes.

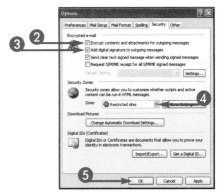

How can I help keep e-mail more secure?

▼ To keep e-mail more secure, here are some principles to follow:

- Use antivirus software that integrates with Outlook.
- Use junk e-mail and spam filters when possible.
- Delete any suspicious e-mail with attachments (even if it claims to be from someone you know).
- Use a secured e-mail application (preferably not an open Web-browser–based system).
- Avoid or limit your use of wireless networking in unsecured public hot spots for e-mail.
- Use a digital ID and encrypt your messages for sensitive e-mail.

How can I keep up-to-date on the latest e-mail virus threats?

▼ You can click Windows Security Center on the Control Panel and then click Get the latest security and virus information from Microsoft, or use your Web browser to go to www.microsoft.com/security. Your virus protection software company will also have information on its Web site.

Should I open e-mail messages that are forwarded to me?

▼ If you know that the forwards are from people you know and trust, you can probably open them. However, many people simply forward you messages that have been forwarded to them. You may want to leave these messages unopened. Ask the person who forwards these messages to you to take you off his or her forward list.

Secure Internet Explorer

Y ou can ensure that you have a more secure Web-browsing experience if you take some time to review Internet Explorer's security settings. The easiest way to do this is to right-click the Internet Explorer icon on the desktop and click Properties. This brings up the Internet Properties dialog box. If you have already launched Internet Explorer, you can also get to this dialog box by clicking Tools and then clicking Internet Options. Several tabs on this dialog box relate to security.

The Security tab on the Internet Properties dialog box enables you to view the setting for each Web content zone. The four categories are Internet (for all sites not put into other zones), Local intranet, Trusted sites, and Restricted sites. The *Internet* zone has a medium level of security so that you have relative safety but maintain functionality. The *Local intranet* zone has your local network and intranet sites, assumes the trust level is high, and allows maximum functionality. The *Trusted sites* zone contains sites other than your local intranet that have a high trust level and, therefore, allow maximum functionality. The *Restricted sites* zone contains sites that may have higher risk, such as external mail and file servers.

Secure Internet Explorer

① Right-click the Internet Explorer icon.

② Click Properties.

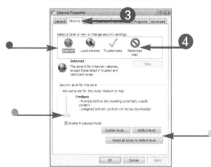

The Internet Properties dialog box appears.

③ Click the Security tab.

● Indicates the Web content zone is selected.

● Click the slider to adjust the security level for this zone.

● Click to make changes to individual settings.

④ Click Restricted sites.

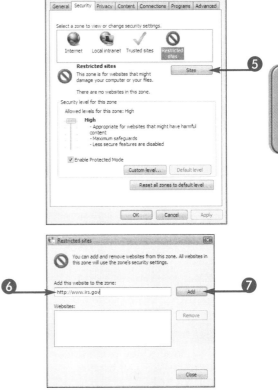

The settings for the Restricted sites Web content zone now appear.

5 Click Sites to add a site to this zone.

The Restricted sites dialog box appears.

6 Type the address of the Web site you want to add to this zone, for example, **http://www.irs.gov**.

7 Click Add.

I want to be notified every time an attempt is made to download an ActiveX control to my computer for the Internet Web content zone. How do I do this?

▼ Click Tools and then click Internet Options. Click the Security tab. Click the Internet zone, and then click Custom Level to open the Security Settings – Internet Zone dialog box. In the ActiveX controls and plug-ins section, find Automatic prompting for ActiveX controls and click Enable (○ changes to ◉). Click OK. If you were using the default level (Medium), it now appears as Custom Level.

How can I get maximum functionality for a specific trusted Web site?

▼ The easiest way to do this is to add the site to your Trusted sites Web content zone. To do so, open the Internet Options dialog box and click the Security tab. Click Trusted sites. Next, click Sites to open the Trusted sites dialog box and type the address of the Web site that you trust. Click Add to add the site to the Websites list. Make sure that the Require server verification (https:) for all sites in this zone option is selected; otherwise, you will be using minimum security with an open protocol — an unsafe procedure.

continued

Secure Internet Explorer *(Continued)*

You can add sites to and remove sites from each of the security zones by selecting the zone and clicking Sites. You can also make changes to individual security settings for each security zone by clicking Custom Level. By clicking Default Level, you can restore any settings to their default values.

The Internet Properties dialog box also has additional security-related settings on the Advanced tab; these are grouped together in the Security section of the Settings list. Although privacy is a security issue, it is a category unto itself as well, and, therefore, it has its own Privacy tab on the Internet Properties dialog box. Web sites often use *cookies* to store information on your computer for later retrieval. While cookies only contain information that you provide, you may want to restrict such information. From the Privacy tab, you can use a slider to set the privacy level from Accept All Cookies (least privacy) through Medium (default level) to Block All Cookies (most privacy). Blocking all cookies considerably reduces functionality on some sites (such as travel reservations), so you should consider the setting that best fits your needs.

- After clicking Add, the Web site added to the Restricted sites Web content zone appears in the Web sites window.

8 Click Close.

9 Click the Advanced tab.

Drag the scrollbar of the Settings window downward until you see the Security settings.

- Click here to restore all advanced settings defaults (not just security).

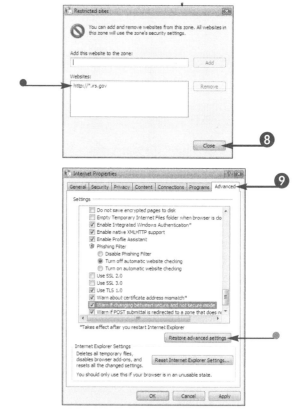

⑩ Click here to delete temporary Internet files every time you close your browser (☐ changes to ☑).

⑪ Click the Privacy tab.

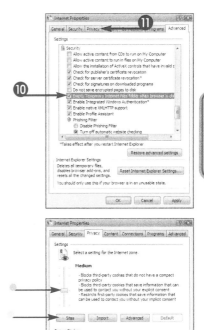

The Privacy tab of the Internet Properties dialog box appears.

◉ Dragging this slider adjusts the privacy level by determining whether to accept certain cookies.

◉ Click Sites to expressly block or allow cookies from a specific Web site, regardless of overall privacy settings.

⑫ Click OK to accept changes.

Are there any other things I should do to secure Internet Explorer?

▼ Yes. Make sure that Automatic Updates are turned on in the Security Center, or frequently click the Tools menu in Internet Explorer and click Windows Update. This takes you to a Microsoft update site where you can check for critical updates (these usually have to do with security). If updates are available, download and install them on your computer. Many times, the update does not specifically fix an Internet Explorer problem but is related to problems that Internet Explorer exposes on your computer.

How can I maintain a high privacy level but allow cookies from one site that I trust?

▼ Click Tools and then click Internet Options to open the Internet Options dialog box. Click the Privacy tab. In the Settings area, move the slider upward and then click Sites, for example, from Medium to High. This displays the Per Site Privacy Actions dialog box. In the Address of website box, type the name of your trusted site and click Allow. Click OK to close the Per Site Privacy Actions dialog box and click OK again to close the Internet Options dialog box.

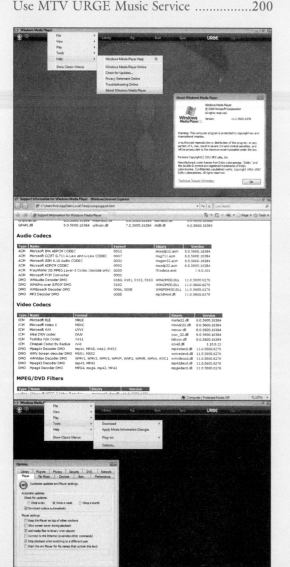

PART III

MASTERING MULTIMEDIA WITH WINDOWS VISTA

11 Creating Digital Content with Windows Vista

12 Enjoying Digital Entertainment with Media Center

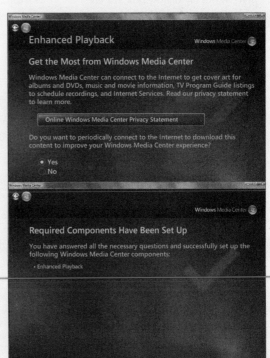

Work with Windows Media Player 11

Windows Vista includes Windows Media Player 11, a program that enables you to play audio and video on your computer, as well as burn and rip CDs and DVDs. See Chapter 10 for more on burning CDs and DVDs. Media Player makes it easy to play back audio whether it is stored on CD, DVD, media player, or file. By default, Windows is configured to launch Media Player any time you insert an audio CD or DVD — such as a DVD from your favorite rock group — or plug in a supported media player. Likewise, when you click an audio file supported by Media Player, such as a Waveform Audio

(WAV) or Moving Picture Experts Group (MPG) file, Media Player launches and plays the file.

You can also use Media Player to play video on your computer. You can use it to play digital video files and DVD discs. With Media Player 11, you can insert a DVD into your DVD drive and watch a movie. You can download and play video clips — thousands, or millions, perhaps, of which are available on the Internet — on Media Player. You also can create home movies and play back the video files using Media Player.

Work with Windows Media Player 11

① To play an audio CD, insert the CD-ROM in the CD tray.

The AutoPlay dialog box appears.

② Click the option to play the audio CD using Windows Media Player.

● You can click this option to have Windows perform this action every time you insert an audio CD (☐ changes to ☑).

③ Press Enter.

The Windows Media Player window appears, with the Now Playing tab displayed.

The first track on the CD begins playing.

④ To pause the track, click the Pause button.

⑤ To stop the track, click the Stop button.

⑥ To move to the next track, click the Next button.

⑦ To mute the sound, click the Mute button.

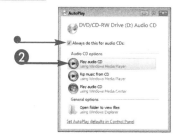

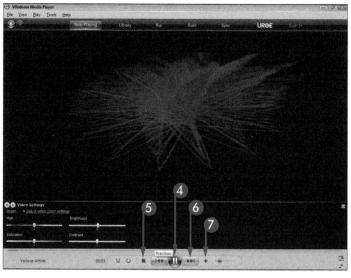

8 Click the Play button to continue playing after you have paused or stopped the track.

9 To move to different parts of a track, slide the Seek slider to the left or right. Or, click the Fast Forward or Rewind buttons.

10 Graphic visualizations can play as your audio file plays. To change a visualization, right-click the visualization area.

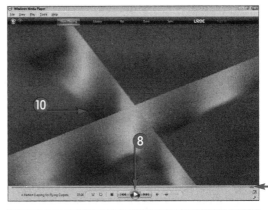

A menu of visualization categories appears.

11 Click a category.

12 Click a visualization name.

The new visualization plays.

PART III

I have Media Player installed, but another program opens when I insert a CD. What can I do to change this?

▼ You must change the file association with your audio file formats. An easy way to do this is to click Start and click Default Programs. Click Change AutoPlay Settings and click the down arrow next to the Audio Files media item. Click Play Using Windows Media Player. Click OK. Now when you insert an audio CD, Media Player is the program that launches to play back your songs.

Are there updates available for Media player? If so, how do I get them?

▼ Microsoft routinely announces updates to Media Player. As of this writing, the latest version of Media Player is 11. To check for Media Player updates, you must have an Internet connection. Next, start Media Player and click Help. From Help, click Check for Updates. Media Player checks your version against the latest one on the Microsoft Web site. If your version is the most current one, a message appears letting you know this. Click OK to confim and to return to the Media Player window. If your version is not the most current one, a wizard appears to download the Media Player update.

Install and View Codecs for Media Player 11

Windows Media Player makes it easy to install codecs for playing audio and video files. *Codecs* are encoded programming code that instructs Media Player how to decompress an audio or a video file when you want to play it back. Codec is short for COmpressor/DEcompressor. Audio and video files are compressed so they take up less room on the media (such as CDs and DVDs) on which they are delivered to your computer and take less time to download from the Internet. Without a codec on your computer, Media Player does not know how to decompress a type of file.

When you install Media Player, some codecs are automatically installed. As newer compression formats are introduced, however, new codecs are written. Some codecs are free, while others cost money. Media Player is set up to download codecs automatically when you attempt to play back a video that uses a codec not already on your computer. You must be connected to the Internet for this to occur.

Media Player also lets you view which codecs are installed. You may want to know this information for troubleshooting playback problems.

Install and View Codecs for Media Player 11

Install a Codec

① To enable Media Player to automatically download and install codecs, right-click the toolbar.

A submenu appears.

② Click Tools.

③ Click Options.

The Options dialog box appears.

④ Click the Player tab.

⑤ Click the option to download codecs automatically (☐ changes to ☑).

⑥ Click OK.

When you open a file that requires a codec not currently on your computer, Media Player automatically searches for the right one to download and install.

View Installed Codec

1 To view the codecs installed, right-click the Media Player toolbar.

A submenu appears.

2 Click Help.

3 Click About Windows Media Player.

The About Windows Media Player dialog box appears.

4 Click the Technical Support Information link.

The Support Information for Windows Media Player page appears.

5 Scroll down the page to the Audio Codecs and Video Codecs lists.

Names and file specifications about each codec installed on your computer appear in these lists.

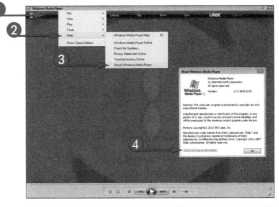

Sometimes when I try to play back an Audio Video Interleave (AVI) video file, I get an error saying it cannot find the DivX codec. Where can I get it on the Internet?

▼ The DivX codec is one of the oldest codecs around used for video files, including Windows Media Video (WMV), MPEG-4, and AVI files. With DivX, video producers can shrink an entire DVD-sized movie to fit on a CD without losing too much of the quality. To download DivX, visit DivX.Com at http://go.divx.com. You can download DivX (which is free and has some features disabled) and DivX Pro. DivX Pro currently costs around $20.

I have a codec but Media Player says it is not installed. Do codecs ever have updates?

▼ Yes, some codecs are updated constantly. A codec may be updated with new user features, have better compression algorithms included, or be ported to other operated systems. When Media Player tells you that it cannot locate a specific codec and you know it is on your system, be sure the option for allowing Media Player to download new codecs is enabled.

Rip Music with Windows Media Player

Media Player makes it very easy to rip music from your audio CDs. When you rip music, you copy the music from the CD to the computer, saving each song (called a *track*) into a file. You can then play back the ripped music as an album, create playlists by combining individual tracks from various albums into your own "album," or copy music to another device.

When you begin ripping music, you select the tracks you want to rip. To rip the whole album, you select all the tracks. To rip only selected tracks, select them in the Rip tab of Media Player. When you start ripping,

Media Player shows you the progress of the ripping process. While you are ripping a CD, you can even listen to it.

When you rip music and you are connected to the Internet, Media Player automatically downloads information about the album. For example, Media Player downloads track title, artist name, music genre information, and other information. Although many CDs have this information available on the Internet, some do not. If the information is not available, Media Player displays labels such as Unknown Artist, Track 1, Track 2, and so on.

Rip Music with Windows Media Player

1 Insert an audio CD into your CD-ROM drive.

Windows displays the AudioPlay dialog box.

2 Click Rip music from CD using Windows Media Player.

- You can click this option to have Windows Media Player to automatically start and rip your audio CDs from now on. However, you may not want to choose this if you plan to play back CDs using Media Player in the future.

3 Press Enter.

The Windows Media Player window displays with the Rip tab open.

- Media Player automatically begins ripping the CD.

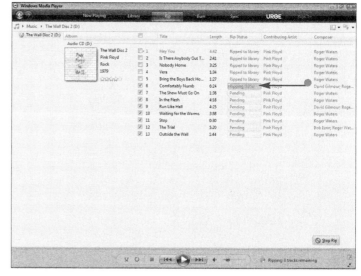

● If you are connected to the Internet, Media Player also downloads artist, track, and license information about the album.

When the CD is finished ripping, the Media Player window appears as shown here. You can play back tracks, record to another media device, create playing lists, or close Media Player.

④ To change ripping options, click the Rip down arrow.

⑤ Click options for ripping your music CDs.

Some of the CDs I try to rip have a copy protection item selected. What is this and how can I play back the tracks?

▼ CDs that have the Copy protect music check box enabled are protected files. You must obtain a license (called *license migration*) to play back the tracks. The license includes information about restrictions on the file. This information depends on the creator of the license but can include restrictions on copying the music to other computers. The license you download while ripping a track is associated with the computer on which you download the license. This license can be played only on the computer where you create the license file.

In previous versions of Media Player, I was able to back up my Digital Rights Managements (DRM) licenses. How can I do this in Media Player 11?

▼ Media Player 11 does not support backing up DRMs. However, if you lose or transfer music to another computer, you may be able to restore the DRM licenses. Click the Online Stores tab in Media Player (the default stores tab is called URGE, for the MTV URGE library). Select a command for that library, such as Restore My Library (this name, if available for the store you choose, may be different) to restore your library. Also, depending on the online store, you may have to limit the number of times you can restore the DRM.

Use Media Player 11 Library

The Media Player Library provides a centralized area to manage your digital music, pictures, and videos that you have stored on your computer. The Library enables you to play back and organize your digital media by different categories, such as artist, album, songs, genre, year, and rating. The Rating category, for instance, is a system by which you can give your media items a star rating from one to five stars. When you save an item in the library, Media Player downloads information about that item and shows a rating based on the site from which the information was downloaded. You can change this rating.

From the Library, you can create a list of items you want to play back as a group, called a *playlist*, and choose items that you want to burn to a CD or DVD, or download to a portable media device. For more information, see the section "Create Playlists," later in this chapter.

To add items to your library, you can rip music CDs or DVDs, download files (such as music or video) from online stores, or add files from your hard drive. In addition, as you play a new file in Media Player, such as from a network drive, that file is added automatically to the Library.

Using Media Player 11 Library

Add Items to the Library

① To manually add items to the Music Library, play a new audio CD in Media Player.

The Media Player window appears with the Now Playing tab showing.

② Click the Library tab.

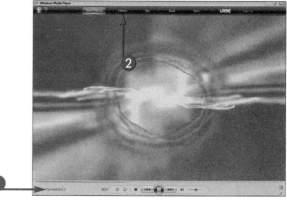

The Library tab appears. Information about the CD appears in the Library.

Change a Rating for an Item

1 To change the star rating for a song, click the Library tab.

2 Right-click the item to modify it.

A submenu appears.

3 Click Rate.

A submenu appears.

4 Click the number of stars you want for the rating.

The Library shows the new rating.

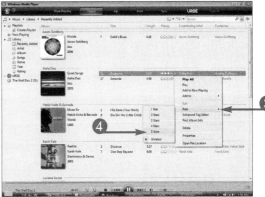

I have some video files in a folder I created that Media Player does not automatically add to the Library. Can I change where Media Player looks for these?

▼ Yes. By default, Media Player 11 looks for media items in specific locations, such as your personal foldes (Music, Videos, and so on). To change this, open the Library tab and click the arrow below the Library tab. On the Add to Library dialog box, click Add to Library and then click Advanced Options. Click Add and then click the folders you want Media Player to monitor. Click OK and then click OK again. Click Close.

Can I access my Library from a network computer?

▼ Yes. With Media Player 11, you can set up Media Sharing to do this. Click the Library tab and then click the arrow under the Library tab. Click More Options. On the Options dialog box, click Configure Sharing on the Library tab to open the Media Sharing dialog box. Click Share my media and click Allow. Click OK to close the Media Sharing dialog box and then click OK again to close the Options dialog box. You must have a network set up and the other computers must be running Windows Vista to access your shared media files.

Create
Playlists

Media Player enables you to create *playlists*, which are customized lists of files that you want to listen to or watch. A playlist can be one song, several songs, one video file, a list of video files, or a complete album.

You can view playlists in the Playlist pane when you have the Library tab selected. Items in a playlist can be played back in order, repeated, shuffled, and sorted. When you shuffle a playlist, Media Player automatically plays files back in random order.

After a playlist is created, you can add files to it. Files can be added to playlists using Media Player or by

selecting files from Windows Explorer or Computer. You can modify (by adding files to it, renaming files, or removing files), resort, or remove the playlist. Another handy way to use a playlist is to burn a CD or DVD using the listed items.

When you use a playlist to create a CD or DVD, the playlist file is not copied to the disc. The contents of the playlist, however, are copied. On the other hand, when you sync content to a media device using a playlist, Media Player copies the content and the playlist to the device, enabling you to use the playlist on the device.

Create Playlists

① To create a new playlist, click the Library tab.

② Click the Library tab arrow.

A submenu appears.

③ Click Create Playlist.

The Playlist pane appears.

④ Type a name for the playlist.

● The Playlist pane instructs you to drag items to it to build your list.

⑤ In the Contents pane of the Library tab, select an item.

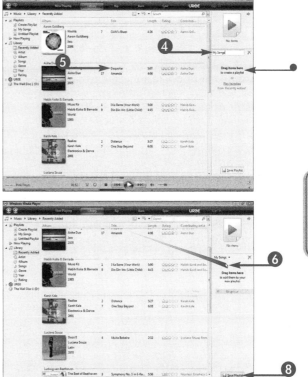

⑥ Drag the track to the Playlist pane.

The file is added to the new playlist.

⑦ Repeat steps **5** and **6** to continue adding files to the new playlist.

⑧ Click Save Playlist.

The new playlist is saved to your computer. To play it, choose the playlist name after you click My Playlists in the Contents pane.

What are Auto Playlists?

▼ *Auto Playlists* are playlists that Media Player creates automatically based on certain criteria that you can select to use for the Auto Playlist. To see Auto Playlists that have been created on your computer, open Media Player and click the Library tab. Click the down arrow next to the Now Playing tab and select Auto Playlists from the menu that appears. Auto Playlists display, including Composer, Date Added, Playcount – Total Weekend, and My Rating. These lists are automatically updated each time you open them in Media Player.

How do I create an Auto Playlist?

▼ Choose the Library tab and click the arrow under the Library tab. Click Create Auto Playlist. The New Auto Playlist appears. Type a name in the Auto Playlist Name name box. Click the green plus signs (+) to choose various criteria for the Auto Playlists. For example, from the first list, click File Type. Click the Contains link and click an option, such as Is. Click the Click To Set link to show a list of file type choices (such as Windows Media Audio, or WMA). Click a type. Continue adding criteria as needed to create your list. Click OK when you are ready to save it. Media Player adds the new Auto Playlist to your playlists.

Sync with Music Devices

One of the most popular inventions over the past few years has been the digital music device, sometimes referred to as the MP3 (MPEG, or Moving Picture Experts Group, Audio Layer III) player. These devices enable users to download music files to a small portable digital player that stores and plays back their music. Many of these devices can hold thousands of individual songs and are about the size of a small cellular telephone. In fact, some cell phones now include digital media players.

Media Player makes it a breeze to download music to your digital music devices. When you do this, it is called *syncing*. In order to sync with a device, you

must have a cable that connects your device to your computer. Some devices use internal, removable flash memory cards that you can insert into a computer or memory card reader. You then use Media Player to copy files to the media device.

The tasks you can perform with the media devices depend on the media player. Some devices let you view track names, the length of tracks, and other information. Other devices may also include features that you let you organize and sort tracks, delete individual tracks, and even download small pictures associated with the artist or album.

Sync with Music Devices

① In Windows Media Player, click the Library tab.

② Connect your device to the computer.

The device appears in the Navigation pane.

③ If it is not selected, click the device.

4️⃣ Click Start Sync.

Media Player copies the items shown in the playlist to the media device. When finished, it displays a label in the Details pane that says Synchronizing 100 percent complete.

5️⃣ Disconnect the media device to listen to the stored music.

I have a portable device that does not hold enough songs. What can I do?

▼ Some devices enable you to expand built-in memory by inserting flash memory cards. Flash memory is similar to a computer's random access memory (RAM) but has the capability of storing information for long periods of time. You can add flash memory cards in the 65MB, 128MB, 256MB, 512MB, or 1GB range to media devices that can be expanded. You have to look at the specifications that came with your media device to see if it allows for expansion memory, the type of memory card you have to use, such as Secure Digital (SD), extreme Digital (xD), Smart Media, and so on, and the maximum size card it can hold.

When I insert my memory card, the media device says it needs to be formatted. How can I do this?

▼ Media devices are essentially devices that hold computer files (like a hard disk or Zip drive) but have the added bonus of including music playback capabilities. So, to format a media device expansion card, open Computer or Windows Explorer and locate the listing for the media device. It appears as a drive name, such as Drive H. Right-click the device name and choose Format. The Format Disk dialog box appears. Click Start to format the drive. After the format finishes, you can use Media Player to copy music to the media device.

Use MTV URGE Music Service

Media Player includes a new access service that enables you to subscribe to a music or other digital content provider to download items to your computer. Media Player then stores and organizes your content so you can access it from your computer quickly and easily.

In a special offering from MTV (Music Television), the MTV URGE service link comes with Media Player. URGE is a digital music service that delivers music to your desktop. You can purchase albums or individual songs using the URGE service. Even though the Media Player

interface includes a tab for URGE, to use it you must pay for a subscription.

With the URGE service, you not only get access to the namesake MTV list of music, which primarily comprises cutting-edge and current tracks, but you also get access to the VH1 (Video Hits 1) and CMT (Country Music Television) music. The VH1 music collections comprise more classic rock and roll music, while the CMT collections focus on country music.

When you first start using URGE, you need to set up your computer for the service and subscribe to it.

Use MTV URGE Music Service

① In Media Player, click the Sign In button to the right of the URGE tab.

The URGE Download Online Store Software window appears.

② Read the online music service agreement.

③ Click I Accept.

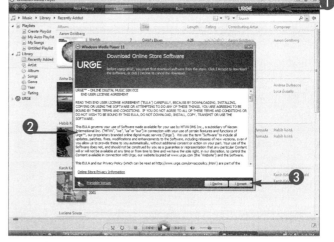

Media Player downloads the required software for the URGE service.

● A Downloading window appears, showing you the progress of the software download.

When the service has downloaded, the Microsoft Windows Media Configuration Utility – Security Warning dialog box appears.

④ Click Run.

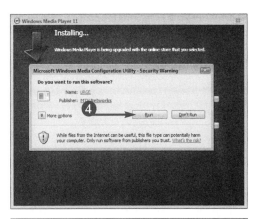

● The Installing window appears, showing that Media Player is being updated for the service you selected, for example, URGE.

When Media Player has been updated, the Media Player window appears.

How much does an URGE subscription cost?

▼ Because costs can change through the course of time, it is difficult to specify the cost you will pay if you subscribe when you read this book. At the time of this writing, however, the cost is $9.95 per month or $99 per year. This gives you access to the service. You also can use the free trial service that lasts for 15 days, and then you must sign up for an account.

Signing up for a subscription requires that you agree to allow URGE to send updates to your computer as the updates become available.

Are there other digital music subscription sites?

▼ Yes. In fact, you can access a list of them from Media Player. Click the URGE tab and then click the arrow under the URGE tab. This displays a submenu. Click Media Guide. The current list of subscription sites appears. Again, you will have to subscribe to these sites as you would to the MTV URGE site. The benefit of using a service like this, however, is that you do not have to worry about converting or ripping albums to create your playlist of music. Most of these sites let you create them as you purchase songs or albums.

continued

Use MTV URGE
Music Service *(Continued)*

To use the URGE music service, you must sign up for an account. At the time of this writing, the URGE service has a trial membership for 15 days. By using a trial membership, you do not have to pay for monthly or annual fees to access the service. After the 15-day trial, however, your downloads will stop working unless you subscribe to the service and purchase the downloaded songs.

During the signup process you can elect to start a standard account, which has a monthly or an annual fee. Because you are paying for the entire year upfront, the annual account is less expensive than the monthly year pro-rated over an entire year

(at the time of this writing, you save about $20 when you purchase the annual account). You can access a number of different genres of music, including alternative, hip-hop, blues, classical, rock, and more. Once you pick a genre, you can click the current hits, the editor's choice, or search for an artist you want to hear.

When you find what you want, such as an album, you click the Download link to download the selection to your computer. Once there, you can access it in the Media Player library to play it back on your computer or copy it to a digital media player.

Use MTV URGE Music Service *(continued)*

⑤ In the Media Player window, click the Sign In button.

The Signing in to URGE window appears.

⑥ Click Create New Account.

The Create Your Account window appears.

⑦ Type your account information in the fields.

⑧ Click Continue.

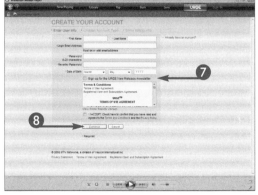

The Choose Your Account Type window appears.

9 Click an account option, for example, the Free Trial button.

The Enter Billing Information window appears.

10 Type your billing information in the fields, or press Cancel to skip.

11 Click Get Started when the Congratulations window appears.

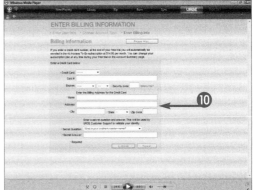

I received e-mail from URGE. Do I have to respond to them?

▼ Yes. The initial e-mail messages are confirmation messages that you are the person who signed up for the URGE account. You must respond within 24 hours to make sure your account stays active. The e-mail message has a validation link that you simply click to connect to the URGE validation page, and that's all you have to do. Other messages you may receive from URGE describe your membership and some of the benefits you get with the subscriptions, as well as the terms and restictions of the service.

Can I find every current and recently released album at URGE?

▼ Probably not. There are some artists who have not joined digital sites for downloading. As with the heavy metal band Metallica, however, some bands that originally stayed away from digital download services have recently begun providing online content. So keep checking with URGE for updates. URGE has more than two million songs from several genres; more than 500 playlists; access to features, profiles, and blogs; and more than 130 radio stations, of which 20 are free.

Install Internal CD or DVD Burners

New PCs usually come equipped with a number of hardware devices, including CD-ROM (Compact Disk-Read Only Memory) drives, DVD (Digital Versatile Discs) drives, a CD burner, and a DVD burner. Some devices include both a CD burner and DVD burner in one device. However, if your computer does not have a CD or DVD burner, or you would like to upgrade your burner to a faster one, you will need to install it using the Windows Vista Add Hardware Wizard. Vista displays this Wizard automatically after you install your new device and start up Windows. The Wizard attempts to locate all the necessary device drivers to allow it to

work with Vista and, if it is successful in doing so, it displays a message in the Notification Area that your new device is working.

You also can use the Control Panel to start the Add Hardware Wizard. Open the Control Panel and change the Control Panel view to the Windows Classic view. Individual icons for each Control Panel applet are now visible. Double-click the Add Hardware icon to launch the Add Hardware Wizard.

Some CD and DVD burners include burning software that you may want to use instead of the built-in capabilities of Vista.

Install Internal CD or DVD Burners

① With your computer shut down, install the CD or DVD burner into it by following the device's instructions.

② Start Windows Vista.

Vista locates the new device and sets up the software automatically. You are done.

③ If Vista does not find your device, click Start.

④ Click Control Panel.

The Control Panel window appears.

⑤ Click Classic View.

The Classic view of the Control Panel window appears.

⑥ Double-click Add Hardware.

The Welcome to the Add Hardware Wizard appears.

⑦ Click Next to continue.

When I started Windows after I installed my CD burner, Windows did not display any screens confirming it installed my new device, but it is working fine. Is this OK?

▼ Yes, many times Windows locates the device automatically, installs the device drivers automatically for that device, and starts up with no indication that a new device was ever found. But if you go into Windows Explorer — click Start and then click Computer — your device appears under the Computer listing. This is also true if you uninstall a device and then later re-install that same device, even if you unistalled the device a year ago. Windows remembers the device and sets up the device automatically for you.

How much can a CD-R or DVD-R hold?

▼ Regular sized CD-Rs (CD-writable) discs can hold up to 700MBs of data. However, do not expect to use all 700MBs of this space when you are burning files to your disc. Some of that space is used by Windows to set up data files that help your computer, and other devices read the files on your disc. Usually you can count on about 680MBs of empty space for your files. When you burn audio to your CDs, you can burn about 80 minutes of music or video to your discs. DVD-Rs (DVD writable discs) can hold up to 4.7GB of data, or 120 minutes of audio or video.

continued

Install Internal CD or DVD Burners *(Continued)*

After you set up your internal CD or DVD burner you can start using it to burn files to discs. To do this, you will need blank CD-R or DVD-R discs that you can purchase at just about any retail store. Look for CD-R discs that are rated for the same or higher speed as your CD burner. For instance, if your burner has a burn rate of 52x, look for CDs that have a rated speed of 52x. 52x means that the CD burner can burn files to your disc at 52 times the original speed of CD burners, which was really slow compared to today's standards. Similarly, your DVD device uses DVD-R or DVD+R discs to burn files. The +

and – in the names refer to different DVD standards. Refer to your DVD device for information on which standard it supports. Some devices support both standards.

Blank CDs are relatively inexpensive if you purchase them in bulk, such as in packs of ten or 20. In fact, the cost of discs can be less than 50 cents apiece in large quantities. It is nice to have a couple of extra blanks available in case one does not copy correctly or if the system should not be able to read the blank when you insert it for burning.

Install Internal CD or DVD Burners *(continued)*

The wizard can help you install other hardware window appears.

8 Click Install the hardware that I manually select from a list (Advanced) (○ to ◉).

9 Click Next to continue.

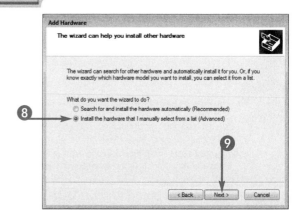

A window appears showing a list of common hardware types you can choose to install.

10 Click the DVD/CD-ROM drive selection.

● Click here if the DVD/CD-ROM drive selection is not listed.

11 Click Next to continue.

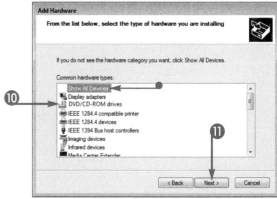

The Select the device driver you want to install for this hardware window appears.

⑫ Select the manufacturer and model of your device.

⑬ Click Next.

The wizard is ready to install your hardware window appears.

⑭ Click Next to continue.

Windows installs your new CD burner device. The Completing the Add Hardware Wizard window appears.

⑮ Click Finish.

My CD burner does not display in the model or manufacturer list when I set up my device. What can I do?

▼ First, contact the manufacturer of your device and request updated device drivers for your CD burner. Make sure the drivers are written for and tested for Windows Vista. Once you have these, repeat steps **1** to **11**. Click the Have Disk button. This opens the Install From Disk window. Use the drop-down list under Copy Manufacturer's Files From to specify the disk name, such as D or E, on which the device drivers reside. Or click the Browse button to locate the files; for example, to find them if they are stored on your hard drive or a network drive. Click OK to close the Install From Disk window and to continue with step **11**.

Why are blank DVDs more expensive than blank CDs?

▼ Blank DVDs are more expensive because they hold more information than CDs. DVDs have the capacity to store large amounts of data, such as large computer programs, music albums — they can include video and music on one disc, for instance — feature-length movies, and backup data. DVDs also can include other features that CDs cannot, such as interactive menus that display when you pop in the disc. You would need several CDs just to fit one two-hour movie. This is why Windows Vista comes on DVDs now and not CDs.

Synchronize with Portable Devices

Windows Media Player enables you to synchronize digital music files with media devices, such as MP3 players. MP3 players are portable devices, like the previously ubiquitous Sony Walkman cassette and CD players, that store and play back digital music files.

You can use Media Player to rip, store, organize, and then copy music to your media device. You use the Sync tab in Media Player to synchronize, or copy, items to the media device. When items are synchronized, you can disconnect the media device and listen to the music.

The type of tasks you can do with the media devices depends on the media player. Some devices let you view track names, the length of the track, the name of the artist, and other information. Other devices may also include features that let you organize and sort tracks, delete individual tracks, and even download small pictures associated with the artist or album.

When you are ready to remove items from the media device, you can delete them from within Media Player or use a file management tool (Computer or Windows Explorer) to complete the task.

Synchronize with Portable Devices

① Start Windows Media Player.

The Media Player window appears.

② Connect the media device to your computer.

The Device Setup window appears.

③ Type a name for your device.

- You can keep the default name, but you may want to make it more descriptive.

④ Click Finish.

The device appears in the Sync pane and shows how much space remains on the device.

⑤ Drag items, such as individual songs or playlists, to the Sync pane to copy them to your media device.

6 Repeat step **5** to continue adding items to your media device.

7 Click Start Sync.

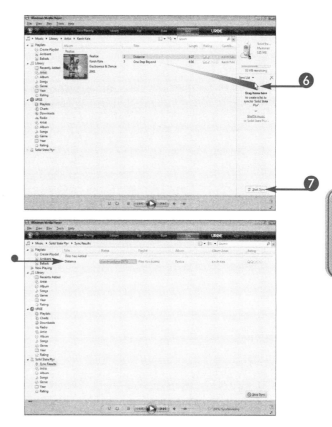

● Media Player adds the item to your media device.

8 When it has finished, disconnect the media device from your computer.

I have a portable device that does not hold enough songs. What can I do?

▼ You can expand the built-in memory in some devices by inserting flash memory cards. Flash memory is similar to a computer's random access memory (RAM) but has the capability of storing information for long periods of time. Media devices that can be expanded let you add flash memory cards from as small as 8MB to as large as 8GB at the time of this writing and depending on the type of flash memory card your device uses. You have to look at the specifications that came with your media device to see if it allows for expansion memory.

When I insert my memory card, the media device says it needs to be formatted. How can I do this?

▼ Like a hard disk or DVD disc, media devices are essentially devices that hold computer files but have the added bonus of including music playback capabilities. So to format a media device expansion card, open Computer or Windows Explorer and locate the listing for the media device. It appears as a drive name, such as Drive H. Right-click the device name and click Format. The Format Disk dialog box appears. Click Start to format the drive. After the format finishes, you can use Media Player to copy music to the media device.

Burn CDs

Media Player makes it easy to burn audio tracks and digital data files to CD. When you burn a CD, you copy files from your computer to a recordable CD disc. You must have a CD-R or CD-RW (ReWritable) device installed on your computer to burn CDs.

Files saved in Windows Media Audio (WMA), MP3, and Waveform Audio (WAV) format can be burned to CD. You can play back Audio CDs you create on most computers, as well as car CD players, home CD players, and portable CD players that support CD-R and CD-RW discs.

To set up a list of items to burn, you can create a burn list that is used just for one-time burning. Or you can select a playlist you have created and burn those tracks to CD. Media Player keeps track of the amount of space available on the CD so you can see if your burn list can fit on one CD. Discs can hold about 72–80 minutes of audio.

Media Player enables you to modify burn settings if you want to increase the quality level of your recordings. If you do this, however, file size for each track increases, so fewer songs can fit on a CD.

Burn CDs

1 To burn a CD, open Media Player.

2 Click the Library tab to view your library.

3 Click the Burn tab.

The Burn pane appears.

4 Insert a blank CD-R or CD-RW into your CD-R/RW drive.

If the CD Drive dialog box appears, click the Close button.

5 Drag items, such as individual songs or playlists, to the Burn pane.

Windows adds these items to the burn list.

6 Repeat step **5** to continue adding items to the burn list.

- The items you add to your burn list appear here.

- The amount of time for your currently selected burn list appears here.

Note: An average CD holds approximately 80 minutes of data.

7 Click Start Burn.

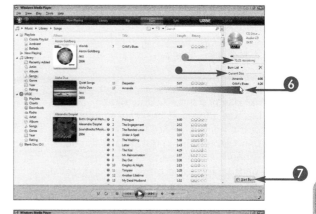

Media Player begins burning your list to the blank CD.

When it has finished, your CD is ejected from the CD-ROM drive and it is ready for you to play on other devices.

How can I make the highest possible quality digital data CDs?

▼ You use the convert setting of the CD drive properties. To see these settings, click the arrow on the Burn tab in Media Player and then click More Options. The Options dialog box with the Burn tab shows. Click Convert To to activate the quality level slider, which you can move to the right to increase burn quality settings. When you do this, however, the amount of space required for the recording is increased, leaving less space for audio tracks. Click OK to confirm your changes. The Media Player window appears.

When I rip music, Media Player saves it in WMA format. However, I want to burn CDs in MP3 format. How can I change this in Media Player?

▼ To change from the default WMA to MP3, click Tools and then click Options from Media Player. Click the Rip Music tab and then click the Format drop-down list. This displays a list of formats that Media Player can rip. Click MP3 and then click OK to save your settings. The audio files you rip now are saved in MP3 format.

Set Up Scanners

Windows Vista makes it easy to install and use digital scanners. Until digital cameras became affordable and easy to work with, scanners were the primary device for transferring photographs and other printed documents to your computer. Scanners enable you to convert hard copy documents, photographs, and other printed material into digital files. When these files are on your computer, you can view them, edit them, transfer them to another computer, e-mail them to other people, or store them for future reference.

When you connect a scanner to your computer, Windows Vista uses the Scanners and Cameras tool to

manage it. After you install and set up your scanner, you can use the Scanners and Cameras Wizard to scan and view documents on your computer.

Windows also includes two programs that let you perform rudimentary editing and viewing of scanned images. The first, Windows Photo Gallery, enables you to view, crop, fix red-eye problems, and adjust brightness and colors. The second, Paint, is a drawing tool that lets you view and modify picture files. You can resize images, save them to different formats, cut selections from an image, or even add text boxes and shapes to a picture.

Set Up Scanners

1 Connect the scanner to your computer.

Note: *Many scanners support connections to Universal Serial Bus (USB) ports, parallel ports, and Small Computer System Interface (SCSI) ports. Refer to your scanner's documentation to find out which port your scanner supports.*

The Welcome to the Scanner and Camera Installation Wizard appears.

2 Click Next to continue.

The next screen asks you which scanner or camera you want to install.

● If your device is not listed here, click Have Disk to install your scanner using the scanner's install disk.

3 Select a manufacturer.

4 Select a model.

5 Click Next to continue.

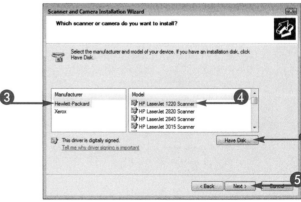

The next screen asks you the name of your device.

- You can type a name to identify your scanner. In most cases, users leave the default name, as shown here.

6 Click Next to continue.

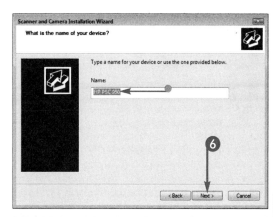

The Completing the Scanner and Camera Installation Wizard window appears.

7 Click Finish in the final screen of the wizard.

After Windows installs your scanner, you may be prompted to shut down and restart your computer. If so, click Yes to restart your computer.

After Windows restarts, you can use the Windows Fax and Scan to scan images to your computer.

Note: See Chapter 15 for more information on scanning.

How can I make changes to scanned photos with Windows Photo Gallery?

▼ You can do some editing of your pictures in Windows Photo Gallery. You can organize, fix colors, adjust brightness, crop photos, delete, and view pictures in Photo Gallery. You also can launch Windows Movie Maker from it to create a movie of your photographs. For more information on editing photos and Windows Photo Gallery, see Chapter 11.

If Windows Photo Gallery does not suit your needs, which is true for most Windows users, even those who do not plan on producing professional quality pictures, you should consider purchasing picture editing software. Some examples of these include Corel PaintShop Pro or Corel PhotoPaint (www.corel.com), and Adobe PhotoShop or Adobe PhotoShop Elements (www.adobe.com).

What formats can I save picture files to in Paint?

▼ Paint enables you to save pictures in BMP, JPG, GIF, TIFF, and PNG format. To do this, open Paint and then open the image you want to convert. Click File and then click Save As. The Save As dialog box appears. Click the Save as type drop-down list and select the file format in which you want to save the picture. The two most prevalent picture formats on the Web are JPG and GIF. These two formats are easily inserted into most e-mail programs and can be viewed by all major Web browsers. Click Save to save the file.

Install a Digital Camera

Windows Vista makes it easy to connect digital cameras to your computer and download pictures to it. In most cases, you just have to plug in the camera using a Universal Serial Bus (USB) cable to the computer's USB port, and Windows walks you through setting up the camera and then downloading pictures. When you have set up the camera on your computer, the next time you connect the camera to the computer, Windows automatically recognizes it. This enables you to start downloading pictures immediately.

If Windows does not automatically recognize your camera, you use the Scanner and Camera Installation Wizard to set up the digital camera. This wizard walks you through installing the camera to work with Windows. Windows prompts you to insert an installation CD or DVD to complete the setup.

After you connect your camera, you can download — or copy — pictures from the camera to your computer. When the pictures are safely stored on the computer, you can delete them from your camera, providing free space to snap more pictures. In addition, with the pictures on your computer, you can edit them, rename them, print them, store them, or delete them.

Install a Digital Camera

① Connect the camera to your computer.

Note: *Many cameras support connections to USB ports. Refer to your camera's documentation to find out which port your camera supports.*

The Scanner and Camera Installation Wizard appears.

② Click Next to continue.

The next screen asks you which scanner or camera you want to install.

● If your device is not listed here, you can click Have Disk to install your camera using the camera's install disk.

③ Select a manufacturer.

④ Select a model.

⑤ Click Next to continue.

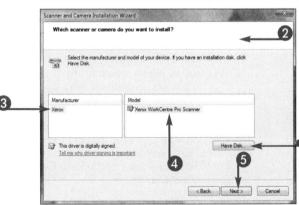

The next screen asks you the name of your device.

- You can type a name to identify your camera. In most cases, users leave the default name, as shown here.

⑥ Click Next to continue.

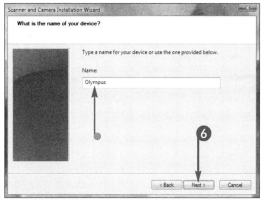

The final screen of the wizard appears.

⑦ Click Finish in the final screen of the wizard.

After Windows installs your camera, you may be prompted to shut down and restart your computer. If so, click Yes to restart your computer.

After Windows restarts, you can use the Import Pictures tool to download pictures from your camera to your computer.

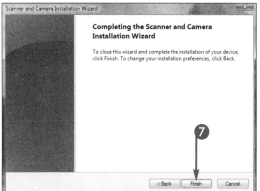

My digital camera uses an extreme Digital (xD) memory card. Can I remove it from my camera and upload pictures to my computer?

▼ Yes, but you must have a device called a *card reader* that enables you to do this. The card reader usually has slots that support multiple sizes of flash memory cards, such as Secure Digital (SD), xD, and so on. You connect the card reader to your computer, insert the flash memory card, and then download pictures to your computer. Card readers are handy because they offer one device that can read several different cards. Plus they use their own power source — or the power source of the USB connection — enabling you to save your camera's batteries.

I have several pictures on my computer but do not know how to organize them. How do I create a slide show on my computer?

▼ Windows includes Windows Photo Gallery, which includes tools for viewing, managing, and editing your photographs. With Windows Photo Gallery, you can set up yout photos to view them as a slide show. To do this, start Windows Photo Gallery and locate your photographs. Next, click the Play Slide Show button at the bottom of the Windows Photo Gallery window. Or press F11. The Windows screen fades to black, and your photographs play as a slide show across the screen. Press Esc to stop the show.

Import Pictures from a Digital Camera

T he primary reason for connecting a digital camera to your computer is to download your pictures onto it. Windows Vista makes this very easy to do with the Import Pictures tool. After you connect and configure your camera to work with Windows Vista, you can start importing your pictures. To do this, connect your camera, select Import Pictures from the AutoPlay dialog box, add a tag for your pictures, and start the import. Tags are words or phrases that describe the content of your picture set.

Import Pictures copies each picture to your hard drive, stores the collection in your Pictures folder, and then displays the full set in Windows Photo Gallery after they are imported. As your photos import, you can watch as a small thumbnail image of each photo displays.

Once your pictures are imported, you can do several things with them, including archive them for posterity, send them to other people via e-mail, create a movie, burn a DVD, print them, add them to Web pages, make a family photo album, use them in research documents, or just view them on your computer screen.

Import Pictures from a Digital Camera

① Connect the camera to your computer.

The AutoPlay window appears.

● You can click here to instruct AutoPlay to always import pictures (☐ changes to ☑).

② Click Import pictures.

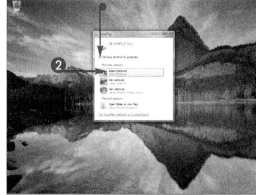

The Importing Pictures and Videos window appears.

● Each picture appears in a thumbnail view.

③ Type a tag for the picture set.

Tags are used by Windows Explorer and Search to help you find and organize your files.

④ Click Import.

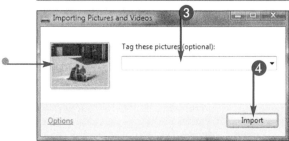

Windows Vista imports the pictures to your hard drive.

When Windows Vista has finished, the pictures display in the Windows Photo Gallery.

PART III

Do I have to add a tag?

▼ No, tags are not required. However, the tag word or phrase you add to your picture import set is added to the name of the file and to the folder that Windows Vista creates to store your picture set. If you use a descriptive tag for the set, you may find it easier to organize your photographs at a later date. The default file and folder names Windows Vista creates without a tag simply are the dates you import the pictures, such as 2007-02-17 001. When you add a tag, such as Ralph Birthday, the file name becomes Ralph Birthday 001, and the folder name becomes 2007-02-17 Ralph Birthday.

My camera includes software for importing images. Can I use it instead of Windows Vista's software?

▼ Yes. In fact, some cameras work better with the software they come with. Some software includes more advanced options than the Import Pictures software offers. For example, some software enables you to rename each picture as you import it, select specific pictures you want to import while ignoring others, apply auto-editing features to each photo, and print straight from the camera to your printer. To use your camera's software, install it and make it your default photo import and editing program. Most programs enable you to choose it as your default as you work through its setup wizard.

Explore Windows Photo Gallery

The Windows Photo Gallery is a new tool provided with Windows Vista. You can use Windows Photo Gallery to view the pictures on your computer as a library of pictures in the gallery or open them individually in the editing window.

The gallery window includes different views by which you can look at your pictures. For example, you can use the Thumbnails view to see a small version of the full photograph. The Thumbnails with Text view

shows the thumbnail plus file information below each photo. This information includes the date and time the photograph was taken.

Another key part of the gallery is the Navigation pane. This pane appears on the left side of the screen. The Navigation pane organizes your pictures and videos into different categories. For example, you might want to view pictures taken on a specific date. To see these, open the Date Taken folder and drill-down to the month and date you want to view.

Explore Windows Photo Gallery

① Click Start.

② Click All Programs.

Note: *After you click All Programs, the name changes to Back.*

③ Click Windows Photo Gallery.

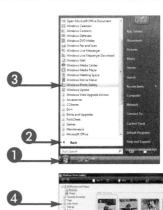

The Windows Photo Gallery window appears.

④ Click the Date Taken folder to expand it.

The Date Taken folder expands to show years in which your stored photographs have been taken.

⑤ Click a year to expand it.

The year expands to show months.

Photos appear in the gallery categorized by months in which a photograph was taken.

⑥ Click Pictures to display all your pictures.

The gallery displays all your pictures.

⑦ Click the Choose a thumbnail view menu to pick a thumbnail view.

A menu appears.

⑧ Click the Thumbnails with Text command to display text under your pictures.

The gallery displays picture information under each photograph.

Can I see a larger version of my photos without opening them in the view window?

▼ Yes, if you want to see a little larger view of a photograph in the gallery, simply hover the mouse over the photograph. Windows Photo Gallery pops up a larger view of the picture, but not quite as large as the full view. This is a quick way to see some details of the photograph but not take the time to fully open the picture. Also, when viewing a photograph in this manner, you get to see the name of the photograph, its tag, its rating by how many stars it has, the date and time it was taken, and the size of the picture file.

Can I send my finished photographs to someone using e-mail?

▼ Yes, you can do this from Windows Photo Gallery or from other places within Windows Vista. For example, to send a photograph to someone while you are using Windows Photo Gallery, click a photograph and then click the E-mail button. The Attach Files dialog box appears. Click Attach. A new mail message from your default e-mail program appears, such as Windows Mail. It includes the selected photograph as a file attachment and the name of the photo as the subject line. Add recipients to the To line and then click Send.

Crop Photos in Windows Photo Gallery

Unless you take perfect pictures every time, you will probably want to edit something in your pictures before you present them to the world — or send them to Aunt Jane. With Windows Photo Gallery, you can perform some basic editing chores on your pictures.

Say that you have a picture that includes a nice close-up of a family member, but there is some unsightly background material — no, not Aunt Jane! — that you would like to remove before sending out the picture. You can use Windows Photo Gallery to crop the image

so you are left with just the part of the photograph you want — the good part.

You might also want to brighten up the photograph if it appears too dark. Use the Adjust Exposure tool in Windows Photo Gallery to increase the brightness and contrast of the photo.

Finally, many of our photographs include that dreaded red eye, where the pupils of our eyes are red and make us look goofier than we already look. You can use Windows Photo Gallery's Red Eye tool to remove that look.

Crop Photos in Windows Photo Gallery

① Click Start.

② Click All Programs.

Note: After you click All Programs, the name changes to Back.

③ Click Windows Photo Gallery.

The Windows Photo Gallery window opens, displaying the gallery.

● You can click here and select a different view of the images.

● You can hover the mouse over a photo to see a larger view of it.

④ Double-click a photo to edit.

The photo displays in the editing view.

5 Click Fix.

The Fix tools pane appears.

6 Click Crop Picture.

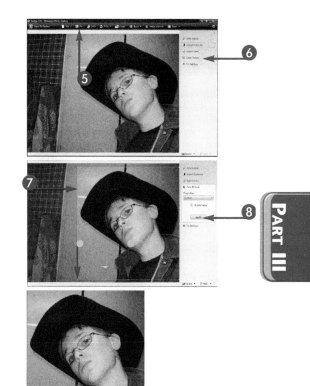

The Crop Picture tools and the cropping frame appear.

7 Move and resize the cropping frame to position it around the area you want to crop.

● You can use the resize handles to shrink or enlarge the cropping frame.

8 Click Apply.

Windows Photo Gallery crops the photograph.

Should I save a copy of my original before I edit it?

▼ Yes: therefore, if you mess up during the editing process, you can return to the original and try again. To do this, open Windows Photo Gallery and click the Pictures button on the left pane. Right-click the photo you want to copy and click Copy. Windows Vista stores a copy of the image to the Windows Clipboard. Next right-click and choose Paste. A duplicate of the image appears at the bottom of your folder listing. If you compare its name to the original, you will see that Windows Photo Gallery attaches the word "Copy" to the end of the file name.

When I double-click a picture in Windows Explorer, Windows Paint opens. Can I change this?

▼ Yes, Paint is the default program for opening picture files, such as Tagged Image File Format (TIFF), Joint Photographic Experts Group (JPG), or Graphics Interchange (GIF). To change this, right-click a picture and click Open With. From the menu that appears, click Choose Default Program. The Open With dialog box appears. Click Windows Photo Gallery, make sure the Always use the selected program to open this kind of file option is selected, and click OK.

Adjust Exposure and Colors in Windows Photo Gallery

Unless you are a professional photographer or an avid hobbyist, you probably do not carry professional lighting for the digital photographs you take. Because of this, some photographs may come out too bright or too dark once you have a chance to import them into Windows Photo Gallery and view them. If this is the case with your photos, use Windows Photo Gallery's Adjust Exposure tool.

With the Adjust Exposure tool, you can increase or decrease the brightness and contrast of your photographs. As you adjust brightness to a picture, you can control how dark or light the overall picture is. With contrast, you can increase or decrease the differences between the brightest and darkest areas on a picture.

Another tool you might try is the Auto Adjust tool. It automatically adjusts the brightness and contrast of a photograph. However, you may find that the Auto Adjust tool's results are not that appealing, so you will have to use the Adjust Exposure tools to find the correct mix.

Finally, you can modify color settings using the Adjust Color tool. You can set color temperature, tint, and saturation.

Adjust Exposure and Colors in Windows Photo Gallery

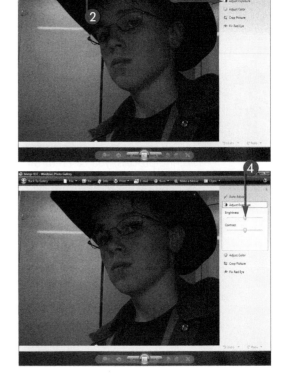

① Open a photograph in the Windows Photo Gallery editor.

The Windows Photo Gallery appears.

② Click Fix.

The Fix tools pane appears.

③ Click Adjust Exposure.

The Adjust Exposure tools appear.

④ Drag the Brightness slider to adjust exposure.

Move the slider to the right to brighten the photo or to the left to darken it.

⑤ Drag the Contrast slider to adjust exposure.

Move the slider to the right to increase contrast or to the left to decrease contrast.

⑥ Click Adjust Color.

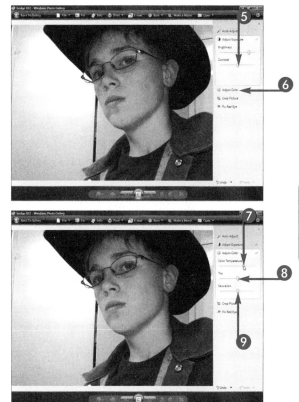

The Adjust Color tools appear.

⑦ Drag the Color Temperature slider to adjust color.

Move the slider to the right to increase color temperature or to the left to decrease it.

⑧ Drag the Tint slider to adjust color.

Move the slider to the right to increase tint or to the left to decrease it.

⑨ Drag the Saturation slider to adjust color.

Move the slider to the right to increase saturation or to the left to decrease it.

Can I undo changes I make to an image?

▼ Yes, to do this click the Undo button at the bottom of the Fix pane. Each time you click Undo, Windows Photo Gallery undoes your most recent edit. If you want to undo all your changes quickly, click the down arrow on the Undo button. This displays a short menu of commands. Click Undo All, or press Ctrl+Shift+Z. All your changes are erased, and you are left with the image as it was before you started editing. It is important to remember that when you return to the gallery or close Windows Photo Gallery any changes you have made to that photograph are automatically saved.

I used Auto Adjust and it made the photo too dark. What can I do?

▼ There are two things you can do. First, click the Adjust Exposure button to reveal those tools. Next, slide the Brightness slider to the right until your photo's brightness satisfies you. Adjust the contrast if necessary. Second, you can undo the Auto Adjust setting by clicking the Undo button at the bottom of the Fix pane. On some photographs, the Auto Adjust tool does not work as well as it does on others. You will have to experiment with it to see which of your photographs work best with Auto Adjust.

Import Digital Video Using Windows Import Video

Windows Vista enables you to view and save video from a digital video camera. Windows makes it easy to connect and set up your digital video camera and then record video clips to your computer.

The video you capture using a digital video camera can be recorded straight to your computer using the Windows Import Video tool. That is, unlike analog video — VHS tapes — you do not have to convert it and then save it to disk. You simply connect your video camera to the computer, such as via a USB or FireWire port, and then begin the transfer.

With Windows Import Video, you can import video, save the video file to disk, import it to Windows Movie Maker 6, or create a DVD from the imported video. You also can view the imported video using Windows Media Player 11.

During the Windows Import Video process, you have the options of recording the entire tape to your computer, recording it to your computer and then straight to DVD, or recording parts of the tape that you specify. After you import the video, Windows stores the file(s) in Windows Photo Gallery.

Import Digital Video Using Windows Import Video

① Connect your video camera to the computer.

This example uses a digital video camera connected to the FireWire port of your computer.

② Turn on the video camera so it is set to playback mode.

The AutoPlay dialog box appears.

● You can click here to have your videos automatically imported when you connect a video camera (☐ changes to ☑).

③ Click Import Video.

The Import Video window appears.

④ Type a name for the video.

● You can click here and select the location of where you want to store the imported video.

⑤ Click Next to continue.

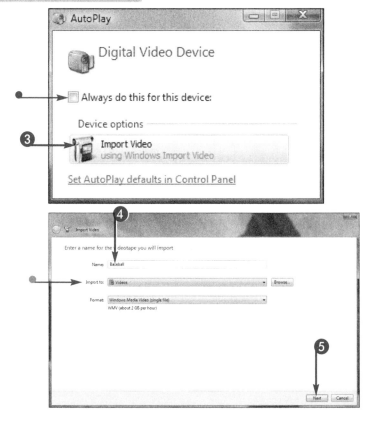

The Import entire videotape or just parts window appears.

6 Click the Only import parts of the videotape to my computer option (○ changes to ◉).

- You can use this option to start the recording anyplace on your tape.

- You can use this option for recording the entire tape to your computer.

7 Click Next to continue.

The Cue the videotape and then start importing video window appears.

- Use these controls to cue your video to the starting point.

8 Click Start Video Import.

Note: *The Start Video Import button changes to Stop Video Import.*

The video begins recording to your computer.

9 Click Stop Video Import.

The import process stops.

Use the cue controls to cue to another part of the tape, if desired.

10 Click Finish.

Windows Photo Gallery displays with the saved video files.

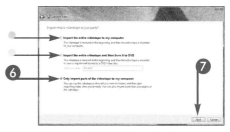

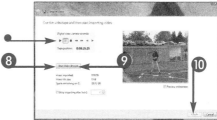

PART III

Import Video Using
Windows Movie Maker 6

Windows Vista is a nice platform for creating digital video files and editing those files. Windows Vista includes an excellent free movie-editing software program called Windows Movie Maker 6. With Movie Maker 6, you can capture video from an external video device, such as a VCR, a digital video camera, an analog video camera, or a Webcam. As you copy video to Movie Maker 6, Movie Maker 6 creates segments of the video so you can manipulate those segments into your own custom movie.

You also can import video files for Movie Maker 6 that you have previously imported using the Windows

Import Video tool. Movie Maker 6 supports several video formats, including the following: ASF, AVI, MLV, MP2, MP2V, MPE, MPEG, MPG, MPV2, WM, and WMV. Another option is to receive video files from another user in one of the preceding formats and import that video into Movie Maker 6.

When you import video files into Movie Maker 6, the files are made into clips. You then can add individual clips to the Movie Maker 6 storyboard to create your movie.

Import Video Using Windows Movie Maker 6

① Click Start.

② Click All Programs.

Note: After you click All Programs, the name changes to Back.

③ Click Windows Movie Maker.

The Windows Movie Maker window appears.

④ Click File.

⑤ Click Import from Digital Video Camera.

The Import Video window appears.

⑥ Click Next to continue.

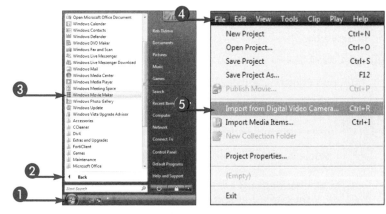

The Import entire videotape or just parts window appears.

7 Click the Only import parts of the videotape to my computer option (○ changes to ◉).

● You can click here to import the entire videotape to your computer.

8 Click Next to continue.

The Cue the videotape and then start importing video window appears.

● Use these controls to cue your video to the starting point.

9 Click Start Video Import.

Note: *The Start Video Import button changes to Stop Video Import.*

Windows Import Video begins recording the video to your computer.

10 Click Stop Video Import.

Use the cue controls to proceed to another part of the tape, if desired.

11 Click Finish.

● The video clip is added to the Windows Movie Maker clip list.

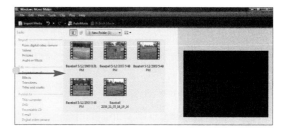

PART III

My video camera does not have a Digital Video Interface (DVi) port. How can I download my clips to my computer?

▼ To copy video content from a video device, you must have a way to download the video to your computer. With a digital video (DV) camera, you usually accomplish this using an IEEE 1394 cable connected between the camera and the computer. IEEE 1394 is also referred to as FireWire. Webcam content, which is live content, is copied to your computer via the Webcam connection. This connection is usually via a USB port. Oder video analog content, such as VHS, requires converter hardware, such as the AVerMedia DVD EZMaker Pro USB 2.0 device.

Can I use other software for capturing and editing video?

▼ Yes, Movie Maker 6 is just one of many video-editing programs available. Movie Maker 6 is free and actually has some very nice features for creating and editing video. If you need more sophisticated features, such as editing pixels in the movie clips, overlays, and other professional-quality options, consider products like Pinnacle Systems' Studio (www.pinnaclesys.com) or Nova Development's Video Explosion Deluxe (www.novadevelopment.com)

Work with Windows Movie Maker 6

Windows Movie Maker 6 enables you to view, edit, and save digital movies on your computer. You can capture video from your video camera, import videos from other sources, import pictures into a movie, and add sound files to a movie. When you create a movie, you can add special effects to the movie, as well as create transitions between scenes.

Windows Movie Maker also enables you to add titles and credits to your movies. This enables you to create movies customized for your family, business, or church without burdening you with costly creation fees from professionals.

Another handy feature of Movie Maker is the AutoMovie tool. This tool takes a clip or set of clips and creates a movie quickly using editing styles you choose. It also incorporates music into the movie. The AutoMovie tool is not something you would want to use every time you create movies, but it is a good tool if you are in a hurry to create a movie based on a collection of clips. It is also a good way to see how different Movie Maker enhancements can be used with your clips.

Work with Windows Movie Maker 6

Edit Movie Clips

1. Start Windows Movie Maker.

2. Import clips from a digital video camera.

Note: To import video clips, see the section, "Import Video Using Windows Movie Maker 6."

3. Click and drag a clip from the Collection area to the storyboard.

4. Repeat step **3** to continue adding clips to the storyboard to create your movie.

5. To add an effect to the movie, click a link in the Edit area.

   The next screen asks where you want to add a title.

6. Click the link to add a title at the beginning of the movie.

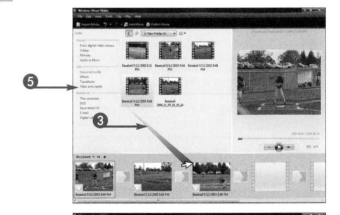

The Enter text for title window appears.

7 Type a title for the movie.

8 Click Add Title to add your title to the movie.

● The title is added to the storyboard.

9 To add a transition between clips, click the link to view video transitions in the Edit area.

● The Transitions window appears.

10 Click and drag a transition to the storyboard, such as the Diagonal, Box Out transition.

● The transition appears on the storyboard between two clips.

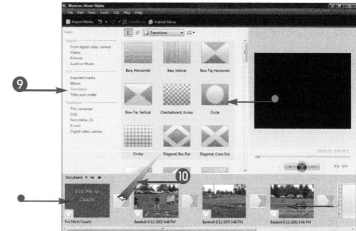

I have looked all over for Movie Maker 6 on my computer. What if I do not have it installed? How can I get it?

▼ Movie Maker 6 is available with Windows Vista. You must also have a graphics card that meets Windows Movie Maker 6's minimum requirements to be able to even start Movie Maker 6. See www.microsoft. com/vista for these requirements. You may need to invest in a new video card before you can start using Movie Maker 6. You also can visit the Movie Maker 6 Web site for tips, tutorials, downloads, and other information. Go to www.microsoft. com/windowsxp/using/moviemaker/ default.mspx.

When Movie Maker 6 is capturing my video, I have the option of creating clips. Why would I want to do this?

▼ Clips are small segments of your video. With clips, you can find parts of your video much more easily and quickly than by looking over one large copy of the video. In addition, clips enable you to move parts of the movie around, perhaps creating a different feel for the finished movie. For example, a clip that was taken at the beginning of the day can be moved to the middle or end of the movie if it better illustrates a point in the movie.

continued ▶

Work with Windows
Movie Maker 6 *(Continued)*

When you create movies with Windows Movie Maker, you can add transitions and special effects to your movies. These types of enhancements give your movies a more finished, somewhat professional look.

Transitions are used between clips to help ease viewers into the next scene. Some of the transitions include Keyhole, Fan, Pixelate, Rectangle, Shatter, and Wipe. Because you can view each clip in the Preview Monitor on the Movie Maker window, you can experiment with each transition until you find the one you want.

Video effects are like special effects you can add to your clips. For example, if you want a clip to look like an old-fashioned clip, use the Film Age, Oldest effect. This adds a layer of dust and other particles to your clip, making it appear older than it is. You can use more than one video effect on a clip. For example, you can use the Speed Up, Double and the Grainy effects on one clip to make it appear like an old speeded-up filmstrip.

To Publish Your Movie

1. To publish your movie, click File.

2. Click Publish Movie.

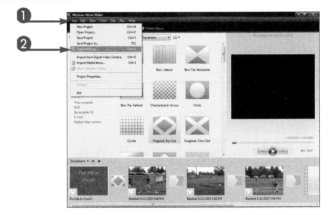

The Publish Movie Wizard appears. This screen gives you choices on where you can save your movie, such as to the hard drive, to a DVD, a CD-R, an e-mail, or a digital video camera.

3. To save to your hard drive, click This computer.

4. Click Next to continue.

The Name the movie you are publishing screen appears.

5 Type a name for the movie project.

6 Click Next to continue.

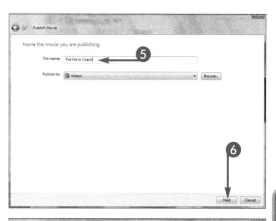

The Choose the settings for your movie screen appears.

● You can control the compression and quality of your finished movie with these choices.

7 Click Publish.

If I am working on a movie and not finished with it yet, how can I save it?

▼ To save an unfinished movie so you can return to it later and edit it, you must save it as a Movie Maker Project. A project keeps the movie as separate clips and lets you continue adding effects, transitions, or titles to it. To save a movie as a project, click File and then click Save Project As. The Save Project As dialog box appears. Type a name in the File name box. Movie Maker gives the file an MSWMM, Microsoft Windows Movie Maker Projects, file extension. Click Save. This saves the movie as a project into your Videos folder. If you later come back and want to edit this project, click File and then click Open Project to open the project file.

I hear voices and other noise on the clips that I have added to Movie Maker. How can I see the audio information for the clip?

▼ The audio that is on a video clip is part of that clip. To isolate the audio — such as if you want to turn it off in parts of the movie — click the Storyboard button at the bottom of the screen. A menu appears. Click Timeline. The Timeline view appears. Click the plus sign (+) next to Video to expand your video file. You now see tracks for Video, Transition, and Audio. These three tracks are for your imported video. You want to concentrate on the Audio track. For example, right-click the Audio track and click Mute to turn off the audio for that clip. You now can overlay music on the Audio/Music track, and the sounds from your video clip will not be heard.

continued

Work with Windows Movie Maker 6 *(Continued)*

When you work on a movie in Movie Maker 6, you build it in a project. The project file allows you to perform editing and creation tasks, such as adding new clips, moving clips on the storyboard, adding titles and credits, and so on. As you create your movie project, you can play back your movie in the small playback window on the main Movie Maker window. This gives you an idea of what your finished movie will look like. The nice thing about projects, however, is that you can save and close them and then come back later to edit them.

When you get your movie project finished, you are ready to publish. Publishing means creating a movie file that can be played outside of Movie Maker. You can choose to publish to several mediums, including to your hard drive, burn to a DVD, make a recordable CD, send as an e-mail attachment, or record to a digital video camera. The medium you choose is what is best for your situation. In many cases, users prefer to publish the movie to their hard drive, view it, critique it, and then move it to another medium if desired, such as to a DVD.

Work with Windows Movie Maker 6 *(Continued)*

The Publishing your movie window appears.

● The amount of time remaining until your movie is ready appears here.

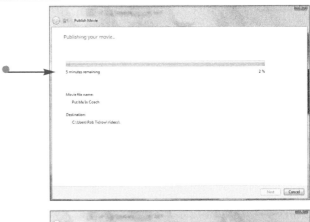

After your movie is created, the Your movie has been published screen appears.

8 Click Play movie when I click Finish to see your new movie (☐ changes to ☑).

9 Click Finish.

The Media Player appears, ready to start playing your movie.

⑩ Click the Play button to start playing back your movie.

The movie plays.

● You can adjust the setting by dragging the Hue, Saturation, Brightness, and Contrast sliders.

⑪ Click the Stop button to stop the movie.

If I choose to create an AutoMovie, what does it add to the movie and how long does Movie Maker take to complete the movie?

▼ The AutoMovie feature lets you select an editing style — such as Music Video — and adds transitions, effects, music, and titles to the movie to make it appear a little more professional looking than what you may do your first time. The length of time it takes depends on how long your clips are. Generally, AutoMovie takes about one-third the total time of your clips to complete the movie.

I created a movie and am trying to send it as an e-mail attachment. Why can my recipients not receive it?

▼ Probably because the movie file is too big. Many companies and services that host e-mail servers put a file-size restriction on the maximum size of incoming e-mail messages so as not to overload the server. For example, some corporations have a cutoff of 5MB. Anything larger than that is rejected, and you may or may not receive notification that the message was rejected. Consider creating small movies, if you want to send them over e-mail. Or publish your movies to a DVD or recordable CD and mail them to your recipients the old-fashioned way.

Burn a DVD Using Windows DVD Maker

There are a number of different ways you can export your digital movies. Probably the most popular and convenient way is to save the movie to a DVD. To do this, you will need a DVD burner and blank DVD-R or DVD-RW discs.

DVDs can store up to 150 minutes of video, audio, or data. In addition, the video on DVDs retains most of its quality even after many playbacks. These issues make DVD a great technology for delivering feature-length movies. Now with the affordable DVD drives and discs, you can take advantage of the DVD medium as well.

Windows Vista includes the Windows DVD Maker to help you burn a movie to a DVD. Windows DVD Maker includes menu styles that you can use to set up menus that play before your movie or after it. These menus are similar to the menus you see when you play back your favorite Hollywood movie on DVD. You can add a disc title to your DVD. This title appears on the title page. You also can rename the buttons users can use for playing back a movie or jumping to specific scenes. There is also a Notes section in which you can enter information for viewers to read by clicking the Notes button on your movie.

Burn a DVD Using Windows DVD Maker

Note: *These steps assume you have a movie you imported or created in Windows Movie Maker 6 that you can burn to DVD.*

① Open Windows Photo Gallery.

The Windows Photo Gallery window appears.

② Click Videos in the Navigation pane.

③ Click the movie or video files you want to burn.

④ Click Burn.

⑤ Click Video DVD.

The Windows DVD Maker appears, with the Add pictures and video to the DVD window open.

⑥ Click Next to continue.

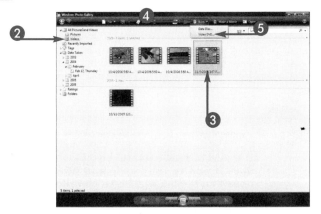

The Ready to burn disc window appears.

7 Select a menu style.

This example uses the Reflections menu style.

8 Click Menu Text.

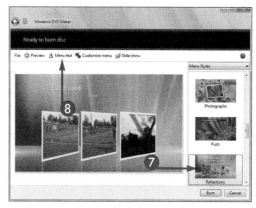

The Change the DVD menu text window appears.

9 In the Disc Title box of the Change the DVD menu text screen, type a new name for the DVD title.

● You can change the phrasing for the Play button and Scenes button items here.

Can I change the font for my DVD menu?

▼ Yes. To do so, work through the preceding steps until you reach step 7. Click Customize menu from the Ready to burn disc window. The Customize the disc menu style window appears. You also can change fonts on the Change the DVD menu text window. In the Font drop-down list, select a different font. Keep in mind that headlines like these menus are easier to read if you use a large font that is Sans Serif, such as Calibri, Latha, Tahoma, and similar fonts. On the other hand, fancy script fonts — like Edwardian Script — can sometimes be difficult to read.

Can I make the DVD-burning process faster?

▼ No. You can, however, limit the amount of data you put on the DVD, but this will shorten your films and decrease the number of pictures you put in a slide show. About the only way to really speed up the burn process is to invest in a fast DVD burner. You can visit online computer sellers or hardware dealers to price these burners, for example, www.cpusolutions. com, www.dell.com, or www.bestbuy.com.

continued

Burn a DVD Using Windows DVD Maker *(Continued)*

When you burn a DVD using Windows DVD Maker, you can customize the DVD menu, usually called the *root menu*. You might want to play a song in the background as the menu displays. On the other hand, as you are shown in the following procedure, you can add notes to the menu so viewers can find out more about the movie they are watching. If you add notes to the DVD menu, make them pertinent to the DVD's contents and strive to make them enjoyable to read.

The amount of space you can use for notes is limited, so do not expect to be able to write lengthy

dissertations about your movie-making exploits. Instead focus on the key information you want to express, such as pointing out when the video was made, reporting any important events you want viewers to look for, or reminding viewers about a funny scene. For lengthier information than what appears on the Notes, consider recording them on your video camera and adding them to your movie as a scene that viewers can click on.

You can add notes to the Notes box on the Change the DVD menu text screen.

Burn a DVD Using Windows DVD Maker *(Continued)*

⑩ Click in the Notes box and type some director notes.

● Notes are optional, but they are fun and your audience will probably enjoy reading them.

⑪ Click Change Text.

The Ready to burn disk window appears, showing your menu changes.

⑫ Insert a blank DVD into your DVD burner.

⑬ Click Burn to start the burn process.

The Burning window appears, showing the burn process.

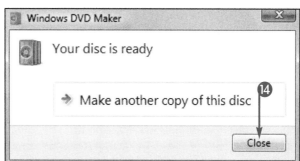

After Windows DVD Maker creates your DVD, it ejects your freshly burned DVD from your computer and displays the Your disc is ready window.

⑭ Click Close.

PART III

Can I set up a template to use for my menus if I customize them?

▼ Yes, you can do to this on the Customize the disc menu style screen, which you can access by clicking the Customize Menu button on the Ready to burn disc screen. On the Customize as new style screen, make changes to the disc menu styles as desired. For example, you may want to change the button styles of the scene buttons. Next, click the Save as new style button. The Save as New Style dialog box appears. Type a name for the new style and click OK. Your style becomes available on the Custom Styles drop-down list on the Ready to burn disc screen.

Can I add a video to the background when my menu is showing?

▼ Yes, this is one way to really add a professional-looking touch to your DVDs. To do this, open the Customize the disc menu style screen. In the Background video box, type the path and file name of a video or picture file that you want to appear in the background. If you are not sure of the full path name, click Browse to find it using the Add Background Video dialog box. Select the file and click Add. Click Change Style to save your background video changes.

Explore the
Media Center

One of the more fascinating aspects of computers has been the convergence of computing technology with entertainment. Users can now connect all sorts of entertainment devices to their PCs and let the computer's operating system and specialized programs manage them. One such program that Windows Vista includes is Windows Media Center.

You can use Media Center to play back music, store album art, create playlists, and watch slide shows as the music plays. Media Center, when used on a computer with a television tuner card, can play and record television programs in Windows Media Center. You can also pause live TV while Media Center records the portion you are missing. Upon returning to the show, you can rewind to the part you have missed or fast-forward through it to catch up with the program.

Users can use Media Center to play back videos and watch pictures on their televisions or other display devices, for example, digital projectors are commonly used for large rooms or conference rooms or training areas. Another option for Media Center is listening to radio broadcasts. With an FM tuner device, you can tune into FM radio stations through Media Center.

To distribute, archive, and transport media files, Media Center enables you to burn and rip CDs; burn DVDs; and store music, photos, television programs, and video. Finally, with the optional Media Center Extender, you can leave the computer in one room and use Media Center features in another. In fact, you can work on other computer tasks while you use the Media Center Extender features. Media Center is best viewed when you have a large television set and the optional Media Center remote control or wireless keyboard.

Media Center Setup Wizards

Windows Vista provides easy-to-use wizards and setup programs to configure your computer and devices to use Media Center. The first time you start Media Center, you are prompted to set up your computer and hardware devices to work with Media Center. You can use the Express setup choice or the Custom setup choice to work through configuring Media Center. The Express setup offers a quicker route to getting your equipment and software set up. However, you may opt for Custom setup if you want more control over configuring your display, sound, and other devices.

Central Management Area

Windows Media Center provides a central place to manage all your digital entertainment files and devices. For example, you can see all your videos, watch recorded television shows, view live TV, listen to music, and start games, all from the Media Center application.

Media Center Devices

Microsoft designs and manufacturers hardware devices to extend your Media Center experience. Two of these devices are the Microsoft Media Center Remote Control and Receiver and the Microsoft Media Center Remote Keyboard. With these devices, you can remotely control your Windows Media Center computer.

You can, for example, situate your computer in the family room where you normally enjoy your television. With the Remote Keyboard, you can sit anywhere in the room and control the Media Center experience as you watch television. You do not have to sit at your computer desk to select Media Center tools and options. The keyboard includes the standard keys, including alphanumeric keys, function keys, and arrow keys. You navigate the screen using the arrow and directional keys.

Media Center Remote Keyboard

The Media Center Remote Keyboard includes a green start button to let you launch Media Center from the keyboard using just a single mouse click. Because you may spend a great deal of your time viewing television with dim or no lights, the Remote Keyboard also includes backlit keys to enable you to see them easily in the dark. With a range of up to 30 feet, the Remote Keyboard can be used from just about anyplace in an average-size room. Finally, when you are not using the keyboard, you can use the lock function on it to lock down the keys to keep other people from using it while you are at the computer working on other tasks.

Media Center Remote Control and Receiver

You can control a number of items on the Media Center window using the Media Center Remote Control and Receiver. On the Remote Control, you can click the power buttons to shut down your computer or put it in standby mode. You can also use the Remote Control to record, pause, and rewind live television. After you view the recorded material, you can use the remote to fast-forward to "catch up" with the live performance.

You can record up to three live TV shows at once and then play them back when it is convenient for you. The Media Center Remote Control makes it easy to set up and begin recording these shows.

Like the Media Center Remote Keyboard, Media Center Remote Control has lighted buttons. The backlit buttons make it easy to see the Remote Control's buttons so you do not to have fumble in the dark for the button you want to press.

Media Center Computers

To use the Media Center Remote Control devices, you must purchase them separately. Windows Vista does not ship with them. However, those computers that are designed and marketed as Media Center computers may have these devices — or at least the Media Center Remote Control and Receiver — available when you purchase the computer.

Purchase Additional Products

You can learn more about these products, and discover how to purchase them, by visiting the Windows Marketplace on the Web. Use Internet Explorer and connect to www.windowsmarketplace.com.

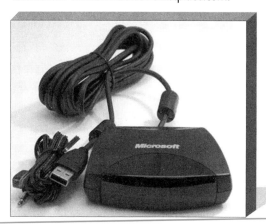

PART III

Configure Media Center

To prepare for configuring Media Center, you need to install and configure the devices you want Media Center to use. For Internet connectivity, make sure your Internet components are working. You will need to have a broadband or faster connection to the Internet. Dial-up does not have the bandwidth capacity to handle the Media Center download.

To network with other devices, you must have your local area network installed and working. Wireless networks are generally the best option for homes because they do not require you to "pull" cable through your house (who wants to cut up her drywall to put in network cables?).

If you want to experience the television and radio tuner features of Media Center, install those adapters into your computer. Because these types of devices are more specialized than what this book covers, you will have to consult the manufacturer of those adapters or other documentation to help you set up those devices.

Finally, set up any audio speakers that your Media Center computer will use. One part of the setup walks you through arranging your speakers.

When you are ready to start using your computer with your media devices, you are ready to configure Media Center.

Configure Media Center

Set Up the Display

Make sure your media devices are connected to your computer and are compatible with Windows Vista.

① Click Start.

② Click All Programs.

Note: After you click All Programs, the name changes to Back.

③ Click Windows Media Center.

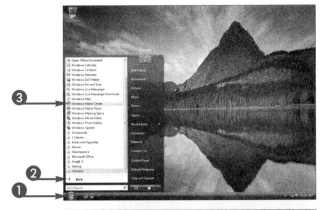

The Welcome screen for Media Center appears.

● You can click the Express setup option, which automatically sets up Media Center, downloads files from the Internet, and signs you up for the Customer Experience Improvement Program.

④ Click the Custom setup option (○ changes to ◉).

⑤ Click OK.

The Welcome screen appears.

6 Click Next.

The Windows Media Center Setup screen appears.

7 Click Next.

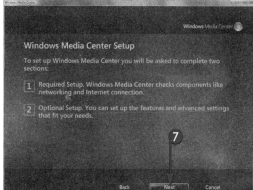

What equipment do I need to extend my Media Center experience?

▼ You need a Media Center Extender, such as a networked DVD player or TV that has Media Center Extender built in. One such device is the Microsoft Xbox 360 gaming device. You also need a network set up in your home. Unless you want to install network cabling in your home, the best option for this is a wireless network. Finally, and this may seem obvious, you need a Media Center computer.

Do I have to join the Customer Experience Improvement Program?

▼ No, this is optional. However, if you do join the program, you can provide feedback, suggestions, and helpful information to the group at Microsoft that is resonsible for designing and implementing the Media Center program. For example, if you discover that a component of the Media Center program does not provide everything you expected (such as the TV recording controls), you can send a message to the Customer Experience Improvement Program explaining your position. As Microsoft improves the Media Center platform, your suggestions may be used in future releases.

continued

Configure Media Center *(Continued)*

When you first launch Media Center, you will probably notice how different it looks from other Windows programs. First, it covers the entire screen. Second, it does not use the normal application paradigm of a menu toolbar, graphical toolbar icons, dialog boxes, or scroll bars. Third, the text is easy to read, large, and in a high-contrasting font.

The reason Media Center looks different from "normal" Windows programs is because it is designed to be used by input and display devices different from those of a regular computer monitor. Although you can use a mouse to interact with Media Center, and can surely use a regular monitor with it, Media Center is designed for larger television sets (or large monitors) where you use a remote control device to select items on the screen.

With a remote control, the large buttons are easy to highlight and pick. Similarly, the large text is easy to read when you are sitting across the room. Even on a 19-inch computer monitor, Media Center is easy to see. Just think what it looks like on a 60-inch High Definition Television (HDTV) set.

Note: *Depending on the Media Center devices you have installed, your setup screens may be different from those shown here.*

The Windows Media Center Privacy Statement screen appears.

● You can click here to read the privacy statement.

⑧ Click Next.

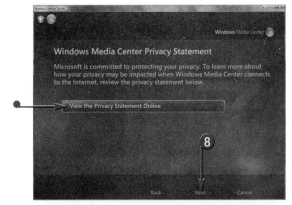

The Help Improve Windows Media Center screen appears.

⑨ Click the No thank you option (○ changes to ◉).

● You can click here to join the Customer Experience Improvement Program.

⑩ Click Next.

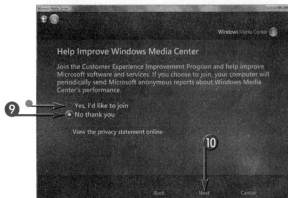

The Enhanced Playback screen appears.

⓫ Click Yes (○ changes to ◉).

● You can click No if you do not want Media Center to connect to the Internet and receive digital content.

● You can click here to read about Windows Media Center privacy.

⓬ Click Next.

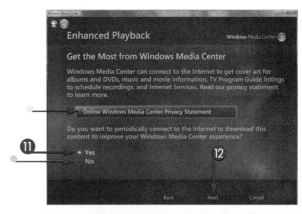

The Required Components Have Been Set Up screen appears.

⓭ Click Next.

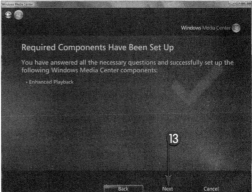

Does Media Center support all music, video, and picture types?

▼ Not all, but it does support all the formats that Windows Media Player 11 supports. Some of these formats include: WAV, SND, AU, AIF, WMA, and MP3 for audio; AVI and WMV for video; and JPG, and JPEG for picture. Of course, Media Center also supports the Microsoft Recorded TV Show format, which is the DVR-MS format. If you are not sure Media Center will play a file, try to play it in Windows Media Player. If you can play it there, you can play it in Media Center.

Can I play back music and videos without Media Center?

▼ Yes. Media Center is designed for users who want to extend Windows' capabilities to other facets of their lives; that is, they want to enhance their non-computing experiences. If you want to enjoy your music and videos as you use your computer, and you have no desire to extend your computer's "reach" to devices outside of the PC (your television, for instance), you can just use Media Player. Click Start, click All Programs, and then click Windows Media Player to start Windows Media Player. All your music and video files are available from the Libraries tab.

continued

Configure Media Center *(Continued)*

The second part of the Windows Media Center setup process involves configuring optional settings. During the Optional Setup phase, you can optimize Windows Media Center display settings; configure the libraries that store your music, videos, and pictures; and set up your speakers.

When you set up your display settings, you have options to choose the type of display you will use for your Media Center viewing. You can choose Monitor, such as for a standard computer monitor. If you have

a flat panel liquid crystal display (LCD) screen, do not pick this choice. Pick the Flat Panel option. Another choice is Built-in display, such as for the display on a laptop computer. For flat panel LCD monitors, choose Flat panel. If you have your television connected as the display, choose Television. It works for regular television sets, HDTV sets, LCD sets, and plasma sets. Finally, if you have a digital projector connected as your Media Center display, choose Projector. These are used giving presentations and displaying television shows, DVDs, and videos in large auditoriums.

Configure Media Center *(continued)*

The Optional Setup screen appears.

⑭ Click the Optimize how Windows Media Center looks on your display option (○ changes to ◉).

⑮ Click Next.

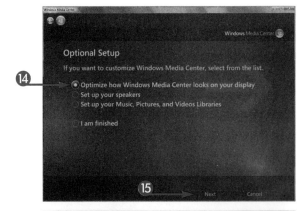

The Display Configuration screen appears.

● Click here to see a video explaining how your display can be configured.

⑯ Click Next.

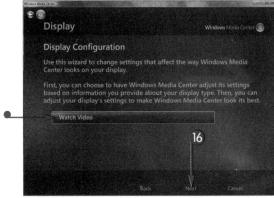

Note: *If you are not in full-screen mode, you are prompted to change Media Center to full-screen mode. Click the Yes option (○ changes to ◉).*

The Is Your Preferred Display Connected? screen appears.

⓱ Click the Yes, I see the wizard on my preferred display option (○ changes to ◉).

⓲ Click Next.

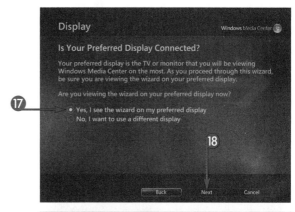

The Identify Your Display Type screen appears.

⓳ Click your display type (○ changes to ◉).

This example uses the digital projector as a display type.

⓴ Click Next.

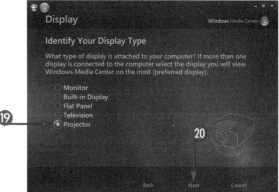

PART III

What if I do not see the wizard on my display, as specified in step 19?

▼ Click the Cancel button on Windows Media Center and click Yes, you want to exit the setup. Shut down your computer and connect or reconnect your display. Restart Windows. If you are prompted to install software or configure any settings for the display device, do so now. After the device is set up, start Windows Media Center and begin the setup procedure again. Windows Media Center should recognize your device now. If it does not, contact the display's manufacturer and ask for help on setting the display to work with Windows Media Center.

How do I know what size my display width is?

▼ Normal television and computer monitor widths have a ratio of 4:3. That means their display is almost square (which would be a 4:4 or 1:1 ratio). Newer television sets and some computer monitors — like wide-screen laptop monitors — have a display width ratio of 16:9. They are noticeably wider than they are tall. Movie theater screens have a 16:9 ratio; many movies on DVD or premium movie channels show movies in the 16:9 ratio (that is why you see black bars above and below the movie on a regular television set).

continued

Configure Media Center *(Continued)*

One of the screens during the Media Center setup program enables you to fine-tune, or calibrate, your display. This is not a required step, but you may want to do this the first time you use a new display device to ensure that device's output is one that you expect. You can change many characteristics of the display during this process.

Onscreen Centering & Sizing enables you to position where the picture displays on your screen. Aspect Ratio enables you to control the way in which shapes appear on your screen. If the aspect ratio is off,

characters and images may look short and squatty, tall and thin, bloated, slightly tilted, or misshapen.

Brightness (Black & Shadows) lets you control how clearly dark colors and shadows appear on the screen. Contrast (White) enables you to control how clearly the color white appears on the screen. Contrast often is overlooked when users adjust the display; they usually adjust just the brightness and color balance. However, the contrast setting can help sharpen images on your display. RGB Color Balance enables you to set color settings on your screen.

Configure Media Center *(continued)*

The Connection Type screen appears.

㉑ Click the cable type that connects to your display (○ changes to ◉).

This example uses Digital Video Interface (DVI), Video Graphics Array (VGA), or High-Definition Multimedia Interface (HDMI).

㉒ Click Next.

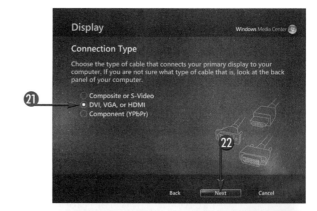

The Display Width screen appears.

㉓ Click your display width (○ changes to ◉).

㉔ Click Next.

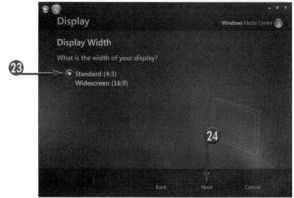

The Confirm Your Display Resolution screen appears.

㉕ Click Yes to keep your current resolution (○ changes to ◉).

㉖ Click Next.

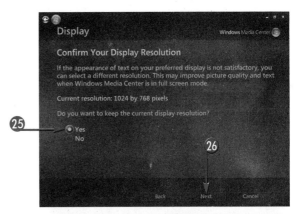

The Adjust Your Display Settings screen appears.

㉗ Click the Adjust display controls option (○ changes to ◉).

㉘ Click Next.

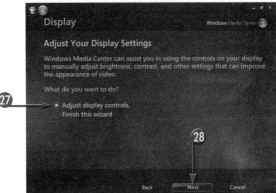

Can I change my display resolution while in the Windows Media Center setup program?

▼ Yes, to do this, click No in step 27 and then click Next. The Select Your Display Resolution screen appears. Pick a different resolution, such as 800 × 600 pixels (if you are currently using a different setting). Click Next when you finish. Note that Media Center screens do not show a great deal of information on them to make them easier to navigate with remote controls. This means you may want to try a lower resolution than what you currently use for your computer.

Do I have to work through all these steps?

▼ No, you can configure Media Center options later by clicking the Run setup later option when you open Media Center the first time. However it is a good idea to do it once so that you are sure all your Windows Media Center devices are working correctly. The last thing you want to do when your favorite television show comes on is to run through the Windows Media Center setup program to get your devices configured correctly.

continued

Configure Media Center *(Continued)*

Users who are heavily into audio experiences invest a great deal of money into getting just the right sound from their stereos, televisions, game consoles, and computers (not to mention their car sound systems). With Windows Media Center, you can optimize the system to handle your speakers. For example, Media Center enables you to specify exactly which type of connection your speakers use to connect to your computer or Media Center device.

Another option configures the number of speakers you have. You can choose two speakers, 5.1 surround speakers, or 7.1 surround speakers. Users who have

home theaters set up in their homes will probably have a 5.1 or 7.1 surround sound system. Media Center can take advantage of this system for an optimum playback experience.

The placement of speakers in your home entertainment arena is very important. Windows Media Center provides a way to configure where you have your speakers in relation to the computer so audio sounds during a movie, game, or television show emit where they are intended. For example, explosions going off on the left side of the screen should not be heard coming out of your front right speaker.

Configure Media Center *(continued)*

The Display Calibration screen appears.

㉙ Click Next.

The second Display Calibration screen appears.

㉚ Click a button to change a display setting.

A check mark appears after you change a setting.

㉛ Click Next when you finish calibrating your display.

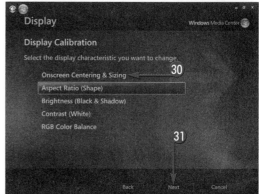

The You Are Done! screen appears.

Note: *This means you are finished optimizing your display. Continue to work on setting up speakers and media libraries.*

③② Click Next.

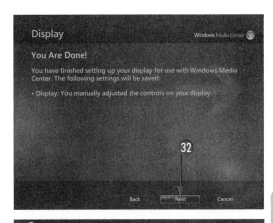

Set Up Speakers

The Optional Setup screen appears.

③③ Click Set up your speakers (○ changes to ◉).

③④ Click Next.

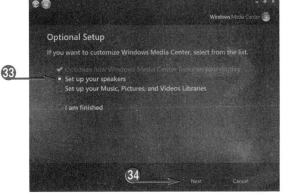

Can I change my setup later?

▼ Yes, you can select the Task item on the main Media Center window and then click the Settings button. The Settings window appears. Click General to open the General window. Here you can click from a number of settings topics. For example, to change the display settings, click Windows Media Center Setup. Next, click Configure Your TV or Montor. You are then taken into the Display Configuration setup area. Click Next to work through those settings.

Can I set parental controls in Media Center?

▼ Good question. Yes, you can. To do this, open the Settings window. Next, click General to open the General window. Click Parental Controls. The Create An Access Code window appears. Type a four-digit access code. Make it difficult to guess. Do not, for example, use 1234 or 9876. Retype the code. The Parental Controls window appears. On this page, you can turn on blocking for specific areas, such as TV-rating blocking. You can set the maximum allowed TV rating (such as TV-14).

continued

Configure Media Center *(Continued)*

When you set up Media Center, you can configure the optimal settings for your speakers to work with your computer. However, before you can even do that, you should make sure your audio adapter, or sound card, functions correctly. If you want to make sure it works correctly, click Start and then click Control Panel. Click the Hardware and Sounds link to open the Hardware and Sound window. Click Sound to display the Sound dialog box.

Click the audio device on the Playback tab and then click Properties. The Properties dialog box for the playback device includes tabs called General,

Supported Formats, Levels, Enhancements, and Advanced. (Your device may have different tabs.) Look on these tabs for settings to enhance your listening experience. For example, on the General tab, if your device shows Jack Information and the selection is for a digital RCA jack or similar, make sure your speakers are plugged into that jack in the back of your computer. Do not use only the standard mini-plug jacks.

You also can find playback settings on the Enhancements tab. Here you can select options like Low Frequency Protection, Virtual Surround, and Room Correction.

Configure Media Center *(continued)*

The Welcome to Speaker Setup screen appears.

35 Click Next.

The Speaker Connection Type screen appears.

36 Click the speaker connection type for your speakers (○ changes to ◉).

37 Click Next.

The Choose number of Speakers screen appears.

38 Click the number of speakers you have (○ changes to ◉).

39 Click Next.

The Test Your Speakers screen appears.

40 Click Test.

41 Click I heard sound from all of my speakers
(○ changes to ⊙).

42 If you did not hear a sound, click this option
and you will be led through steps to
troubleshoot your speakers and sound settings.

43 Click Next.

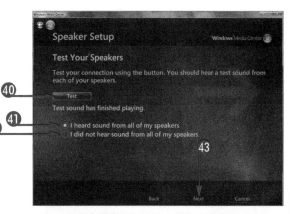

The You Are Done! screen appears.

44 Click Finish.

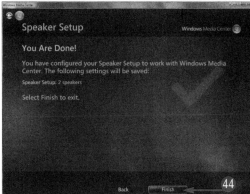

What types of sound adapters should I look for when I am upgrading?

▼ When you are looking to invest in a new sound system, look for ones that support Dolby Digital 5.1, Dolby Digital 7.1, or Digital Theatre Systems (DTS). These are common sound systems that you will find with many movies and DVDs. Another one you can look for is the Pulse Code Modulation (PCM) system. This type of system requires different jacks when connecting the speakers to the computer, so you may have to also upgrade your speakers, or at least purchase adapters that fit over the jacks your speakers currently use.

Do I have to invest a lot in speakers to enjoy Media Center?

▼ No, but if you plan to set up your Media Center computer to run your movies, videos, television, games, and radio devices, consider investing in some good speakers. Many users purchase state-of-the-art sound cards for their new computers but rely on dinky standard (and analog, not digital) speakers that do not do justice to the program. You can find a good resource for speakers on the Web at the Bose Systems site at www.bose.com. Click the Home Theater Systems link.

continued

Configure Media Center *(Continued)*

Windows Media Center enables you to access your music, pictures, and videos and play them back. You can set up Windows to monitor specific folders and automatically add music, video, and picture files from those folders to your Media Center libraries. This is handy if you want to keep your Media Center and Windows Media Player libraries in sync automatically, and not try to remember to update Media Center each time you input a media file.

For example, as you import photographs from a digital camera, you can tell Media Center to automatically add those files to Media Center as well as to your Windows Photo Gallery folders. During the

Media Center Library Setup stage, the setup program shows all the user folders (the Documents folder, for example) and drives on your computer. You can then drill down on those drives and folders to specify subfolders you want Media Center to monitor. Media Center automatically monitors your Pictures, Music, and Videos folders.

You can set up Media Center to watch local folders (those stored on your computer), a shared folder (those stored on a network computer), or both. If you specify a shared location, you must have a network connection and permission to access files on that share.

Configure Media Center *(continued)*

Set Up Media Libraries

The Optional Setup screen appears.

45 Click Set up your Music, Pictures, and Videos Libraries (○ changes to ◉).

- You can click here if you do not want to set up your media libraries in Media Center.

46 Click Next.

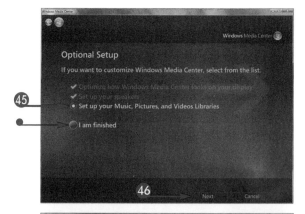

The Music, Pictures and Videos Folders screen appears.

47 Click Add folder to watch (○ changes to ◉).

48 Click Next.

The Add folders screen appears.

49 Click Add folders on this computer (○ changes to ●).

● You can click here to set up shared folders to watch.

● You can click here to set up both local and shared folders to watch.

50 Click Next.

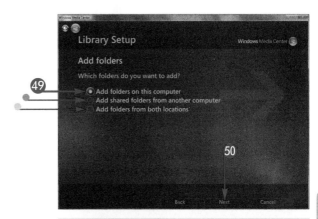

The Select folders that contain media screen appears.

51 Click the folders to monitor.

52 Click Next when finished.

Can I set Media Center to stop monitoring a folder?

▼ Yes, for example if you do not want Media Center to monitor your Pictures folder, you can remove the option that tells Media Center to monitor that folder. To do this, click the Tasks item on the main Media Center window and then click Settings. Click Library Setup on the Settings window and then click Stop watching a folder on the Library Setup window. Click Next. Click to remove the check mark next to a folder you want Media Center to stop watching. Click Next and then click Finish to save your setting.

A folder on the network does not show up. How can I see it?

▼ First, make sure you are connected to the network and that you have permssion to access the folder. You will have to switch out of the Media Center setup program to do this. Also, you may want to set up a drive mapping to the shared folder by opening Windows Explorer, clicking Tools, clicking Map Network Drive, and filling out the Map Network Drive dialog box. You assign a drive letter to the shared folder so that it appears just like a drive in the listings when you go to set up the shared folders to monitor.

continued

Configure Media Center *(Continued)*

After you configure Windows Media Center, you can start using it to enjoy your entertainment media. Even if you do not have the latest HDTV and TV tuner to record television, pause live TV, or access the latest television information, you can still enjoy Media Center's features. For example, if you have a multimedia projector, you can set it up to play back a video you have created in Windows Movie Maker without the need to burn the movie to a DVD first. If you have a remote control for the projector, you can use it to access the easy-to-read buttons and options on the Media Center screens, even from across the room.

Another use for Media Center that does not require an investment in a TV or radio tuner is the Online Media feature. Here you can download information about TV and movies, music and radio, news, sports, games, and lifestyle. For example, you can find special offers for XM satellite radio or discover the latest online game that you can play.

Configure Media Center *(continued)*

The Add folders screen appears.

● You can click this link to see the folder you selected to monitor.

53 Click Finish.

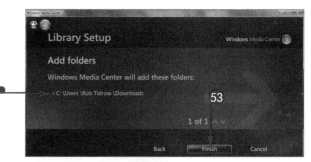

The ADDING MEDIA window appears.

54 Click OK.

The Optional Setup screen appears.

55 Click I am finished (○ changes to ◉).

56 Click Next.

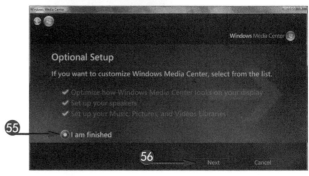

The You Are Done! screen appears.

57 Click Finish.

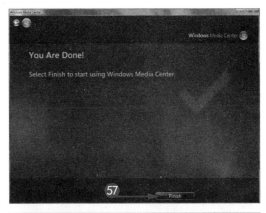

The main Media Center window appears.

Do I have to run setup each time I use Media Center?

▼ No, when you start Media Center the next time after you have gone through the steps of configuring it, you are presented with the main Media Center window, the final screen shown in the steps here. You can, however, access the Media Center settings by clicking Tasks on the main window and then clicking Settings. You can then change options for your TV, pictures, music, and other Media Center items, without navigating the entire setup program. This is handy if you change display types, such as if you purchase a new television set for your home.

When I set up Media Center to store my pictures, can I view them separately?

▼ Yes, Media Center enables you to show individual pictures while you are in the Picture Library. You simply select a picture and Media Center displays it. You also can view a slide show of all your pictures, which is a common thing people do when family or friends are over for a party get-together. Turn on the Media Center computer and show your slide show of pictures on your new big-screen TV (or your regular-size one as well).

Navigate Media Center

As you first use Media Center, you may notice that it is a little different from your normal Windows program. In fact, you may be a little uncomfortable by the interface because it does not have the usual Windows items.

However, there are some basic navigation rules you can follow to help you get over the learning curve when you first start using Media Center. One rule is that each screen does not show a lot of information. You will not find extraneous words or pictures thrown around on the screens. Instead, you find basic navigation buttons, task buttons, pop-up images that

are hot-linked, short titles, and snippets of key information (dates of photographs, for example).

When you want to choose something on-screen, you move the pointer over the item and click. You use a standard computer mouse to select an item, or, better yet, use a remote control that a Media Center–compatible device provides to move the pointer around. A remote control provided by some television sets and digital projectors enables you to move the mouse and make selections without sitting right next to the computer. Place the Media Center computer in the corner of the room and control your system from the comfort of the couch or easy chair.

Navigate Media Center

① Start Media Center.

The Media Center Start window appears.

② Move the mouse to the top of the main list.

An up arrow appears.

③ Hold the mouse over the up arrow.

The main list scrolls.

● Move the mouse off the up arrow when the item you want to select is in the selection area.

● You also can click an item for it to appear in the selection area.

④ Click the selection.

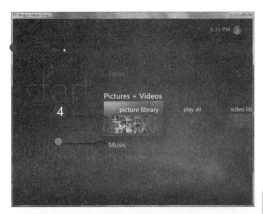

Media Center displays that selection's window.

This example shows the Picture Library.

⑤ Click the back arrow.

◉ You can click here to return to the previous window.

How do I get to the main screen in Media Center?

▼ As you traverse the various features in Media Center, you may find that you just want to go back to the main Media Center screen. To do this, click the Windows Media Center icon that sits at the top left of the screen. The symbol is a circle with a green background and the ubiquitous Windows flag. Regardless of how many clicks you have made away from the Start page, simply click that icon to go directly to the home page. On some configuration windows, however, you cannot go directly to the main Media Center page without finishing or canceling the configuration you're working on.

Why do the controls disappear?

▼ Media Center displays the controls, such as the navigation controls, VCR-type controls, and other items, for just a short period of time. Then they disappear. This enables you to enjoy the content on-screen without the buttons and extraneous stuff getting in your way. To get them back, simply move the pointer (with a remote control or the mouse). The controls pop back on-screen. It is also good to know that if you want the controls to disappear, simply stop moving the mouse. After about five seconds, the controls disappear.

Set Up an Internet Connection in Media Center

One of the first things you may want to do with Media Center is check to make sure it is set up for the Internet. Although your computer may be connected to the Internet, Media Center may not be set up for it yet. Also, the Express setup or Custom setup processes do not lead you through setting up the Internet connection for Media Center. You have to do it manually.

To do this, you go into the Tasks area, click General, and then click the Settings features. You then go into the Windows Media Center Setup area and click Set Up Internet Connection.

By having an Internet connection, Media Center can download system updates, media files, TV listings, and other files. Before you go into the Internet Connection page, test your Internet connectivity by opening Internet Explorer and displaying a Web page. If everything displays, you can feel assured that setting up Media Center will go smoothly. If not, troubleshoot your Internet connection (sometimes just shutting down and restarting Windows Vista does the trick) and then go into Media Center.

Set Up an Internet Connection in Media Center

1 Select Tasks in Media Center.

2 Click settings.

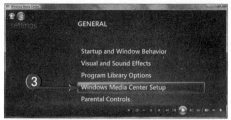

The settings window appears.

3 Click Windows Media Center Setup.

The WINDOWS MEDIA CENTER SETUP window appears.

4 Click Set Up Internet Connection.

The Set Up Your Internet Connection window appears.

5 Click Next.

The "Always on" Internet Connection window appears.

⑥ Click Yes (○ changes to ◉).

● Click No if your service shuts down.

⑦ Click Next.

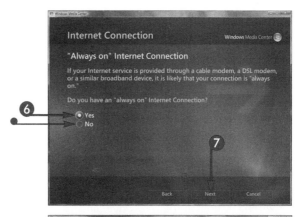

The Test Your Internet Connection window appears.

⑧ Click Test.

● Media Center tests your Internet connection.

⑨ Click Next.

A final window appears.

⑩ Click Finish.

● You can click the Media Center icon to return to the main Media Center window.

Can I use a modem with Windows Media Center?

▼ No, the Media Center requires a high-speed Internet connection, such as a cable, DSL, satellite, or T1 (dedicated local area network, or LAN) connection. This is because Media Center downloads large files of data and artwork for the Media Center Guides. Dial-up modems are not fast enough for these files. If you do not have this type of connection, you need to contact your local service provider (such as your cable television provider) and ask if they provide high-speed Internet services. See Chapter 16 for more on configuring Windows Vista for broadband Internet service.

Are there any network settings I can change in Media Center?

▼ No, all Media Center does when you set up the Internet connection is test to see if your connection is on. To change the settings for the Internet, click the Windows Start button, click Network, and then click the Network and Sharing Center toolbar button. Click Manage Network Connections in the Tasks pane. Right-click your Internet connection and click Properties. On the Properties dialog box, you can change differnet network settings as needed. Also, if you do have connection problems, you may want to turn off the Windows Firewall. See the section "Manage Windows Firewall" in Chapter 8.

Use Media Center to Play DVDs

Media Center makes it easy to kick back and enjoy a DVD in your computer. With Media Center, you can play back the DVD full-screen or inside a window. As you start the DVD, a row of controls is available on the bottom of the screen. These controls let you pause, play, stop, fast-forward, and reverse through the DVD.

One great feature of Media Center's DVD player is that you can stop the DVD (keep it in the DVD drive) and go to different areas of Media Center. You can then

return to the DVD and click Play. The DVD picks right back up to where you stopped it. You can even perform configuration changes to Media Center, and it will not disturb your place in the DVD.

The DVD player controls for fast-forward and reverse have different speeds at which you can move through a DVD. For example, click the fast-forward button once to speed up the playback. Click it again to double the speed. Click it again to double that speed, and so on.

Using Media Center to Play DVDs

① Start Media Center.

② Select TV + Movies.

③ Click play dvd.

The PLAY DVD window appears.

④ Insert a DVD into your DVD drive.

⑤ Click OK.

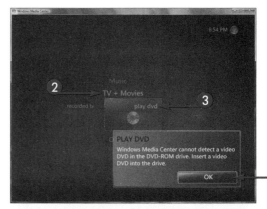

The play dvd item displays.

⑥ Click play dvd.

The DVD begins.

Your DVD may have different menus and options available.

7 Click a menu item.

The menu item plays.

Use pop-up controls to navigate through the DVD.

PART III

Do I have to use Media Center to play DVDs?

▼ No, you can use other DVD player programs to run your DVDs. WinDVD is one such program. If you do not want to use Media Center for DVD playback, you can set up the AutoPlay feature to launch the other player program when you insert a DVD. To do this, click Start and then click Default Programs. Click Change AutoPlay Settings to display Choose What Happens When You Insert Each Type of Media or Device. Select the DVD Movie drop-down list and then click Play DVD Movie Using *the program name* in the list. Do the same for the Enhanced DVD Movie item. Click Save.

How can I find the next chapter in a DVD?

▼ If your DVD has menus (not all of them do), click the next chapter button (to the right of the play/pause button), and Media Center jumps to the next chapter. You can also use the main DVD window that displays when you launch your DVD. You can access this by right-clicking the movie and choosing Title Menu from the menu that appears. This takes you to the DVD menu. Also, some remote controls that come with DVD players or TV devices have next chapter buttons and DVD Menu buttons that navigate to the menu.

Use My Music to Enjoy Music

The Media Center offers a centralized place to access music stored on your computer. With Media Center you can play individual tracks or play your playlists. When you first set up Windows Media Center, you have the choice of allowing Media Center to monitor folders so that when you add new tracks or playlists, Media Center adds them as well. This is handy when you rip a CD in Windows Media Player and know that Media Center will take care of updating your folders as well.

For albums you store in Media Center, you can display album cover art that Media Center downloads (or if you rip in Windows Media Player, Media Player

downloads the art). You can click the album in the Music Library to display the Album Details window. Here you can view additional information about the album. Media Center displays the name of the album, its artist, each track from the album that is stored on your system, the total number of tracks, the elapsed time of each track, the total time, and the album release date.

From the Album Details window, you can select a song to play, play the album, add the album to the Media Center queue, burn a song or the album to disc, edit the album details information, or delete the album.

① Click a Music item.

② Click music library.

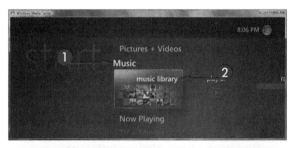

The music library window appears.

③ Click an album.

The album details window for that album appears.

④ Click a title.

The song details window appears.

⑤ Click Play Song.

The now playing window appears while the song plays.

● Use the controls to navigate through the song.

Can I use another program to play music?

▼ Yes, Windows Media Player can play back your music. Click Start and then click All Programs. From that menu, click Windows Media Player. Click the Library tab to see a listing of the music in your library. If you have Media Center watch your folders for new music, your Media Player Library and the Media Center Music Library should contain the same songs and albums. Double-click a song to play it using Media Player.

What kind of information can I add to the song details?

▼ When you display the song details window for a song, click Edit Info. This displays the edit song window. You can change the Song Title, Artist Name, and Rating. After you change the information, click the Save button. This takes you back to the song details window. If, however, you want to erase your changes, click the Cancel button. You return to the song details window.

Use My Pictures to View Pictures

With Windows Media Center, you can display your pictures in a slide show or view individual ones. You access your pictures from the Picture Library after you click the Pictures + Videos item on the Media Center main window.

Once inside the Picture Library, you can view your pictures in a couple of different ways. First you can view pictures by folders. These are the folders in which you store pictures. For example, when you import pictures using the Windows Vista Import Picture tool, Windows groups the pictures from that set into one folder. By default, Windows names that folder using

the date (such as 2007-04-11) and a tag you give it. In Media Center, you can view those pictures by clicking the folder name.

You also can view pictures by tags. This is a tag you give to the entire picture set (during import, for instance), or individual tags you add to each picture.

Finally, you can view pictures by their date. Windows Media Center uses the date the picture was taken, not when it was imported. You can view photos by date by clicking the Date Taken button and then clicking a month and year (such as Apr, 2007).

Using My Pictures to View Pictures

① Click Pictures + Videos.

② Click picture library.

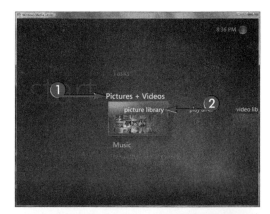

The picture library window appears.

③ Click folders.

Pictures are organized by their folder name.

④ Click a folder.

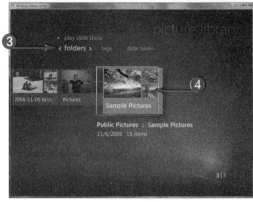

The folder opens.

5 Click a picture.

The picture appears.

You can use pop-up controls to return to the previous window.

How do I play a slide show of my pictures?

▼ Organize your pictures in the order in which you want to play them. When you display pictures, click Folders, Tags, or Date Taken. This determines the order in which pictures display during the slide show (if you want to view all your pictures in a show). Or, if you want to see a subset of them, click the pictures you want to view (such as Apr, 2007 when viewing by Date Taken). Click Play Slide Show. Media Center displays each picture in a slide show.

Can I delete pictures in Media Center?

▼ Yes, to do this, display the picture in a group, such as open them by folder name. Right-click the picture. A small menu appears. Click Delete. The Confirm Delete dialog box appears. Click Yes. Media Center deletes the picture from your computer and places it in the Windows Recycle Bin (if you want to restore it later). You also can leave Media Center and manage your pictures using Windows Photo Gallery or Windows Explorer.

Use Media Center to Play Recorded TV

Often our favorite television shows come on when we are not at home or we are doing something else. Windows Media Center helps so you do not have to miss any of your favorite shows. Media Center enables you to record television programs and then play them back. You need a TV tuner and a connection to television services (such as cable TV) to use this feature. When you record TV items, Media Center saves the files in Microsoft recorded tv show format, which has the .dvr-ms extension.

When you install Windows Vista, Media Center provides a sample from a recorded television program.

To play this, you navigate to TV + Movies, select the recorded tv item, and then click the sample. At the time of the writing, the sample was called Jewels of the Caribbean. The sample on your system may be different.

By default, Windows stores recorded TV files in the recorded tv folder. You can find these files by clicking the Public folder and then clicking recorded tv. If you want to share these files with other users on a network, make sure you allow the sharing of the Public folder (click the Sharing Settings button when you view Public in Windows Explorer, for example).

Using Media Center to Play Recorded TV

① Select TV + Movies.

② Click recorded tv.

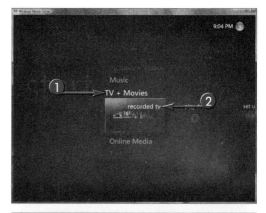

The recorded tv window appears.

③ Click a TV or movie clip.

The program info window appears.

4 Click Play.

The recorded TV clip plays.

Where should I back up recorded TV files?

▼ As you can imagine, recorded TV files can be very large and will take up a lot of storage space on your computer. To make sure the entire program that you want to record has enough space on your computer, consider purchasing additional hard drives or flash drives for your backup purposes. Some hard drives attach to your computer from the outside via Universal Serial Bus (USB) ports. These will work fine as long as they are USB 2.0 (USB 1.x may be too slow to work well for you). If you are on a network that has larger servers, ask if you can store files there. Make sure you get permission from your LAN administrator first.

How big are recorded TV files?

▼ Big. When you record television shows, remember that they are high-quality video files. For Windows Media Center to reproduce this quality, the files must contain a great deal of digital data. Also, most programs also have sound, which adds to the overall size of the video. To help you calculate the amount of space needed, look at the samples furnished with Media Center. They are approximately two minutes long and of very high quality. Each file one is about 50MBs. With this in mind, consider using about 25MBs per minute when recording.

Set Up Your TV Signal to View Television

W hen you equip your computer with a TV tuner, Media Center enables you to watch, record, and play back TV shows on your computer. Depending on the type of TV tuner you purchase, you can access cable, satellite, and over-the-air signals on your computer. This lets you view shows, download information about upcoming shows, record shows and play them back, watch and stop live TV, and more.

TV tuners usually connect to your computer in one of two ways. Internal tuners are Peripheral Component Interconnect (PCI) adapter cards that require that you to open the computer case, locate an empty PCI slot,

and insert the card. If your computer does not have any empty slots (some newer PCs, for example, have only two slots to begin with), you must remove a device you no longer need and then insert the tuner adapter card.

An alternative to the internal tuner is an external one that you attach to your computer via a USB port. Simply plug in the device, configure it, and then start using it.

The following steps assume you have the TV tuner attached to your computer and that it is compatible with Windows Media Center.

① Select Tasks from the main Media Center window.

② Click settings.

The settings window appears.

③ Click TV.

The TV settings window appears.

④ Click Set Up TV Signal.

The TV SIGNAL SETUP window appears.

5 Click Yes.

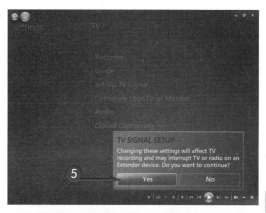

The Set Up Your TV Signal window appears.

6 Click Next.

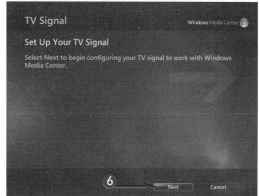

My tuner worked with Windows XP, but does not with Vista. What should I do?

▼ The best thing to do is contact the tuner's manufacturer. Many times the manufacturer will have updated device drivers that you can install on Windows Vista to configure your tuner. If the tuner is an internal one, you might also try removing the card while the computer is shut off. Restart your computer and let Windows Vista start up. Shut down Windows and your computer. Re-insert the card and restart Windows. When prompted for the new hardware (Windows thinks it is new), specify that Windows should try to locate the proper software for it.

Can I use media software that came with my tuner?

▼ Yes, but it will not work with Windows Media Center. That is, you can watch television using the media software that was bundled with your tuner, or you can use Media Center. Which one you choose depends on the features and peformance of the software. You already know that Windows Media Center can let you record, play back, view, and stop live television. If you want those capabilities and your bundled software does not include those features, give Windows Media Center a try.

continued

Set Up Your TV Signal to View Television *(Continued)*

As you set up your TV signal to view television shows with Windows Media Center, you must specify the region. During the setup procedure, Windows Media Center downloads setup options for your region. The region is used to configure the local television shows you will receive through your computer and TV tuner. Windows Media Center provides 260 regions from which you can choose, including places like the United States, Benin, Greece, and Kuwait. If the default region that appears on the Confirm Your Region window is incorrect, make sure you click No, I want to select a different

region and then click Next. This displays the Select Your Region window, from which you can select a different region. Select a region and click Next.

You can specify to have Windows Media Center set up your TV signal automatically, or specify that you will set up the signal manually. It is up to you whether you want to use the automatic or manual feature, but you may want to let Windows attempt to set up the signals automatically. Then if Windows cannot locate the signals itself, you can go back and set them up manually.

Set Up Your TV Signal to View Television *(continued)*

The Confirm Your Region window appears.

⑦ Click Yes, use this Region to configure TV services (○ changes to ◉).

● Click here to specify a different region.

⑧ Click Next.

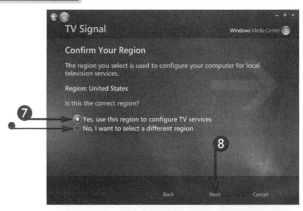

The Download TV Setup Options window appears.

● This download process can take a few minutes to complete.

The Automatic TV Signal Setup window appears.

9 Click Configure my TV signal automatically (Recommended) (○ changes to ◉).

10 Click Next.

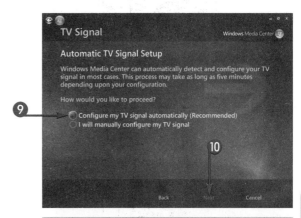

The Examining your TV Signal Setup window appears.

11 Click Next.

PART III

Windows Media Center cannot locate a signal. What should I do?

▼ Make sure your adapater is connected to your TV source. For a digital or satellite TV system, connect the TV tuner to the set top device that feeds your television. For televisions that use an antenna, connect the tuner to the antenna. You may need to purchase a booster device for your antenna to increase reception. Also, you should place antennas near windows or other open areas, and away from computer monitors and other strong electrical-current devices.

Can I manually configure the TV signal?

▼ Yes, in step 9, select I will manually configure my TV signal (○ changes to ◉), press Next, and select the type of TV signal (cable, satellite, or antenna). Depending on the choice you make, Windows Media Center displays a series of windows guiding you through setup. For example, if you choose cable, you need to specify if you have a set top box. Work through each setup screen. For the antenna choice, you will need to pick analog or digital antenna.

continued

Set Up Your TV Signal to View Television *(Continued)*

Windows Media Center uses the Electronic Program Guide (EPG) service to provide you with electronic TV listing information. These listings include information about each show (at least most of the shows) available in your area. You can find out names of shows, the channels they broadcast on, air times, actors' and actresses' names, synopses of shows, and other information. Use this information to find the shows you want to watch, as well as to set up Media Center to record your favorites.

At the end of the Set Up Your TV Signal procedure, you have the option of setting up the program guide.

The program guide may have already downloaded once to your system in the background when you were configuring Windows Media Center. If you had not set up the Internet connection for Media Center, you may not have the EPG information on your system. Or you may want to manually download the information again to ensure it is the most current information as you start using Media Center for television and recording.

Depending on your connection speed, the program guide may take a few minutes to download to your computer.

Set Up Your TV Signal to View Television *(continued)*

The You Are Done! window appears.

⑫ Click Set Up Guide Listings (○ changes to ◉).

⑬ Click Next.

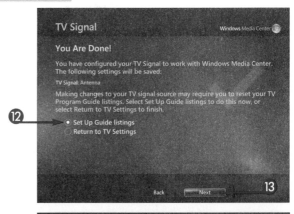

The Set Up Your TV Program Guide window appears.

⑭ Click Next.

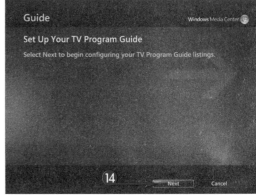

The Guide Privacy window appears.

⓯ Click Yes (○ changes to ◉).

● Click here to read the Guide privacy statement.

⓰ Click Next.

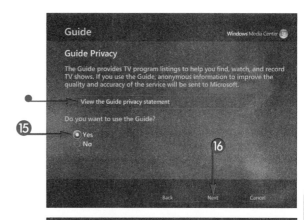

The Guide Terms of Service window appears.

⓱ Click I agree (○ changes to ◉).

⓲ Click Next.

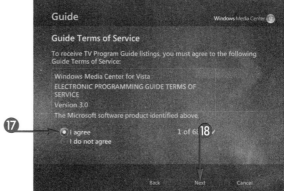

What kind of information does Microsoft know about me after I get the Program Guide?

▼ To download the TV Program Guide, you must agree to allow Microsoft to have access to some of the information about you and your computer, such as your computer's IP address, access times that you get the program guide, and, of course, geographic information. The geographic information includes your country and ZIP code (which you provide during setup) and may include other information. They do not gather personal information about you, such as your name, address, and phone number.

How much does the EPG cost?

▼ At this time, the EPG is a free service when you use the Windows Media Center software. With other "media center" software programs, you may be given a 30-day trial, after which you must subscribe to the service on a monthly or annual basis. If you read the terms of service on the Guide Terms of Service window, you will read that Microsoft does have the right to start charging for the service in the future.

continued

Set Up Your TV Signal to View Television *(Continued)*

The TV listings in the Program Guide contain up to 14 days of programming. After you download the guide, you can use it to specify which shows you want to view. You can read through it, looking for a show that catches your eye or viewing it in categories. For example, you can click the Categories button on the left side of the guide and select from Most Viewed, Movies, Sports, Kids, News, and Special.

Although you will find the Program Guide very handy for finding programs to play on your TV tuner, you can elect not to download it to your computer. You

may want to do this if you decide that the information that is sent back to Microsoft is too great or that it infringes on your privacy too much. To disable it, click the Tasks item on the main Windows Media Center window and click Settings. Click General and then click Privacy. The Privacy window appears.

On the Privacy window, click the Privacy Settings button. The Privacy Settings window appears. Click to clear the Use the Guide and Send Anonymous Information to Microsoft To Improve the Quality and Accuracy of the Service option. Click Save.

Set Up Your TV Signal to View Television *(continued)*

The Enter Your ZIP Code window appears.

⑲ Type your ZIP code.

⑳ Click Next.

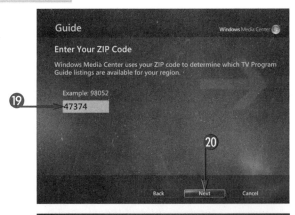

The Download Provider Information window appears.

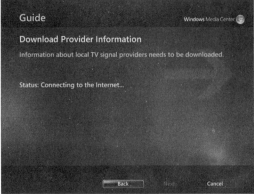

The Download complete window appears after the Program Guide downloads to your computer.

㉑ Click Next.

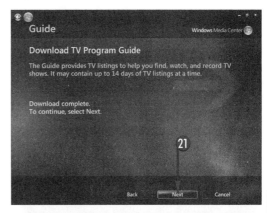

The TV settings window appears.

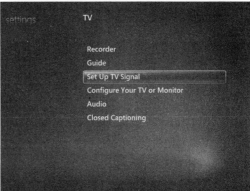

How do I manually download the guide again?

▼ Return to the TV settings window and click Guide. On the Guide window that displays, click Get Latest Guide Listings. The Guide Listings window dialog box appears. Click Yes. The download starts in the background. You can do other tasks at this point, such as watch TV, view a DVD, or view pictures. After the Program Guide downloads, a dialog box apppeas that informs you that the Guide has been updated. Click OK to remove the dialog box, or wait about ten seconds and the box disappears on its own.

Can I burn a DVD while I download an updated Guide?

▼ It is not a good idea. Any time you burn a DVD or CD, your system devotes a lot of resources (CPU cycles, memory, hard drive input/output, and so on) to the burning process. Any resources you take away from that process may jeopardize the disc-burning process. Although the Guide is downloaded using the Internet, your hard drive, CPU cycles, and memory are also used. In the end you may be left with a DVD or CD that does not burn correctly.

Burn DVDs or CDs with Media Center

Windows Media Center includes the capability to burn CDs or DVDs. This is handy when you have a movie or set of pictures you want to record to a disc. Windows Vista includes other areas from which you can burn CDs or DVDs, including Windows Photo Gallery, Windows Media Player, and Windows Explorer.

Before you set up the files that you want to burn, make sure you have the appropriate hardware set up and that it is configured to work with Windows Vista.

For example, to burn to a DVD, you must have a DVD-R, DVD+R, DVD+RW, or DVD-RW device. You will also need to have a blank DVD disc (or blank CD disc, if you want to burn a CD) on which to place the files.

If you are in Windows Media Center and insert a blank DVD or CD disc, Media Center asks if you want to burn a disc. This example shows how users can burn DVDs or CDs from the main Media Center window and assumes you already have a disc in your disc drive and have answered No to that query.

Burn DVDs or CDs with Media Center

① Click Tasks from the main Windows Media Center window.

② Click Burn CD/DVD.

The Select Disc Format window appears.

③ Select a format (○ changes to ◉).

This example uses the DVD Slide Show format.

④ Click Next.

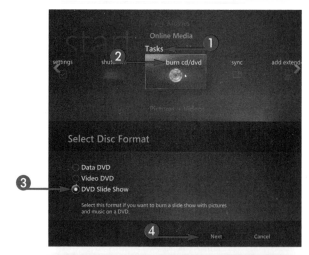

The Name This DVD window appears.

⑤ Type a name for the disc.

● You can use the numeric keypad to name the disc if you are using the Microsoft Remote Control.

⑥ Click Next.

The Select Media window appears.

7 Select a library from which to select files
(◯ changes to ◉).

This example selects the Picture Library.

8 Click Next.

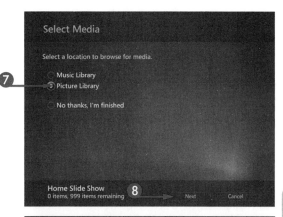

The Choose Pictures window appears.

9 Select the files you want to burn to disc.

10 Click Next.

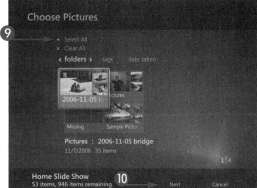

Can I burn television shows on a DVD?

▼ Media Center enables you to burn TV
shows to DVD. However, legally you must
inquire about that from the owner or
producer of the television show. In most
cases, you are not allowed to. However,
some educational programs, such as ones
that air on Public Broadcasting Service
(PBS), CSpan, Discovery, and other
stations, provide free-use licenses for
teachers or educators to record and show
programs during class time. However,
users cannot present those shows at other
functions, such as after-school events,
"home" movie parties, and the like.

**Can I set up a list of pictures to burn
first?**

▼ Yes, you can organize your pictures in the
Media Center Picture Library first and then
burn them using this organization. To do
this, go to Picture Library and organize the
pictures you want to burn. For example,
organize them by Tags or Date Taken.
Right-click the folder. Click Burn. Insert a
blank disc and click Retry. Windows Media
Center burns your disc with the selected
pictures.

continued

Burn DVDs or CDs with Media Center *(Continued)*

After you have selected the files you want to burn, the Review & Edit List window appears. You can view the file names of the individual files you have selected by clicking a plus sign (+) next to a folder in the right column of the list of files. This displays the contents of the folder you selected. If you want to delete a file from the list, click the Close box next to a file. This immediately removes the selected file from your list. To re-select it, you must click Add More and then select the file from the Choose Pictures or Choose Movies window.

After you burn one DVD or CD, you can burn another using the same files you used on the first disc. To do this, wait for Media Center to eject your finished first disc, insert another blank disc into your drive, and then click Burn on the Completing Burn dialog box. The Burn Progress dialog box appears. Continue this process until all the discs you want to burn are completed.

The Review & Edit List window appears.

⑪ Click Burn DVD.

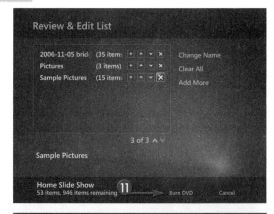

The INITIATING COPY dialog box appears.

⑫ Click Yes.

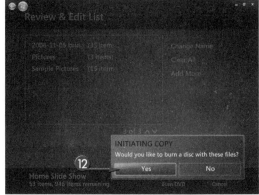

The BURN PROGRESS dialog box appears.

It may take a long time to finish the burn process.

● When the process has finished, Windows Media Center ejects your finished disc.

The COMPLETING BURN dialog box appears.

⑬ Click Done.

Do I have to leave my PC alone during the burn process?

▼ No, but it is a good idea. However, if you want to go on to other things, such as watching television or playing music with Media Center, click OK on the Burn Progress dialog box to do so. Also, consider turning off the screen saver function so your computer resources are not diverted to the screen saver during the DVD burn process. See the section "Select a Screen Saver" in Chapter 5.

Can I add a fade to my slide shows?

▼ Yes, click Tasks on the main Media Center window and click Settings. On the Settings window, click Pictures to display the Pictures window. Under the Transition Type heading, click Cross Fade. You may need to click the down arrow to see all the selections on this window. Click Save. Now when you burn your CD or DVD with a slide show, Windows Media Center uses the cross fade transition instead of the animated transition.

Use the Program Guide

Y ou learned earlier that the Program Guide is used to display a list of upcoming televisions shows in your area. When you get ready to watch a show or record one using a TV tuner, display the Program Guide to find the show you want.

The Program Guide displays information as a multicolumn and multirow table. By default, the table displays the current date, current time, and shows that are scheduled to air during the next two half-hour increments (such as 11:00 PM and 11:30 PM).

The table displays each station or channel and the name of the program under the time column when it

will air. You can use this format to see which shows are coming on during which time slot, or use it to see which shows are coming on for a particular channel. For example, to see all the shows scheduled for Lifetime, find the Lifetime channel and view the shows appearing in the row to the right of it. Move the mouse over a listing to see a short synopsis of it under the table.

Another handy Program Guide tool is the Categories button. Click this to display shows in general categories, such as Movies or Sports.

Using the Program Guide

① Select TV + Movies from the main Windows Media Center window.

② Click guide.

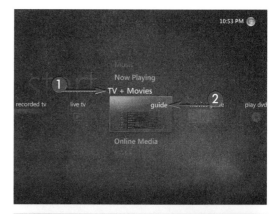

The guide window appears.

● Hover the mouse pointer over a show to see details for it.

③ Click a station.

The station window appears.

④ Click a show.

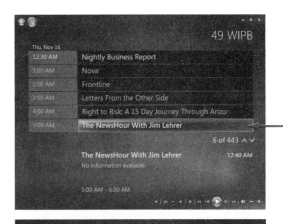

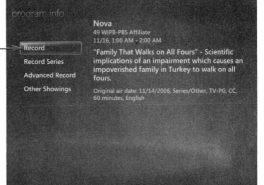

The program info window appears.

● Click here to set up Media Center to record the show.

How do I find what is showing on a particular station?

▼ You can use the Program Guide to find listings for a station. To see a drill-down of all the shows listed for a station, click the name of the station in the Program Guide window. A window appears showing each time slot and the show scheduled to show during that time. To see shows that fall in time slots after the ones displayed on the screen, click the down arrow. This displays another five time slots and the shows for those times.

Can I see if a show is on other days of the week?

▼ Yes, click a station to drill-down to the show you want to investigate. You should be looking at the Program Info window (see step 4 in the previous set of steps). Click Other Showings on the left side of the window. The Other Showings window appears, listing all the dates and times that program is scheduled to show during the next two weeks. Click a particular show to get more details about it.

Watch Live TV Shows

A useful feature of Windows Media Center is its capability to allow you to watch live TV shows through your computer. In many cases, you will run your Media Center computer in your "entertainment" room (such as your living room or family room) and have it hooked up to your television set. You will then use your computer to record shows, pause live shows, and play back these shows.

Media Center provides three ways to watch a live TV show. First, you can select a show from the Program Guide. When you find a program you want to watch in the Program Guide, simply select it and Windows Media Center displays it on your screen. It is that easy.

Second, if you have the Microsoft Remote Control device, press the Live TV button. Media Center turns on the television tuner and displays the show for the currently selected station. On the Remote Control device, you can click the Ch – and Ch + buttons to navigate up and down through channels, or press a number for the station number. Press Enter to return to the previous channel.

Third, select TV + Movies from the main Media Center window. Click Live TV to turn on the tuner.

Watching Live TV Shows

Using the Program Guide

① Select TV + Movies from the main Media Center window.

② Click guide.

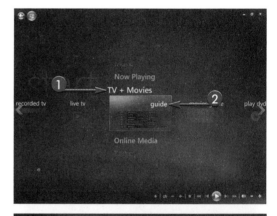

The guide window appears.

③ Click a show.

The show appears on your screen.

④ Click Ch + on your remote control device to change to the next station.

The station you selected appears on your screen.

Can I show subtitles on-screen?

▼ Yes, if that show includes them as part of the programming. To turn on subtitles (also called *Closed Captioning*) in Media Center, click Tasks on the main Media Center window and then click Settings. On the Settings window, click TV and then click Closed Captioning. Click the minus sign (–) under Caption Display until the On setting displays. Click Save. By default, subtitles appear when you mute the volume while watching a show.

When I watch TV, the show seems slow at times. Why?

▼ It is probably due to your computer speed and hardware. In short, Windows Vista by itself requires a great deal of system resources. When you start playing TV, recording TV, and peforming other tasks (such as downloading movie information from the Internet), a slow computer will not perform as you would like. If you plan to use your computer for home entertainment, consider investing in a high-speed, state-of-the-art one that includes 2GB of RAM, a 64-bit or higher graphics card with 128MB of RAM on it, a hard drive with more than 200GB of free space, and a super-fast processor (more than 2.5 GHz).

Use the Movie Guide

Along with the TV Program Guide, Media Center provides you with the Movie Guide. With the Movie Guide, Media Center displays all the movies that are scheduled to air on TV for the next two weeks (the length of time that the Program Guide displays information).

For each movie listed in the Movie Guide, Media Center downloads a picture of the DVD front cover (if one is available for that movie), the name of the movie, the year it was released, the channel it is scheduled to appear on, and the date and time of the showing.

Click a movie image, and Media Center displays additional information about the movie on the Movie Details window. Here you can click a button to see the cast of the movie, set up Media Center to record the movie, see if the movie is scheduled to show during other times, and read a short synopsis of the movie.

Media Center provides categories in the Movie Guide to help you locate a movie in a genre. For example, click Fantasy to get a listing of movies in that genre. Finally, use the Title, Year, Rating, and Start Date buttons to organize movies by those criteria.

Using the Movie Guide

1. Select TV + Movies from the main Media Center window.

2. Click movies guide.

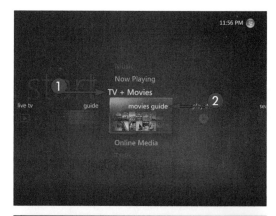

The movies guide window appears.

3. Click Fantasy.

Movies in the fantasy genre are shown.

④ Click a movie.

The Movie Details window appears.

● Click here for additional information about the movie.

● Click here to set Media Center to record the movie.

● Click here to see when it is showing next.

How can I find all the movies showing on a particular day?

▼ Display the Movie Guide and click the Start Date button. This organizes the movies by when the movie is scheduled to show. The day and date appear vertically on the Movie Guide next to images of the DVD box that represents the movie. If a movie is showing on more than one station at the same time, the movie appears that number of times so you can see that it is showing on multiple stations (for example, some areas can get multiple Fox Network stations that air the same program).

I do not need images showing. Can I turn that option off?

▼ Yes, display the Movie Guide and right-click a movie. Click View List. This removes the image for each movie and displays just its name. When you right-click a movie like that, you also can set the option to display large images of the boxes, which makes them easier to read from across the room and lets you see movie details, set up Media Center to record the movie, and more. To turn images back on, right-click a movie name and select View Small or View Large.

Update Media Center Content

Much of what Media Center does is behind the scenes — you do not see it happening, but it takes place anyway. For example, when you display the Movie Guide, you do not tell Media Center to download the information about each movie, its play time, and images of the DVD covers. Media Center does all this without your involvement, usually when you initially start Windows Vista.

You can, however, configure Media Center so that you can manually download content from the Internet. This is a good idea if you have a slower computer system or a busy Internet connection and you want to

control when Media Center downloads content. When you set up Media Center for manual downloads, do not be disappointed if information in your Program Guide and Movie Guide becomes outdated if you forget to manually download it for several days or weeks. To keep this information updated, set up a recurring task in a Windows Calendar that prompts you every few days to run the download. (See Chapter 14 for information on setting up recurring tasks.)

To configure manual downloads, you use the Automatic Download Options window on the Settings area.

Update Media Center Content

1 Select Tasks from the main Media Center window.

2 Click settings.

The settings window appears.

3 Click General.

The GENERAL settings window appears.

④ Click Automatic Download Options.

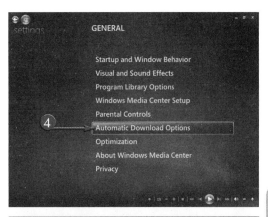

The AUTOMATIC DOWNLOAD OPTIONS window appears.

⑤ Click Manual Download (◯ changes to ◉).

⑥ Click Download Now when are ready to download.

⑦ Click Save.

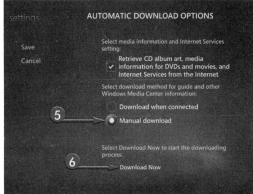

Can I keep automatic downloads on, but stop Media Center from downloading album covers?

▼ Yes, on the AUTOMATIC DOWNLOAD OPTIONS window, click to clear the option under Select media information and Internet Services settings (☑ changes to ☐). This configures Media Center so it does not download CD album art, information for music DVDs and movies (distributed on DVDs), and Internet Services. Click Save to retain your settings. If you decide later that you want the album art, information, and so forth downloaded, return to the AUTOMATIC DOWNLOAD OPTIONS window and select the option under Select media information and Internet Services setting (☐ changes to ☑). Click Save.

Is there a way to optimize Media Center?

▼ Yes, select Tasks on the main Media Center window and click Settings. The Settings window appears. On the Settings window, click General to display the General window. Click Optimization. The Windows Media Center Optimization window appears. Click Perform Optimization. In the Optimization Schedule area, type the hour and minute of the time you want the optimization to occur. For example, to optimize Media Center at 3:00 AM, type that in the Optimation Schedule area. During this time you will not be able to use Media Center or Media Center Extender. Click Save.

15 — Making Use of Windows Vista Fax and Scan Features

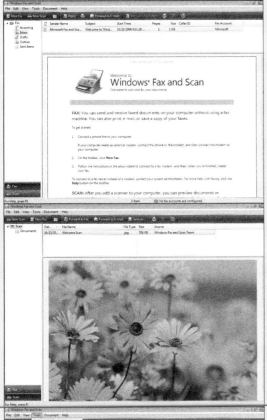

Configure Windows Mail

Microsoft Vista includes a new mail program called Windows Mail. It is an update to the previous e-mail program, called Outlook Express, which so many users got comfortable using to send, receive, and manage e-mail; manage addresses; and communicate with Internet newsgroups. Windows Mail is essentially the same program as Outlook Express, with a few minor changes and a small face-lift to its interface and dialog boxes.

Before you can start using Windows Mail, you need to configure it for your e-mail account. You will need an Internet account. You can use a dial-up or broadband connection for e-mail. Contact a local Internet service provider (ISP) to set up an account.

When setting up your Internet account, ask for an e-mail address. The e-mail account must support POP3 (Post Office Protocol) and SMTP (Simple Mail Transport Protocol). Your ISP will give you information on your e-mail account and e-mail account settings.

Your ISP will provide you with your username — which is usually the same as the first part of your e-mail address — and a password. You must use both when you log on to your ISP mail server to send and receive e-mail. You can set up Windows Mail to store these items so you can log on automatically each time you get and send mail.

Configure Windows Mail

① Click Start.

② Click All Programs.

Note: After you click All Programs, the name changes to Back.

③ Click Windows Mail.

The Windows Mail window appears.

Note: You may see the Internet Account window instead of the main Windows Mail window. If so, go to step 6.

④ Click Tools.

⑤ Click Accounts.

The Internet Accounts window appears.

6 Click Add.

The Select Account Type window appears.

7 Click E-Mail Account.

8 Click Next.

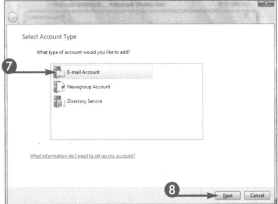

PART IV

Can I switch between e-mail accounts as I did with Outlook Express?

▼ No, the Switch Identies feature is not available with Windows Mail. The primary reason for the change is a concern for security. When users could switch between e-mail identities, Outlook Express did not require users to enter passwords for the identities. Passwords could be saved in the account settings. This could cause serious privacy concerns for users who did not want other users viewing their e-mail, deleting messages, or sending bogus messages in their name.

How can I set up different e-mail accounts for my children and spouse?

▼ You use Windows Vista's user accounts feature to create separate user accounts for each person using your computer. See Chapter 6 for more information on setting up user accounts. After you set up the accounts, each user needs to log on to his or her separate Windows Vista user account to launch Windows Mail and send and receive mail. If you are upgrading from Outlook Express and you had multiple identities created, Windows Mail displays a wizard to help you import your identities into separate user accounts.

continued

Configure Windows Mail *(Continued)*

When you configure Windows Mail with your e-mail account information, the first item you enter is a display name for the account. This name is the one that appears on the From field when you send a message to another person. For most accounts, it is best to use your complete name — first and last name. This way, your recipients will know who sent the message. If you just enter Bill in the Display Name field, your message From field says "Bill."

The next item you enter is your e-mail address. This comes from your ISP and is in the form of

bsmith@mail.com, where bsmith is your username and mail.com is your ISP's mail domain name. You also must include the @ symbol so your e-mail program knows the address is an e-mail address.

Windows Mail then asks you for your e-mail server information. Here you enter the POP3 account information. Some ISPs use a format like pop.mail.com for their incoming mail servers. Their outgoing mail servers may use the same name or a different one, such as smtp.mail.com. You must ask your ISP for this information.

Configure Windows Mail *(continued)*

The Your Name window appears.

⑨ Type a display name.

The example shown is Bill Smith.

⑩ Click Next.

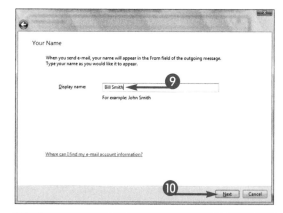

The Internet E-Mail Address window appears.

⑪ Type your e-mail address.

The example shown is bsmith@mail.com.

⑫ Click Next.

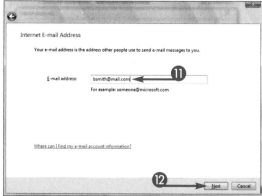

The Set up e-mail servers window appears.

⑬ Type your ISP's incoming mail server information.

⑭ Type your ISP's outgoing mail server information.

⑮ Click Outgoing server requires authentication (☐ changes to ☑).

Your e-mail provider may not require you to fill out authentication information. If not, skip to step 19.

⑯ Click Next.

The Internet Mail Logon window appears.

⑰ Type your e-mail username.

⑱ Type your e-mail password.

⑲ Click Next.

The Congratulations window appears.

● Click here if you do not want Windows Mail to download new messages after you click Next.

⑳ Click Finish.

Windows Mail connects to your e-mail account to confirm your account information.

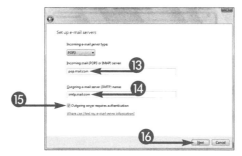

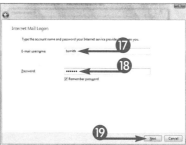

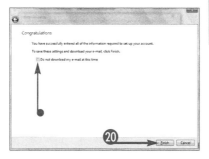

Can I use my Hotmail account in Windows Mail?

▼ No, Windows Mail does not support Web mail as Outlook Express did. You will need to acquire an e-mail account that supports the POP3 and SMTP protocols. Hotmail does provide a POP3 service now, but you must pay an annual fee to access it. If you have a Hotmail account, you can still use your Web browser — usually Internet Explorer — to access that account to send, receive, and manage e-mail.

What if I type in the wrong information. Can I go back and redo it?

▼ Yes, while you are using the Internet Account wizard, click the Back button to return to a previous window. The Back button appears at the top left of the wizard. Also, you can modify your account anytime after you create it by clicking Tools and clicking Accounts. Select your account and then click Properties. The properties dialog box for your account appears. You can read more about this in the "Manage Mail in Windows Mail" section.

Send Mail with Windows Mail

After you set up Windows Mail, you can start using it to send, receive, and manage e-mail messages. To send a message, you must know a recipient's e-mail address. You can find this out several ways. You can ask that person for his or her address. Make sure the address is in the format of susie@mail.com. Usually e-mail addresses are in all lowercase.

You can look for the recipient's address on the Internet using Internet Explorer. Many sites include the e-mail addresses their employees or points of contacts. Some sites, including 411.com, Bigfoot.com, Addresses.com,

and Yahoo! People Search (http://people.yahoo.com), are devoted to listing directories of e-mail addresses.

You can also look at the e-mail address of a user who sends you messages. The address appears in the From line next to the account name. Windows Mail includes the e-mail address of a sender in < >, such as <joe@email.com>.

Another way is to guess what the address is. For example, if a recipient works at a company named Acme, you might use the format name@acme.com to send a message. However, this does not always work, as the company may use a different format, such as firstinitial_lastname@acme.com or some such.

Send Mail with Windows Mail

① Start Windows Mail.

The Windows Mail main window appears.

② Click Create Mail.

The New Message window appears.

③ Click To.

You can type the recipient's e-mail address in the To line. Use commas to separate e-mail addresses if you send the message to more than one person.

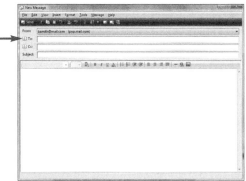

The Select Recipients dialog box appears.

④ Click a recipient.

⑤ Click To.

⑥ Repeat steps **4** to **5** to add more recipients.

⑦ Click OK.

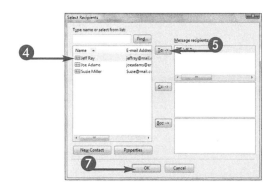

The new message window appears.

● Input e-mail addresses for carbon-copied recipients.

⑧ Type a subject.

⑨ Type your message.

● Use formatting tools to change text formats.

⑩ Click Send.

Windows Mail places the message in the Outbox and then sends the message to your recipient(s).

PART IV

What are carbon-copied recipients?

▼ The Cc line in the New Message window means that you want to send a message to someone, but they are not the primary intended recipients. Carbon-copied (Cc) recipients receive the same message as everyone else, can read it like a regular message, and even reply to it as normal. You may decide to Cc your manager, a team member, or other person on a message if you want that person to get the message but not necessarily feel the need to respond back. Also, if your main recipient sees that you have Cc'd someone, he or she may be more inclined to respond to your message in a professional manner.

Can I send a blind carbon copy?

▼ Yes. When you send a blind carbon copy, or Bcc, the Bcc recipients are the only ones who know you sent the message to them. This is handy if your manager or another adminstrator has asked you to copy all your outgoing messages to him or her to keep track of a project, personnel problem, or other matter. To see the Bcc line for a message, click View and then click All Headers. Fill out the Bcc line as you do the To and Cc lines.

Receive Mail with Windows Mail

Windows Vista enables you to receive your electronic mail in one place — the Windows Mail Inbox. The Inbox is a folder automatically set up to receive messages when you install Windows Vista. After you receive messages in your Inbox, you can move or copy messages to subfolders, copy messages to your hard disk as Enterprise Markup Language (EML) or text files, respond to or forward messages, or delete messages.

When you receive a message, you can read it by clicking the Subject line in the Message pane and reading it in the Preview pane. The Preview pane appears below the Message pane. You can move it to beside the Message pane as well.

As you receive messages, you may want to remove them from Windows Mail to keep your folders from becoming too cluttered. One way to do this is to save messages as files. Windows Mail file format is .eml. If you do not want to store e-mail messages in Windows Mail indefinitely, you can save the files as EML files to retrieve them later, archive them in a backup, or provide links to them in a Web page.

Receive Mail with Windows Mail

① Start Windows Mail.

The Windows Mail main window appears.

② Click the Send/Receive button.

● Windows Mail connects to your e-mail provider and downloads any new mail.

● New messages appear in the Inbox folder.

New messages appear in bold until you read them.

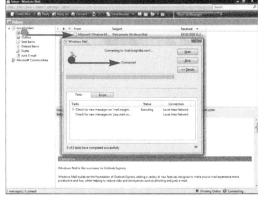

③ Click a message in the Inbox.

The message appears in the Preview pane.

④ Double-click a message.

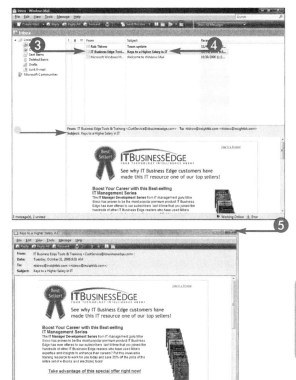

The message appears in a new window.

⑤ Click the Close box.

The message window closes, and the main Windows Mail window appears.

Can I move the Preview pane to the side?

▼ Yes, to do this choose the View menu and click Layout from the menu that appears. The Window Layout Properties dialog box appears. In the Preview pane area, click Beside messages (○ changes to ◉). Click OK. Now when you click a message in the Message pane, you can read it in the Preview pane on the right side of the window. This has the advantage of showing longer messages and having more of your Inbox, or other folder, contents showing in the Message pane.

Can I receive mail without sending it?

▼ Yes, to do this, open Windows Mail and then click Tools. From the menu that appears, click Send and Receive. Another menu appears. Click Receive All from that menu to instruct Windows Mail to receive, but not send, messages. This is handy if you are sending out messages from your Outbox that you do not want to deliver yet, such as an invitation to a meeting that you are not ready to announce yet.

Manage Mail with Windows Mail

O ver a short period, you will probably accumulate a great number of e-mail messages in your Windows Mail mailboxes. Although Windows Mail can handle about as many messages as you want to stuff in there, you may find it increasingly difficult to find the messages you need just because of the sheer volume of mail to weed through. When you find yourself spending a lot of time looking for a message, consider performing some simple management tasks.

One of the first management tasks you can do is to remove old messages from your Inbox. When you do

this, you delete them and Windows Mail stores them in the Deleted Items folder. This folder is similar to the Recycle Bin you can use in Windows Vista. If you delete a message and later find out that you really want it, open the Deleted Items folder, and drag it back to the Inbox or the folder in which you want to store it.

Another management task you can perform in Windows Mail is responding to messages. To do this, open a message, click Reply or Reply All, enter your message, and click Send.

Delete a Message

① Start Windows Mail.

The Windows Mail main window appears.

② Select a message to delete.

- Windows Mail displays the message in the preview mail.

③ Click the Delete button.

You also can press Delete on your keyboard.

- Windows Mail sends your message to the Deleted Items folder.

Respond to a Message

① Select the message to which you want to respond.

   ● Windows Mail displays the message in the preview mail.

② Click Reply.

   ● Click Reply All to reply to all recipients of the original message. Reply sends a reply only to the sender.

The message appears in a separate window.

   ● Windows Mail puts Re: in front of the subject to denote it is a reply.

   ● The original message has a greater than sign (>) or a solid black line to the left of it to separate it from your new message.

③ Type your message above the old message.

④ Click Send.

Windows Mail sends your message to the recipient(s).

Windows Mail cannot connect to my e-mail server and download mail. What should I do?

▼ First, make sure you followed the instructions for configuring your e-mail as specified in the "Configure Windows Mail" section. Second, click Tools and then Accounts. Select your mail account, click Properties, and check over your account properties to ensure they are correct. Check your Internet connection by opening Internet Explorer and navigating to a Web page. If it displays fine, then your Internet connection is okay. Third, if your Internet connection is fine, click File and then click Exit to close Windows Mail. Restart Windows Mail. Finally, if none of these methods work, contact your ISP and ask for assistance.

Can I send a reply message to someone other than the person who received the original message?

▼ Yes, this is called *forwarding,* and a lot of people do this when they receive messages they want to share with others. To do this, select the message you want to forward. Click Forward from the toolbar. Windows Mail displays the message with a blank To line. The message subject changes to show an Fw in front of the subject name. Fill out the To line with an address, add a message to the top of the message area if you want to add a comment or message, and click Send.

Manage Folders with Windows Mail

When you are managing the mail in your Windows Mail folders, you will probably want to set up new folders in which to store your mail. Windows Mail makes it easy to create, rename, and delete folders. You cannot change or delete the folders that Windows Mail sets up automatically — Inbox, Outbox, Sent Items, Deleted Items, Drafts, and Junk E-mail.

You create new folders by going to the folder in which you want to set up subfolders, such as the Inbox, and then clicking the File menu. Click New and then click Folder from the submenu that appears. The Create

Folder dialog box appears. Type a name for your folder. If you did not select the folder in which you want the new folder to reside earlier, you can still select it in the Create Folder dialog box. Click OK. Windows Mail creates the new folder.

You now can move or copy messages into the new folder to help organize messages. Windows Mail does not include an Undo command, so if you move a message to a folder you did not intend to, you have to open that folder and manually move the message back out of there.

Manage Folders with Windows Mail

Add a New Folder

① Start Windows Mail.

The Windows Mail window appears.

② Click File.

③ Click New.

④ Click Folder.

The Create Folder dialog box appears.

⑤ Click a folder.

Windows Mail creates the new folder inside the selected folder.

⑥ Type a name.

This is the name of your new folder.

⑦ Click OK.

● Windows Mail creates the folder and
displays it in the folder pane.

Move Messages

❶ Select a message.

Windows Mail highlights the message.

❷ Drag the message to a folder.

❸ Drop the message into the folder.

● Windows Mail moves the message
to the new folder.

**Can I automatically delete messages from
a specific sender?**

▼ Yes, you do this by setting up Message
Rules. To set up a message rule, click the
Tools menu, click Message Rules, and then
click Mail. On the New News Rule dialog
box, click the conditions for your rule —
such as messages from specific senders —
click the actions to perform — such as
Delete It — and then select the sender by
clicking the hot link in the Rule Desciption
area. Click OK and then click Apply Now.
Click Select All and then click Apply Now
in Apply Mail Rules Now. After the rule
runs, click OK, click Close, and then
click OK.

Can I rename a folder?

▼ Yes, to do this, open Windows Mail and
select the folder you want to rename.
Right-click it and click Rename. You also
can click the File menu, click Folder, and
then click Rename. The Rename Folder
dialog box appears. Type a new name for
the folder and click OK. Windows Mail
changes the name of the folder. You
cannot rename the Inbox, Outbox, Sent
Items, Deleted Items, Drafts, or Junk E-mail
folders. These are standard folders that
Windows Mail creates when Windows Vista
is installed.

Manage Contacts with Windows Contacts

One of the new features included with Windows Vista is the Windows Contacts tool. This tool lets you store your personal contacts in one area, the Contacts folder. The Windows Contacts tool is a folder and it includes an interface for adding contacts.

To see your contacts, open your Documents folder by clicking Start and then clicking Documents. A Windows Explorer window appears, with the Documents folder selected. Above that folder in Windows Explorer is the Contacts folder. Click it to see your contacts.

You can use contacts in the Windows Contacts folder to insert recipients' e-mail addresses when you create

new messages, respond to messages, or forward messages from Windows Mail. Windows Contacts also lets you create a new message while you are viewing a contact in the Windows Contacts folder. Click E-Mail on the Windows Contacts toolbar to open a new message with the selected contact's e-mail address in the To line.

If you have a new message window open in Windows Mail, click To to see the Select Recipients dialog box. The contacts listed in the Type Name or Select From List area are contacts you stored in your Windows Contacts folder.

Manage Contacts with Windows Contacts

Add a Contact

① Click Start.

② Click All Programs.

Note: After you click All Programs, the name changes to Back.

③ Click Windows Contacts.

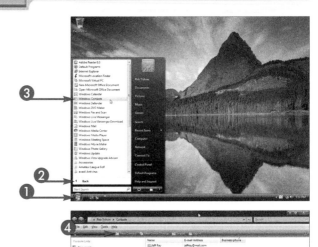

The Windows Contacts window appears.

④ Click New Contact.

The Contacts Properties dialog box appears.

⑤ Click in the fields and type to fill in the information under the Name and E-mail tab.

● The minimum fields you should fill out include First, Last, and E-mail.

⑥ Click Add to add the e-mail address.

⑦ Click OK.

Windows Contacts adds the contact to your Windows Contacts folder.

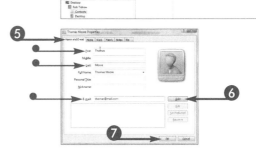

Delete a Contact

① Repeat steps **1** to **3** to open Windows Contacts.

② Select a contact to delete.

③ Click Delete.

The Delete File dialog box appears.

④ Click Yes.

Windows Contacts deletes the contact.

Can I share my contacts?

▼ Yes, to do this open Windows Contacts and select the contacts you want to share. Click Export on the Windows Contacts toolbar. The Export Windows Contacts window appears. Click vCards and then click Export. Select a folder to store the exported contacts. Click OK. Windows Contacts exports the contacts to a file in the folder you selected. Click OK when it finishes. Click Close. Next, send the export file to the other person. Instruct this person to copy the file to her computer, click Import in Windows Contacts, and select the vCard file option from the Import To Windows Contacts window. Select the vCard file, click Open, and then click OK. Click the Close button to finish.

Can I use my old Address Book information?

▼ Yes, as long as you import the addresses into Windows Vista's new contact manager, Windows Contacts. With Windows Contacts, you can store, edit, add to, and delete from your contacts in an easy-to-use program. Windows Contacts is essentially a subfolder in your Documents folder from which you can view your contacts without necessarily opening a separate program to do so — although you can if you want. You simply open a Windows Explorer window and drill-down to the Documents\Contacts folder. It is that easy.

Use the Windows Mail Junk E-Mail Filter

Many times, you receive mail that you do not want, such as sales messages, marketing mail, and so on. This is called *junk mail,* and it is synonymous to the junk mail you receive every day in your regular postal mail. Windows Mail includes a tool that enables it to block unsolicited mail from your Inbox and send it to the Junk E-mail folder. If you want, you can have the junk e-mail filter delete these messages as soon as they arrive, but you may want to review the messages first just to be sure that Windows Mail is not throwing out legitimate mail.

By default, Windows Mail uses the lowest junk e-mail filter on messages you receive. The Low setting catches the most obvious mail that is considered junk. However, you can set the filter to use the High setting so that Windows Mail catches more junk mail, but also moves legitimate mail over to the Junk E-mail folder as well.

Another option is to have Windows Mail set up to send only Safe Sender messages to your Inbox. Everything else is moved to the Junk E-mail folder. The Safe Sender list includes the e-mail addresses of people you specify as safe to send you messages.

Use The Windows Mail Junk E-Mail Filter

① Start Windows Mail.

The Windows Mail main window appears.

② Click Tools.

③ Click Junk E-mail Options.

The Junk E-mail Options dialog box appears.

④ Click the Options tab.

The Options dialog box appears.

⑤ Click Safe List Only (○ changes to ◉).

⑥ Click the Safe Senders tab.

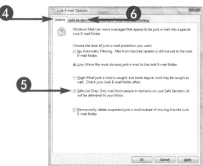

The Safe Senders dialog box appears.

7 Click Add.

The Add address or domain dialog box appears.

8 Type an e-mail address or domain.

Enter e-mail addresses for messages from senders you determine are okay for delivery to your Inbox.

Enter domains, such as microsoft.com, if you approve of all senders from that domain name.

9 Click OK.

The Safe Senders dialog box appears.

10 Click OK when you are done.

Can I send suspected phishing messages to my Junk E-mail folder?

▼ Yes, to do so click the Tools menu and then click Junk E-mail Options. The Junk E-mail Options dialog box appears. Click the Phishing tab. Click Move phishing E-Mail to the Junk Mail folder option. Click OK. Now Windows Mail sends messages that have hyperlinks in them that are deemed to be potential phishing sites. You can review the Junk E-mail folder and delete those messages, or keep them if you know the hyperlink is not a phishing site, such as if it is your own bank's Web site address.

Do I have to use the junk e-mail filter?

▼ No, you can disable it. Do so by clicking the Tools menu and then clicking Junk E-mail Options. Click the Options tab of the Junk E-mail Options dialog box. Click the No Automatic Filtering option. Click OK. Now Windows Mail does not examine the incoming messages for possible unsolicited messages. The Junk E-mail folder still resides in your folder list, and any messages that you had there remain as well.

Use Windows Mail to Block Senders

Another way to block unsolicited or unwanted e-mail coming into your Inbox is to use the Blocked Senders list. You customize this list by adding the addresses of users you deem are sending you junk e-mail messages. All messages from these senders are automatically placed in the Junk E-mail folder.

With the Blocked Senders feature, you can specify individual e-mail messages, such as mail@junk.com. Windows Mail sends all messages from that user to the Junk E-mail folder as soon as you download the message.

You also can specify complete domains from which you do not want to receive messages in your Inbox. For example, instead of entering 20 individual e-mail messages for the Junk.Com company, enter just the domain name, junk.com. This tells Windows Mail you do not want any mail from any senders with the junk.com address delivered to your Inbox. Of course, if there is at least one user who resides at junk.com from whom you want to receive mail, perhaps mom@junk.com, you have to specify every other e-mail address individually, you cannot specify "block everyone but my mom."

Use Windows Mail to Block Senders

① Start Windows Mail.

The Windows Mail window appears.

② Click Tools.

③ Click Junk E-mail Options.

The Junk E-mail Options dialog box appears.

④ Click the Blocked Senders tab.

The Blocked Senders dialog box appears.

5 Click Add.

The Add address or domain dialog box appears.

6 Type an address or domain.

Enter e-mail addresses for messages from senders you determine should be blocked.

Enter domains, such as junk.com, if you disapprove of all senders from that domain name.

7 Click OK.

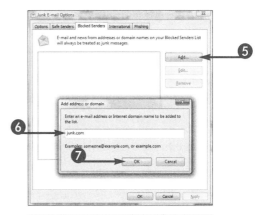

The blocked e-mail address or domain name appears in the list.

8 Repeat steps **5** to **7** to add more blocked addresses or domains.

9 Click OK when you are done.

Can I take someone off the Blocked Senders list?

▼ Yes, to do this click Tools and then click Junk E-mail Options. The Junk E-mail Options dialog box appears. Click the Blocked Senders tab. Your list of blocked senders appears. Select the address or domain name you want to remove and click Remove. Windows Mail removes the blocked sender. Click OK to close the dialog box. Windows Mail will now start sending messages from the previously blocked sender to your Inbox.

I get messages in different languages. How can I block them?

▼ Use the International tab on the Junk E-mail Options dialog box. Display that dialog box and click the International tab. Click Blocked Top-Level Domain List to display the Blocked Top-Level Domain List dialog box. Select the countries or regions you want to block. For instance, to block messages from Armenia, click AM. Click OK and then click OK on the International tab. Messages sent from addresses ending in AM, or the country you specify, will be moved to the Junk E-mail folder upon arrival.

Configure Newsgroup Accounts with Windows Mail

Although they are not as popular as they once were, Usenet newsgroups are still a widely used way for users to communicate over the Internet. *Usenet newsgroups* are electronic bulletin boards that enable users to post messages for others to read and respond to. You can use Windows Mail to participate in newsgroup activities.

The Internet offers thousands of newsgroups. Newsgroups are categorized into areas of interest or subjects. They are available for users who want to discuss different tastes in music, sports, hobbies, computer topics, and similar discussions.

To participate in newsgroups, users must have access to them from their Internet service provider (ISP).

Some larger ISPs no longer offer support for newsgroups, but many still enable users to access them. In addition, some companies provide community newsgroups for technical support and other communications. For example, you can subscribe to the Microsoft Communities newsgroups. When you set up Windows Mail for newsgroups, you instruct it to connect to a news server (information provided by your ISP), download a list of the newsgroups available, and then subscribe to a given newsgroup. After you subscribe to a newsgroup, you can download message headers that are similar to e-mail message headers. You then can download and read entire messages by downloading the body of the message.

Configure Newsgroup Accounts with Windows Mail

① Start Windows Mail.

The Windows Mail window appears.

② Click Tools.

③ Click Accounts.

The Internet Accounts window appears.

④ Click Add.

The Select Account Type window appears.

5 Click Newsgroup Account.

6 Click Next to continue.

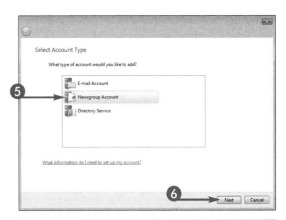

The Your Name window appears.

7 Type your name or a name that you want to use for others to know who is posting a message.

Note: *You do not have to use your real name here. In fact, many users, and especially children, do not.*

8 Click Next to continue.

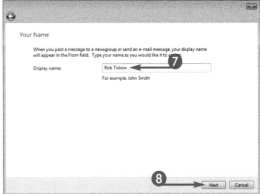

My ISP does not offer newsgroups. How can I get them?

▼ Some ISPs do not have access to newsgroups through their own services. If this is the case for your ISP, you can find news servers on the Internet by searching for them on the Web at Yahoo! or Google. When you locate a server, you can use that information to set up Windows Mail to access those servers and download messages. Some of these news servers are free, while others charge a fee to access them.

Some newsgroup articles have attachments I cannot open. Can you help?

▼ Sometimes messages include binary files — such as picture files — that Windows Mail can display as part of the message body. If Windows Mail cannot display the binary file as part of the body, you can save the file to your computer and then display the file in another program. For example, some messages include sound files that Windows Mail cannot play back. To use these files on your computer, download the message and save the attachment to your computer, such as to the Music folder. Open the Music folder and double-click the file to play it back in Windows Media Player.

PART IV

continued

Configure Newsgroup Accounts with Windows Mail *(Continued)*

When you use Windows Mail for accessing newsgroups, you can use the synchronize tool to have Windows Mail automatically download content from selected newsgroups.

You control this feature by clicking Tools and then clicking Synchronize All or Synchronize Newsgroup when viewing your subscription to newsgroups. Click Get Next 300 Headers from the Tool menu to download the next 300 headers, which are the subjects of the newsgroup postings. You download the headers first; then if, after you have read the header, you want to download the entire message, you can do so by double-clicking the header information. This

saves you from downloading hundreds or thousands of postings that you may not want to download.

After you read a message, you can post a reply to the message by clicking Reply Group on the Windows Mail toolbar. This opens a reply window that displays the original message. You can type your response at the top of the window and then click Send. Your reply is sent to the newsgroup, where other users reading the newsgroup message can now read and respond to your message. You can send a reply just to the original sender by clicking the Reply button on the Windows Mail toolbar. The reply will go to that sender's e-mail address and not to the newsgroup.

Configure Newsgroup Accounts with Windows Mail *(continued)*

The Internet News E-mail Address window appears.

9 Type your e-mail address.

The e-mail address is used so other participants who read messages posted by you can send you e-mail messages directly.

10 Click Next to continue.

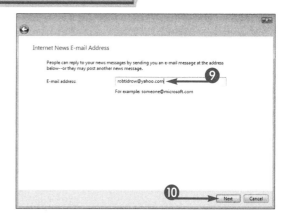

The Internet News Server Name window appears.

11 Type the news server name.

12 Click Next to continue.

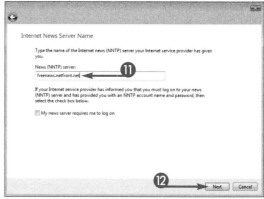

Windows Mail checks to ensure you can connect to the newsgroup. The Congratulations screen appears.

⓭ Click Finish.

● Windows Mail adds the news server account to the News section of the Internet Accounts window.

⓮ Click Close to continue.

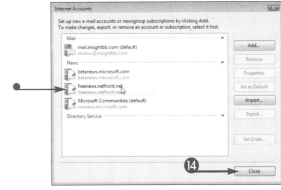

I do not use Windows Mail for e-mail or newsgroups. Can I remove it from my computer?

▼ Windows Mail is an integral part of Windows Vista and so you cannot remove it without altering the Windows subsystem. You can, however, remove access to Windows Mail from the Windows Start menu. To do this, click Start and click All Programs. Right-click the Windows Mail icon and click Delete. When you are prompted if you are sure you want to delete it, click Yes. You now do not see an icon for it on your Start menu.

Are there any newsgroups that allow me to participate without using Windows Mail?

▼ Yes, you can use Internet Explorer to access some newsgroups. In fact, Microsoft has hundreds of newsgroups that are easily accessible using Internet Explorer. To find these groups, start Internet Explorer and visit www.microsoft.com/communities/ newsgroups/default.mspx. Here you can choose from several categories — such as Application Center, Office, and Windows Storage Center — and find specific newsgroups relating to these categories. As an example, click the Windows Vista link to see newsgroups associated with Windows Vista and Windows Vista technologies.

continued

Configure Newsgroup Accounts with Windows Mail *(Continued)*

Some news servers require you to have a username and password to access them. This is a common practice for companies with employee newsgroups that they make available on the Internet. With these types of news servers, employees can connect to the news servers from any location as long as they have Internet access, and can then read and respond to newsgroup postings.

The username and password are maintained by the network administrator and may be the same credentials you use to log on to your e-mail or domain. ISPs that allow newsgroup access also will require users to input usernames and passwords to access the news servers. This keeps unauthorized users from connecting to that news server, or at least those who do not have an Internet account with the ISP.

You can add username and password information to your news server as you configure the newsgroup account. You also can enter your user credentials each time you start a newsgroup session and download header information from your groups. When you click a newsgroup, Windows Vista displays the Windows Vista Credentials window into which you enter your username and password to access that news server.

Configure Newsgroup Accounts with Windows Mail *(continued)*

The Windows Mail dialog box appears, asking if you want to download newsgroups from the news server.

 Click Yes.

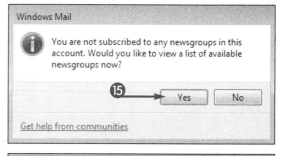

Windows Mail connects to the news server and downloads a list of newsgroups available from the news server. This list can be very large.

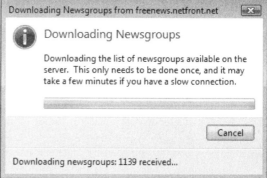

The Newsgroup Subscriptions window appears after the newsgroups are downloaded.

⑯ Double-click the newsgroups to which you want to subscribe.

⑰ Click OK.

● The Windows Mail window appears with the newsgroups listed.

I need to set up a username and password with my news server, but I do not want to enter it each time. Can I change my account configuration?

▼ Yes, in Windows Mail click Tools and then click Accounts. The Internet Accounts dialog box appears. Click the newsgroup account to modify and click the Properties button. The Properties dialog box appears. Click the Server tab and click This server requires me to log on. Type your username in the Account name box and type your password in the Password box. Click Remember password. Click OK to save your settings.

Can I download more than 300 headers at a time?

▼ Yes, 300 is the default setting that Windows Mail uses when you install Windows Vista. You can modify this number to be higher or lower depending on your needs. To change this value, click the Tools menu and then click Options. The Options dialog box appears. Click the Read tab and change the value in the Get 300 headers at a time option. You can type a new number or use the up and down arrows on the option to change the value. Click OK to save your settings.

Read Newsgroup Postings with Windows Mail

After you configure a newsgroup account in Windows Mail, you can subscribe to newsgroups. Subscriptions to newsgroups are free. When you subscribe to a newsgroup, you become a member of that group, which enables you to read messages, called *postings,* to the group, reply to postings, and create your own postings.

Depending on the newsgroups you subscribe to and the activity in those groups, there may be dozens or even thousands of postings available. Usually there is a frequently asked questions (FAQ) posting that enables you to learn about the newsgroup before you start posting your own comments and queries.

For example, some newsgroups are designed for expert-level discussions of a topic, such as music or gardening. These groups include basic-level information in the FAQ, and members are expected to understand this information before posting questions that are already covered in the FAQ.

Newsgroups offer an area where diverse opinions and thoughts, as well as expert commentary, can be expressed. With this in mind, some postings may not be to your liking, because of terse or vulgar language, for example. If a newsgroup you subscribe to is not one you particularly care for, unsubscribe from it.

Read Newsgroup Postings with Windows Mail

① Start Windows Mail.

The Windows Mail window appears.

② Click the newsgroup you want to participant in.

Windows Mail downloads a list of newsgroup headers.

③ Click the header of a posting you want to read.

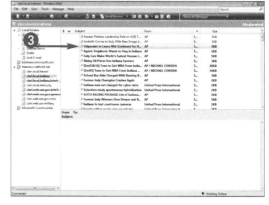

Windows Mail downloads the posting.

④ Click Reply Group to reply to a posting.

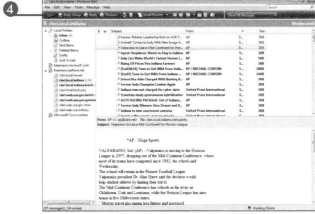

A reply window appears.

⑤ Type your posting reply.

⑥ Click Send.

Windows Mail posts your reply to the newsgroup.

Can I start my own newsgroup?

▼ Yes, but you must have a news server (NNTP) on which to place the newsgroup. You then can allow the newsgroup to be available to any other news server that wants to carry it. Sometimes you can find free news servers on which to create newsgroups, or can pay a nominal fee for the server to host your group. Creating and maintaining a newsgroup that provides a nice forum for people to interact in takes a lot of time, so be forewarned if you decide to undertake this task.

Are newsgroups like Weblogs?

▼ No, Weblogs provide an online forum for people to post messages, thoughts, questions, and other information related to a subject or query. They use Web pages to enable users to transmit information. Newsgroups, on the other hand, use the NNTP Internet protocol to enable users to create and post messages to groups. The format of newsgroup messages is similar to the format of basic e-mail messages that users send to each other using e-mail programs, such as Windows Mail. Learn more about Weblogs at http://en.wikipedia. org/wiki/Blog.

Set Up Appointments in Windows Calendar

Windows Calendar is a new program that comes with Windows Vista. It enables you to keep track of your daily activities, set up meetings, and perform other scheduling functions. With Windows Calendar, you can display your appointments and tasks in different views. For example, if you prefer to see just a day's worth of appointments, you can use the Day view. If you want to see an entire week's schedule, use the Week view. The Work Week view shows your schedule by your workweek — by default this is set to Monday through Friday. Finally, to see an entire month, use the Month view.

Windows Calendar lets you set up appointments for any time of day or on any day of the week. You also can create recurring appointments, which are regularly scheduled appointments that occur every day, week, bi-weekly, monthly, or another schedule. For example, you may have a staff meeting that occurs at 9 a.m. each day. With Windows Calendar, you can set up the appointment once, and then configure it as a recurring appointment that occurs every day.

Other actions you can perform with Windows Calendar include setting up tasks, setting alarm reminders for scheduled items, sharing your calendar, and importing other users' calendars.

Set Up Appointments in Windows Calendar

1 Click Start.

2 Click All Programs.

Note: After you click All Programs, the name changes to Back.

3 Click Windows Calendar.

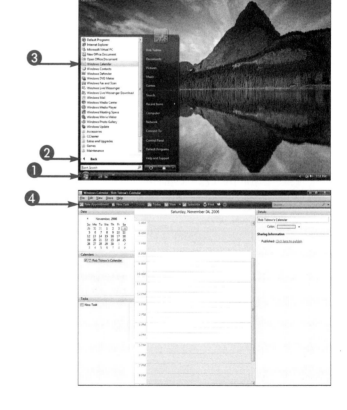

The Windows Calendar window appears.

4 Click New Appointment.

A New Appointment item is added to the current time.

● The Details pane appears.

⑤ Type a name for the appointment.

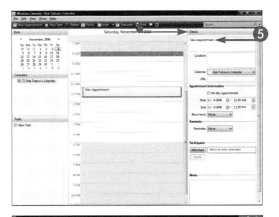

● The example uses Lunch with Manager.

⑥ Press Enter.

● The new appointment appears in the Windows Calendar window.

Can I remove an appointment from Windows Calendar?

▼ Yes, to do this locate the appointment in the calendar and click Delete on the toolbar. Be sure you really want to delete the appointment, because Windows Contacts does not include an Undo command. Once you have removed an appointment, task, or event, it is gone. If the appointment is a recurring one, Windows Calendar prompts if you want to remove the entire recurring series, or just the one occurrence. Click Delete the series or Delete this occurrence, depending on which you would like to delete.

Can I move an appointment?

▼ Yes, you can move an appointment from one time slot to another by simply dragging the appointment from one time slot and dropping it in another. When you view Windows Calendar in Day view, you can move appointments within the same day; when you view it in Work Week or Week view, you can drag and drop appointments in the same week; and when you view it in Month view, you can drag and drop appointments from one day to another in the Month view.

Configure Windows Calendar

Windows Calendar provides several configuration options for changing the way it works, appears, and reminds you of your appointments. To configure Windows Calendar, you use the Options dialog box from the File menu. The Options dialog box is divided into three main areas: Calendar, Appointments, and Tasks.

In the Calendar area, you can change the start day of the week and start day of the workweek. Many users prefer starting the calendar week on Sunday, but the workweek on Monday. However, you can change this to any combination. What you use depends on your personal preferences.

Other options include the start and end times of your day. By default, Windows Calendar uses 8 a.m. to 5 p.m., but you can modify this to suit your workday. For example, some people set up early-morning breakfast meetings at 7 a.m. and end their days at 6 p.m. Others may have "swing shift" workdays, which start at 3 p.m. and end at 11 p.m.

Appointment options include setting the default length for one-hour appointments and specifying when reminders should display for an appointment. Task options include setting how many days completed tasks remain on the Tasks lists, reminder times, and the overdue tasks color.

Configure Windows Calendar

Change Work Day and Times

① Start Windows Calendar.

The Windows Calendar window appears.

② Click File.

③ Click Options.

The Options dialog box appears.

④ Click the Start of workweek down arrow.

A list of days appears.

5 Click a day.

6 Click the Day start down arrow and click a time for the workday to begin.

7 Click the Day end down arrow and click a time for the workday to end.

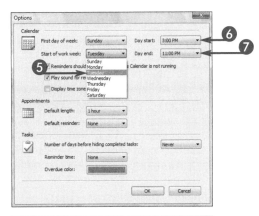

Change the Overdue Task Color

1 Click the Overdue color drop-down list.

The Color dialog box appears.

2 Click a color.

3 Click OK.

The Overdue color drop-down list shows the new color.

4 Click OK.

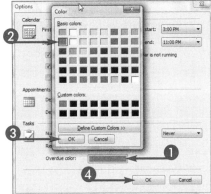

When I have completed a task, Windows Calendar keeps it showing. Can I change this?

▼ Yes, to do this open the Options dialog box. In the Tasks area, click the Number of days before hiding completed tasks drop-down list. A list appears. You can click Never, 1 Day, 2 Days, 4 Days, 1 Week, or 2 Weeks. Click the option you want and then click OK. If you select 2 Days, for example, Windows Calendar shows your completed tasks for two days after you complete them and then removes the tasks from the calendar.

Can I change when reminders display for an appointment?

▼ Yes, to do this, open the Options dialog box and click the Default reminder drop-down list. A list of times ranging from None, which is the default and means no reminder displays, to 2 Weeks. By the way, 0 is not the same as None. Zero (0) means that the reminder goes off at the time the appointment is to start. A good setting for most in-house meetings is 15 minutes. Use a longer time, 30 minutes or one hour, if the appointment requires you to travel a short distance. Click OK after you select the reminder time.

Change Calendar Appointment Settings

You can modify each appointment you create, changing start and end times, and reminder times if they differ from the default of one hour. Windows Calendar lets you modify other appointment settings. With Windows Calendar appointments, you also can specify if the appointment is recurring.

A recurring appointment is one that occurs at the same time every day, week, month, or year. For example, a weekly staff meeting may be held every Tuesday morning from 9 a.m. to 11 a.m. Instead of

setting up this meeting manually for every Tuesday on the calendar, you can click Recurrence drop-down list and specify Weekly. Windows Calendar uses a circular double-arrow icon on the appointment item in your calendar to specify the item is recurring.

You also can specify attendees for an appointment. Windows Calendar lets you use the Windows Contacts tool to select names that you want to add to your appointment and then invite them via e-mail. For more information, see the "Send E-Mail Invitations" section.

Change Calendar Appointment Settings

① Start Windows Calendar.

The Windows Calendar window appears.

② Click to display a day that has an appointment.

③ Click an appointment.

The Details pane shows details about the selected appointment.

④ Click inside the Location box and type a location.

Press Enter to insert additional lines.

⑤ Click the Recurrence down arrow and select the recurrence of the appointment.

⑥ Click Attendees.

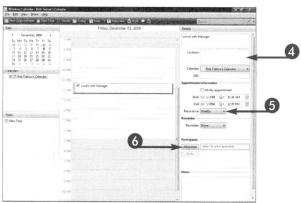

The Windows Calendar Contacts window appears.

7 Click a name.

8 Click To.

The name is added to the Attendees list.

9 Repeat steps **7** and **8** for each contact you want to invite.

10 Click OK when you have finished.

● Windows Calendar lists the names of the attendees in the Participants area.

● This icon denotes that attendees are to be invited to the appointment.

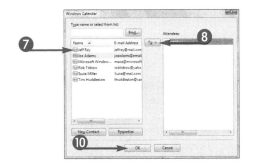

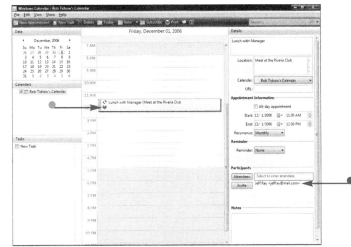

I want reminders to pop up even when Windows Calendar is not running. Can I do this?

▼ By default, Windows Calendar can display reminders even if it is not running. You can set this option if you think it has been disabled by you or someone else in the past. Click the File menu and then click Options. The Options dialog box appears. Click Reminders should show when Windows Calendar is not running (☐ changes to ☑). Click OK. When a reminder goes off, Windows Calendar opens, the Reminder dialog box displays, and a sound plays. Click Dismiss to close the Reminder dialog box. Windows Calendar remains open.

Can I change the color of the calendar items?

▼ Yes, to do this click anywhere on a calendar that is not an appointment or task. The Details pane shows only the Color and Sharing Information items. Click the Color drop-down list and select a color for the appointments and tasks in Windows Calendar. To see additional colors, click More colors. That displays the Color dialog box, from which you can choose a color or define a custom color. Click OK when you are finished.

Set Advanced Recurring Appointment Times

Windows Calendar enables you to set advanced recurring appointment times. For example, say you have a project team meeting that you want to recur every Wednesday for six weeks, because you have been given six weeks to finish the project.

You can use the Advanced option on the Recurrence drop-down list in the Details pane to specify the series specifics for the recurring appointment. To repeat the meeting every week, you would specify one week for the Repeat every option. Next, you would want to set

the number of times to repeat the appointment to six. Finally, you would set Wednesday as the day on which to repeat the appointment. When you click OK to save your settings, Windows Calendar sets up the recurring meeting every Wednesday for six weeks.

You can also use the Advanced options settings for recurring appointments that need to meet every other week from now until a set date, such as January 1, 2008. You can even set up recurring appointments that occur once on the first day of the month, or every year on the same date.

Set Advanced Recurring Appointment Times

1 Start Windows Calendar.

The Windows Calendar main window appears.

2 Create a new appointment.

3 Click Recurrence.

A drop-down list appears.

4 Click Advanced.

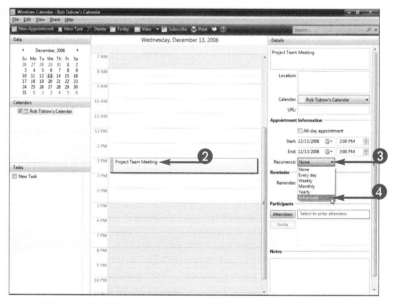

The Recurrence dialog box appears.

5 Type **1** in the Repeat every box.

6 Click the frequency of time down arrow.

A list appears.

7 Click Weeks.

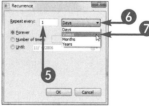

A set of day buttons appears in the dialog box.

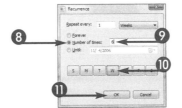

8 Click Number of times (○ changes to ◉).

9 Type **6** to indicate the frequency.

10 Click W for Wednesday.

11 Click OK.

● Windows Calendar sets up the recurring meeting, and the Calendar window appears.

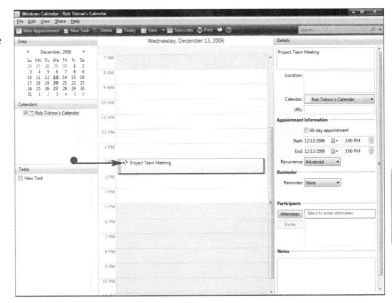

Can I set up a recurring meeting for every second Monday of each month?

▼ Yes, to do this create an appointment on the first Monday you want the meetings to begin, such as the second Monday in January. Click Recurrence and click Advanced. In the Recurrence dialog box, click Months from the Repeat every drop-down list. At the bottom of the dialog box, click 2nd Monday of the month. The options you see here change depending on the day of the month on which your original appointment is created. Click OK when you have finished.

I set up a recurring meeting for every week, but one week I have to cancel it. How can I do that?

▼ To cancel a specific meeting in a recurring appointment series, display the meeting you want to cancel. You cannot cancel the first meeting in the series, by the way. Right-click the meeting and click Delete. A Windows Calendar dialog box appears. Click Delete this occurrence. Important: Make sure you do not click the Delete the series button. If you do, you will delete the entire recurring meeting schedule. Windows Calendar deletes the individual meeting but retains all the other meetings in the recurrence series.

Send E-Mail Invitations

The Participants area of the Details pane in Windows Calendar enables you to send out appointment invitations to other people. Invitations are sent using e-mail.

To use the invitation feature, make sure you have Windows Mail configured to send and receive e-mail messages. See Chapter 17 for more information. You will need to have an e-mail account configured, store contacts in the Windows Contacts list that includes e-mail addresses, and have a connection to the Internet or a local area network.

When you invite someone to a meeting, Windows Calendar creates an iCalendar (ICS) file. These types of files are downloadable calendar files that many

calendar programs can use, including Windows Mail and Microsoft Office Outlook 2007. When someone receives an invitation from you, he opens it and Windows Calendar automatically sets up the appointment in his calendar. Another feature of iCalendar files is that if you need to change the appointment details, such as time or date, you can send an update file for that appointment to your attendees. The iCalendar can then modify the appointment setting on their calendars as well.

Send E-Mail Invitations

① Start Windows Calendar.

The main Windows Calendar window appears.

② Create a new appointment.

③ Click Attendees.

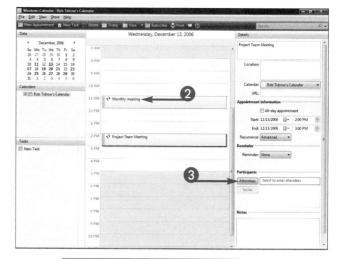

Windows Calendar dialog box.

④ Click a name.

⑤ Click To.

● The name appears in the Attendees list.

⑥ Click OK when you have finished.

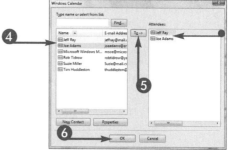

The Windows Calendar window appears with the names in the Invite box.

7 Click Invite.

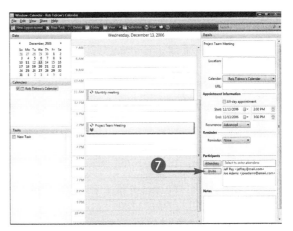

The INVITE: message window appears.

● Invited members appear here.

● The ICS file is attached.

○ You can add a message here.

8 Click Send.

The invitation is sent to the invitees.

When I click Invite, a different mail window appears. Why does this happen?

▼ This happens because your system is set up with a different e-mail program than Windows Mail as its default ICS mail program. To change this, click Start and then click Default Programs. Click Set your default programs. The Set your default programs window appears. Click Windows Calendar, click Set this program as default, and then click Choose defaults for this program. Click Select All to include the .ics and WEBCAL choices. Click Save. Next click Windows Mail, click Set this program as default, and then click Choose defaults for this program. Click Select All. Click Save and then click OK.

I do not have my Windows Contacts set up yet. Can I still enter e-mail addresses?

▼ Yes, to do this click inside the box to the right of Attendees on the Details pane. Type the full e-mail address of your recipient, such as bsmith@mail.com. Press Enter. Windows Calendar adds the new address to the box next to the Invite button. Add as many e-mail addresses to this box as you need. As you will see, once you add several names to this book, you may be inclined to set up Windows Contacts, enter those names there once, and then reuse them in your Windows Calendar and Windows Mail programs.

Receive E-Mail Invitations

Not only can you send out e-mail invitations for appointments, but you can also receive them and integrate them into your Windows Calendar. To do this, make sure your Windows Mail account is working and that someone has sent you an e-mail message that includes an invitation with an ICS file attached to it. You can see the name of the file in the Attach box when you open the e-mail message in Windows Mail.

After you receive an ICS file, you open it in Windows Mail to import it into your Windows Calendar program. You are presented with an Import dialog

box that gives you two choices. You can import the appointment invitation to a new calendar. This choice creates a new calendar and imports the appointment details to that calendar. Alternatively, you can import the appointment invitation into your existing calendar. This latter option integrates the appointment information with appointments already set up on your calendar. Depending on how you manage your calendars, you may want to have all your invitations appear on a separate calendar so you can track them more easily. Or, you may prefer to have all your appointments, including ones to which you are invited, appear on one calendar.

Receive E-Mail Invitations

① Start Windows Mail.

The Windows Mail main window appears.

② Double-click to open the e-mail invitation.

The INVITE: message window appears.

③ Double-click the ICS file attachment.

The Mail Attachment window appears.

④ Click Open.

The Import window appears.

⑤ Click the Destination down arrow.

⑥ Select your calendar from the Destination list.

⑦ Click Import.

- Windows Calendar imports the calendar item.

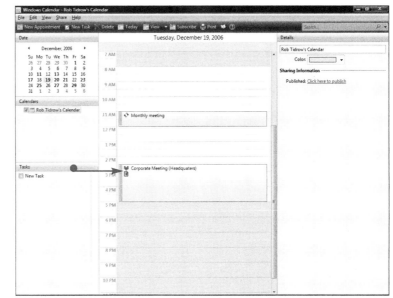

My calendar is too busy. Can I set up a separate calendar for these invitations?

▼ Yes. For example, when you import an iCalendar item, you can do it as part of the import process. Use the preceding steps up to step **6**. Instead of clicking your calendar from the Destination list, click Create new calendar. Click Import. The new calendar appears with the imported meeting in a different color than your normal calendar items. Also a second calendar appears on the Calendars pane on the left side of the Windows Calendar window. Your primary calendar includes all appointments, but your new calendar includes only the imported appointment.

When I import the iCalendar file, Windows Calendar does not appear. Another program does. What causes this?

▼ This is a similar problem to the one covered in the first Tip in the section called "Send E-mail Invitations," earlier in this chapter. You need to ensure that Windows Calendar is set up as the default calendar program for iCalendar (.ics) files. Go through the steps detailed in the Tip to see how this is done. After you do this, re-import the iCalendar file from Windows Mail. Windows Calendar should appear when you open the iCalendar file.

PART IV

Create Tasks

Windows Calendar enables you to create tasks, specify them as completed when you finish them, and set reminders to help you remember when they are due. You may have different ways of tracking and managing your to-do lists. Some use little notes or reminders of things that have to be done. Some keep a separate notebook to enter daily tasks. Windows Calendar can make managing and tracking these to-do items a little easier. Windows Calendar calls them *tasks,* and they appear on the left side of the main Windows Calendar window.

When you create tasks, Windows Calendar includes different options in the Details pane than when you create an appointment. For instance, with tasks you can check the Completed box when you have completed a task so you know you have finished the job. You also can set High, Medium, Low, or None depending on the priority for completing this task.

For tasks that need to be completed by a specific date, you specify when the task needs to be completed. Windows Calendar provides a way to set reminders when a task is due. Finally, you can specify when you want to start this task, or input the actual date that it was started if that date is in the past.

Create Tasks

1 Start Windows Calendar.

The Windows Calendar main window appears.

2 Click New Task.

A new task box appears.

3 Type **Pay Utilities**.

4 Press Enter.

The new task name appears.

The new task's Detail pane appears.

5 Click the Priority down arrow and select Medium.

6 Click the Due date check box (☐ changes to ☑).

7 Click the Due date down arrow and select a date in the future.

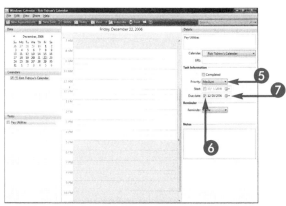

⑧ Click the Reminder down arrow.

⑨ Click On date.

A reminder date appears.

⑩ Enter a new reminder date one day earlier.

⑪ Click in the Notes box and type your task.

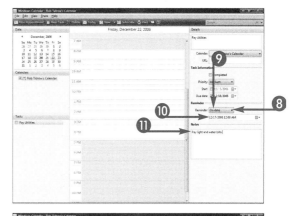

⑫ Click anywhere outside the Details pane.

Windows Calendar saves your new task.

Can I turn off the Tasks area?

▼ Yes. In Windows Calendar, the area on the left side is called the Navigation pane. You can turn this off, but you will also turn off the Date and Calendars area as well. To do this, click the View menu and then click Navigation pane. The pane disappears and you are left with the calendar view and the Details pane. You can press Ctrl+I to turn on the Navigation pane, or choose View and then click Navigation pane.

What happens when a reminder displays for a task?

▼ The Reminder dialog box appears. This is the same dialog box you see when an appointment reminder displays. If more than one reminder is issued at the time the Reminder dialog box appears, all the reminders display in the dialog box. You can select a task or appointment and click View Item to see the details about the task or appointment. If you do not want to see additional reminders for the task, click Dismiss. Otherwise, click Snooze to be reminded again later.

Set Up Shared Calendars

Windows Calendar enables you to share your calendar with other users. You might be someone who tends to overbook your life. You might have sporting events, choir recitals, church meetings, fund-raising events, and other appointments to attend. Not to mention all the work-related stuff you have to do. By sharing calendars, team members, family members, and other people can see the appointments you have set up in your Windows Calendar, and schedule around or with you to make life a little less complicated.

To use shared calendars, you need a place on the Internet to publish them. If you do not have a site to which to publish your calendar, click the Share menu and then click Publish. In the Publish Calendar dialog box, click the Where Can I Publish This Calendar link. It provides information on sites to publish your calendar. You also can visit the iCalShare Web site at www.icalshare.com to set up an account so you can share your iCalendars.

To add a layer of security to your shared calendar, you can set a password on it and then provide that password only to those you want to view your calendar.

Set Up Shared Calendars

① Start Windows Calendar.

The main Windows Calendar window appears.

② Click Share.

③ Click Publish.

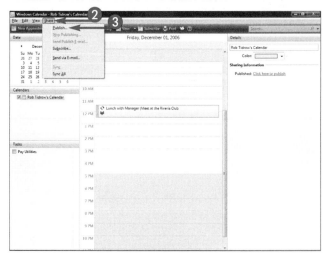

The Publish Calendar dialog box appears.

④ Type the server name.

● Click Browse to locate a server on your local area network.

⑤ Click Automatically publish changes made to this calendar (☐ changes to ☑).

⑥ Click all Calendar details to include check boxes (☐ changes to ☑).

⑦ Click Publish.

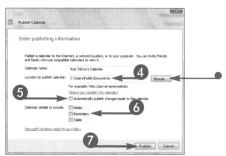

Windows Calendar connects to the server and uploads your calendar to it.

8 Click Announce.

A Subscribe to my calendar e-mail message appears.

9 Fill out the To field.

10 Click Send.

Windows Mail sends your announcement.

The Publish Calendar window reappears.

11 Click Finish.

Can I use my Live Mail account to publish my calendar?

▼ Microsoft's Live Mail e-mail account is an update to the Hotmail accounts that have been around for several years. At this point, neither Live Mail nor Hotmail includes a way to publish your Windows Calendar. Live Mail, however, does have its own calendar that you can use while online and share with other users. To find out more, go to www.hotmail.com and sign up for a free account.

Windows Calendar shows an error when I click Publish. What can I do?

▼ There are a number of reasons why Windows Calendar cannot publish your calendar. First, click the back button to return to the Publish Calendar dialog box. Make sure the Location to publish calendar box is filled in correctly. Also, make sure your Internet connection works by starting Internet Explorer and testing the connection by going to a Web page. Finally, you may need to shut down and restart Windows Calendar, particularly if you have made several changes to your calendar and to the interface.

Subscribe to Shared Calendars

Not only can you share calendars with others, but you also can subscribe to calendars shared by other users. This is handy if you belong to an organization that regularly updates a shared calendar, for example, your church or local youth league. You can download the shared calendar into Windows Calendar using the subscribe feature.

In order to use the subscribe feature, you need to know the Internet or network address of the shared calendar. You also have to have permission to access the shared calendar. Just as you announced your shared calendar in the preceding section, you may receive an announcement from another user about accessing his or her calendar.

Make sure you know the exact path and file name of the calendar to which you want to subscribe. Windows Calendar does not provide a Browse button to go looking for a shared calendar. Better yet, if you receive a shared calendar announcement, highlight the path in the e-mail message, press Ctrl+C to copy the path to your Windows Clipboard, and then press Ctrl+V with the cursor in the Calendar to subscribe to box of the Subscribe to a Calendar dialog box. This pastes the exact path into the dialog box.

① Start Windows Calendar.

The Windows Calendar main window appears.

② Click Share.

③ Click Subscribe.

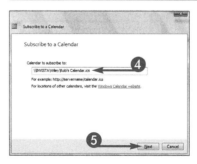

The Subscribe to a Calendar dialog box appears.

④ Type the calendar path.

Note: *The path and file name must be exact, or Windows Calendar will not find it.*

⑤ Click Next.

Windows Calendar connects to the shared calendar.

The Calendar Subscription Settings
dialog box appears.

6 Click the Update interval down
arrow and select Click Every
15 minutes.

7 Click Include reminders
(☐ changes to ☑).

8 Click Include tasks (☐ changes
to ☑).

9 Click Finish.

● The shared calendar appears
in your Windows Calendar
window.

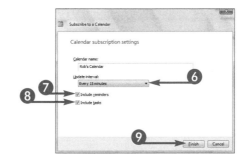

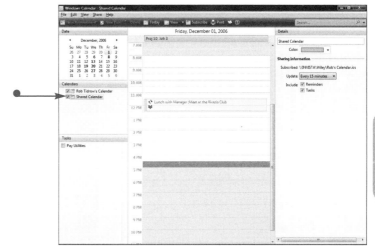

Can I stop publishing my calendar?

▼ Yes, to do this you must unpublish your
calendar. Open Windows Calendar and
click your calendar name in the Calendars
list in the Navigator pane. Click the Share
menu and then click Stop Publishing. A
Windows Calendar window appears. Keep
the Delete calendar on server option
selected if you want your calendar
removed from the server — this is a good
idea. Click the Unpublish button. Windows
Calendar removes the calendar from the
server and stops publishing any new
updates to it.

Can I set the update schedule to a longer time?

▼ Yes, to do this open Windows Calendar
and click the shared calendar in the
Calendars list in the Navigator pane. In the
Details pane, click the Update drop-down
list. Select a longer time, such as Every
hour or Every day. Because each Windows
Calendar goes out to the network or
Internet to get an update, your system
may slow down until after the update task
is completed. So it is a good idea to find
the best update setting for your system
and network connection.

PART IV

Start Windows Fax and Scan

Windows Vista includes a new program for sending and receiving faxes and scanning documents or photos called Windows Fax and Scan. It installs automatically when you install Windows Vista.

When you use Windows Fax and Scan to fax documents, you can use a modem that is connected to your computer, or use a network fax server. Usually users who fax documents from home, a small office, or a stand-alone computer will use a connected modem. Users in larger computing environments, such as those

in a large office or those using a community computer, may have a company- or organization-wide fax server to handle incoming and outgoing faxes.

To scan documents, you can set up Windows Fax and Scan to use a local scanner, one connected to your computer, or use a network or public scanner. Most home and small office users have local scanners that they connect directly to their computer. In larger offices or public environments, such as a library or hotel, scanners are usually set up for sharing, which eliminates the expense of purchasing multiple scanners.

Start Windows Fax and Scan

① To start Windows Fax and Scan, click Start.

The Windows Start menu appears.

② Click All Programs.

Note: After you click All Programs, the name changes to Back.

③ Click Windows Fax and Scan.

The Windows Fax and Scan window appears.

④ To use the fax features of Windows Fax and Scan, click Fax in the bottom left pane.

The Fax tools and folders appear.

⑤ To use the scan features of Windows Fax and Scan, click Scan in the bottom left pane.

The Scan tools and folders appear.

I have Windows Vista Home, but do not see the Windows Fax and Scan program. Why not?

▼ Windows Fax and Scan is available with the Windows Vista Business, Vista Enterprise, or Vista Ultimate versions. If fax and scanning are an important part of your business or outside life, consider upgrading to one of these versions to get Windows Fax and Scan. You also can use other faxing and scanning programs that are available as third-party programs. For example, Symantec's WinFax Pro software provides a nice alternative to Windows Fax and Scan (www.symantec.com). For scanning, you can use the Windows Photo Gallery tool. See Chapter 11 for more on creating digital content.

Can I send a fax from my computer through another computer that is not set up as a fax server?

▼ No. To use Windows Fax and Scan's network feature, you must have a network fax server and that server's address. The address is in the form of \\networkname\faxservername. You also need to make sure you have permission to access the fax server. Contact your network administrator for this information. If you decide to set up a fax server, understand that not all fax machines or fax modems can be configured to be network servers. Consult the fax device's documentation or contact the manufacturer to learn more about the device's capabilities.

Configure Windows Fax and Scan for Faxes

Windows Fax and Scan enables you to set up support for a fax modem to send and receive faxes. A fax modem is a hardware device that enables your computer to act like a fax machine. The fax modem can be an internal modem or external modem. In addition, Windows Fax and Scan supports networked fax devices. The following instructions, however, assume you have a fax device connected directly to your computer, either internally or externally.

Internal modems are ones that are installed inside your computer as expansion boards or are a built-in components of the motherboard. External modems

connect to your computer via a serial or a Universal Serial Bus (USB) port. Both types require that Windows be configured to recognize the modems. Most fax modems include setup CDs or DVDs that help you configure the hardware part of the modem.

After you install the fax modem, you must set up a fax account for Windows Fax and Scan so it can handle incoming faxes, send outgoing faxes, display your faxes, and store the faxes. By default, Windows Fax and Scan automatically installs when you install Windows.

Configure Windows Fax and Scan for Faxes

① Start Windows Fax and Scan.

Note: For more information on starting Windows Fax and Scan, see the section "Start Windows Fax and Scan."

② Click Tools.

③ Click Sender Information.

The Sender Information window appears.

④ Type your sender information in the required fields.

- You must include at least your name and fax number.

⑤ Click OK.

⑥ Click Tools.

⑦ Click Fax Accounts.

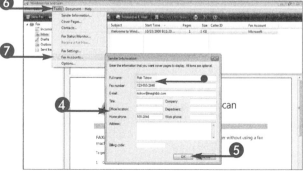

The Fax Accounts window appears.

⑧ Click Add.

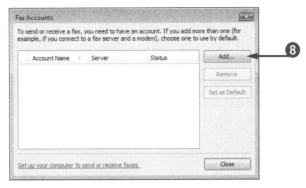

The Fax Setup wizard window appears.

⑨ Click Connect to a fax modem.

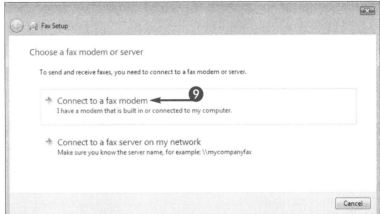

I have a fax machine at work. Why would I need a fax modem?

▼ You may not. If you send a lot of faxes, fax machines are the easiest and most efficient way to send faxes. This is especially true if you send a lot of faxes of signed documents or hard-copy forms. If you just have a fax modem, you need to scan the document into Windows and then fax the document from there. Another reason to have a fax machine is that you can share that machine with others in the office or department. Sharing the services of a fax modem is not as easy.

What are reasons to have a fax modem?

▼ Fax modems are very convenient for users who send a log of unsigned documents to other fax machines. You can create a document in Word, for example, and then simply fax it to another person while still within Word. You do not have to print out the document first and then fax it. Another benefit of a fax modem is that you can receive a fax from other fax modems or fax machines and then store that document as a file. This is handy if you want to then e-mail that document to another user, eliminating the need to scan the document before sending it.

continued

Configure Windows Fax and Scan for Faxes *(Continued)*

To start using Windows Fax and Scan to send or receive faxes, you must set up a fax account. The fax account includes the name of the account, the fax device type, and where the device is located, such as connected to a USB port on your computer.

You can have more than one fax account set up on your computer, but you must specify one as the default fax account. This is handy in offices, for example, if you have a local fax modem on your computer, but your company also has a fax server. Set

up both in case one experiences problems, or if you want the fax server to handle company-wide faxes you may receive, while your local one handles faxes sent specifically to you.

You use the Fax Setup wizard to guide you through setting up a fax account. During the fax account setup, you specify the type of fax you are connecting to: local fax modem or fax server. In the following steps, you learn how to set up a fax for a local fax modem. Before you set up a fax account, install and test the fax modem to ensure it is working correctly.

The Choose a modem name window appears.

⑩ Type a name for the modem.

⑪ Click Next to continue.

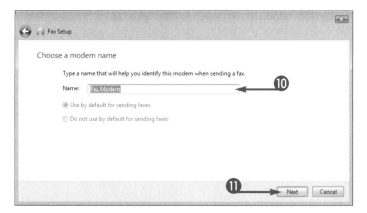

The Choose how to receive faxes window appears.

⑫ Click Answer automatically (recommended).

This option sets Windows to answer calls as incoming faxes after five rings.

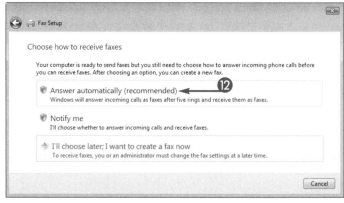

The Windows Security Alert window from Windows Firewall may appear. It warns you that Firewall can block or unblock network users from using your new fax account.

⑬ Click Keep blocking.

The Fax Accounts window appears, displaying your new fax account.

⑭ Click Close.

Do I have to set up a fax account if I just want to receive faxes?

▼ Yes, Windows Fax and Scan uses the fax account information to determine which fax modem or fax server you want to use for incoming and outgoing faxes. When a call comes in, and you let the phone ring for five rings, Windows Fax and Scan automatically assumes the call is from another fax modem or fax machine and connects to receive the fax message. Without a fax account set up, Windows Fax and Scan will not answer.

Do I have to use Windows Fax and Scan for fax services?

▼ No, there are many fax software products that you can use as an alternative to Windows Fax and Scan. However, Windows Fax and Scan has some very nice features for handling faxes. First, all your faxes are stored in the Incoming mailbox until they are completely received. Then they are stored in the Inbox. You can forward a received fax as an e-mail using the Forward As E-Mail tool. And you can store all your faxes and scanned images in one spot, which can be useful for documents you scan and then want to fax to someone.

Send a Fax

After you get a Windows Fax and Scan account set up, you can send and receive faxes. Windows enables you to do this by using the Fax View. The Fax View is a single interface that you can use to view and manage incoming, outgoing, and stored faxes.

Windows uses Windows Contacts as its default address book to store and display fax numbers. If you have Microsoft Office Outlook 2003 installed, then Fax can use the Outlook Address Book (OAB) as well. Address books enable you to store and retrieve contact information, including a contact's fax number. When

you set up a new fax message, you just need to retrieve the recipient's fax number and other information from your address book.

To send a fax, you specify the recipient of the fax — who must have at least a valid fax number — insert a subject for the fax, type in a fax message, and click Send. If you want, Microsoft Fax and Scan also enables you to create a cover page for the fax. Cover pages you can use are FYI (For Your Information), Urgent, Confident (for Confidential), or Generic. Fax cover pages help route a fax to its proper recipient, while providing a cover for the contents of the actual fax.

Send a Fax

① Start Microsoft Fax and Send.

② Click Fax on the left pane to display the Fax view.

The Fax view appears.

③ Click New Fax.

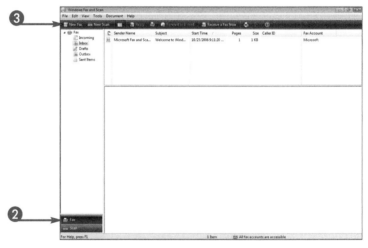

The New Fax window appears.

④ Click To.

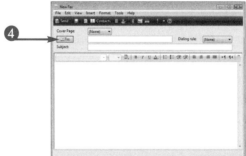

The Select Recipients window appears.

5 Click a recipient.

6 Click To.

- The recipient's name appears in the To box.

You also can double-click a name to add it to the To box.

7 Click to add additional recipients, if necessary.

8 Click OK.

The New Fax window appears, with the recipient's name in the To field.

9 Type a subject.

10 Click the Cover Page drop-down arrow and then select Urgent.

The Urgent cover page area appears.

11 Type a cover letter message.

12 Type a fax message.

13 Click Send.

Windows Fax and Send sends your new fax message.

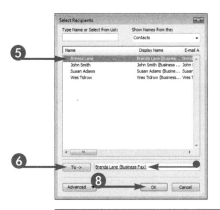

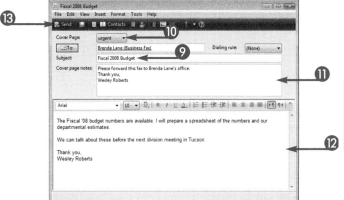

I have a fax modem installed on my computer. Can I use it to connect to the Internet?

▼ Yes, but you cannot be online and send or receive faxes at the same time. Internet services exist that allow faxing via the Internet, but they use Internet technology to send and receive your faxes and do not use your fax modem to do the faxing. To send and receive a fax, you need to disconnect from the Internet, just as if you were making a phone call with the telephone line.

Microsoft Word and other word processors have fax cover sheet templates. Can I use these with Windows Fax and Scan?

▼ Yes, and, in fact, using these kinds of templates makes creating and sending your faxes easier. To see an example of a fax cover sheet template, open Microsoft Word 2007 and click File. Then click New. The New Document pane appears. Click General Templates. Click On My Computer and then click Letters & Faxes from the Templates window. This shows fax templates and the Fax Wizard. The Fax Wizard is handy for walking you through setting up a new fax document.

Receive a Fax

You can use Windows Fax and Scan to receive faxes. When you receive them, the Incoming folder of the Fax View appears. Here you can see the start time of the fax, the ID of the caller — such as the fax number or name — the status of the fax, the current page that is being received, the size of the fax, and other information. This gives you an idea of what type of fax you are receiving and who is sending it.

Windows Fax and Scan automatically receives an incoming call as a fax if you let the phone ring five times. You also can click Receive a Fax Now on the Fax toolbar to manually instruct Windows Fax and Scan to pick up a fax. Use this feature when you know someone is sending you a fax, and you do not want the phone to ring five times before Windows Fax and Scan picks up.

When the fax is received, you can view it from the Inbox folder. The Inbox folder stores your faxes until you delete them. The following task shows how to manually receive a fax and view it in the Fax View window.

Receive a Fax

① Start Windows Fax and Scan.

② Click Fax in the left pane.

The Fax view appears.

③ Click Receive a Fax Now.

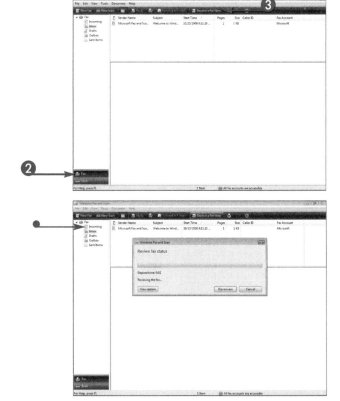

The Review fax status window appears.

● Click here to see the status of the incoming fax.

④ Click the Inbox.

The received fax appears in the Inbox.

⑤ Click the new fax.

● The new fax appears in the Preview area.

Can I set my fax to pick up after three rings?

▼ Yes, you can set Windows Fax and Scan to pick up after the first ring or 99th ring. To set the number of rings, open Windows Fax and Scan, click Tools, and then click Fax Settings. The Fax Settings dialog box appears. On the General tab, make sure the Automatically Answer After option is selected. Next, change the value in the Rings box to 3, or the number of times you want the phone to ring before Windows Fax and Scan picks up. Click OK.

How do I get Windows Fax and Scan to not play a sound after I send a fax?

▼ To do this, make sure Windows Fax and Scan is started. Click the Tools menu and then click Fax Settings. Click the Tracking tab on the Fax Settings dialog box. Click Sound Options to open the Sound Settings dialog box. Click to clear the A Fax Is Sent option and click OK. Click OK to close the Fax Settings dialog box. Now Windows Fax and Scan makes a sound when it detects an incoming call ringing, receives an incoming fax, or detects a problem with a fax.

Manage Faxes

O nce you send and receive some faxes, the Windows Fax and Scan folders start filling up with fax messages. A couple of faxes are easy to manage, but after you get several, your Inbox and Sent Items can become cluttered and unmanageable.

You can remove faxes, save the faxes to disk, or e-mail the faxes to another person. After you e-mail or save them to disk, you can delete them to make it easier to locate other faxes. When you save a fax to disk,

Windows Fax and Scan converts it to a tagged image file (TIF). This enables you to view the fax in an image-editing or a viewing program, such as Windows Paint or Windows Photo Gallery.

Another task you can do to preserve your faxes is to print them. After you print them, you can archive them in file folders in your desk or file cabinet. Many times this is the best way to transfer faxes — print them out and hand deliver them to another person, particularly for users who are not as adept at computing as you are.

Manage Faxes

1 Start Windows Fax and Scan.

2 Click Fax in the left pane.

The Fax View appears.

3 Click the Inbox.

The Inbox contents appear.

4 Select a message to save.

The message is highlighted.

5 Click File.

6 Click Save As.

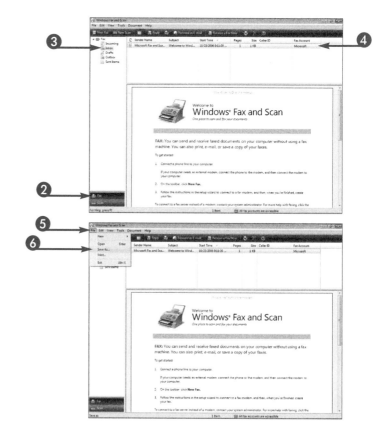

The Save As dialog box appears.

7 Type a file name.

8 Click the Save in down arrow to select a new location.

9 Click Save.

Windows Fax and Scan saves the fax message as a TIF file.

10 To print a fax, select a fax message in the Inbox.

11 Click the Print button on the toolbar.

The Print dialog box appears.

12 Click Print.

13 To delete a fax, select a fax message.

14 Press Delete on the toolbar.

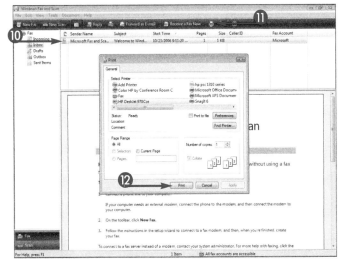

Can I forward a fax to an e-mail recipient?

▼ Yes, to do this, open Windows Fax and Scan and click Fax on the left pane to display the Fax View. Select the Inbox folder and select the fax you want to forward. Click Forward As E-Mail to display your default e-mail program's new e-mail message window. For example, if you use Windows Mail, a new Windows Mail message window appears. Your fax message automatically attaches as a file attachment as a TIF file. Fill in the rest of the e-mail window and click Send.

A fax in my Outbox appears with a red circle with an X in it. What does this mean?

▼ It means that Windows Fax and Scan experienced a problem when sending that fax. You can leave the message in the Outbox; Windows Fax and Scan continues to try to send the message once every ten minutes. The problem may be an issue with your fax modem, a connection issue with the recipient's fax device, or a bad telephone connection. To remove the fax, select it and then click Delete.

Configure Vista Scan

Windows Vista makes it easy to install and use digital scanners. Until digital cameras became affordable and easy to work with, scanners were the primary device for transferring photographs and other printed documents to your computer. Scanners enable you to convert hard-copy documents, photographs, and other printed material into digital files. When these files are on your computer, you can view them, edit them, transfer them to another computer, e-mail them to other people, or store them for future reference.

When you connect a scanner to your computer, Windows Vista manages it using the Scanners and Cameras tool. After you install and set up your

scanner, you can use the Windows Fax and Scan program to scan and view documents on your computer.

Windows also includes two programs that let you edit and view scanned images. With Windows Photo Gallery, you can view, rotate, zoom in on, save to a different format, adjust colors and brightness, fix red-eye problems, or delete photo files. Paint, the other program, is a drawing tool that lets you view and modify picture files. You can resize images, save them to different formats, cut selections from an image, or even add text boxes and shapes to a picture.

Configure Vista Scan

① Make sure the scanner is connected to and configured for your computer.

Note: If the scanner is not configured for your computer, use the Add Hardware tool in the Control Panel to set it up.

② Click Start.

③ Click All Programs.

④ Click Windows Fax and Scan.

The Windows Fax and Scan window appears.

⑤ Click Scan in the left pane.

The Scan view appears.

⑥ Click Tools.

⑦ Click Scan Settings.

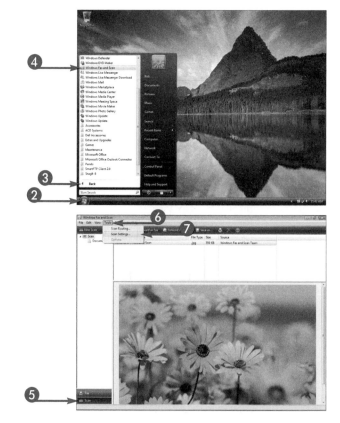

The Scan Profiles dialog box appears.

⑧ Select a scan profile.

⑨ Click Set as Default.

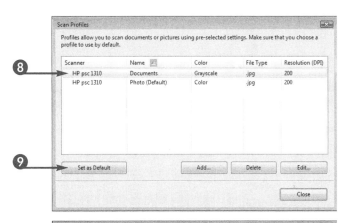

- The word (Default) appears next to the profile.

⑩ Click Close.

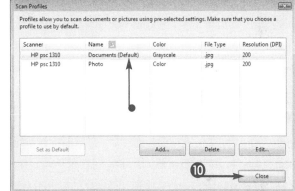

My scanner is working fine, but I want to make some changes on the scanned picture. How can I do this with Windows Photo Gallery?

▼ Open the photograph in Windows Photo Gallery and click Fix on the toolbar. This displays five tools: Auto Adjust, Adjust Exposure, Adjust Color, Crop Picture, and Fix Red Eye.

You also can use Paint to do some editing, such as changing pixel-level colors, cropping, and resizing. If Paint does not suit your needs, which is true for most Windows users, even those who do not plan on producing professional-quality pictures, you should consider purchasing picture-editing software. Some examples of these include PaintShop Pro (www.corel.com) and Photoshop Elements (www.adobe.com).

What formats can I save picture files to in Paint?

▼ Paint enables you to save pictures in bitmap (BMP), Joint Photographic Experts Group (JPG), Graphics Interchange (GIF), icon (ICO), Tagged Image File Format (TIFF), and Portable Network Graphics (PNG) format. To do this, open Paint and then open the image you want to convert. Click File and click Save As. The Save As dialog box appears. Click the Save as type drop-down list and select the file format in which you want to save the picture. The two most prevalent picture formats on the Web are JPG and GIF. You can easily insert these two formats into most e-mail programs, and they can be viewed by all major Web browsers. Click Save.

Scan a Graphic

Once you get your scanner set up to work with Windows Fax and Scan, you can start scanning pictures and documents. In this section, you learn how to use Windows Fax and Scan to scan a graphic/photograph to create a file. In the next section, you see how to scan a document into Windows Fax and Scan.

When you scan a graphic, you usually want to maintain much of the original photograph's colors and quality. One thing you will notice as you scan

photographs: they can create very large files. A small 4 × 6 photograph, for example, can take up as much as 50MB of disk space. For that reason, compression graphics format are used to compress files so they consume less space on your hard drive and do not consume all the memory when you view them. Some of the most popular compression formats include JPG — good for skin tones — and GIF. Formats like TIFF and BMP are not compression formats; you will notice that files stored in those formats are larger than JPG and GIF.

Scan a Graphic

① Start Windows Fax and Scan.

② Click Scan in the left pane.

The Scan view appears.

③ Turn on your scanner and place a photograph on the scanner bed.

④ Click New Scan on the Windows Fax and Scan toolbar.

The New Scan dialog box appears.

⑤ Click Preview.

A preview of the image appears.

6 Move the cropping handles to select only the photograph.

A box appears around the photograph.

7 Click Scan.

Windows Fax and Scan scans the photograph.

● The scanned picture appears in the Preview window.

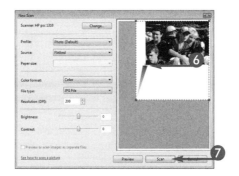

PART IV

Can I scan from other programs?

▼ Yes, in fact you can scan using Windows Photo Gallery, Windows Paint, Microsoft Office Word 2003, and a number of different programs. Windows Fax and Scan is handy because it combines what has been historically two of the most difficult computing features to configure and get to work correctly: faxing and scanning.

If you want to scan from Windows Photo Gallery, click File and then click Import from Camera or Scanner. Select the scanner from the Import Pictures and Videos dialog box and then click Import. Click New on the New Scan window and scan your photo.

After I scan a photo in Windows Photo Gallery, where is it stored?

▼ Windows Photo Gallery stores its scanned images in the Pictures folder. You can find this by opening Windows Explorer or Computer. Double-click your user folder, such as Frank. The Pictures folder is a subfolder there. By default, Windows Photo Gallery looks in this subfolder to locate pictures that it can display in the Photo Gallery window. After you scan a photo, the photo appears in the Photo Gallery window as well.

Scan a Document

Windows Fax and Scan enables you to scan documents. When you scan a document, change the scan profile to the Document profile. This scans the document in grayscale. Unlike most of the photographs you scan, the vast majority of the documents you scan can be done in grayscale, which makes the file smaller for storage.

You can use documents you scan for many different purposes. For example, some companies scan all receipts and invoices to save a digital archive of the

item. This retains the quality of the document for many years, unlike paper and ink that can fade over time.

Scanned documents make it easy to share important documents. For all those paper documents — such as contracts, federal forms, and company policies — you need to share with other employees, consider scanning them into JPG files that you can then e-mail to all employees, or create an internal Web site users can visit to read them.

Scan a Document

① Start Windows Fax and Scan.

② Click Scan in the left pane.

The Scan view appears.

③ Turn on your scanner and place a document on the scanner bed.

④ Click New Scan on the Windows Fax and Scan toolbar.

The New Scan dialog box appears.

⑤ Click the Profile drop-down list.

A list of profile choices appears.

⑥ Click Documents.

⑦ Click Preview.

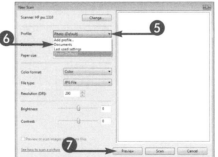

A preview of the image appears.

⑧ Move the cropping handles to select only the document page.

A box appears around the document.

⑨ Click Scan.

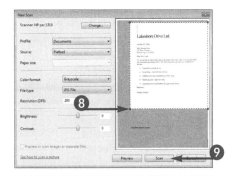

Windows Fax and Scan scans the document.

● The scanned document appears in the Preview window.

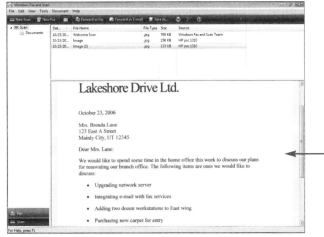

When I scan a document, it comes in dark. Can I make it brighter?

▼ Yes, after you click Preview on the New Scan window and before you click Scan, move the slider next to the Brightness option on the left side of the New Scan window. To make the image brighter, move the slider to the right a little. Click Preview. Continue moving the slider in small increments until the preview looks clear enough to scan. Click Scan to scan your document.

Can I fax a document straight from the scanner?

▼ Yes, select the Tools menu and then click Scan Routing to open the dialog box for setting up automatic forwarding of scanned files. To e-mail the scanned image, click Use E-Mail. In the E-Mail Addresses box, enter the full e-mail address of the mailbox to which you want the scanned files to be sent. Enter your e-mail address in the Mark As From box. Enter the server name of the e-mail server and the port number. You may need to ask your network administrator for these values. Click OK.

Manage Scanned Files

After you have scanned your photographs and documents using Windows Fax and Scan, you can use the Scan view to manage your files. Some of the actions you can perform on scanned files include renaming files, deleting files, adding new subfolders in the Documents folder to store your scanned images, printing files, and forwarding them via fax or e-mail.

Probably the first task you will want to do after scanning is rename the file. By default, Windows Fax and Scan does not know what to call the scanned file, so it names it Image. Subsequent files are named Image (2), Image (3), and so on. You can right-click a file, click Rename, and type in a more descriptive name.

You can print scanned images from the Windows Fax and Scan program. To do this, click an image in the Documents folder, click File, and then click Print, or click Print on the Scan toolbar. From the Print Pictures dialog box, you can select the printer to print to and then click Print.

Finally, if you no longer need an image in the Document folder, right-click it and click Delete. This deletes the file from your computer.

Manage Scanned Files

1 Start Windows Fax and Scan.

2 Click Scan in the left pane.

The Scan view appears.

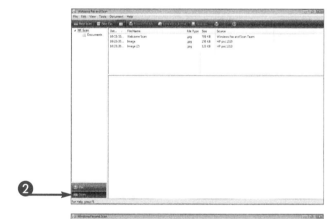

3 To rename a scanned image, right-click an image in the list area.

A menu appears.

4 Click Rename.

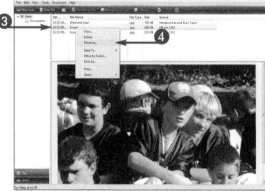

The Rename File window appears.

5 Type a new name for the image.

6 Click OK.

● The new name appears in the File Name column.

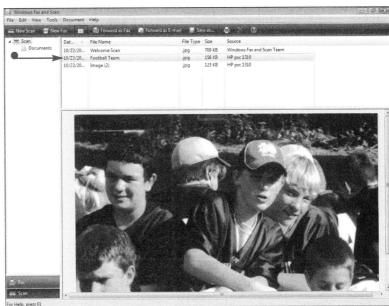

Can I fax a document straight from the scanner?

▼ Yes, to do this, start from the Windows Fax and Scan window and click File, click New, and then click Fax From Scanner. The New Fax window appears. Add a recipient to the To field and then click Send. You also can forward a scanned image that is already stored in your Documents folder. To do this, select the scanned document to fax and click Forward as Fax. The New Fax window appears, with the image inserted as an attachment. Add a recipient and click Send.

I have two pictures on one page that I want to scan. Can I scan them as two different files?

▼ Yes, click New Scan on the Windows Fax and Scan window to display the New Scan window. Click Preview or scan images as separate files. Some scanners do not support this feature, so it will be grayed out and you will not be able to use this feature. Click Preview to preview the pictures and then click Scan when you are ready. The images will scan as separate files.

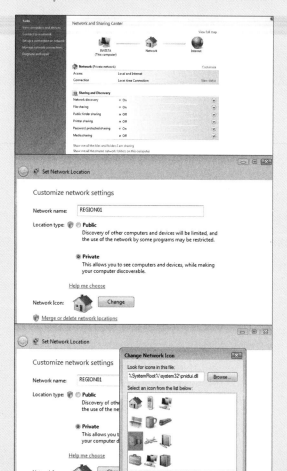

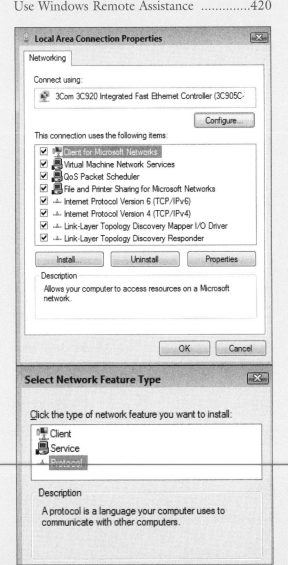

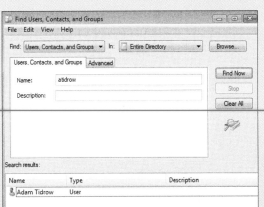

Configure LAN Connections

Windows Vista makes configuring your computer for network connections much easier than it was in previous Windows editions — even easier than Windows XP! With Windows Vista, you can configure your computer to work on local area networks (LANs), be part of wide area networks (WANs), and connect to the Internet using broadband connections.

Setting up a network requires hardware and software components. For hardware, your computer must have an installed network interface card (NIC). A NIC has an opening in which a network cable is attached, or is a wireless device that receives network data using radio signals. The network cable connects your computer to another computer on the network.

Although you can get cables that connect two computers together directly, usually a third piece of hardware is used: a switch. A switch is a device in which network cables from two or more computers are connected, and it directs network traffic to each computer on the network. Finally, you need at least one other computer connected to your switch to complete your network.

The software you need for a network includes network protocols, network services, and a network operating system. All of these software requirements are built in to Windows.

Configure LAN Connections

Connect to a Network

① Click Start.

② Click Network.

The Network folder appears.

③ Click Network and Sharing Center.

The Network and Sharing Center window appears.

④ Click Connect to a network.

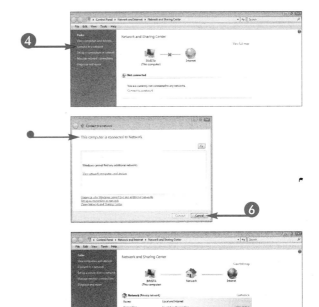

The Connect to a network window appears.

⑤ Connect the network cable to your NIC.

Note: *For wireless users, see the section "Work with Wireless Networks" in Chapter 23.*

● Windows finds your new network connection and sets up the software for it. A message appears in the window saying, "This computer is connected to Network," or the name of your network.

If additional networks appear, you can click one and then click Connect.

⑥ Click Cancel to start using your network.

The Network and Sharing Center window reappears.

Can I set up a network at home even if I do not have a network server?

▼ Yes. Windows Vista enables you to connect two or more Windows computers together even if you do not have a server; this is called a *peer-to-peer network*. You can use Windows Vista with Windows XP, Windows 98, and other operating systems. It enables you to share files, printers, and drives with other users. You also can use some of Windows' built-in communication tools, such as Windows Remote Desktop and Windows Remote Assistance to troubleshoot problems on networked Vista and XP computers. A server, however, is very useful because it enables you to share large quantities of files, allows for centralized backups and maintenance, and provides other network services.

How many computers make up a network?

▼ Networks can be as small as two or large as millions, in the case of the Internet. Your company may have a network that includes computers that allow for sharing of files, printers, scanners, and other resources.

Some networks are layered: One large network encompasses many smaller networks. A large company may have individual networks for marketing, sales, design, accounting, and so on. Each smaller network has specialized needs. Design may need access to high-quality printers. Marketing may need access to some sales data but not to everything that sales does. To complete the network, a large corporate-wide network (WAN) connects all these networks together for corporate requirements, such as Internet access and e-mail.

Configure LAN Connections
(Continued)

Windows Vista makes it painless to set up and configure your LAN connections, provided you have all networking devices working and installed properly. It seems that the biggest problem with configuring LANs under Windows Vista is getting that hardware layer established correctly. To eliminate most of the guesswork, however, you should always consider purchasing new hardware components that meet the Windows Vista hardware requirements.

Another item of concern for any network is to have the workgroup named correctly. You can use just about any name within reason, although organizations that have multiple types of Windows versions installed should use shorter names, under 14 characters.

Sometimes organizations like to create workgroup names that correspond to the employees' responsibilities in the organization, for example, Sales or Marketing, or the team to which employees belong, for example, Project.

Finally, if you have more than one network in your organization or home, consider naming each one a unique name — this is different from a workgroup name. The default network name that Windows Vista uses is simply NETWORK. Here you see how to change the name to a more specific one, as well as how to change the default "home" icon picture to a more professional-looking icon.

Configure LAN Connections *(continued)*

Name Your Network

① On the Network and Sharing Center window, click Customize.

The Customize network settings window appears.

② Type a name for your network.

③ Click Change.

The Change Network Icon dialog box appears.

4 Click an icon.

5 Click OK.

The Customize network settings window appears.

6 Click Next to continue.

The Successfully set network settings window appears.

7 Click Close.

The Network and Sharing Center window reappears.

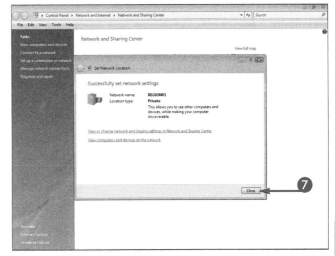

Can I run Active Directory from my copy of Windows Vista Ultimate?

▼ No. Windows Vista Ultimate, or any version for that matter, is not designed to be a domain controller (DC) on a Windows network. You must have Microsoft Windows 2000 Server or Microsoft Windows Server 2003 to run Active Directory. You can, however, use some tools to manage server resources from your Windows Vista computer. For example, you can use the Computer Management, Services, and Event Viewer tools from the Control Panel's Administrative Tools folder to view and manage server processes and disks.

When I change network settings, I have the choice of making the connection a public or private one. Which one should I use?

▼ In most cases, you can make the network connection a private one. This sets up Windows Firewall, if enabled, to use the Home and Office firewall settings. Essentially a private network enables you to see other network devices on the network, such as computers and printers, and enables your computer to be discovered by other network users. You should use the public network option when you connect to networks in public places, such as Internet cafés, airports, hotels, and the like. This keeps your computer from being seen by other network users.

Configure Internet Broadband Connections

Windows Vista enables you to set up access to the Internet using a broadband connection. *Broadband connections* are those connections that are rated at high speeds and are usually cable, satellite, DSL (digital subscriber line), or T1 connections. For most homes or small businesses, cable, satellite, or DSL are the most affordable broadband solutions. T1 connections are dedicated digital telephone lines that can cost as much as $1,000 per month, leaving them for medium to large companies, public libraries, schools, and the government.

Before you begin setting up a broadband connection, contact a local Internet service provider (ISP) and obtain a broadband account. Many times, you also must have the ISP arrange for you to receive additional hardware, including a router, sometimes referred to as a *cable modem*, cable or telephone wiring, and sometimes connection software.

You need to set up any required hardware for your broadband connection before you can follow the steps in this task. Because hardware devices differ in their features and configurations, you must consult the hardware manuals for setup information. These steps assume you already have the hardware installed and connected to your computer.

Configure Internet Broadband Connections

1 Click Start.

2 Click Network.

The Network folder appears.

3 Click Network and Sharing Center.

The Network and Sharing Center window appears.

④ Click Set up a connection or network.

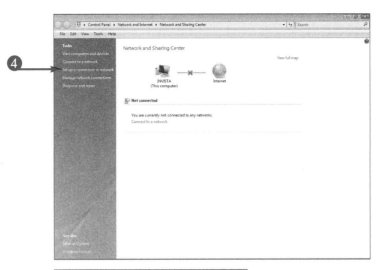

The Choose a connection option window appears.

⑤ Click Connect to the Internet.

⑥ Click Next to continue.

If my ISP gives me a setup CD, why do I have to use these instructions?

▼ You do not have to use the instructions shown here. In fact, use the instructions the ISP provices. They are usually ones customized specifically for your ISP and, in some cases, specifically for your computer. In addition to the customized ISP instructions, companies that manufacture the cable modems required to access many broadband connections provide instructions. Again, refer to the instructions provided with the cable modem; they may be customized for that particular cable modem device. The instructions provided in this section should be used by those readers who do not have specific instructions from their ISP or their hardware manufacturer.

I cannot get Windows to connect to my broadband ISP. What should I do?

▼ The best thing to do is to contact your ISP. Customer Service can walk you through troubleshooting steps that may uncover problems you have with your connection or setup. Many times the problem is with the TCP/IP (Transmission Control Protocol/ Internet Protocol) settings of your computer. To see those settings, open Network and Sharing Center, click Manage Network Connections, and then right-click your Internet connection. Click Properties, click Internet Protocol Version 4 (TCP/IPv4), click Properties, and then examine the TCP/IP settings. Make sure these match what your ISP has given you.

continued

PART V

Configure Internet Broadband Connections *(Continued)*

Windows Vista enables you to access Internet resources over a fast broadband connection. The speeds with which you can access the Internet vary depending on the service in your area. Generally, the underlying cabling hardware the ISP uses determines the speeds for cable modems — cable lines connected to routers.

The average speed for broadband is around 1.5 Mbps to 3 Mbps (megabits per second), which is much faster than a dial-up modem. Recently some service providers have announced broadband speeds of more than 10 Mbps, with one ISP offering 15 Mbps.

Broadband speeds are listed as two speeds — a download speed and an upload speed. Usually the download speed is much faster than the upload one. A number like 10 Mbps/1 Mbps means that the download speed is 10 Mbps, while the upload speed is only 1 Mbps, which is still extremely fast compared to dial-up speeds. Dial-up modem speeds are measured in kilobits per second — kilo is thousands, whereas mega is millions. The standard modem speed is 56 Kbps, much slower than most broadband connections.

Configure Internet Broadband Connections *(continued)*

The How do you want to connect? window appears.

⑦ Click Broadband (PPPoE).

The Type the information from your Internet service provider (ISP) window appears.

⑧ Type your account name.

⑨ Type your account password.

⑩ Type a descriptive name.

This example uses Internet Connection as the new name.

Note: *If you have multiple network and Internet connections, be sure to make the name descriptive enough to distinguish it from other connections.*

⑪ Click Connect.

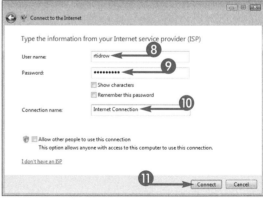

Windows Vista searches for your broadband devices and sets up a connection to the Internet.

⑫ Click Close.

● The Network and Sharing Center window appears, showing a connection to the Internet.

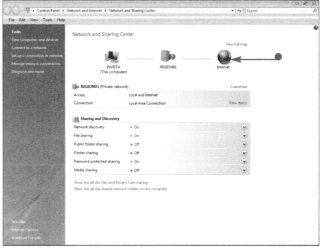

What if I do not have a broadband connection? Can I connect to the Internet using a modem?

▼ Yes. Windows Vista enables you to configure and connect your modem to a dial-up Internet connection. Dial-up connections are substantially slower than broadband connections. However, dial-up connections are more widely available, especially to those users in rural areas. For areas that do not offer cable or DSL connections for high-speed Internet, look for satellite companies that offer high-speed Internet. One such company is HughesNet (www.hughesnet.com).

My broadband connection works but is slow. How can I speed it up?

▼ First contact your broadband network provider and ask them to run a system test on your cable line. The amount of traffic that can flow over broadband cable — called *bandwidth* — may be reduced after you reach a daily threshold of downloaded bytes. This is called a *fair usage policy* and may apply in your situation.

Also look for extraneous programs running while Windows is running. These programs are called spyware, malware, or adware. Download Ad-Aware SE Personal (www.lavasoftusa.com) and Spybot Search & Destroy (www.safer-networking.org/en/download); run these programs weekly to find and delele malicious software that can slow down Internet connections.

Configure Dial-Up Connections

Another type of connection you can have to the Internet uses a modem and regular telephone wire. This is called a *dial-up connection,* and Windows Vista makes it very easy to set up these types of connections. You need a username, password, and dial-up number to set up a dial-up account.

To access the Internet with a dial-up connection, you must have a modem installed and configured to work with Windows Vista. Usually modems are installed inside your computer as a separate adapter or as part of your computer's motherboard. If your computer

does not have an internal modem, you can purchase one and install it inside your computer. Another option is to purchase an external modem that connects to your serial communications port, also called a *COM port*. These devices do not require you to open your computer case for installation.

When setting up a new dial-up account, consider the method of payment. Most national ISPs, such as AOL, NetZero, and PeoplePC, require a credit card to sign up a new account. Some local ISPs, such as those in your town or a nearby town, can set up an account for you and then bill you each month via invoice.

Configure Dial-Up Connections

1 In the Network window, click Network and Sharing Center.

Note: To access the Network window, click Start and then click Network.

The Network and Sharing Center window appears.

2 Click Set up a connection or network.

The Choose a connection option window appears.

③ Click Set up a dial-up connection.

④ Click Next to continue.

The Type the information from your Internet service provider (ISP) window appears.

⑤ Type the ISP phone number.

⑥ Type your username.

⑦ Type your password.

⑧ Click Create.

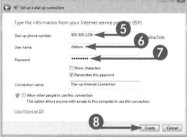

Windows Vista creates a dial-up connection to the Internet.

⑨ Click Close.

The Network and Sharing Center window reappears.

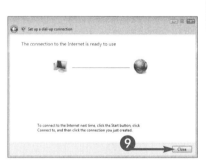

My ISP requires me to contact them over the Internet before setting up my account. How can I do this without first setting up Windows for an Internet connection?

▼ Make sure your modem works and then dial into the ISP setup modem. These are special modem accounts used by ISPs, such as PeoplePC and AOL, that let you set up and configure new accounts. After your account is set up, you download setup software that you then run to complete your initial setup. After this happens, the ISP disconnects you from the first modem and then allows you to dial up and reconnect using your new account. In most cases, the first modem you dial is a toll-free number; subsequent connections use local phone numbers.

I connected a regular telephone to my modem line, and I hear a lot of noise. What can I do to eliminate it?

▼ First you must contact your local telephone provider. Ask them to run a line test, which usually requires a field technician visit your home or office and run tests on the line. Some line tests can be conducted from the main office, but they may not pick up all noise on your individual line. Usually line noise is a result of older copper lines being used instead of newer fiber optic or state-of-the-art copper lines. If your area is experiencing population growth, line noise also can be a result of additional customers being placed on your line. When line noise is recognized, the telephone service technician needs to fix the problem, or new telephone wire needs to be installed in your area.

Configure Internet Connection Sharing

Windows Vista enables you to share an Internet connection with multiple computers on your network using a feature called Internet Connection Sharing (ICS). ICS is handy when you have several computers but only one Internet connection. Internet connection sharing is best used when you have a broadband or faster connection. This enables multiple computers to be downloading information without compromising bandwidth.

Bandwidth is the amount of data that can be uploaded and downloaded from an Internet connection. The higher the bandwidth, the more data

that can be "pushed" through a connection at one time. As you share an Internet connection with more computers on your network, the bandwidth for each computer decreases, thereby slowing down each connection.

To set up ICS, your computer must be part of a local area network. When ICS is set up, the computer on which ICS is configured is given a static IP address of 192.168.0.1. Other computers in the network are then given addresses in the same range, such as 192.168.0.2, 192.168.0.3, and so on.

Configure Internet Connection Sharing

1 Set up two network connections, one to your local area network and one to the Internet.

Note: *To set a network to your local area network and the Internet, see the "Configure LAN Connections" and "Configure Internet Broadband Connections" sections.*

2 In the Network and Sharing Center window, click Manage network connections.

The Network Connections window appears.

3 Right-click the network connection you want to share.

4 Click Properties.

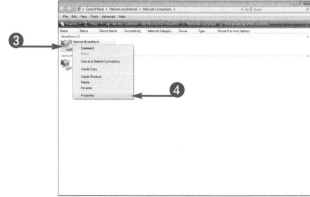

The Properties dialog box for the connection appears.

5 Click the Sharing tab.

6 Click the option to allow other network users to connect through your computer's Internet connection (☐ changes to ☑).

● Select this option to enable your connection to dial automatically when another computer on the network attempts to access external resources (☐ changes to ☑).

● Select this option to allow other network users to enable or disable the shared Internet connection (☐ changes to ☑).

7 Click Settings.

● In the Advanced Settings dialog box, you can set other options that users can modify, such as SMTP (Simple Mail Transfer Protocol), FTP (File Transfer Protocol) server, and other settings.

8 Click OK to close the Advanced Setting dialog box.

9 Click OK in the Properties dialog box to save your settings.

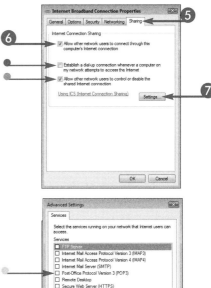

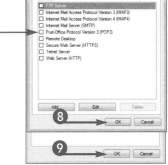

My ISP said I can have only one computer connected to my Internet account simultaneously. Can I work around this with ICS?

▼ You can try, but using your Internet account in this manner may not be a good idea. If your ISP requires separate accounts for individual computers, contact them and inquire about a package deal they may offer for bulk connections. Some ISPs give discounts.

I have two networks set up in my company. Is there a way to share an Internet connection with both networks?

▼ Yes. You can use ICS to set up a network bridge, which enables you to connect two or more networks together to share one Internet connection. This type of sharing is especially helpful if you have a wired and wireless network set up in your house, company, or workgroup.

Why is it important for my network administrator to know that my IP address has changed since adding ICS to my computer?

▼ This is important if your computer needs to be configured with a different IP address, or needs to have a dynamic address. If so, let your network administrator know so she can set up the local domain server so that your computer is recognized using the 192.168.0.1 address.

Manage IPSec

Windows Vista includes IPSec (Internet Protocol Security) as a way to help secure traffic over a VPN (Virtual Private Network). A VPN is a secure network configuration that uses the Internet to enable you to connect to another network or server using a private, secure connection. Many times VPNs are used to enable remote users to access secure data on a corporate network by traveling over the Internet. The remote computer connects to the Internet, establishes a VPN connection to the corporate computer, and then navigates on the corporate network as if the user were using a computer inside the corporation.

The IPSec tools provide system administrators with a way to manage their secure environments in a much broader way than they could in the past. With IPSec, administrators do not have to manage security for individual programs, which can be daunting in organizations with a number of different programs and newer programs being installed periodically.

IPSec provides a secure "language" for VPN connections to occur. With Windows Vista, you can perform some management tasks as a user. To manage IPSec, you can use the Microsoft Management Console (MMC). You can then install MMC Snap-Ins to control the IPSec features.

Manage IPSec

① Click Start.

② Click All Programs.

Note: After you click All Programs, the name changes to Back.

③ Click Accessories.

④ Click Run.

The Run dialog box appears.

⑤ Type **mmc**.

⑥ Click OK.

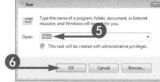

A blank Console window appears.

7 Click File.

8 Click Add/Remove Snap-in.

The Add or Remove Snap-ins dialog box appears.

9 Click IP Security Monitor.

10 Click Add.

● The IP Security Monitor item is added to the Add or Remove Snap-ins dialog box.

11 Click IP Security Policy Management.

12 Click Add.

Do I need to use IPSec to access basic Internet resources?

▼ No. IPSec is a feature that you can use as an additional layer of security for a VPN connection. VPN connections are used by many companies to ensure that employees have access to internal network resources as if they were actually connected to the local LAN (local area network). For example, an employee in an office in Dallas can use a VPN to connect to a branch office's LAN in Chicago. IPSec provides an additional layer of security for this transaction. If you do not have a VPN connection, you do not have to worry about IPSec.

My college allows VPN connections for laptop users. How can I set up my laptop to access their VPN?

▼ Because each VPN configuration can be different, there is not one way to set up a laptop for a VPN. You can use Windows Vista's Connect To a Workplace Wizard to walk through setting up a VPN connection. To start, open the Network and Sharing Center window. Click Set Up a Connection or Network and click Connect To a Workplace. Click Next. Click the type of connection you want to use, such as Use My Internet Connection (VPN). Type the Internet address into your company's VPN and click Next.

continued

Manage IPSec

(Continued)

When you use IPSec, Windows Vista provides the MMC (Microsoft Management Console) program to manage the IPSec resources. You can use the IP Security Monitor and IP Security Policies snap-ins to monitor IPSec activities — such as statistics, filtering tasks, and security associations — and to create and manage IP security policies.

IP security policies enable you to create security rules to determine when Windows Vista should invoke specific security actions based on communication activities. For example, you can create a new IP security rule that is invoked when you connect to any network connection, a local area network (LAN), or to a network via remote access. An IP filter can be created that enables you to filter IP traffic based on the source of the IP, such as from a specific DNS name or DHCP server.

After you set up your IP security policies using the IPSec snap-in tools, you should save the MMC snap-in so you can return to your console to review security activities or to modify a security rule. Windows Vista enables you to save MMC to any location on your system. You may find, for example, that saving the console to your desktop lets you access it quickly by just double-clicking the MMC shortcut icon.

The Select Computer or Domain screen appears.

⑬ Click the local computer option (○ changes to ⊙).

⑭ Click Finish.

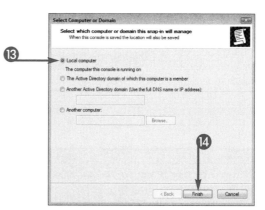

● The IP Security Policy Management item is added to the Add or Remove Snap-ins dialog box.

⑮ Click OK.

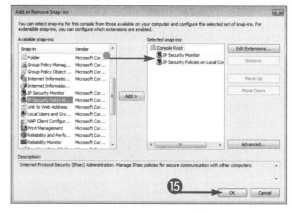

- The Console window appears with the IP Security Monitor and IP Security Policies on Local Computer items showing.

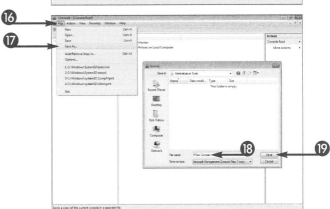

16 Click File.

17 Click Save As.

18 In the Save As dialog box, type a name for the console.

19 Click Save.

Windows saves the console so you can return to it later without reinstalling the IPSec snap-ins.

Note: Some of the management tasks you can do include setting up a new IP Security Policy, managing client IPSec policies, and viewing server IPSec security settings.

Is there a way to get statistics on the IPSec activities?

▼ Yes, you can use the IP Security Monitor snap-in in MMC. To see the statistics, double-click IP Security Monitor to expand it. Next, double-click the computer on which you want to view the statistics. Usually this is your local computer's name. Double-click the Quick Mode folder to expand it. Finally double-click the Statistics folder. The middle pane displays several parameters that IP Security Monitor tracks, such as Active Tunnels, Bytes Sent In Tunnels, and Offloaded Bytes Sent. The Statistics column shows you data for these parameters.

Can I create IP security policies for my computer?

▼ Yes, the IP Security Policies on Local Computer snap-in provides a wizard that walks you through creating IP security rules. Right-click the snap-in in the Console window and click Create IP Security Policy. The IP Security Policy Wizard appears. Click Next. Provide a name for the policy and click Next. Click an option to activate the security policy and then click Next again. On the Completing the IP Security Policy Wizard window, click Finish. This sets the properties for the IP security policy. The new IP security policy Properties dialog box appears.

Configure Wireless Networking

Windows Vista enables you to set up your computer on a wireless network using the Mobility Center. Wireless networks use radio signals to link computers, handheld devices — such as personal digital assistants, or PDAs — wireless printing devices, and mobile phones. With wireless networks, you do not need the standard cables to connect your devices together.

Wireless networking makes it convenient for those users who travel a great deal with laptops or other devices. You have probably heard of cyber cafés. Many hotels and airports, some restaurants, and even entire cities provide access to wireless networks to enable users to connect to the Internet when they are away from the office. This is handy if you need to check your e-mail, browse a Web site, or connect to your office.

To use the wireless networking features of Windows Vista, your computer must be equipped with a wireless NIC. This can be either an internal one that is housed inside your computer, or an external one that is connected to your computer using a Universal Serial Bus (USB) port. The wireless network also must have a wireless hub or router — called an *access point* — that connects your computer to the network or Internet.

Configure Wireless Networking

① Click Start.

② Click Connect To.

The Select a network to connect to window appears.

③ Click the wireless network to which you want to connect.

④ Click Connect.

For networks that are not secure, such as a home network, a window appears telling you that.

5 Click Connect Anyway.

Windows connects to the network. The Successfully connected to window appears.

6 Click Save this network (☐ changes to ☑).

7 Click Close.

The Connected To icon appears in the Notification bar of the taskbar.

8 Click Network and Sharing to display the Network and Sharing Center window.

The Network and Sharing Center window appears, showing the connected wireless network.

● Look here for the wireless signal strength.

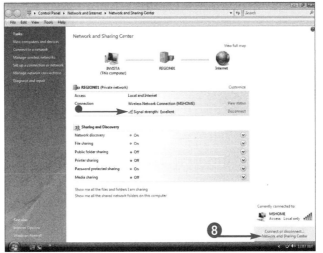

I have heard of several different wireless terms, such as Wi-Fi and hotspots. What are these?

▼ Wi-Fi is short for *wireless fidelity*. This term is used in reference to wireless networking specifications known as the *802.11 networks*, which include 802.11a, 802.11b, 802.11g, and 802.11n. To connect to a Wi-Fi network, a computer must be able to locate *Wi-Fi hotspots*. These are wireless access points offered by companies, organizations, and local governments that enable consumers or workers to connect to the wireless network.

How can I find hotspots?

▼ One place to begin looking for them is from the Hotspots Directory on the Web at www.jiwire.com/search-hotspot-locations.htm. If a restaurant, hotel, or airport has wireless networking available, it usually posts information about these hotspots on doors, signs, menus, and brochures. Finally, you can call and ask a place of business if it offers wireless hotspots. If it does, you can ask the rate per hour for connecting to the hotspot.

Also, if you have Windows set up to receive wireless communications, when you enter a hotspot zone, Windows can display a message that you are in a hotspot area.

Set Up a Sync Partnership with a Network Folder

Windows Vista includes the new Sync Center tool, which enables you to keep synchronized multiple versions of a file that are stored in different locations. This enables you to modify or delete a file that is stored in one location and have Windows Vista modify or delete the same file that is stored in the other location when you want to synchronize those files.

Files in a shared folder can be made available for offline access, which sets up a sync partnership. Files that are located on a network drive will be downloaded to your computer so you can modify

them when you are not connected to the network folder. When you finish working on the file and re-connect to the network folder, Windows Vista Sync Center synchronizes the offline file with the file stored in the network folder.

To set up a sync partnership, you must have access to a shared folder on a network server or computer, or have a device to which you can synchronize. See Chapter 7 for more information on setting up shared folders. You can read about syncing devices in Chapter 9.

Set Up a Sync Partnership with a Network Folder

① Click Start.

② Click Network.

The Network window appears.

③ Double-click a shared computer.

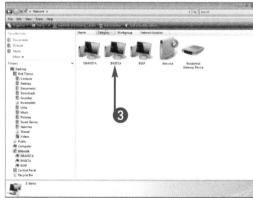

The Shared Folders window appears.

④ Right-click a shared folder.

⑤ Click Always Available Offline to set up a sync partnership.

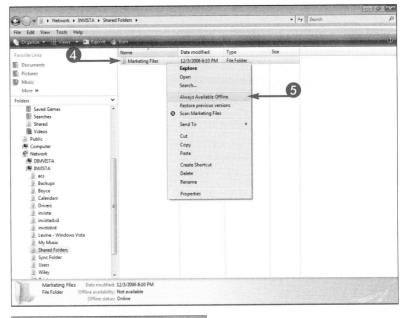

The Always Available Offline window appears.

⑥ Click Close to close the window.

The sync partnership is set up.

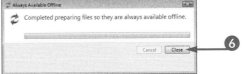

How can I change a folder so that it is no longer in a sync partnership?

▼ Before you change the folder, be sure no one is in the process of syncing with the folder. To stop the sync partnership, open the Network folder and right-click the folder that you want to change. The Always Available Offline command has a check mark next to it. Click Always Available Offline. The Always Available Offline window appears, telling you that Windows Vista has completed changing files in the folder so that they are no longer available offline.

How can I tell if I have offline folders set up?

▼ There are a couple of ways to find this out. First, if you right-click a folder and the Always Available Offline command has a check mark next to it, you know it is set up as an offline folder. Second, look at the icon for the folder. Offline folders include a green circle with two yellow swooping arrows. Third, open Control Panel, click Network and Internet, and then click Offline Files. Click View your offline files. Finally, you can view sync partnerships in the Windows Vista Sync Center, which is discussed in the section "View Sync Partnerships in Sync Center" in this chapter.

View Sync Partnerships in Sync Center

You can use Sync Center when you store files on your computer's drive and store the same file on a network drive, a mobile device, or in programs that support Sync Center. Once you have at least one sync partnership set up, you can use the Windows Vista Sync Center to view your sync partnerships. See the section "Set Up a Sync Partnership with a Network Folder."

In the Sync Center, Windows Vista displays a folder named Offline Files for the files you have set up to be available offline. In the Offline Files folder, you can view all the items within the sync partnership. For example, if you have two folders set up for offline access, you see two folders when you view the contents of the Offline Files folder in the Sync Center. The Sync Center displays the name of the folder, the status of the sync, and a progress bar. The progress bar displays the progress of a sync process, which is discussed in the section "Sync Offline Folders Using Sync Center," later in this chapter.

View Sync Partnerships in Sync Center

① Click Start.

② Click Control Panel.

The Control Panel window appears.

③ Click Network and Internet.

The Network and Internet window appears.

④ Click Sync Center.

The Sync Center window appears.

⑤ Double-click the Offline Files folder to open it.

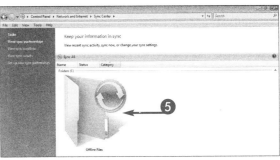

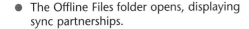

● The Offline Files folder opens, displaying sync partnerships.

Do all the files I want to sync need to be stored in one network folder?

▼ No, in fact that is one reason Sync Center is such a powerful tool. It remembers all the folders in which files are stored. You may, however, want to limit the number of folders set with a sync partnership if you notice the sync process is taking a long time to complete. This means that Windows Vista is having to look in many different network folders to copy files, which over slow or busy network connections can lengthen sync times.

Can I specify that some files in a folder set with sync partnership not be synced?

▼ No, you should keep in mind that all files in a folder set up as a sync partnership are synced. So if you have any files you do not want synced, you need to move them out of the folder set up in a sync partnership. For example, if your Marketing folder includes confidential documents that should not be distributed to other computers, move them to a different folder that is not set up as a sync partnership.

Sync Offline Folders Using Sync Center

Windows Vista enables you to synchronize files stored in folders that are set up as sync partnerships; that is, available for offline access. You use the Sync Center tool to start the sync processes. You also can stop the sync process, browse the contents of shared folders, and set up a schedule for the syncing folder. You use the Sync All button to initiate the sync process. During the sync, Windows Vista compares the files in each location, for example, on your hard drive and on the network location. If the files differ, Sync Center determines which file to save and copies it to the other location.

Sync Center uses the file's last modification date to determine the most up-to-date file to keep in both locations.

If the files in both locations have been updated since the last sync, then you are prompted by Sync Center to determine which file should be kept. For example, you have worked on the file in your offline folder and someone else has worked on the file from the original network folder. This is known as *sync conflict*. See the section "View Sync Conflicts" for more information on sync conflicts.

Sync Offline Folders Using Sync Center

① Open the Sync Center.

Note: *To access the Sync Center window, refer to steps 1 to 4 in the previous section, "View Sync Partnerships in Sync Center."*

② Double-click the Offline Files folder to open it.

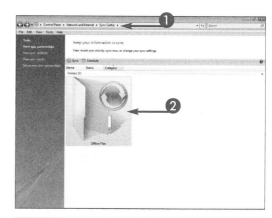

The Offline Files window appears.

③ Click Sync All to synchronize offline files.

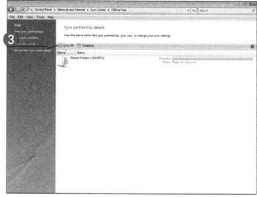

● Windows Vista synchronizes the files in the sync partnership.

④ Click View sync results to display the results of the sync.

● The Sync Results window appears.

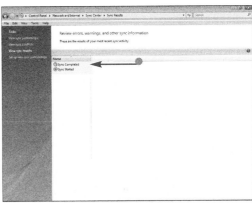

Can I see anymore information about my sync results?

▼ Yes, you can display additional columns of data for the sync results. To see these columns, click the View sync results link in the Tasks pane of the Sync Center window. Right-click the Name column. A menu appears. Click a column name. Repeat this for all the columns you want to display. You can display Details, Date created, Partnership, More details, Sync item, and Severity. To remove a column, right-click a column and select Remove.

I right-clicked a sync name in the View sync results window and chose Ignore. The sync name disappeared. How can I see it again?

▼ Click View sync partnerships in the Task pane of the Sync Center window. Double-click the Offline Files folder to see the Sync partnership details window. Click Sync All to sync the offline folders. After the sync has completed, click View sync results in the Tasks pane. The sync name appears again in the View sync results window.

View Sync Conflicts

When you are using Sync Center to synchronize your sync partnerships, you may encounter conflicts with files. With the Windows Vista Sync Center, you can view these conflicts and resolve them.

A sync conflict occurs when Sync Center cannot reconcile which version of a file should be saved to a location. In some cases, this is because a file has been modified in both locations since the last sync was performed. Another conflict can arise if a sync partnership folder is renamed on one of the locations. Sync Center displays a sync conflict and prompts you to choose a way to fix the conflict. For example, there

may be two different versions of a marketing document you are working on, and the Sync Center cannot determine which is the most recent one. If the same marketing document is modified and saved on the other location, and a sync has not occurred since one or the other file was saved, a conflict arises.

When this happens, Sync Center displays a sync conflict and displays a conflict on the View sync conflict window. To complete the sync, you must resolve all conflicts. Click the Resolve button on the View sync conflicts window and select a resolution, such as picking a version of the file to copy to the other location.

View Sync Conflicts

1 Open the Sync Center.

Note: To access the Sync Center window, refer to steps 1 to 4 in the section "View Sync Partnerships in Sync Center."

2 Double-click the Offline Files folder to open it.

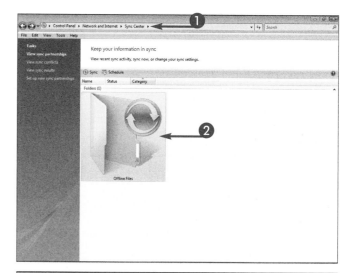

The Offline Files window appears.

3 Click Sync All to synchronize offline files.

- Windows Vista synchronizes the files in the sync partnership, except for those files that have conflicts.

④ Click View sync conflicts.

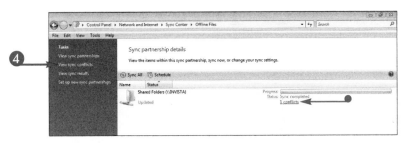

The Conflicts window appears.

⑤ Click a file in the Offline Files column.

⑥ Click Resolve to resolve the sync conflict.

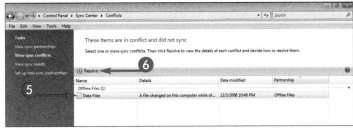

The Resolve Conflict dialog box appears.

⑦ Click Keep this version and copy it to the other location.

Sync Center copies the file to the other location and removes the sync conflict from the Conflicts window.

Does Sync Center delete files?

▼ Yes, if you delete a file in one location, Sync Center deletes that file from the other location. This is because Sync Center is designed to keep both files in both locations in sync, including if one file is deleted in one location. You should always keep this in mind when you are modifying files in a location. If you want to delete the file, say on your local computer while offline, remember that Sync Center will delete that file on the network folder the next time you run a sync.

I keep getting sync errors. Why is the Resolve button not working for it?

▼ Sync errors and sync conflicts are two different things. A *sync conflict* occurs when Sync Center cannot reconcile which file should be stored in a location. *Sync errors*, on the other hand, occur when a problem prevents the sync process from starting or completing. This is usually due to a hardware problem, such as a device not being plugged in, a network problem that does not allow your computer to access a shared folder, or other such problem. You will have to troubleshoot these errors.

Discover Internet Explorer 7's New Features

One of the most popular software applications used by millions of users is a Web browser. A Web browser enables users to connect to the Internet and browse the millions of pages and resources available on the World Wide Web, also called the Web or WWW. The Internet is a collection of networked computers around the world. The Web is a part of the Internet that provides users with pages of information. These pages can have text, pictures, audio, animation, forms, and other features.

To use the Web, users must have an Internet connection and a Web browser. Once they are on the Web, users enter specific addresses to display Web pages or other items, or click specially designed *hyperlinks,* usually called just *links,* to navigate from page to page. Most Web pages are made up of text, graphics, and links.

Microsoft's Internet Explorer is the most popular Web browser on the market, and Microsoft started including Internet Explorer in prior versions of Windows. Windows Vista includes a new upgrade to Microsoft Internet Explorer, version 7. It includes several new features that make your Web browsing easier, safer, and more dynamic.

Tabbed Browsing

New with Internet Explorer 7 is tabbed browsing. Tabs enable users to display multiple pages in the same Internet Explorer window. On each tab, users can display different Web pages in order to compare prices, search for information from multiple search sites, view one page while others are downloading, or do other things at once. Prior to Internet Explorer 7, users could display multiple pages but each page had to be in a separate Internet Explorer window. This meant users had to open a new iteration of Internet Explorer for each site or page they wanted to view. Now with tabs, users simply click the last tab — Internet Explorer 7 always includes a blank one ready for use — enter an Internet address, and press Enter to view that page.

Quick Tabs

Along with tabbed browsing, Internet Explorer 7 includes a feature called *Quick Tabs*. Users can click the Quick Tabs button to display a page of thumbnail views. Each thumbnail presents a snapshot of each page on the tabs users have open. To navigate to a page, users simply click that page to display it in Internet Explorer 7. Quick Tabs also lets users close a tab by right-clicking its thumbnail and clicking Close on the menu that appears. Or, users can right-click a thumbnail and click Close Other Tabs to close all tabs except the one they are right-clicking. Finally, Quick Tabs let users *refresh* — instruct Internet Explorer to re-download — a page or all pages.

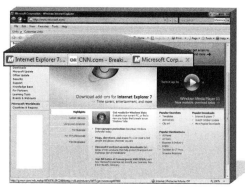

Tab List

The Tab List button is another new Internet Explorer 7 feature. It resides between the Quick Tabs button and the first page tab. You click the Tab List to reveal a list of the Web pages currently opened in separate tabs. To display one of these tabs, you click its name in the Tab List. Internet Explorer displays that tab.

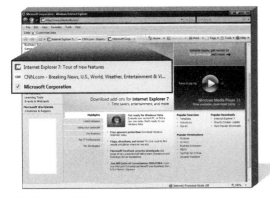

Phishing Filter

Some Web pages are not what they seem. In fact, some are designed solely to rip you off. These are known as *phishing* sites. They include forms that provide places for you to fill out personal and confidential information so that the owner of the site can steal your data. They are "fishing" for your data, so to speak. Internet Explorer 7 includes the Phishing Filter tool to alert you to sites that have been reported as possible phishing sites. You can turn the Phishing Filter on to scan every page you visit, manually scan a specific page, or turn off the filter altogether. You also can report sites that you suspect are phishing sites.

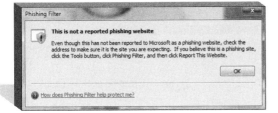

RSS Feeds

Internet Explorer 7 provides a way to receive updates to your favorite *blogs* — short for Weblogs — and Web sites automatically. It does this by using a technology called RSS feeds, also known as Really Simple Syndication. Users can sign up to receive RSS feeds — they actually subscribe to them — and then have Internet Explorer display the feed in the RSS Feeds pane of the Favorites Center. Feeds usually are short snippets of information — including headlines, weather reports, blog statements — that have links to full pages of information. In addition, with the RSS Feeds tool, Internet Explorer 7 recognizes if the sites users visit have an RSS feed available, and helps users quickly and easily set up the feed.

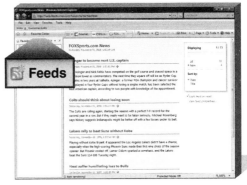

Search

Probably one of the most useful features of the Web is searching. Users can search for information on just about any topic they can think of, from astronomy to medieval literature to Zubird. Internet Explorer 7 makes searching for Web content easier by providing the Search Bar. It enables a user to enter a search term in the Internet Explorer interface and use her favorite *search engine* — a Web site devoted to searching — rather than requiring that user to open a page to that search engine before commencing the search.

Use Internet Explorer 7 for Web Browsing

The primary reason to use Internet Explorer is to browse Web sites. When you start Internet Explorer 7, a home page appears in the main viewing area. The home page provides a starting point for your Web browsing. By default, Microsoft makes the home page the MSN.com site, which Microsoft owns. Some computer companies may alter this home page on new computers they sell. For example, Dell points users to a Dell.com home page, which sells laptops, desktops, and network servers.

Once a Web page appears in the Internet Explorer viewer, users can read the page's content, click on a

hyperlink to another page, download a file, view a picture, fill out a form, or close Internet Explorer altogether. You can also open a new tab and browse to a page on that tab.

To locate Web pages on the Internet, users must enter addresses. These addresses are called Web page addresses or Uniform Resource Locators (URLs). Sometimes users enter these addresses, such as when they want to go directly to a page. Other times a hyperlink stores the Web address and activates when users clicks the link.

Use Internet Explorer 7 for Web Browsing

① Connect to the Internet.

② Click Start.

③ Click Internet.

The Internet Explorer 7 window appears. The Web page set up as your home page displays in the Internet Explorer viewing area.

④ Click a link.

The links you click may be different from the ones shown here.

Internet Explorer displays the linked Web page.

● When you hover the mouse over a link, the mouse pointer changes to a hand icon.

⑤ Click the Back button.

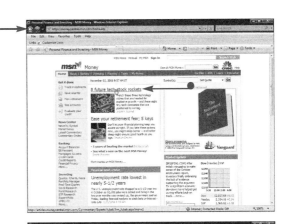

Internet Explorer displays the previous Web page.

● You can click Home to display the Home Page.

When I start Internet Explorer, my home page is different from the one discussed here. Can I change this?

▼ Yes. To change the home page, start Internet Explorer, click the Tools menu, and then click Internet Options. The Internet Options dialog box appears. On the General tab, click inside the Home Page text box. Delete the home page address that is there now. Next, type the complete URL of the page you want to use as your home page. An example is http://www.microsoft.com, if you want to use Microsoft's Web site as your home page. Click OK. The next time you click Home or open Internet Explorer, your new home page appears.

My Web page is slow. Can I make it faster?

▼ The best way to improve Web page speed is by connecting to the Internet using a high-speed connection, usually called a *broadband connection*. You will need to contact Internet service providers (ISPs) in your area to ask if they offer high-speed Internet for your location. Households that can access cable TV services usually can get broadband cable service to the Internet. Households in rural areas may have high-speed wireless services they can access, or may use satellite Internet service. See Chapter 16 for more on configuring broadband connections.

PART V

Enter a Web Address in Internet Explorer 7

Each page on the Web has its own Web address. Web addresses include specific information that tells your Web browser, Internet Explorer in this case, where the page exists out on the Internet. A typical Web address, also called a URL, format is http://www.microsoft.com/index.htm.

The http:// signifies that the address is a Web address. HTTP stands for *hypertext transport protocol*. The :// specifies that the information is on a network somewhere. With Internet Explorer, you do not have to enter http:// for every Web site; Internet Explorer assumes you want it as part of the address. However, if you experience trouble accessing a site, it is not a bad idea to enter the entire address, including http://, to ensure Internet Explorer is attempting to locate the correct address.

The next part of the address, www.microsoft.com, specifies the domain name of the site. Domain names are registered by a company, an individual, an organization, a school, a government, and so on.

At the end of the address is the specific Web page you want, shown such as index.htm. Some pages end in .html, .asp, .mspx, and other names. These just denote the type of file format for the page.

Enter a Web Address in Internet Explorer 7

1 Connect to the Internet.

2 Click Start.

3 Click Internet.

The Internet Explorer 7 window appears.

4 Click inside the Address Bar and type **www.microsoft.com**.

5 Press Enter.

The Web page appears.

● The Address Bar retains the address of the current site.

● Internet Explorer's title bar displays the name of the Web page.

6 Click the down arrow on the Address Bar.

● A list of previously typed Web addresses appears.

You can click an address to displays the Web page.

PART V

Sometimes when I enter a URL and go to that page, the name changes in the Address Bar. Why does it do this?

▼ This is caused by the operator of the Web site automatically re-routing Internet Explorer, and other Web browsers, so that it goes to a different page on their Web site. Usually Web site operators do this because the address you have entered is an outdated one and they have a newer one set up now. Another reason for re-routing viewers is to display pages that have special purposes, such as daily site news, advertisements, hot topics, or other announcements.

What if I do not know a Web site address of a page I want to view?

▼ You can try two things. First, guess at the site name. For example, most established businesses and organizations have Web sites that use their names as the domain name, such as cnn.com, foxnews.com, target.com, and so on. Try entering an URL like www.companyname.com in the Address bar to see if it takes you to the site you are looking for. Second, type the company name in the Search Bar and press Enter to locate pages and sites of interest. Searching is discussed in the "Search Sites in Internet Explorer" section, later in this chapter.

Use the Favorites Center in Internet Explorer 7

S ay you have a Web page you want to visit often, if not daily. You can make that page your home page, but perhaps you have another page that serves well as your home page. Another option is to make a link to that page in the Favorites folder located in the Favorites Center. These links are commonly called *bookmarks,* much like the bookmarks you use in books to mark a page to return to again.

Internet Explorer enables you to save a bookmark to any page on the Web to your Favorites listing. You just specify that you want to store the page as one of your favorites, and Internet Explorer does the rest. Your

Favorites page stores the name and address of the site, when you last visited the site, when you created the bookmark, and the number of visits you have made to the site.

When you want to view a page stored in your Favorites, open the Favorites Center and then click an item located in the Favorites list. Internet Explorer connects to that page and then displays it in the viewing area.

Use the Favorites Center in Internet Explorer 7

① In Internet Explorer, go to the page you want to store in Favorites.

Internet Explorer displays that page.

② Click the Add to Favorites button.

You also can press Ctrl+D to add a page to the Favorites list.

The Add a Favorite dialog box appears.

3 Click Add.

Internet Explorer adds the page to your Favorites.

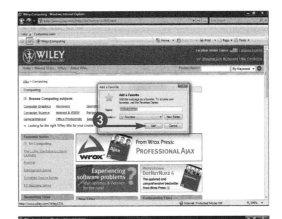

4 Click the Favorites Center button.

● The Favorites Center appears.

5 Click the Web page you want to display.

Internet Explorer displays the Web page.

How do I display the Favorites menu on the Menu Bar in Internet Explorer?

▼ You can turn on the Internet Explorer Menu Bar so that it appears below the Address Bar and above the viewing area. To have this toolbar appear each time you open Internet Explorer, right-click an area below the Address Bar, but do not click the viewing area. A menu appears. Click the Menu Bar option. When you do this, the Menu Bar with File, Edit, View, Favorites, Tools, and Help appears. You can now click the Favorites menu to access your saved bookmarks.

Can I share my Favorites list with another user?

▼ Yes, but you have to export it to a file first. To do this, click the Add to Favorites button and click Import and Export. The Import/Export Wizard appears. Click Next to display the Import/Export Selection window. Click Export Favorites and click Next. Click Next again because you want to export all your favorites. The Export Favorites Destination window appears where your export file will be saved — your Documents folder. Click Next and then click Finish. Click OK when it is done. Give the saved export file to the other user on disk or send it via e-mail. He or she can use the Import/Export Wizard to import your Favorites list.

Select a History Item in Internet Explorer 7

Internet Explorer saves a list of every page you visit on the Web in its History list. The History list enables you to quickly go back to that page later. By default, Internet Explorer stores the list of previously visited sites for 20 days. After that, the page is deleted from Internet Explorer's History list.

To see the History list, open the Favorites Center and then click History. By default, each site you have visited appears as a separate entry in the History list. You can expand each site to see the specific page or pages you visited on that site. To return to a page,

click that page and Internet Explorer connects to it and displays it in the viewing area.

Internet Explorer enables you to display the History list in four different ways. Choose the By Date option to view visited pages by the date you visited each. Use the By Site option to see pages listed by site name — this is the default view. To display sites in order of the number of times you have visited them, click By Most Visited. Finally choose By Order Visited Today to see the order of the sites you visited today.

① Start Internet Explorer.

The Internet Explorer 7 window appears.

② Click the Favorites Center button.

  ● The Favorites Center pane appears.

③ Click here to pin the Favorites Center open.

④ Click History.

  ● The History list appears.

The Favorites Center pane stays open.

5 Click a site.

The site expands to show all the pages you have visited for that site.

6 Click a page.

Internet Explorer displays the page.

Can I delete items in my History?

▼ Yes, you can do this by opening the History list and then right-clicking the item you want to delete. A context menu of commands appears. Click the Delete command. A Warning message appears asking you if you are sure you want to delete the history item. Click Yes to remove it. If you want to remove all of your history items, click the Tools menu and then click Internet Options. On the Internet Options dialog box, click Delete to open the Delete Browsing History dialog box. Click Delete History and then click Yes. Click Close and then OK.

Is there a way to delete the History list every day?

▼ Yes. This is helpful to keep your History list easier to navigate and less cluttered. Click the Tools menu and then click Internet Options. On the General tab, click Settings in the Browsing History area. The Temporary Internet Files and History Settings dialog box appears. In the History area, set the Days to keep pages in history setting to 1. Click OK and then click OK again. Internet Explorer deletes items in the History list that have not been visited within the past 24 hours.

Search Sites in Internet Explorer 7

Probably the most frequently accessed Web sites on the Internet are search sites. *Search sites*, or *search providers*, enable you to enter a keyword or phrase to locate items on the Web. The keywords or phrases you enter are called *search criteria*. Search criteria can be as simple as a single character, or as complex as an advanced Boolean search.

Many search sites exist on the Web. Often you will hear search sites referred to as a *search engines*. The search engines are simply the technology used to generate searches and locate the information you are looking for. You can use Internet Explorer to open a search site in a browser window, type in the search criteria, and then have the search engine return results. You can then peruse the results and click links to navigate to that document or site.

Internet Explorer 7 provides the Search Bar so you can enter your search criteria on the Internet Explorer window without having to open a search site in the browser. This handy tool lets you specify which search providers you want to use to search the Internet. By default, Internet Explorer uses Live Search, a Microsoft search provider.

Search Sites in Internet Explorer 7

1. Start Internet Explorer.

   The Internet Explorer window appears.

2. Click in the Search Bar.

   The Search Bar changes to white.

3. Type your search criteria.

   This example uses *Gardening* as the search word.

4. Press Enter.

   ● You also can click here to start your search.

Internet Explorer connects to the Search provider and displays search results.

⑤ Click a link.

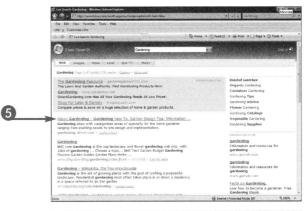

Internet Explorer displays the page you want.

What are some of the most popular search sites?

▼ The Internet has a number of search sites for general or specific searching. Some sites let you search for anything, including images, maps, videos, and text. Others are specific to a topic, such as a medical site for searching medical-related topics. The following is a list of search sites that you may find useful:

Search Sites	Address
About.com	www.about.com
Ask.com	www.ask.com
Google	www.google.com
HotBot	www.hotbot.com
Live Search	www.live.com
Lycos	www.lycos.com
Yahoo!	www.yahoo.com

Can I change the search provider in the Search Bar?

▼ Yes. You do this by clicking the Search Bar down arrow to show a menu of choices. Click Find More Providers. Internet Explorer displays a Web page of search providers. Click a search provider link, such as Google. The Add Search Provider dialog box appears. Click Make this my default search Provider and click Add Provider. Now when you search from the Search Bar, Internet Explorer uses that provider to return search results.

Use Tabbed Browsing

The Web offers so much information that a normal person could never access all of it. However, during the course of a Web session, you may find multiple pages that you would like to open at once. For example, you may be looking to purchase a car and you want to compare the features of two different makes and models. Instead of opening a page at a time and navigating back and forth to the pages you are reading — for example, using links in Favorites, the Back button, and History — you can use Internet Explorer 7's new tabbed browsing feature.

Tabbed browsing provides you with multiple pages in the viewing area of Internet Explorer that you can use

to display separate pages. This enables you to open one Internet Explorer window, but have multiple Web pages displayed. To use tabbed browsing, you simply click a blank tab and specify a page to open. You can enter the URL of a Web page, click a Favorites link, click a link in History, or start a search from the Search Bar.

Another way to start a new tab is by right-clicking a link on page and clicking Open in New Tab from the menu that appears.

Use Tabbed Browsing

1 Start Internet Explorer.

The Internet Explorer window appears.

2 Click the second tab.

● A blank tab appears.

By default, Internet Explorer enables you to include a blank tab after your last page.

3 Open a Web page in the new tab by typing its URL in the Address Bar, clicking a link in your Favorites, opening History and clicking a link, or using the Search Bar.

● Internet Explorer displays the page in the tab.

④ To close a tab, click the Close Tab button.

Internet Explorer closes the tab.

Can I move a tab?

▼ Yes. To do this, display at least two tabs in Internet Explorer. Move the mouse pointer over the tab that you want to move. Press and hold down the left mouse button. Drag the tab to its new location. A small black indicator line appears at the location where you can place the tab. Also, the mouse pointer changes to include a small index card icon to indicate that you are moving a tab. Release the mouse button when you find a new location for the tab. After you move a tab, it stays open for you to view.

Can I turn off tabbed browsing?

▼ Yes. Do this by clicking the Tools menu and then clicking Internet Options. The Internet Options dialog box appears. On the General tab, click Settings in the Tab area. The Tabbed Browsing Settings dialog box appears. Click the Enable Tabbed Browsing option to deselect it — it is selected by default when you install Windows Vista. Click OK. Click OK again. Click the File menu and then click Exit. If you have multiple tabs open, a prompt appears asking if you want to close all tabs. Click Close Tabs. Internet Explorer shuts down. Click Start and then click Internet to start Internet Explorer without tabs showing.

Use
Quick Tabs

When you open two or more tabs filled in Internet Explorer, the Quick Tabs tab appears. Clicking this tab displays a page of small thumbnail images of each of the tabs you have open. The Quick Tabs tab appears to the left of the first tab you have open. It appears only when you have pages displayed on two or more tabs. If you have only one page open in Internet Explorer, you will not see the Quick Tabs page.

To use Quick Tabs, click the Quick Tabs page. You then can click a tab to make it active, click the Close Tab button on a tab to close it, right-click a tab's

thumbnail and click Close Other Tabs to close all other tabs except the one you are right-clicking, and to refresh the tab you are viewing.

Along with the Quick Tabs tool, Internet Explorer includes the Tab List. This small down arrow appears between the Quick Tabs page and the first tab in Internet Explorer. Click the Tab List to see a list of opened tabs in the Internet Explorer viewing area. To jump to that tab, click it in the Tab List. Internet Explorer opens that tab.

Use Quick Tabs

① Start Internet Explorer.

The Internet Explorer window appears.

② Open Web pages on three tabs.

You can open a Web page in a tab by typing its URL in the Address Bar, clicking a link in your Favorites, opening History and clicking a link, or using the Search Bar.

Each tab appears in Internet Explorer.

③ Click the Quick Tabs tab.

Internet Explorer shows the Quick Tabs page.

④ Click a thumbnail.

Internet Explorer displays the tab.

How do I refresh pages from the Quick Tabs page?

▼ Right-click the thumbnail and click Refresh. The thumbnail for that tab goes blank and an animated circular icon appears showing that the page is being refreshed. When the process is finished, refreshed information appears in the thumbnail view and on the tab itself. You will have to click the thumbnail to display the full page. You also can right-click a thumbnail in the Quick Tabs page and click Refresh All to refresh all tabs. Internet Explorer re-downloads each page again, so for several pages, you may want to do each one individually.

Can I close all tabs except the current one?

▼ Yes. Click the Quick Tabs page to display thumbnail images of your open tabs. Right-click the thumbnail of the page you want to keep open. A menu appears. Click the Close Other Tabs command. Internet Explorer closes all other tabs you have open, and keeps the current tab open. It still appears as a thumbnail, but you can click it to enlarge it to its full size.

Subscribe to RSS Feeds

You can use Internet Explorer to not only go out and find information, but also to receive information sent to you. With RSS feeds (Really Simple Syndication), Internet Explorer can display updates from Web sites, blogs, and other sources that deliver information as RSS feeds.

RSS is delivered in a data format called XML (Extensible Markup Language) as a Web feed or RSS feed. Internet Explorer 7 includes built-in tools to let you discover if a Web site offers RSS feeds and reads RSS feeds delivered to your computer. You use the

Favorites Center to view RSS feeds. Feeds usually have limited information, including a headline, date of feed, a short three or four line synopsis, and a link to more information. An RSS feed for the *USA Today* Web site, for example, includes synopses of top stories, datelines, when the stories were posted, such as 18 minutes ago, and links to them.

When you visit a site that offers RSS feeds, Internet Explorer displays the Feeds toolbar button. You can click this button to subscribe to one or more feeds on that site.

Subscribe to RSS Feeds

① Start Internet Explorer.

The Internet Explorer window appears.

② Type **www.first.gov** in the Address Bar.

③ Press Enter.

The FirstGov Web site appears.

The Feeds button activates.

④ Click the Feeds button.

The Web site's RSS feeds page appears.

⑤ Click Subscribe to this feed.

The Subscribe to this Feed dialog box appears.

⑥ Click Subscribe.

The Subscribe to this Feed dialog box closes.

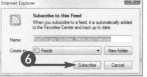

Note: To learn how to read RSS feeds, see the section "Read RSS Feeds."

How much do RSS subscriptions cost?

▼ RSS feed subscriptions are usually free. Some sites may require a fee, but they are not as popular as the free sites. Many sites that provide RSS feeds are advertiser supported, so they disseminate information to the general Web users for free anyway. RSS feeds are just another way for the company to generate Web traffic to the site. Sites such as government institutions generally do not charge for RSS feeds because their budgets for providing the RSS feeds are taxpayer subsidized.

How can I find out more information about RSS?

▼ Sites using RSS have rapidly increased over the past few years. One of the first developers of the RSS technology was Dan Libby, who started the MySpace.com Web site. Some of the sites devoted to helping users understand and create their own RSS feeds are "Introduction to RSS" at www.webreference.com/authoring/languages/xml/rss/intro and "RSS Tutorial" at www.mnot.net/rss/tutorial/.

PART V

Read
RSS Feeds

Once you have an RSS feed subscription set up, Internet Explorer begins receiving updates from the RSS feed. You can then read the information on the RSS feed. You use the Favorites Center to read and manage your RSS feeds. Click the Favorites Center button and then click Feeds. The RSS Feeds pane appears.

From the RSS Feeds pane, you can view the list of RSS feeds to which you have subscribed. If you have multiple feeds from a single Web site, Internet Explorer organizes them into a folder for that site. Notice that at the top of the list is a folder called Microsoft Feeds.

This folder contains the feeds that Internet Explorer automatically subscribes to for you when you install Windows Vista.

To read an RSS feed, click its name. For example, to see one of the Microsoft feeds, click Microsoft Feeds and then click Microsoft at Home, or another of the feeds. The Microsoft at Home RSS feed appears.

When you click the Favorites Center button on the Internet Explorer window, you may want to click the Pin the Favorites Center button to keep the Favorites Center open. This makes it easier to see your RSS feeds and to click them.

Read RSS Feeds

① Start Internet Explorer.

The Internet Explorer window appears.

② Click the Favorites Center button.

The Favorites Center appears.

③ Click Pin the Favorites Center.

The Favorites Center appears as a pane on the left side.

④ Click the Feeds button.

Internet Explorer displays your subscribed to feeds.

⑤ Click a feed.

Internet Explorer displays the feed in the viewing area.

⑥ Click the Go To Full Article link.

Internet Explorer opens the full article for the selected feed article.

How often are RSS feeds sent to me?

▼ By default, Internet Explorer receives RSS feeds once a day. For feeds that update once a day, this setting is fine. However, if you subscribe to a feed that updates several times a day, or even several times an hour, consider setting Internet Explorer to get feeds at shorter intervals. To do this, right-click an RSS feed in the Favorites Center. Click Properties. On the Feed Properties dialog box, click Settings and then click a new time in the Every drop-down list. For example, for news sites that change rapidly, consider 30 minutes as the time for Internet Explorer to automatically check feeds for updates. Click OK and then click OK again.

Can I unsubscribe from an RSS feed?

▼ Yes, to do this, open the RSS Feeds pane in the Favorites Center. Right-click a feed that you want to delete to show a menu. Click Delete. Internet Explorer removes the RSS feed from your computer.

How can I find RSS feeds?

▼ When you display a Web site that has an RSS feed, Internet Explorer displays the orange and white View Feeds icon on the Internet Explorer toolbar. To find RSS feed information on a Web page itself, look for the orange and white RSS icon, a text icon that says RSS, an icon that says XML, or links to areas that describe how to sign up for subscriptions.

Use a Phishing Filter to Check a Web Site

Identity theft is one of the most dangerous aspects of the Web. To help you combat this problem, Internet Explorer 7 includes the Phishing Filter tool. The Phishing Filter lets you check a Web site against a centralized list of known or suspected phishing sites to help you avoid these creepy sites.

What are phishing sites? *Phishing sites* are ones that appear to be legitimate sites, but are set up to steal information from unsuspecting users. A site can pose as a banking institution, government office, not-for-profit charity, retail establishment, or any other site that asks for confidential information.

Unsuspecting users who reach phishing sites are prompted to fill out forms containing confidential information. Some sites ask for passwords, Social Security numbers, credit card numbers, mothers' maiden names, and so forth.

With the Phishing Filter, Internet Explorer can automatically check the Web sites you access to see if they have been reported as suspected phishing sites. You also can check a site manually with Internet Explorer. If the site has been reported, Internet Explorer displays a message to that effect, so that you can proceed with caution to it or click away from it.

Use a Phishing Filter to Check a Web Site

1 Start Internet Explorer.

The Internet Explorer home page appears.

2 Click in the Address Bar and type an address.

3 Press Enter.

The Web site appears in your Internet Explorer window.

4 Click Tools.

A menu appears.

5 Click Phishing Filter.

A submenu appears.

6 Click Check This Website.

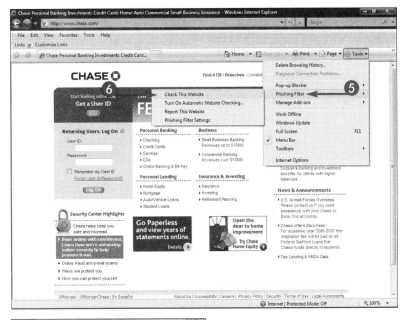

Internet Explorer checks the site against a list of potential or known phishing sites that Microsoft maintains.

Internet Explorer displays a message as to the safety of the site.

7 Click OK.

Can I turn off the Phishing Filter?

▼ Yes. To do so, click Tools, click Phishing Filter, and then click Phishing Filter Settings. The Internet Options dialog box appears, with the Advanced tab showing. Scroll toward the bottom of the list of settings to the Phishing Filter area. Click Disable Phishing Filter. Click OK. When you do this, Internet Explorer can usually display each page faster, but will not automatically check any sites for phishing. However, you can perform a manual check as is described in this task's steps. Follow steps 4 to 7 to manually check a site.

How do I report a site as one I suspect is a phishing site?

▼ If you encounter a Web site that you suspect is a phishing site, report it immediately. To do so, click Tools and then click Phishing Filter. From the submenu that appears, click Report This Website. Internet Explorer opens a new Web browser window, not just a new tab, but a new window, and connects to the Microsoft Phishing Filter Report a Website page. Click the I Think This Is a Phishing Website option. Finally, click Submit. Microsoft adds the site to its suspected phishing sites and then Microsoft Phishing Escalation Reviews will review the site and verify if it is a phishing site or report the site as safe.

PART V

Share and Manage Printers

Windows Vista enables you to share printers across a network. If you do not have a printer directly connected to your computer, you can use a printer that is connected to another computer on your network. You can do this provided the printer is shared on the computer to which it is attached. You also have to set up software on your computer to be able to access that shared printer.

The installation process for setting up a shared printer is much the same as setting up a local printer. The main difference is you have to know the name of the printer to which you are connecting, or at least know the type of printer you want to set up. You can then usually find the printer in the network directory.

In this task, however, you see how to use Windows Vista to set up a printer that is located on your network. To set up a shared printer, you need to install the printer as you would a local printer. Then, during the installation process, you can decide to set it up as shared.

① Click Start.

② Click Control Panel.

③ In the Control Panel window, click Printer.

The Printers window appears.

④ On the toolbar, click Add a printer.

The Add Printer window appears.

⑤ Click Add a network, wireless or Bluetooth printer.

⑥ Click Next to continue.

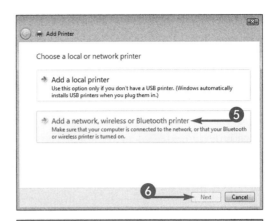

● The Searching for available printers screen appears. Windows shows all the printers it finds on your network.

⑦ If the printer you want to set up appears, select the printer and go to step **14**. If the printer you want to set up does not appear, click The printer that I want isn't listed option and then go to the next step.

⑧ Click Next to continue.

Note: You may need to look at the printer or printer documentation for the exact name of the printer model. Be sure you pick the driver for your printer model.

In my office we each have our own printer. Why should we share them?

▼ You may decide to share a printer if you have the only color laser printer in your general office area. Or, you may have a printer set up that is designated as the only one that prints office letterhead. Finally, knowing how to share printers is invaluable if one of those printers quits working during a critical time of your work. Instead of moving files to a different computer to print them, simply change the print destination to one of the shared ones and print. You will be the hero, or heroine, of the office.

My printer is already set up as a local one. Can I set it up as a shared one now?

▼ Yes. To do this, open the Printers folder and right-click the icon of the printer you want to share. Click Sharing on the menu that appears. The Sharing tab of the printer's Properties dialog box appears. Click Share This Printer. Type a share name in the Share name field. Make this name descriptive enough so other users know the printer is set up to your computer. You can name a color laser printer connected to the budget computer "Budget Color Laser," for example.

continued

PART V

Share and Manage Printers *(Continued)*

Windows Vista enables you to name your printer during the printer sharing procedure. The name you pick should be one that is descriptive to you and to others on the network. A name that is generic, such as "Printer," is not the best one to use.

Instead, use a name that describes the printer and describes its location. For example, a high-speed color inkjet printer may be connected to a computer in the Advertising department. A good name for this printer would be "Ad_Dept_Color_Inkjet."

Windows enables you to manage print jobs that are sent to a printer you share. Some printers provide their own management software that is installed as part of the printer installation routine.

If your printer does not provide management software, or if the management software is limited in what it can perform, you can use the Windows Vista management features. Windows Vista uses the printer window to display print jobs, the size of print jobs, the status of the job, and the owner. To display the printer window, double-click your printer icon in the Printers and Faxes window of the Control Panel.

Share and Manage Printers *(continued)*

9 Click the Select a shared printer by name option (○ changes to ◉).

10 Type \\ and then the computer name and printer name in the field provided.

- You can also click the Browse button to search for a network printer.

The \\ indicates that the computer name is located on the network.

11 Click Next to continue.

The Printers window appears and instructs that you must set up a printer driver for this printer to work.

12 Click Install driver.

Windows copies the driver files and sets up your new printer.

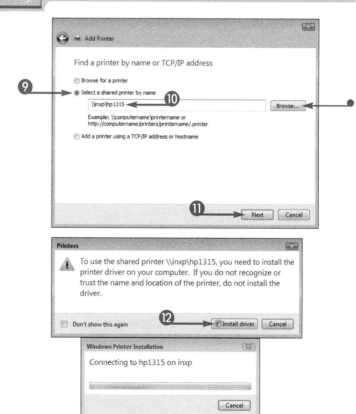

The Type a printer name screen appears.

⑬ Click Next.

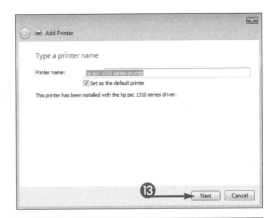

A screen appears telling you that Windows successfully added the printer to your Printers folder.

● You can click here to send a test job to the printer.

⑭ Click Finish.

After I set up the printer, why should I finish by sending a test job? I would think the printer would work fine now.

▼ The printer test is a great way of confirming that your printer is set up and working the way that it should be. If you take the time to test the printer now and find it is not working correctly, you will not be surprised, or aggravated, later when you need to send a document to the printer.

I understand what software is, but can you tell me what a printer driver is?

▼ Yes. It is a program designed to allow the printer to work with your computer and with Windows Vista. Windows has what is called a *printing subsystem* that is designed to recognize some general printers. However, most printers have more features than the standard generic printer handled by Windows. Manufacturers write printer drivers to take advantage of these features, as well as make it easier for users to use their printers. In short, if you do not have the correct printer driver for your printer and version of Windows, your printer will probably not work correctly.

PART V

Troubleshoot
Network Errors

Windows Vista provides tools that enable you to troubleshoot network errors. You can solve some errors you encounter by tweaking something inside Windows, such as adding a different network protocol to Windows. Other problems are a result of hardware problems. One common problem users have occurs with network cabling. Sometimes a cable goes bad, causing the network connection not to operate properly.

As you encounter network errors, you should approach them in some sort of hierarchical manner. That is, do not assume that the problem is always an advanced problem that requires you to examine the deepest reaches of the Windows Registry to solve. Instead, look at the most obvious problems first. The first item you should address is determining if all the network cables are plugged into your computer and network jack, usually a network jack wall plug. Also, determine if you have access to this kind of equipment, and if the network switch has power and is operational. Sometimes just turning off and turning back on the switch will fix connectivity problems. For wireless access, make sure the wireless access points are powered on as well. Shutting down and restarting Windows often helps fix connectivity problems.

Troubleshoot Network Errors

Troubleshoot the Local Area Network Connection

① Click Start.

② Right-click Network.

③ Click Properties from the menu that appears.

The Network and Sharing Center window appears.

Note: Your connection may be named something else.

④ Click View status.

The Local Area Connection Status dialog box appears.

⑤ Click Properties.

The Local Area Connection Properties dialog box appears.

- Make sure this is the correct network adapter for your computer.

- If not, click Configure and set up a new adapter.

- The network items list should have at least one network client and a protocol for Internet connections.

6 If a required item is not listed, click Install.

The Select Network Feature Type dialog box appears.

7 Click Protocol

8 Click Add.

The Select Network Protocol dialog box appears.

9 Click a protocol.

10 Click OK.

The protocols are installed and listed on the General tab of the network properties dialog box.

11 Click OK.

12 Click Close.

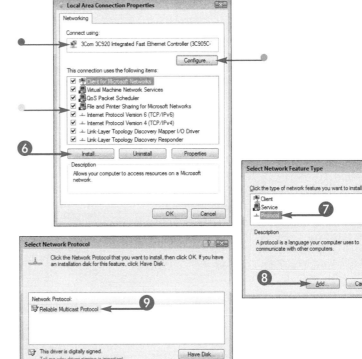

My network is not working correctly. Are there some other problems I should be looking at?

▼ One common problem to look for is that a virus may have attacked your computer, the network servers, or both. To look for viruses, you must have an antivirus program installed on your computer. Run an antivirus program on your computer to scan for any viruses. If any are found, delete the files that contain the viruses. Rerun your antivirus software to make sure the virus has been removed from your system. Shut down and restart your computer.

I recently began getting pop-up messages on my screen. Could these be causing my network problems?

▼ Some spyware programs have been known to cause network problems. These programs are notorious for changing network settings, including IP address settings, firewall protection settings, and proxy configurations. Spyware tools such as Microsoft Windows Defender, Spybot Search & Destroy, and Spy Sweeper find and terminate these and other spyware programs. These tools are available as downloads from the Internet.

continued

PART V

Troubleshoot Network Errors *(Continued)*

A number of different types of errors can cause problems with Windows networking. If you have all the correct protocols on your network, examine the Transmission Control Protocol/Internet Protocol (TCP/IP) protocol. Click it and then click Properties while you are looking at the General tab of the Network Connection Properties dialog box.

On the Internet Protocol (TCP/IP) Properties dialog box, the Obtain an IP address automatically and Obtain DNS server address automatically options should be selected. These are the default settings for networks using Dynamic Host Control Protocol (DHCP) and Windows Internet Name Service (WINS),

which are common for networks running Windows Server 2003. If you are not sure if these options should be selected, ask your network administrator.

One of the most useful tools for troubleshooting network errors is the Event Viewer. This tool is provided with Windows and gives you a glimpse of the activities and events that are happening within Windows. When something happens in Windows, which can be several times every second, Windows logs the event. An Event Viewer has five types of events: Information, Success audit, Warning, Failed audit, and Error. Although you probably do not want or even need to see every event, you can isolate just the bad events, called *Warnings and Errors,* which occur.

Troubleshoot Network Errors *(continued)*

Troubleshoot with the Event Viewer

① Click Start.

② Click Control Panel.

③ In the Control Panel window, click System and Maintenance.

The System and Maintenance window appears.

④ Click View event logs in the Administrative Tools category.

The Event Viewer appears. Event logs appear in this area. It may take a few minutes for Windows Vista to collect and display the event logs.

⑤ Click Windows Logs to view Windows system and application events.

⑥ Click Application.

A list of application log categories appears. The middle pane displays Application events.

⑦ Double-click an event that appears next to an Error event.

The Event Properties dialog box appears.

● You can see details about the event, including when it occurred, the event ID, the computer name, and a description of the event. If a link appears in the description, click it for more information.

⑧ Click Close.

You may continue opening events in Event Viewer to read about them.

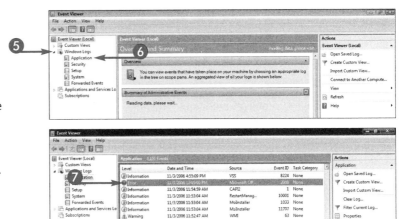

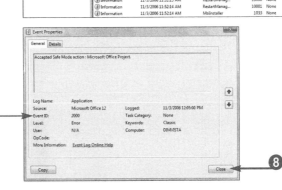

I have seen the network administrator use Event Viewer to help solve problems on the LAN. Why would I want to use Event Viewer on my own computer?

▼ Event Viewer does not provide any options or tools that enable you to change settings or program behavior. Instead, Event Viewer simply shows you what has happened. This information is critical for helping you diagnose what a problem is. In some cases, the Event Viewer, in tandem with www.Microsoft.com, can provide you information on how to solve the problem. Again, however, you cannot make the change from within Event Viewer. To learn more about Event Viewer, visit the EventID Web site at www.eventid.net.

Event Viewer is nice, but it does not always give me information on the error. Can I download or purchase other network error tools?

▼ Yes, there are dozens of these types of programs available. Some are designed to run locally — that is, on your computer — while others must be installed and run from a network server. The first kind is what you want. These programs are usually designated for "client" or "host" computers. Generally, they analyze the network from a client computer, not from a server. To find this type of software, go to Google or another search engine and type **Windows Vista Network Utilities**.

Use Network Diagnostics

Windows Vista includes the Diagnose tool to help you find problems with your network configuration. When you display the Network and Sharing Center, you can click View status. This opens the Local Area Connection Status dialog box. From here, you can click Diagnose. Windows searches your network connections and settings to determine problems with the connections.

One such error that Windows may return is that the DHCP client is disabled. If this is so, you can start it by clicking the link on the Windows Network Diagnostics window. Windows starts up the DHCP client on your computer.

Another common problem you might encounter with networks is that the wrong workgroup name is specified. To correct this, click the down arrow next to the Network Discovery item on the Network and Sharing Center window. Click Change Settings next to Workgroup to show the System Properties dialog box. Click Change and specify a different workgroup name in the Workgroup field. Click OK twice and then click Apply when you are back on the Network and Sharing Center window.

① Click Start.

② Right-click Network.

③ Click Properties.

The Network and Sharing Center window appears.

④ Click View status.

The Local Area Connection Status
dialog box appears.

5 Click Diagnose.

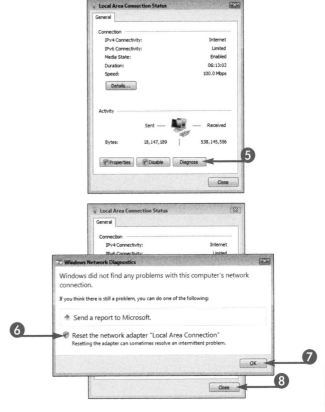

Windows searches for common
problems with your network adapter
and network connection, including
Internet.

6 Click a link to attempt to solve the
network problem. If no errors are
found, click Reset the network
adapter to re-acquire a new IP
address.

7 Click OK.

8 Click Close to close the Local Area
Connection Status dialog box.

**My Internet connection worked earlier
this week, but not now. The Windows
Network Diagnosis tool did not find any
problems. What can I do?**

▼ Most Internet Service Providers (ISP) require
users to re-acquire an Internet Protocol (IP)
number every 24 to 48 hours. If this is the
case, you can do a couple of things. First,
shut down and restart Windows. This
almost always works because it clears out
the old IP address and requests a new one
when you connect to the Internet. Second,
on the Local Area Connection Status dialog
box, click Disable. This shuts off your
network interface and drops the IP address
that it uses.

**A coworker wants to use some of my
shared folders. How can I see which
folders and files I am sharing?**

▼ In the Network and Sharing Center, click
the Show Me All the Shared Network
Folders On this Computer. This displays a
Windows Explorer window with the icons
of the folders and files that are being
shared from your computer. If the folder
you want to share is not part of that
group, locate the folder in the left pane
of the Windows Explorer window and
right-click it. Click Share, specify the
username who wants to access the folder,
and click Share.

Configure Remote Settings

Windows Vista includes two applications that allow two computers to connect to each other remotely over a network or the Internet. With Remote Desktop Connection, users can connect to your computer and use your computer as if they were sitting in front of it. On the other hand, you can use Remote Desktop Connection to connect to another user's computer over a network or Internet connection and use it as if you were sitting in front of it. This is handy if you need to access a resource that is available only from that other user's computer. Likewise, another user could use your computer to tap into a remote resource or application to which only you have access.

With Remote Assistance, you allow another user to access your computer — and take it over — to help diagnose problems, install updated software, or perform other maintenance tasks.

Before you can begin using Remote Desktop Connection or Remote Assistance, you must enable remote access on your computer. If you do not do this, Remote Desktop Connection or Remote Assistance will allow others to connect to your computer.

Configure Remote Settings

① Click Start.

② Right-click Computer.

③ Click Properties.

The System window appears.

④ In the System window, click Remote settings.

The Remote tab of the System Properties dialog box appears.

5 Click the Allow Remote Assistance connections to this computer option (○ changes to ◉).

6 Click the Advanced button to open the Remote Assistance Settings dialog box.

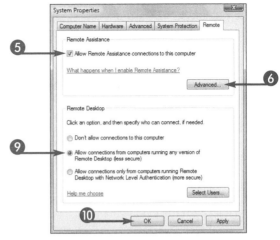

The Remote Assistance Settings dialog box appears.

7 Click the Allow this computer to be controlled remotely option.

8 Click OK to close the Remote Assistance Settings dialog box.

9 In the System Properties dialog box, click Allow connections from computers running any version of Remote Desktop.

10 Click OK to save your changes.

Your computer is now set up for Remote Desktop Connection and Remote Assistance sessions.

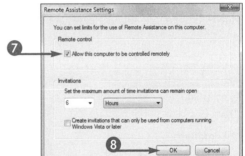

Why does not Windows Vista automatically allow people to connect remotely to my computer?

▼ Because of security issues. When you enable the remote settings, you are allowing other computers to "see" your computer over a network or Internet. This can make it vulnerable to attacks from outsiders. To combat this, set up users in your network who can have access to your computer via Remote Desktop Connection. You must have a network domain. On the Remote tab of the System Properties dialog box, click the Select Users button. Specify the users in the Remote Desktop Users dialog box and click OK.

How do I shut off the sleep mode so others can access my computer when I'm not using it?

▼ If you have sleep mode turned on, choose the Start button and click Control Panel. In the Control Panel window, click System and Maintenance to display the System and Maintenance Control Panel applications. Click the Change when the computer sleeps option under the Power Options category. The Change settings for the plan window appears. From the Put the computer to sleep drop-down list, select Never. Click Save Changes. Now your computer will not go into sleep mode.

Find Your
IP Address

I n order for users to access your computer using Remote Desktop Connection, you must provide them with your computer's IP address. The IP address is a unique address that identifies your computer on a network. The IP address is given to your computer either by your Internet service provider (ISP) or network administrator, or it is automatically configured using a DHCP server. A DHCP server allows a network administrator to divvy out IP addresses as computers connect to the Internet.

Your computer then leases the IP address for a specified amount of time. Sometimes the lease time is forever. Usually, however, IP address leases are for a

one-week period, after which your computer has to renew the IP address lease. The renewal is automatic and happens when your system shuts down and restarts. Large companies use system-wide management software to shut down and restart all computers in the company, usually on a weekly basis. This is when IP addresses are renewed for those situations.

If you want to access your home computer from work, your work computer from home or when traveling, or allow others to access your computer, you must know the IP address. You can find it quickly using the Command Prompt window.

Find Your IP Address

① Click Start.

② Click All Programs.

Note: After you click All Programs, the name changes to Back.

③ Click Accessories.

④ Click Run.

The Run window appears.

⑤ Type **cmd** in the Open field to specify the program to run.

⑥ Click OK or press Enter to start the Command Prompt program.

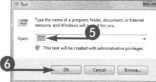

The Command Prompt window appears.

⑦ Type **ipconfig** to specify the command to run.

⑧ Press Enter to start the command.

The ipconfig command returns values about your computer's IP address.

⑨ Copy down the numbers in the IPv4 Address line.

Note: *IP addresses are in the format xxx.xxx.xxx.xxx*

⑩ Click the Close box to close the Command Prompt window.

I want to connect to someone else's computer. Can I find her IP address from my computer?

▼ No, you have to ask her to obtain the IP address from her computer using the same steps shown in the "Finding Your IP Address" section. When she finds it, she can send you an e-mail that includes the IP address of her computer. Make sure you take steps to keep the IP address confidential so unauthorized users do not copy down her IP address and attempt to connect to her computer remotely.

What if my IP address at work changes before I can connect remotely?

▼ That may occur, especially if you are away from the office for several days or weeks. In those cases, contact your manager or security officer in your company to inquire about how you should obtain the address. It may require someone logging on to your computer and using the ipconfig command to access your address. This is not a good idea, because you will have to give that person your Windows logon password, which can be cause for dismissal in some organizations. Your information technology (IT) department may be able to ascertain the IP information from a DHCP report on the server.

PART V

Establish a Remote Desktop Connection Session

Remote Desktop Connection enables you to remotely control your computer from another location. This is handy if you want to access your home computer from the office, such as to obtain files you forgot at home. Conversely, you can set up Remote Desktop Connection on your work computer so you can access it from home.

To use Remote Desktop Connection, you must have Windows Vista installed on the computer you plan to use as the host computer — one that can log on to other computers. The remote computer can be running Windows XP, Windows 95, 98, 98 SE, or Me

but must be running the Remote Desktop Connection client software. Those versions of Windows can act only as remote computers, not hosts. For example, if you are running Windows Vista at work and only Windows XP at home, you cannot connect from the XP computer to the Vista computer. However, you can connect from the Vista computer to the XP computer. If both computers are running Windows Vista, either one can serve as a host or remote computer.

You also must have a network connection for connecting to computers inside a company, or have an Internet connection to connect to computers via the Internet.

Establish a Remote Desktop Connection Session

① On the remote computer, click Start.

② Click All Programs.

Note: *After you click All Programs, the name changes to Back.*

③ Click Accessories.

④ Click Remote Desktop Connection.

⑤ In the Remote Desktop Connection window, type the TCP/IP address of the computer to which you want to connect.

⑥ Click Connect.

Remote Desktop Connection connects to the remote desktop and displays the Enter Your credentials window, which prompts you for a username and password.

⑦ Type the username.

⑧ Type the password for the remote computer.

⑨ Click OK to log on.

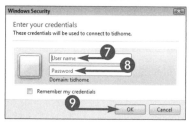

A view of the remote desktop appears.

Note: If you also have the remote computer nearby, you will see that the computer goes into lockdown mode. You cannot have a remote session and local session at the same time.

Navigate around on the remote computer as needed.

⑩ When you are finished with the remote session, click the Close box to close the remote desktop window.

The Disconnect Windows session dialog box appears.

⑪ Click OK.

The remote session closes.

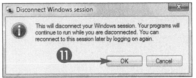

Where can I get the is the Remote Desktop Connection software for other versions of Windows?

▼ To obtain the software, go to the Microsoft.com Download Web site at www.microsoft.com/downloads. Type **Remote Desktop Connection** and click Go. Click the Remote Desktop Connection Software link. The Windows Vista Remote Desktop Connection software page appears. Click Download to download the client software. The file you need to download is called MSRDPCLI.EXE and is about 3.5MB in size. After the download is complete, run the MSRDPCLI.EXE file to install the client software. This software enables older Windows computers to connect remotely to a computer running Windows Vista Professional with Remote Desktop Connection enabled.

I tried accessing my work computer from home but cannot do it. What should I try next?

▼ Sometimes network administrators do not allow Remote Desktop to work across their networks. The main reason is security. If your company has a firewall installed, the port for Remote Desktop Connection and similar remote access software has probably been blocked. You can ask your network administrator if running Remote Desktop Connection on your computer at work is authorized. In some businesses, it is not.

PART V

Use Windows Remote Assistance

Windows Remote Assistance enables other users to access your computer and assist you. Conversely, if you are an experienced user or one who feels comfortable helping others fix their own computers, Remote Assistance can help you be a fix-it star.

With Remote Assistance, you send an invitation to another user to allow them to connect to your computer and see what is on your screen. You can continue to work on your computer while the other person is connected to it. You and the other person can communicate with each other using Remote

Assistance chat tools. The other person can ask you questions and you can respond using the Remote Assistance chat tool.

A remote user also can request permission from you to take over your machine. This enables the remote user to perform maintenance tasks, install programs, and do any action on your machine that you can do. In many organizations, Remote Assistance is a great tool for IT workers to use to administer desktops throughout the company.

Before you start, you must have an e-mail program, such as Windows Mail or Microsoft Office Outlook 2007, set up.

Use Windows Remote Assistance

Invite Someone to Help You

1 To invite someone to help you, click Start.

2 Click All Programs.

Note: After you click All Programs, the name changes to Back.

3 Click Maintenance.

4 Click Windows Remote Assistance.

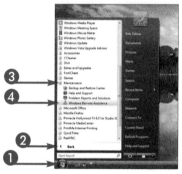

The Windows Remote Assistance window appears.

5 Click Invite someone you trust to help you.

The How do you want to invite someone to help you? window appears.

6 Click Use e-mail to send an invitation.

● Click here to save the invitation to a file, which you can use to send to others if you use a Web-based e-mail program, such as live.mail.com.

The Choose a password for connecting to your computer window appears.

7 Type a password that the other person will use to access your computer.

Note: *Do not enter a password that you use to access Windows, the network, or any other program. Use a password that you can share with someone else.*

8 Retype the password.

9 Click Next.

Remote Assistance starts your e-mail program and creates a Remote Assistance file and e-mail message.

10 Type the e-mail address of the invited user in the To: field.

11 Click Send.

Remote Assistance sends the invitation via e-mail to the other user.

The Waiting for incoming connection window appears on your computer.

12 Contact the other user and tell him or her the password to access your computer's Remote Assistance session.

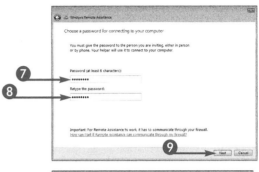

PART V

Do I need Windows Messenger to use Windows Remote Assistance?

▼ No, Windows Remote Assistance is built on a communications platform that does not require Windows Messenger. In fact, Windows Vista does not include Windows Messenger support, as previous versions of Windows did. If you send a Remote Assistance invitation to a user on Windows XP, that user will have Messenger installed on his or her computer, and will use it to connect to your computer with Windows Remote Assistance and assist you with your problem.

Can I set a time limit for how long a session lasts?

▼ Yes. Although you can set a password for the invitation, you do not want to expose your computer for an indefinate amount of time in case another user figures out the password and connects to your computer. Click Start, click Control Panel, click System and Maintenance, and click System. Click Remote Settings and then click Advanced. On the Remote Assistance Settings dialog box, set the maximum amount of time setting to a lower number, such as two hours. Click OK twice.

continued

Use Windows Remote Assistance *(Continued)*

You initiate a Remote Assistance session by sending an e-mail invitation to another user. This invitation includes a Microsoft Remote Assistance Incident Ticket, or RATicket, file attached to it.

If you do not want to send out an e-mail invitation, such as if you do not have a Simple Mail Transport Protocol (SMTP) e-mail account, such as Microsoft Windows Mail, set up on your computer, you can instruct Remote Assistance to create a RATicket file that you can then attach manually to a Web-based e-mail message. For example, you can use a Windows Live Mail account to send out the invitation to the other

user. Or, you can copy the file to a shared folder on your network for someone to access. This can be a problem if the shared folder is available to people other than the one you invite. Someone besides the intended person can pick up the ticket, masquerade as that person, and access your computer via the Remote Assistance tool.

To use Remote Assistance, you must have one computer running Windows Vista, Windows XP, or Windows Server 2003 that receives assistance and another computer running Vista, XP, or 2003 that provides assistance.

Use Windows Remote Assistance *(continued)*

To Accept an Invitation

① To accept an invitation to provide Remote Assistance, double-click the RATicket file.

The other user's Remote Assistance program connects to your computer and displays a password screen on his computer.

② Type the password to access your computer's Remote Assistance session.

③ Click Yes.

The Remote Assistance window appears with your computer's desktop displayed on the right side of the window.

④ Click in the Message Entry area and type a message.

⑤ Click Send.

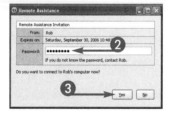

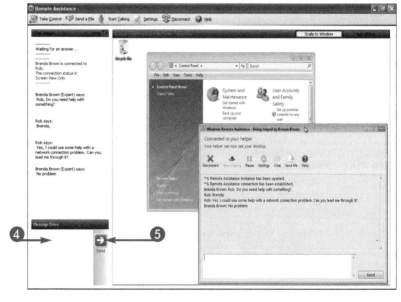

Remote Assistance sends the message to your computer.

6 On your computer, type a response.

7 Click Send.

8 Continue using the Remote Assistance session to allow the other user to help you diagnose and fix your problem.

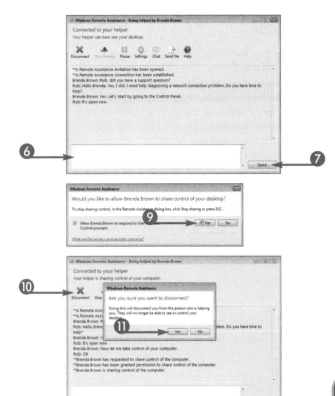

9 Click Yes to enable another user to take control of your computer.

The other user now can control your computer with you. The other user must click Release Control, or press Esc or press any Esc+ key combination, such as Esc+Tab, to give up control.

10 At the end of the session, click Disconnect in the Remote Assistance window.

A message appears asking if you are sure you want to end the session.

11 Click Yes.

PART V

Is Windows Remote Assistance the same as Windows Remote Desktop?

▼ No. Windows Remote Assistance enables users to communicate with each other using chat, as well as enables other users to take control of the your computer, or vice versa if you offer the help. Remote Assistance also is available only to the user with the latest invitation (RATicket), not by a computer name or IP address. With Windows Remote Desktop, on the other hand, other users can take control of your desktop, but not send you messages while they are connected to your computer. You are essentially "frozen out" of your computer while someone is connected with Remote Desktop.

Why should I use Remote Desktop when I have Remote Assistance?

▼ Remote Desktop is ideal for a couple of reasons. First, your computer is locked during a Remote Desktop session. Someone walking up to your computer while Remote Desktop is working cannot use your computer. Remote Desktop can be used by you if you need to access files on your work computer while you are away from the office. Second, Remote Desktop automatically logs on to your computer — users do not have to ask permission to take over the computer. This is ideal for remote help desk or IT workers who need to access your computer while you are not sitting there, such as after hours, weekends, vacations, or when you are sitting in a long meeting.

Install and Configure a Web Server

With Internet Information Service (IIS), you can set up and maintain a Web server on your computer. You can use the Web server to publish Web pages and other Web content on the Internet, to an intranet, or both. If you have an account with an Internet Service Provider (ISP), you can publish information on the Internet so users connected to it can access your content. You can use an intranet to publish information for an internal Web site, such as one for a small office or home.

To manage IIS, you use the Microsoft Management Console (MMC) snap-in, or run the IIS program from the Control Panel. With the MMC, you have the option of displaying and working with multiple snap-ins from one window. This is handy for managing several services at once.

Before you even begin to set up IIS, you should make sure that you have a working network for your organization. All the computers that access your IIS Web site must be connected to this network. If you plan to connect your Web site to the Internet, make sure your machine is connected to the Internet, and that you have access to the Internet using a high-speed connection.

Install and Configure a Web Server

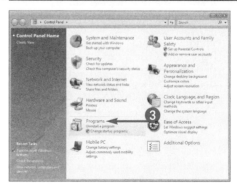

1 Click Start.

2 Click Control Panel.

The Control Panel window appears.

3 Click Programs.

The Programs window appears.

④ Click Turn Windows features on or off.

The Windows Features dialog box appears.

⑤ Click the expand (+) button next to Internet Information Services.

The IIS components appear.

⑥ Select the components you want to install with IIS.

⑦ Click OK to install the selected IIS components.

Windows installs the components, showing you the progress of the installation. When the installation is finished, the Programs window appears.

How can I run a Web server on a dial-up connection?

▼ You cannot. You must have a connection that is on 24 hours a day, 7 days a week. With most dial-up connections, this is not possible. In fact, many ISPs shut off your connection every few hours to thrwart users from setting up private Web servers. Another reason you must have a 24/7 Internet connection is so that you can have a fixed, or static, Internet Protocol (IP) address, which your ISP gives you. An IP address is a unique identifying number that is given to your computer so other computers via the Domain Name System (DNS) can find your Web site.

What is a Web server?

▼ A Web server is software that enables you to publish information on the Internet. A Web server can also refer to the physical computer on which Web server software resides.

Can I run a Web server for my office only?

▼ Yes, this is called an *intranet* and has some advantages over running IIS for Internet connections. First, you can assign yourself an internal IP address. Second, because the site is private, you will not be overwhelmed by users trying to access your site. And third, if you keep your site away from the Internet, you do not have to invest in a firewall to keep out intruders.

continued

PART V

Install and Configure a
Web Server *(Continued)*

You can publish Web pages, files, and other content to your IIS Web server. Standard Web pages are created in hypertext markup language (HTML) and saved as HTML or HTM files. You can use a number of different programs to create HTML files, including Windows Notepad, Microsoft Word, Microsoft FrontPage, Adobe GoLive, and Macromedia Dreamweaver.

HTML is not a programming language like Visual Basic, Java, or C++. Rather a scripting language includes instructions to Web browsers on how information should appear. For example, if you want a line of text to be boldface, you add an instruction at

the beginning of the line to apply boldface, and then add another instruction at the end of the line to turn it off.

Web browsers, such as Microsoft Internet Explorer and Netscape Navigator, interpret the HTML code and display information as scripted in the HTML file. Although these two Web browsers are the most popular, others are available, including Mosaic, Mozilla FireFox, and Opera. All Web browsers display basic HTML code. When extended coding and features are part of a Web site, such as Java and style sheets, not all Web browsers display these items correctly. The most common browser is Internet Explorer.

Install and Configure a Web Server *(continued)*

⑧ Click Start.

⑨ Right-click Computer.

A submenu appears.

⑩ Click Manage.

The Computer Management window appears.

⑪ Double-click Services and Applications.

The Services and Applications section expands.

⑫ Double-click Internet Information Services in the middle pane.

The Internet Information Services item appears.

⑬ Click Internet Information Services (IIS) Manager.

The IIS Manager details appear in the middle pane.

⑭ Right-click the Web server in the Connections column.

A submenu appears.

⑮ Click Stop from the menu that appears.

The IIS Manager server stops so you can configure it.

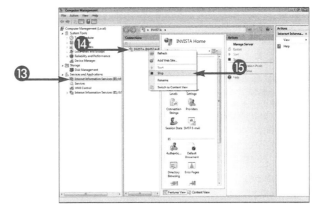

When I create a Web page in Notepad, it saves it as a TXT file. How do I change this to HTM?

▼ The best way to do this is to make sure you can see and edit file name extensions. Open Computer and click Tools and then click Folder Options. In the Folder Options dialog box, click the View tab and deselect the option to hide extensions for known file types. Click OK. Create your Web page in Notepad and click File and then click Save. Name your file and click Save. Open Computer and right-click the file and click Rename. Change TXT to HTM.

Are there any free HTML editors that I can try?

▼ Yes, there are several that you can download and use for free or try for a specific period of time before you must decide to purchase the product or remove it. One popular, full-featured editor you can download for free is Serif Web Plus (www.freeserifsoftware.com/Software/ WebPlus/download.asp). You can also look for free and trial editors on the Tudogs shareware Web site (www.tudogs.com). You must sign up by using an e-mail address.

continued

Install and Configure a
Web Server *(Continued)*

You can learn how to create HTML pages by looking at the HTML code of other pages. To do this, when you open a Web page in Internet Explorer, click the Page menu and then click View Source. This shows the HTML code in a Notepad window.

At first, the code may look a little strange to you. However, if you take the time to examine it, you should find that it is straightforward in its design. For example, code that appears as part of the Web page falls under the heading named <html>.

Anything that is within the < and > is called a *tag* in HTML language. Therefore, the first tag in a Web page is the <html> tag. If you look at the bottom of the source document, you find a tag that looks like this: </html>. Notice the /. This means that the tag is an end tag.

Every tag with a few exceptions in HTML has an end tag. Therefore, if you want to make a table in your Web page, you add the tag <table> to start the table, use the correct HTML tags to add rows and cells, and then end the table with </table>.

Install and Configure a Web Server *(continued)*

⑯ Right-click the IIS connection, for example, INVISTA.

   A shortcut menu appears.

⑰ Click Add Web site.

An Add Web Site dialog box appears. You can configure and view your Web site settings here.

⑱ Type a name for your Web site.

⑲ Type the physical address for the Web site.

⑳ Click here and select the IP address for your Web site.

㉑ Type the port you want to use for your Web site.

㉒ Click OK to confirm your changes.

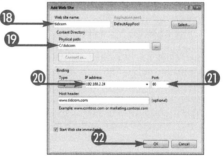

㉓ Click the arrow to the left of the Connections item.

The IIS window expands the connections.

㉔ Click the arrow next to Web Sites.

The Web Sites folder expands.

● In the Internet Information Services window, the name of your Web site appears.

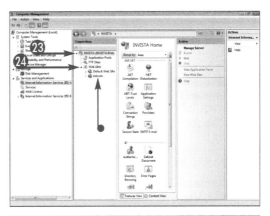

㉕ Right-click the Web service.

㉖ Click Start from the menu that appears.

IIS starts your Web site so you can test it.

I am using the Windows Vista Basic version. Can I install IIS 7?

▼ No, IIS 7 is not part of the Windows Vista Basic package. To get IIS 7, you must have the Windows Vista Business or Windows Vista Ultimate versions.

How can I find out more about HTML and Web page authoring?

▼ The first place you should start is a site on the Web called W3C, which stands for the World Wide Web Consortium (www.w3.org). This organization is responsible for approving and expanding HTML and other specifications of the Web. A number of excellent books are also on the market that can help you understand HTML authoring.

I have read about security problems from hosting your own Web site with IIS. What can I do to make sure my IIS site is secure?

▼ Microsoft introduced new security features with the previous release of IIS (6.0) and has further increased those features in this release, version IIS 7. The most critical update is that the default Web site no longer automatically starts when you initially install IIS. Instead you must start it manually. Even with the security features expanded, there is an area you may want to limit access to. Open Computer or Windows Explorer and delete the c:\inetpub\iissamples folder. This folder contains sample script files that are vulnerable to hacking attacks.

Install and Configure an FTP Server

With a File Transfer Protocol (FTP) server, you can allow users to transfer binary files to your Web site, and copy files from your site. It is has been one of the most stable and popular Internet protocols since the Internet was created in the late 1960s.

To configure and manage an FTP server, you use the Internet Information Services (IIS) window. You can set identification features of the FTP server, set connection setting defaults, configure site operators, create an FTP site banner message, and set up other features. In this section, you learn how to set up the FTP server to get it running.

Once your FTP server has been set up, users can transfer files to it. To transfer files using FTP, users can use Internet Explorer or the built-in FTP Command Prompt tool. For most users, using Internet Explorer is easier because it provides a graphical user interface during the FTP exchange. The FTP Command Prompt tool requires users to type commands to initiate transfers. You also can use Windows Explorer to navigate an FTP server. When you connect to an FTP site with Internet Explorer, click Page and then Open FTP Site in Windows Explorer.

Install and Configure an FTP Server

① Open the IIS window from the Computer Management window.

② Click the expand arrow next to Internet Information Services (IIS) 6.0 Manager.

③ Click the expand arrow next to FTP Sites.

The Default FTP Site (Stopped) item appears.

④ Right-click the FTP Sites and click Properties from the menu that appears.

The Default FTP Site (Stopped) Properties dialog box appears.

⑤ Type a name for the FTP site.

⑥ Click here and select the IP address for your FTP server.

⑦ Click OK to confirm your changes.

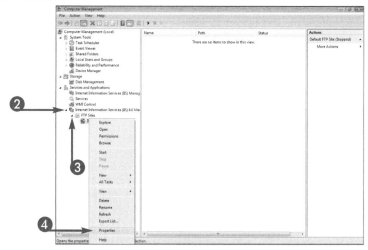

In the Internet Information Services (IIS) 6.0 Manager window, the name of your FTP site now appears, instead of Default FTP Site.

8 Right-click your FTP site.

9 Click Permissions.

The Security tab for the selected FTP site appears.

10 Click Edit.

I want to test my FTP server, but am not sure what to do. What are some commands that I can use?

▼ Because FTP has its roots in the Unix operating system, the commands for FTP can be a little intimidating for some users to learn. To start the FTP tool, click Start, click All Programs, and then click Accessories. Click Command Prompt to start a DOS window. Type **FTP** and press Enter. The command to start a session is **Open** and then the name of the site. To end a session, type **Close**. To see a complete list of commands you can use with FTP, type **?** and press Enter.

What kind of security concerns should I be aware of when hosting an FTP server on my computer?

▼ Just having an FTP server installed on your Web server can open you up to receiving dangerous files, including viruses that can damage or delete vital files. You should never allow anonymous users to access your FTP site. Instead, allow only specific users, such as coworkers, technical support people, and other trusted users, access. You also should run an antivirus program on your computer at all times. This way files are scanned as they are being uploaded to your computer.

continued

PART V

Install and Configure
an FTP Server *(Continued)*

Windows Vista enables you to set up an FTP server on your computer to allow others — usually users from the Internet — to access your computer to transfer files. One of the most important aspects of setting up and running an FTP server is security. Because others will access your computer via FTP, you should pay special attention to who accesses it and how folder and file permissions are set up.

When you set up folder permissions, you tell Windows to which folders users can have access. In addition, you can configure which users have access to which folders. For example, you may want to grant outside sales people access to a folder called SALES-DATA. Other users, such as team managers, also may be given access to the SALES-DATA, as well as PROJECT, folders.

By setting up file permissions, you tell Windows what types of actions users can take on files. File permissions include read-only, read and write, and full. Read-only permission allows users to download files from the FTP site. Read and write permission allows users to download files from and upload files to the FTP site. Full permission allows users to download, upload, and delete files on the FTP site.

The Permissions for ftproot dialog box appears.

⑪ Select a user to change FTP access permissions.

⑫ Select a permission for the user, such as by clicking the Allow check box next to Modify (☐ changes to ☑).

The user now is allowed to modify files on the FTP site.

⑬ Click OK.

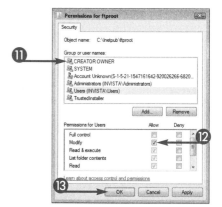

The Security tab appears.

⑭ Click OK.

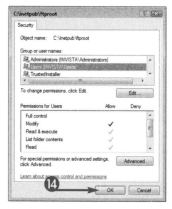

The Computer Management
window appears, with the
Internet Information Server (IIS)
application showing.

⑮ Right-click the FTP site.

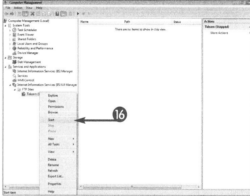

A submenu appears.

⑯ Click Start.

The FTP site starts.

I have IIS installed and started on my computer. How can I test that it is running, including my FTP server?

▼ An easy and quick way is to use the Ping command from another computer. From the other computer, open a Command Prompt window. Type **PING** and the name of your FTP server. Press Enter. The PING command connects to your FTP server and displays a message that it was successful and shows the connection speed to the FTP server. If the PING command cannot find your FTP server, it displays a message that the host — your FTP site name — could not be found.

I have permissions set up for some folders on my FTP site. How do I copy files to those folders?

▼ When your computer acts as both your working computer — the one on which you do your daily work — and your FTP server, copy files from other folders into the folders set up for the FTP site using Windows Explorer. Click Start, click All Programs, click Accessories, and then click Windows Explorer. Expand the Computer icon and find the drive that has the files you want to copy. Expand the folder in which the files you want to copy reside and then copy them to the FTP server folder.

Install and Configure
an SMTP Virtual Server

IS 7 enables you to set up a Simple Mail
Transport Protocol (SMTP) virtual server. SMTP is
an Internet protocol that enables users to send
messages from one computer to another on a
network. This allows you to use the Internet to send
messages within an organization or across the world.

With the SMTP virtual server on your computer, you
can host your own e-mail server. As soon as you set up
an SMTP virtual server on your computer and start
receiving messages, you need an e-mail server, such as
Microsoft Exchange Server, to help you deliver and
route messages to end-users' e-mail programs, such as
Microsoft Outlook or Microsoft Windows Mail.

The SMTP server also enables you to send e-mail from
a Web application. For example, you might create a
Web site that includes Web mail applets, forms, and
other items that allow users to send e-mail messages
from your Web site.

Many of the options available on the SMTP virtual
server go beyond the scope of this introduction. To
understand how to configure and run the SMTP virtual
server, consult online documentation or a book
specifically on SMTP.

Install and Configure an SMTP Virtual Server

① Open the Internet Information Server (IIS)
management window.

② Click Internet Information Services (IIS)
Manager.

The Web server components appear in the
middle pane.

③ Scroll down the list of components.

④ Double-click SMTP E-mail.

The SMTP E-mail component pane appears.

You can click and drag its border to the right to increase the size of the SMTP E-mail component pane.

5 Type the e-mail address of the SMTP server in the E-mail address box.

6 Type the name of the SMTP server in the SMTP Server box.

● You can click here to specify a pickup directory for e-mail, instead of an e-mail address as you specify in step 5.

7 Click Apply.

A message appears in the Alerts pane saying that the changes have been saved.

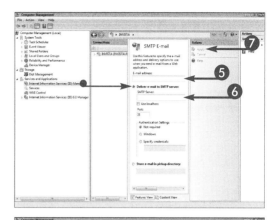

Do I have to install the SMTP virtual server on the same computer that runs my Web server?

▼ No. In fact, most organizations separate the two servers so as not to overwhelm one computer. Also, because users send and receive messages to your domain name, your SMTP virtual server may be vulnerable to outside attack.

Is there a way to set up authentication on the SMTP server?

▼ Yes. On the SMTP E-mail component pane, click the Windows or Specify credentials options under the Authentication Settings label. With the = Windows authentication setting selected, you use Windows' built-in authentication. The Specify credentials setting requires you to set up a username and password that users must know before e-mail is authorized.

Is there a way to limit spam and other unwanted messages from entering my SMTP virtual server?

▼ This is the million-dollar question many administrators get. The short answer is that you cannot stop spam altogether. However, you can do things to reduce the number of unwanted messages your company gets. One thing to do is use a hardware device in front of the SMTP server that contains the number of recipients per message to a small number, such as ten. This way messages sent to your domain that have a large *bulk* address list with several hundreds or thousands of e-mail addresses are denied entrance to your site.

Configure a Default Document

When users navigate to your Web site, they must know either the home page URL or a specific document on the site. For example, to visit the CNN news Web site, you can type in **www.cnn.com**. Or, you can type in **www.cnn.com/index.html**. Either way you end up at the CNN home page. By specifying the default document for a site, the Web server knows that the first address should present the index.html page.

The default document is a Web page, such as an HTML, HTM, ASP (Active Server Page), or other page that a site manager wants as the default page that users navigate to if only the top-level address is given. The reason for this is that users may know a company or organization's domain name, for example, www.nn.com, but may not know what the full name of the first page is.

With IIS, you can specify this default document. You can also specify additional default documents in case the primary one is not available, such as down for maintenance. Documents are listed in order of preference using the Default Document component.

Configure a Default Document

① Open the Internet Information Server management window.

② Double-click the Default Document component.

The Default Document component appears in the middle pane.

③ Click in the File name(s) box.

④ Type the name of the document you want to use as the primary default document.

Use the full document name, such as index.html.

⑤ Add additional documents to use in case the primary default document is not available.

⑥ Click Apply.

IIS saves your default document settings.

Can I specify any document as the default one?

▼ Yes, but your default document should be in a file format that a Web browser can view. In addition, if you are looking to maximize your visits, make the default page one the majority of Web browsers on the market can read. For example, if you want to pull in the most viewers, documents saved with .html or .htm extensions are best. This way users with just about any browser and on any type of computer will be able to read your home page.

I notice that many sites use Macromedia Flash files as default pages. Can IIS do that?

▼ Yes, you can specify that the default page use a Flash file as the opening page. You must use a flash editor to create the file because IIS cannot create the file itself. In many cases, although a Flash file is the preferred home page for many sites — Flash files are animated and jazzy looking — some users do not want to view these files. You may want to provide a link on the home page that enables users to choose which type of home page they want to view — Flash or plain HTML.

PART V

Configure Windows Vista for a Domain

Windows Vista enables you to connect to a Windows domain. Domains are similar to networking workgroups but provide additional administration and networking features. In addition, when you want to connect to a domain, you must provide proper authentication — username and password — to be allowed on the domain. Domains are established on a computer running network operating systems, such as Microsoft Windows Server 2003.

Network administrators in charge of domains are responsible for creating domain accounts for all users who need to access the domain network. Just because

you create an account on your computer does not mean you can necessarily access a domain. Your network administrator determines that.

To connect to a domain, your Windows Vista must have permission to do so. Your network administrator must grant you this permission, which includes a username and password that the administrator sets up in the Windows Active Directory. Active Directory is the directory service for Windows 2000 Server and Windows Server 2003. It collects and stores information about network objects. It is also what administrators primarily use to manage these objects and the server itself.

Configure Windows Vista for a Domain

① Click Start.

② Right-click Computer.

③ Click Properties.

The System window appears.

④ Click Change settings.

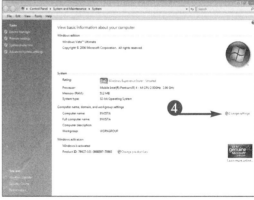

The System Properties dialog box appears.

5 Click Change.

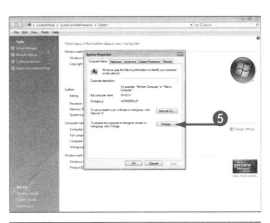

The Computer Name/Domain Changes dialog box appears. Here is where you can change your computer's name, as well as change whether it connects to a workgroup or domain.

6 Click Domain (○ changes to ◉).

7 Type your domain name in the Domain text box.

Note: You can obtain the domain name from your network administrator.

8 Click OK.

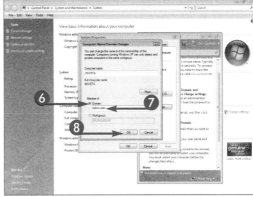

PART V

Can I manage features of a domain from within Windows Vista?

▼ Yes, but you are limited to what you can do on the Windows Vista client. One of the administrator duties you can perform is viewing remote Event Viewer items. This is handy if you want to see information regarding warnings and errors that occurred on the server. To use this feature, open the Control Panel and click System and Maintence. Click View Event Logs. Click Action and then click Connect To Another Computer. The Select Computer dialog box appears. Type the name of the domain server — you need to know the computer name for this server — and click OK. The Event Viewer window shows the events associated with the server.

When I attempt to connect to a domain, I receive a message saying the domain is unavailable. What should I do?

▼ This can be caused by a few things. First, make sure your computer is connected to your network. Second, make sure you typed in the domain name, username, and passwords correctly. Passwords are case-sensitive, so be sure you enter your password exactly as given to you by your network administrator. Another item to look at is the computer name. Each computer on the network must have a unique name. If your computer name is the same as another one on the domain — even if the other computer uses a different operating system — change your computer name.

Configure Windows Vista for a Domain *(Continued)*

When you set up your computer on a domain, the Windows server checks to see if another computer on the network has used your computer name and other computer ID. For that reason, the Computer name field on the Computer Name/Domain Changes dialog box must contain a unique name for your network. In some organizations, the computer names may be as simple as Marketing-01. However, some organizations that have thousands of desktops to manage must use names that at first glance may appear as random numbers and letters, such as E43- W2-3876. In this example, the name may stand for the 43rd branch

office in the East region, wing number 2, computer number 3876.

Domains offer several advantages over workgroups. The threshold many information technology workers like to meet to determine when a domain is needed is when there are 15 or more computers in an environment. Two of the most critical reasons for domains include user control and access rights. With a domain, network administrators can specify which users have access to the network — a workgroup does not have this capability. Each user, then, can be configured to have only certain permissions on the network, such as accessing a specific folder or printer.

The Computer Name/Domain Changes dialog box appears. You must log on with your username and password to complete the changes.

⑨ Type your username.

⑩ Type your password.

⑪ Click OK.

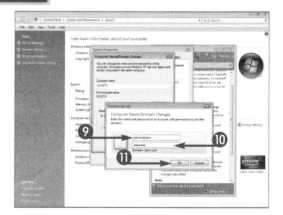

Windows logs on to the domain to authenticate your username and to ensure your computer has permission to connect to the domain.

⑫ Click OK when Windows welcomes you to your domain.

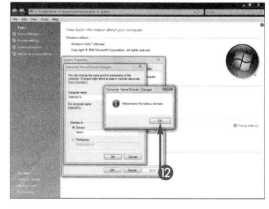

A message box appears saying that to apply these changes you must restart your computer.

⑬ Click OK to continue.

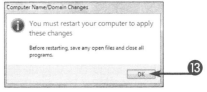

The System Properties dialog box appears.

⑭ Click Close to continue.

A dialog box appears.

⑮ Click Restart Now to shut down and restart Windows.

Windows shuts down, and your computer restarts to the Windows log on screen.

The Member of and Workgroup options on the Computer Name/Domain Changes dialog boxes are grayed out. How can I change them?

▼ You must be logged on to Windows Vista using an administrator username and password. If you have an administrator account and privileges, choose Start, click the right power arrow, and then click Log Off. When the Windows Welcome screen appears, click the administrator account name, enter the password for that account, and press Enter. Now perform the steps described in the "Configure Windows Vista for a Domain" section.

I carry a laptop to work and take it home at night. Will I need my domain available at home to start Windows Vista?

▼ No, when you log on at home, Windows Vista will start fine, but the network resources will not be available. For example, your company may have a program, such as a database, that runs on only its network. When you log on at home, you will not be able to use your database program. Programs that reside on your hard drive, such as Microsoft Office 2007, can be used. Other network resources, such as printers, and sending and receiving e-mail messages also will not be available.

Connect to a Domain

After you configure Windows Vista to reside on a domain, you must connect to the domain. Upon restarting Windows — either after changing from workgroup to domain setup or simply starting your computer to begin working — the Windows logon screen appears. You must press Ctrl+Alt+Del to access the screen in which you can enter your authentication information.

One of the main reasons organizations incorporate domains into their environments is to capitalize on Windows 2003 security. Unlike versions of consumer-oriented Windows before the release of Windows XP, Windows Vista is a secure operating system. That means if a password is required, and most domains require one, you must enter the

password to gain access to the Windows desktop and programs. Previous versions, such as Windows Me and Windows 98, allowed you to bypass the logon screen by clicking Cancel or pressing Esc. You could then access local files and programs as if you had logged on. Networking resources still required users to log on to access information and objects, even in a simple Windows 98/Me workgroup network.

Not only do most organizations require a password to access the domain, but also passwords generally have to adhere to stringent guidelines. For example, users should have passwords that are at least six characters long, have both numbers and letters, have at least one uppercase letter, and be difficult to guess.

Connect to a Domain

① Start your computer.

② When the Windows screen appears, press Ctrl+Alt+Del.

The Windows log on screen appears.

③ Type your password in the password field.

④ Press Enter.

Windows logs on to the domain
and then displays the Windows
desktop.

**After I press Ctrl+Alt+Delete, I do not see
my username. What can I do?**

▼ Windows Vista displays all the users who
have logged on to this computer. So if
your domain username is different from
your workgroup name, click Switch User.
If your username appears on the screen
that appears, click it and enter your
password. If not, click Other User. Type
your username into the User name field
and your password into the Password field.
Press Enter to start Windows. The next
time you start Windows, this will be the
username that appears after you press
Ctrl+Alt+Delete.

**Why does my desktop look different
when I log on to the domain account?**

▼ Because Windows Vista treats you as a
different user account, and each user
account has a different set of environment
configurations, including desktops,
program settings, User folder, and so on.
After you log on to Windows Vista and
connect to a domain for the first time, you
will have to set up your desktop the way
you like it, configure programs, and add
bookmarks to Internet Explorer. You will
also have to set up connections to your
network resources, such as network
printers.

Disconnect from a Domain

Windows Vista enables you to disconnect a computer from a domain. This is helpful if you move the computer to a different location that does not require domain authentication, if a domain is removed from your network, or if you need to perform administration tasks that require you to be off the domain for that time.

After you disconnect from a domain, you log on to Windows using the Welcome screen. On that screen, you select a user account and, if it is configured to have one, enter the user account password to start Windows. When you disconnect from a domain, you

set up access to a workgroup. Even if you are setting up your computer in a stand-alone environment — no other computers connected to yours — you should still set up the computer in a workgroup. If you do not have a workgroup name, use a generic one such as Workgroup.

To disconnect Windows from a domain, you must be currently logged on to the domain using an authorized user account. After a computer is disconnected from a domain, the resources available on that domain are no longer available for that computer until the computer is reconnected to the domain.

Disconnect from a Domain

① Click Start.

② Right-click Computer.

③ Click Properties.

The System window appears.

④ Click Change Settings.

The System Properties dialog box appears.

⑤ Click Change.

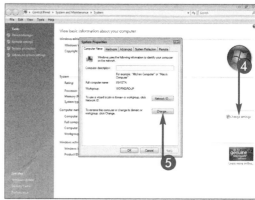

⑥ In the Computer Name/Domain Changes dialog box, click the Workgroup option (○ changes to ⊙).

⑦ Type the name of a workgroup, for example, **WORKGROUP**.

⑧ Click OK.

Windows disconnects from the domain and then connects to the workgroup you named in step 7.

A Welcome screen appears when the workgroup is located.

⑨ Click OK.

A dialog box prompts you to restart your computer to apply the change.

⑩ Click OK.

⑪ Shut down and restart your computer.

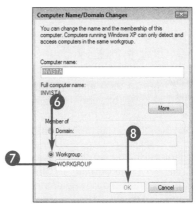

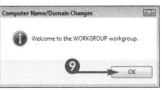

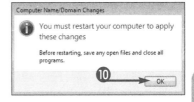

When I am on a domain, how can I find its name?

▼ The domain is listed on the System window. To see this, click the Start button and right-click Computer. Click Properties on the menu that appears to display the System window. On the System window, look under the heading named Computer name, domain, and workgroup settings. An entry named Domain lists the domain name. This information comes in handy if you attempt to log on to a resource that requires you to use your domainname\ username and password to log on. Sometimes intranet pages require this information.

How do I know what workgroups are available on my network when I disconnect from the domain?

▼ Sometimes organizations keep a list of workgroups in a centralized location, such as on a department bulletin board or in the system administrator's office. If you do not know a specific workgroup name when you disconnect from a domain, create a new workgroup name by typing that name in the Workgroup text box. The default Windows Vista workgroup name is WORKGROUP. If in doubt, you can use that name and you will probably locate other members of this workgroup in your organization.

Search for Users

Windows Vista enables you to search for users within your domain. This is handy if you want to find the username for a particular person in your organization. You also may want to do a search if you are setting up new users for your organization and want to make sure they have unique names on the domain. In this example, simply search for the proposed new usernames. If Windows cannot find a username, then you can use the new name. On the other hand, if a match is made for the username you are searching, you know you must come up with a different username for the new user.

Windows Vista includes the Find Users, Contacts, and Groups tool to help you find resources on your network. Sometimes you may see windows and help articles that refer to these resources as objects. When you use the Find Users, Contacts, and Groups tool, you can search the domain on to which you are logged, or the entire directory. The entire directory means your domain, any local directories you have stored on your computer, and any directories where you are in other domains that you have user permissions to search.

Search for Users

① Click Start.

② Click Network.

The Network window appears.

③ Click Search Active Directory.

The Find Users, Contacts, and
Groups window appears.

④ In the Name text box, type the
name of the user you want to find.

⑤ Click Find Now.

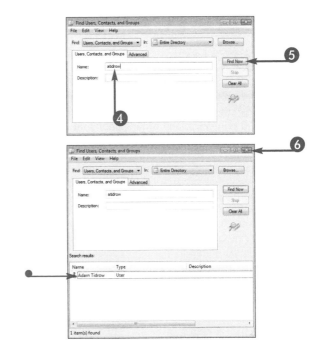

● If a user is found in the domain
that matches the name you
entered, Windows displays it in
the Search results area of the
Find Users, Contact, and
Groups window.

⑥ Click the Close box to close the
window.

**Are there ways to narrow a user search
to department?**

▼ Yes, the Find Users, Contacts, and Groups
tool includes the Custom Search feature.
To access this, click the Find drop-down list
and click Custom Search. The Custom
Search tab appears where the Users,
Contacts, and Groups tab was. Click the
Field drop-down list. From this list, you can
search on user or group attributes, such as
Computer Name, Contact, Group, and so
forth. The upside to this is that you can
perform your searches very quickly if you
can narrow your search to one of these
attributes. The downside is that in some
organizations, user and group attribute
fields are not routinely filled in or updated
as much as they should be.

**On the Field list of the Custom Search
tab on the Find Users, Contact, and
Groups window, I see a drop-down list
called Group. What is a domain group?**

▼ A *domain group* is a collection of users,
computers, and other groups. The network
administrator can create groups to help
manage security permissions and e-mail
distribution lists. Users can be in one group
or be put into many groups, depending on
the rights they need. For example, some
users have only standard user permissions,
while others may have standard
permissions as well as power user
permissions.

Search for Printers

Another useful feature of Windows Vista that you can use in a domain is to search for shared printers. Many organizations set up shared printers so several users can use one printer. Also, shared printers enable one user to use many printers. For example, you may have a laser printer attached to your computer that prints only in black and white. Another user, who may be down the hall from you, may have a color printer that is shared. You can connect to the color printer for those times you need a color printout.

When you search for printers over a domain, Windows sends a request out over the network to return all printers that are set up as shared. Depending on the size of your network, speed of the connections, the number of shared printers, and speed of your computer, this search may take several minutes to complete.

When a printer is found, you can set it up on your computer so you can access it for printing. Sometimes the search may not yield the printer you want or any printers at all. Contact your help desk or IT department for a list of network printer names and locations.

Search for Printers

① Click Start.

② Click Control Panel.

The Control Panel window appears.

③ Under the Hardware and Sound category, click Printer.

The Printers window appears.

④ Click Add a printer.

⑤ In the Add Printer window, click Add a network, wireless or Bluetooth printer.

The Searching for Available Printers window appears while Windows searches for all available printers on the network.

⑥ Click Next to continue.

The Find a printer by name or TCP/IP address screen appears. Here you can browse for a printer, specify a printer to connect to, or specify a printer using an Internet address.

⑦ Click Select a shared printer by name (○ changes to ◉).

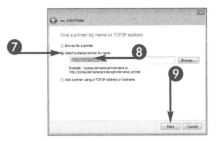

⑧ Type the path for the printer, including the \\computername to indicate the name of the computer to which the printer is attached.

⑨ Click Next to continue.

The Type a printer name window appears.

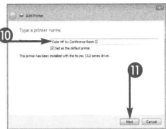

⑩ Type a name for the printer.

Use a name that makes it easy for you to remember the printer's location.

⑪ Click Next.

A window appears announcing you have set up the printer correctly.

⑫ Click Finish.

The Printers window appears.

PART V

Last week I set up a network printer but now I cannot print to that printer. What can I do?

▼ You can do a couple of things. First, make sure you are connected to the domain properly. Look for a shared file or folder, or try to access your corporate e-mail. If all these things are OK, make sure the shared printer is turned on. This may mean you need to walk around to the printer and check its power switch. Or if the printer is situated next to someone in your office, ask him or her if the printer is turned on. Of course, a common problem is that the paper tray is empty. Fill it to continue printing.

I know a printer is on the network, but I cannot find it using the Search feature. How do I find it?

▼ To find a printer on the network requires that the printer be shared and be listed in the directory. When the printer is set up, these options are configured. If these conditions are not met, the printer will not show up in the Search window. Ask a colleague to print something to that printer to see if the printer is working. If so, you should be able to locate the printer as well. Shut down and restart Windows. Re-logging on to Windows may set up access to the printer.

Redirect the Document Folders

You may want your folders, such as your Documents, Desktop, and Start Menu, to be available to you regardless of the computer to which you log on. To do this, you can use a Windows Vista feature called Folder Redirection. With Vista, you can redirect up to ten folders.

With Folder Redirection, you can redirect a folder so it is on a network server. To use Folder Redirection, you must have a user group policy set up. For more information on group policies, see Chapter 6.

After a user group is established, you can use the Folder Redirection policy to establish which folder is redirected and to which location it is redirected. Usually the folder is redirected to the main server that the user normally accesses. For example, if you have a mobile user on your sales team who generally logs on to a server to download sales worksheets at his home office, you can locate the redirected folder on that server as well. This way Windows Vista does not have to access multiple servers when a user logs on at the home office.

Redirect the Documents Folder

① Click Start.

② Click All Programs.

Note: After you click All Programs, the name changes to Back.

③ Click Accessories.

④ Click Run.

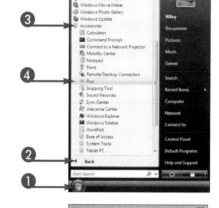

The Run dialog box appears.

⑤ Type **gpedit.msc**.

⑥ Click OK.

The Group Policy Object Editor appears.

⑦ Double-click Windows Settings.

The Windows Settings options expand.

⑧ Double-click Folder Redirection.

Folders that you can redirect appear.

⑨ Double-click the folder that you want to redirect, for example, AppData.

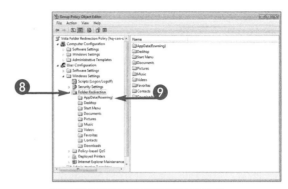

The folder's Documents Properties dialog box appears.

⑩ Click the Target tab.

⑪ Click the Setting down arrow and select the basic option to redirect everyone's folder to the same location.

⑫ In the Security Group Membership area, click the option to redirect to the local user profile location.

⑬ Click OK to confirm your changes.

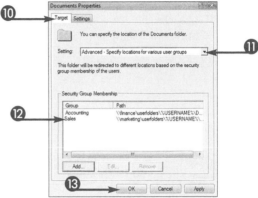

As the system administrator, I have to set up each of the redirected folders. Each user has several folders I want to redirect. Can I do them in a batch?

▼ Unfortunately, Windows requires that you set up each redirected folder separately. You also must redirect each user's folders separately. This can take some time, so do not plan on doing them all in one morning if you have dozens of users, each requiring several folders to be redirected. Also, you may want to issue an e-mail to users about these folder redirection changes. Explain what the folders are and why you are allowing these folders to be redirected.

As the system administor, I plan to use roaming profiles and redirected folders on my network. What kind of performance issues do I have to consider?

▼ Good question. Roaming profiles can consume a great deal of resources — real memory and processor cycles. The main reason for this is that anything stored by the users onto their computers — files, environment changes like desktop changes, and so on — are saved to the network server. Each time the user logs on, those files must be downloaded to the local computer. For this reason, consider establishing limits to the amount of information that a user can save to his Documents folder, such as 100MB. This way the user must pare down his saved files when he reaches that threshold.

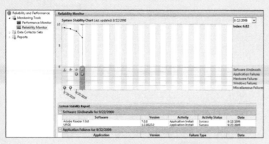

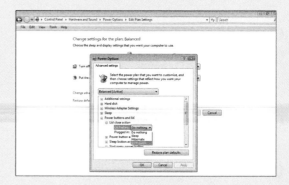

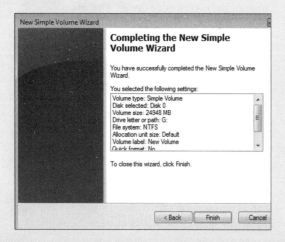

25 Troubleshooting Windows Vista

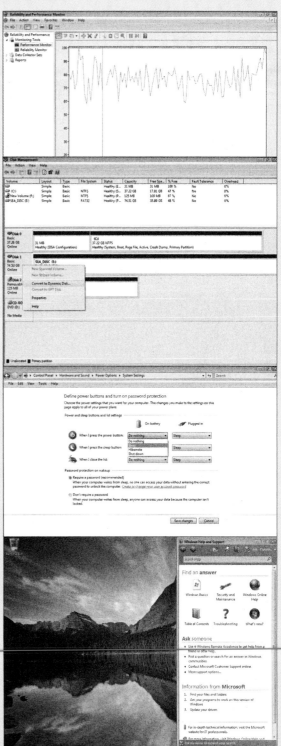

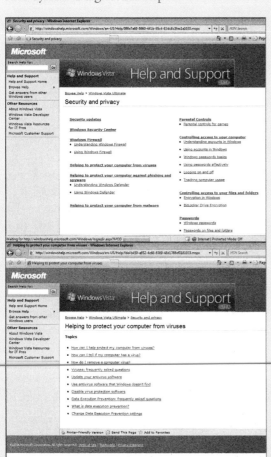

Display System Information

You can readily view information about your PC using the System Information tool. You can launch the tool from the Run command either by typing msinfo32.exe or by navigating from the Start menu by clicking All Programs, clicking Accessories, and then clicking System Tools. A more basic command-line tool also exists, if you prefer. It is called systeminfo.exe, and it includes a subset of the information available in the System Information tool.

When you launch the System Information tool, it searches for and collects pertinent system data and then displays System Summary information. With System Summary selected, the right pane of the System Information window displays the most basic system data. You can navigate the tree structure in the left pane to find the information you are looking for by category, or you can use the Search feature to find all instances of a text string. From the File menu, you can export data displayed to a text file or print it. From the Tools menu, you have access to these system tools: Net Diagnostics, System Restore, File Signature Verification Utility, DirectX Diagnostic Tool, and Dr Watson.

① Click Start.

② Click All Programs.

Note: *After you click All Programs, the name changes to Back.*

③ Click Accessories.

④ Click Run.

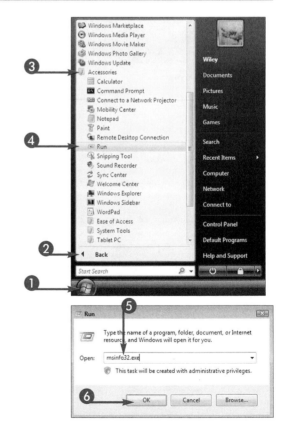

The Run dialog box appears.

⑤ Type **msinfo32.exe**.

⑥ Click OK.

The System Information window appears.

● System Summary lists basic system information.

● Detailed additional system information is grouped by categories that can be viewed by expanding the tree and then selecting a subcategory.

7 Type a text string here, for example, **NTFS**.

8 Click Find.

The System Information tool takes you to the first instance of NTFS.

9 Click Find to find the next instance of the text string you typed.

10 Click the Close box to exit System Information.

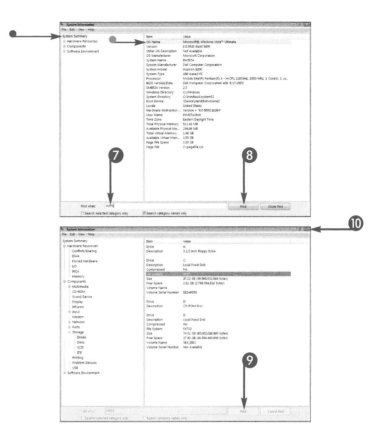

Can I find information about hardware conflicts and problems with the System Information tool?

▼ Yes. Click Hardware Resources in the navigation pane and then click Conflicts/Sharing to review resource conflicts. Resource conflicts include direct memory access, interrupt, and input/output device settings. You can also click Components and then click Problem Devices. If any plug-and-play (PNP) devices have problems, you see a list with the description of the device, a PNP Device ID, and the relevent error code.

Can I find my Internet Protocol (IP) address here?

▼ Yes. In the navigation pane, click Components, click Network, and then click Adapter. You see your IP address and subnet mask, and other relevent information.

When I search using a keyword, I do not find what I am lookin for. Are there ways I can improve my chances?

Probably the first thing to do is to remove the check mark in the Search Category Names Only check box (☑ changes to ☐). This enables Windows to search all the details in the System Information tool, not just the category names.

Manage Devices

Y ou can manage components of your PC's hardware and logical devices with Device Manager. To access it, right-click Computer and click Manage to bring up the Computer Management window. From there you can click Device Manager to display a list of categories of devices connected to your PC, including the mouse, the keyboard, disk drives, network cards, display adapters, and so on. Each category has a plus sign to its left; clicking this button expands the tree and shows individual devices within any given category.

For each device, you can perform several operations, depending on the type of device. By right-clicking the individual device, you can scan for hardware changes, update the device's driver, uninstall the driver, or disable or enable the device. You can also click Properties to bring up a dialog box for the device in question, usually with several tabs, depending on the device. The first tab to display, the General tab, has a device status box indicating whether the device is working properly. From this tab, you can disable or enable the device. Click the Driver tab to view the version and origin of the driver, as well as to update, roll back, or uninstall a driver.

Manage Devices

① Click Start.

② Right-click Computer.

③ Click Manage.

The Computer Management window appears.

④ Click System Tools.

⑤ Click Device Manager in the left navigation pane.

● A list of device categories is displayed in the right pane.

⑥ Click the plus sign (+) next to a device category to view the individual devices in that category.

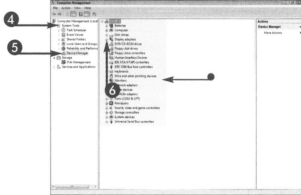

⑦ Right-click a device, for example, Dell 8200.

⑧ Click Properties.

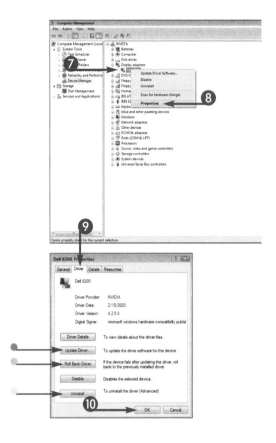

The Properties dialog box for the device appears.

⑨ Click the Driver tab to view the date, version, and provider of the driver.

● Click here to update the device driver to a newer version.

● Click here to roll back to a previous version.

● Click here to Uninstall.

Note: *It is preferable to use the Add Hardware tool for this operation.*

⑩ Click OK to confirm your changes.

How can I tell if there is a new driver?

▼ If you click Update Driver, you have the option of checking via the Windows Update site. You must have a working Internet connection to use this feature. Often you will be directed by a support technician to download a new driver from a hardware manufacturer to fix a problem.

If a new device driver is located, make sure it is newer than the one you are replacing. You can find out this information by comparing the file names. Usually the newer ones will have more recent dates associated with them — see the Drive Date label for your current driver's date — and they will have higher version numbers.

How do I disable a device?

▼ Right-click the device and click Disable. A red X appears over the device's icon in the display indicating that it has been disabled, which is not the same as uninstalling it. To enable it again, just right-click the device's icon and click Enable. Not all devices can be disabled. Also, sometimes a device cannot be re-enabled from Windows. If you notice a device does not re-enable, try shutting down and restarting Windows. Usually this reinstalls the drivers for that device so that it works when Windows starts up.

Manage Tasks

You can examine running applications, processes, CPU (Central Processing Unit) performance, and network performance with Task Manager. You can also use Task Manager to switch between applications or end an application if it is locked up.

Task Manager has six tabs: Applications, Processes, Services, Performance, Networking, and Users. The Applications tab of Task Manager enables you to see how many applications, or instances of applications, are currently running on your PC. From this tab, you can also switch between applications, or close an application. From the Processes tab, you can view the system processes that are currently running. Processes are a more detailed representation of programs that are currently executing on your computer, including those run by the system and utilities such as virus-scanning software and Task Manager itself. You can also end a process from this tab, but this can cause your system to become unstable. The Services tab shows the Windows services that are currently running. The Performance tab graphically represents your CPU's utilization as well as that Page File usage and memory details. The Networking tab measures network activity. The Users tab shows the user account information.

Manage Tasks

Note: *In this example, Paint and Media Player have been launched prior to running Task Manager to show sample applications running.*

1 Click Start.

2 Click All Programs.

Note: *After you click All Programs, the name changes to Back.*

3 Click Accessories.

4 Click Run.

The Run dialog box appears.

5 Type **taskmgr.exe**.

6 Click OK.

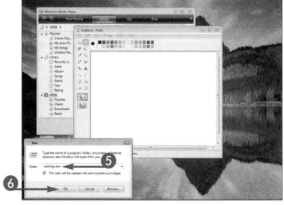

The Windows Task Manager appears, showing processes that are currently running.

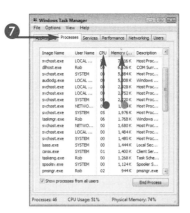

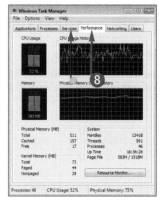

7 Click the Processes tab to view the programs that are executing.

- The current percentage of CPU usage appears here.

- Memory usage by process enables you to identify those processes using significant memory.

8 Click the Performance tab.

The Performance tab appears, showing a graphical representation of CPU and Page File usage in real time, as well as other performance measurements.

- To view the Windows services that are currently running, click the Services tab.

9 Click the Networking tab.

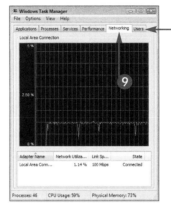

The Networking tab appears, showing local area network name, utilization, link speed, and connection status.

- To view user account information, click the Users tab.

I am running an application that is not responding to my input. How can I close the application?

▼ To shut down a program that no longer responds, you must use the Windows Task Manager program. To open Task Manager, press Ctrl+Alt+Del. Windows Vista displays a window similar to the log on Window. Click Start Task Manager. Windows Vista displays Windows Task Manager. Click the Applications tab and then click the application that no longer responds. If you're not sure of its name, look for an application that has Not Responding in the Status column. Click End Task.

How can I find out whether one of my currently running applications is taking up substantial memory?

▼ Use the Windows Task Manager program again. Click the Applications tab and then right-click the application you want to check on. From the menu that appears, click Go To Process. This takes you directly to the corresponding process in the Processes tab of the Task Manager, with the percent of CPU usage and memory usage for that process.

View
Events

Y ou can use Event Viewer to analyze your
system. Event Viewer is particularly useful for
troubleshooting. It keeps three logs of events:
one for the system, one for applications, and one for
security. The log entries contain information about
each event to help you identify issues easily.

Windows Vista has dramatically changed Event Viewer
from its previous releases. In fact, Event Viewer is now
more useful than older versions, which can help you
troubleshoot problems quicker. Event Viewer displays
Application, Security, and System logs. When you click
a log, you see a list of most recent events for that

category. There are several categories of events: Error
indicates that an error occurred; Warning indicates a
condition to watch; Information logs a normal event,
Success Audit, in the Security log, indicates a
successful attempt to get through a security
checkpoint; and Failure Audit, also in the Security log,
indicates a failed attempt to get through security.

Each event records such information as date, time,
type, user, computer, source, category, event ID, and
description. Some events also contain additional
data — useful to programmers and IT specialists.

View Events

1 Click Start.

2 Right-click Computer.

3 Click Manage.

The Computer Management window
appears.

4 Click Event Viewer in the left
navigation pane.

- A list of event logs appears at the
bottom of the middle pane.

5 Double-click System in the Log
Summary window.

- A list of System events appears in
the right pane.

6 Click an event.

The Event information appears on the General tab at the bottom of the pane.

● You can click here to copy the event information displayed to the Clipboard.

7 Click the Details tab.

Detailed system information about the error appears.

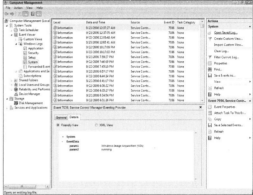

Can I find a recent error in an application to send to the tech support staff in my company?

▼ Yes, this is usually possible if the error is recent enough. If you know the date and time of the error, you can open the Application log and look for an error at that date and time. Errors are easy to spot: They have a red icon with a white exclamation point. Open the event entry by double-clicking it. Click Copy Details as Text from the Actions pane, and then paste it into your e-mail to your tech support staff or paste it into a text file using Notepad.

I just want to view error and warning events. Can I do that?

▼ Yes. You can filter the log entries by clicking Filter Current Log on the Actions pane. The Filters tab of the Filter Current Log Properties dialog box for that event log appears. Clear the check boxes for all event types except Error and Warning and then click OK. Note that this filter stays on until you next check all the check boxes or click Clear on the Filters tab of the Properties dialog box.

PART VI

461

Monitor Performance

Y ou can monitor your system performance with the Reliability and Performance Monitor. If you type **perfmon.msc** from the Run command and press OK, you launch Microsoft Management Console (MMC) with the Reliability and Performance Monitor. The Performance Monitor enables you to view system performance graphically and numerically in real time. The Reliability Monitor shows the system stability to help you analyze it. These tools are useful for identifying areas where your system is performing poorly so that you can address the performance bottlenecks. You can choose from various performance counters and performance objects to zero in on a problem.

Clicking Reliability and Performance in the left navigation pane brings up the Resource Overview, which shows CPU, Disk, Network, and Memory usage. When you click Performance Monitor, you see a real-time graph of your system's performance. By adding different counters to this graph, you can track CPU processes, print queues, disk usage, and many more areas of your system. When you click the Reliability Monitor in the left pane, the System Stability Chart and a report of software installations, application failures, Windows failures, and more appears.

Monitor Performance

① Click Start.

② Click All Programs.

Note: *After you click All Programs, the name changes to Back.*

③ Click Accessories.

④ Click Run.

The Run dialog box appears.

⑤ Type **perfmon.msc**.

⑥ Click OK.

The Reliability and Performance Monitor of MMC appears, with the Resource Overview displaying CPU, disk, network, and memory performance graphically in real time.

● Numeric data and a key to performance counter settings appear here.

⑦ Click Performance Monitor in the left pane.

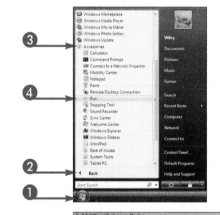

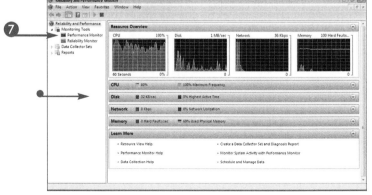

● A graph appears, showing Windows real-time performance for the counter listed at the bottom of the graph.

⑧ Click Reliability Monitor.

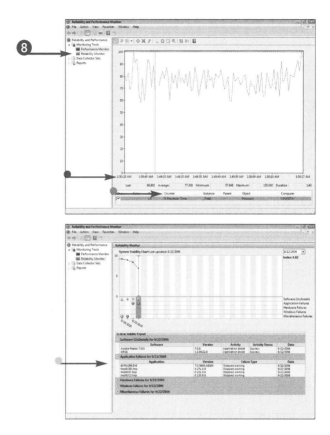

● The System Stability Chart appears, providing a history of software, application, hardware, and other failures and uninstalls.

Are there any diagnostics of the system that I can view from the Reliability and Performance Monitor?

▼ Yes, you can use the Data Collector Sets. Double-click Data Collector Sets in the left pane. Click the arrow next to System, and then right-click the category of Collector Set you want to review. Click Start. In the middle pane, details of the Data Collector Set appear for you to analyze. For example, by starting the Wireless Diagnostics Data Collector Set, you can view reports about your wireless configuration.

How do I select additional counters for the Performance Monitor?

▼ Right-click anywhere in the Performance Monitor pane. Click Add Counters. On the Add Counter dialog box, double-click an item in the Available Counters list to expand it to show specific counters. Click a counter and then click the Add button to display the counter in the Added Counters list. Continue adding counters as necessary. You should probably keep the number of counters to a minimum so that the resulting graph is still easy to understand. Click OK.

Configure and Control Services

You can configure and control services with the Services MMC snap-in. *Services* are programs that run in the background on your system locally or as part of network- or Internet-based client server applications. Depending on the type of service, you can start, stop, pause, resume, disable, or enable services from the Services snap-in. You can also configure how services behave in a given situation, or turn services on and off based on a specific hardware profile.

To launch the Services tool, type **services.msc** from the Run command and press OK. This brings up the local Services window. The Extended tab shows a

description and a list of available commands for the selected service. The Standard tab does not display the description and list of commands, but shows more fields. To control a service, click its name. In the Extended tab, the description and basic commands appear. For more detailed configuration options — such as what to do when the service fails, alternate behavior with different hardware profiles, and so on — double-click the service. Use caution when manually controlling services. Read any warnings carefully and understand any program interdependencies before stopping or disabling a service.

Configure and Control Services

① Click Start.

② Click All Programs.

Note: After you click All Programs, the name changes to Back.

③ Click Accessories.

④ Click Run.

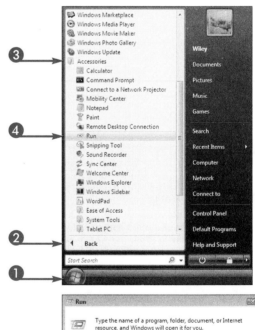

The Run dialog box appears.

⑤ Type **services.msc**.

⑥ Click OK.

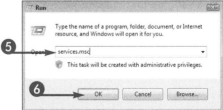

The Services window of MMC appears, showing service descriptions.

● Click the Standard tab to remove the Description pane on the left side.

⑦ Click the service (FTP Publishing Service, in this example).

● A description of the service's function appears here.

⑧ Click one of the basic commands you can perform on the service.

The status changes to Paused.

⑨ Click Resume the service.

⑩ Click the Close box to close the Services window.

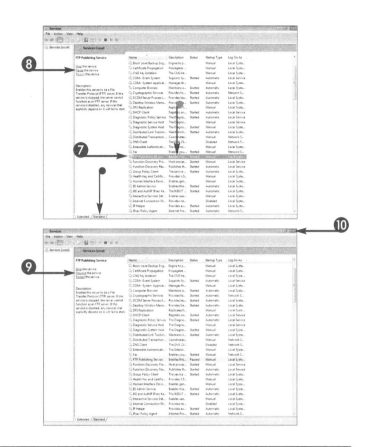

How do I disable a service for a specific hardware profile?

▼ Launch the Services snap-in. Double-click the service name from the list. The properties dialog box appears. Click the Log On tab and choose the hardware profile for which you want to disable the service. Click Disable. Click OK. Before you disable a service, make sure you do not need it for Windows and your applications to run properly. For example, the humble-looking DHCP Client service (Dynamic Host Configuration Protocol) simply registers and updates IP addresses and Domain Name System/Server (DNS) records. For some users, that does not mean much. But if you turn it off, you will not have Internet connectivity on your computer, even if you use a dial-up modem.

How do I change the behavior when the service fails?

▼ Launch the Services snap-in. Double-click the service name from the list. The properties dialog box appears. Click the Recovery tab. Choose an action from the drop-down list for the first, second, or subsequent failures. You can elect to take no action, attempt to restart the service, restart the computer, or run a program. If you elect to restart the computer, click Restart Computer Options for access to more parameters. If you elect to run a program in a failure situation, fill in the information in the Run Program section.

PART VI

Schedule Tasks

You can schedule your PC to run tasks at a specific time in the future or at regular intervals using Task Scheduler on the Control Panel. The easiest way to access this tool is to click Start, click Control Panel, switch to Classic View, and then click Scheduled Tasks. If you want more ready access to this tool, you can right-click the Scheduled Tasks icon in the Control Panel and click Create Shortcut to create a shortcut on your desktop. The Task Scheduler window appears, listing scheduled tasks and an Add Scheduled Tasks item. If you have antivirus software running or are working in an organization with IT support, you probably already have some scheduled tasks listed.

If you want to modify or reschedule an existing task, double-click the task. If you want to disable the task temporarily, but do not want to get rid of it entirely, right-click the task in the Task Scheduler Library and click Disabled. To reschedule a task, click the Triggers tab for the task and modify the date and time settings accordingly. To make changes to how the scheduled task operates based on power or idle time, click the Settings tab.

Schedule Tasks

① Click Start.

② Click Control Panel.

The Control Panel appears.

③ Click System and Maintenance.

④ Click Schedule tasks.

The Task Scheduler window appears.

● To change settings to an existing task, double-click the task.

⑤ Click the Create Basic Task action in the Actions pane.

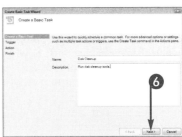

The Create Basic Task Wizard appears.

⑥ Click Next.

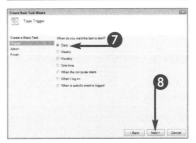

The Task Trigger window appears.

⑦ Select when you want the task to run (○ changes to ◉).

⑧ Click Next.

How do I schedule an existing task to occur just once?

▼ In the Task Scheduler, double-click the task from the list in the Active Tasks list folder to display the tasks in the Task Scheduler Library. Double-click the task at the top of the middle pane to display its properties window. Click the Trigger tab and click Edit. The Edit Trigger dialog box appears. Click One time in the Settings list, set the date and time, and click OK. Click OK again to close the tasks properties window. In the Task Scheduler Library list, the Triggers column shows the one date and time at which the task will run.

Is a task automatically removed from the list if it is not set to run again?

▼ No, but you can set it so that it is deleted if it is not going to run again. Double-click the task to display its properties window. Click the Settings tab. Click the If the task is not scheduled to run again, delete it after option. Select Immediately from the drop-down list next to this option. Click OK to save your settings. After the last scheduled run time, the task is removed from the list.

PART VI

continued

Schedule
Tasks *(Continued)*

To add a new task, click Create Basic Task. The Create Basic Task Wizard launches and walks you through the steps to creating a new task. First, it asks you to enter a name and description for the new task. Then it asks you to specify when and what time you want the task to execute. For example, you can set tasks to run daily, weekly, monthly, one time only, when the computer starts, or when you log on. Next, you specify the type of task, such as running a specific program, you want to run. First, it asks you

to select a program for Windows to run as a scheduled task. Click Browse if you do not see the program you want in the list. You have now completed the steps to build a task.

The final screen of the Scheduled Task Wizard confirms your task information — program, date, time, and frequency. You can view the properties of this task by clicking Open the Properties Dialog For This Task When I Click Finish. Click Finish and the task appears in the list.

Schedule Tasks *(continued)*

A window appears, letting you specify start and recurrence times.

⑨ Click to select the date and time when the task will run.

⑩ Click Next.

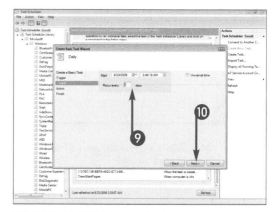

The Action window appears.

⑪ Click the type of task you want to perform (○ changes to ◉).

⑫ Click Next.

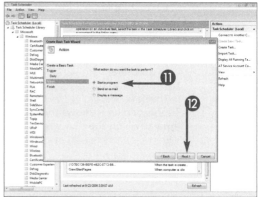

468

The Start a Program window appears.

⑬ Type the program/script to run, or click Browse to select it.

⑭ Click Next.

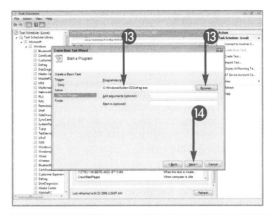

The Summary window appears.

⑮ Click Finish to close the Create Basic Task Wizard.

⑯ Click the Close box on the Task Scheduler window.

Can I make the task run even if my computer is in Sleep mode?

▼ Yes, you can do this provided your hardware supports the Sleep feature. To specify that the task should wake the computer when the task runs, double-click the task in the Task Scheduler Library. Click the Conditions tab of the dialog box that appears. Click the Wake the computer to run this task option. Click OK. When the task is scheduled to run, it will wake up the computer if the computer is in Sleep mode. Of course, the computer must be turned on for the task to run. It cannot run without Windows started.

Can I run a task right now rather than at the scheduled time?

▼ Yes. Right-click the task and click Run. The task launches immediately. In addition to launching a task immediately, you can end a task immediately. Right-click the task and click End. You will want to be careful ending a task prematurely if the task is responsible for disk-related copying or moving that could damage files if the task ends before the files are saved properly.

Diagnose Memory Problems

You can diagnose memory problems several ways. One way is to use the System Information tool provided by Windows Vista. You can launch the System Information tool from the Run command either by typing msinfo32.exe or by using the Start menu. The System Information tool lists the memory address of the hardware device, a description of the device, and the status of memory. Every hardware device uses a portion of memory in Windows. This is called the *memory address*. Each device must have its own memory address allocated in Windows Vista or an error can occur, usually one that causes Windows Vista to stop functioning when you attempt to use that hardware device.

The System Information tool can show resource conflicts. If such a conflict occurs, you can use the Device Manager to troubleshoot the problem. One way to resolve the conflict is to modify one of the devices manually to use a different memory address. Updating the device driver may also solve the problem. Finally, you may have to remove one of the devices, shut down and restart Windows Vista, and then reinstall the device to allow it to set up in a different memory address. See the section "Manage Devices."

Diagnose Memory Problems

① Click Start.

② Click All Programs.

Note: After you click All Programs, the name changes to Back.

③ Click Accessories.

④ Click Run.

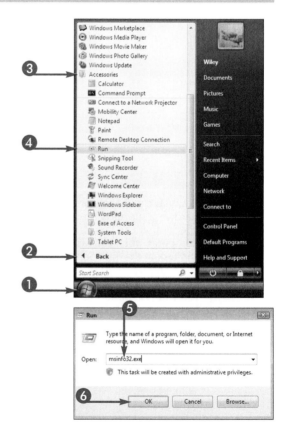

The Run dialog box appears.

⑤ Type **msinfo32.exe** in the text box.

⑥ Click OK.

The System Information window appears.

7 Click the expand button (+) to show subentries.

8 Click Memory.

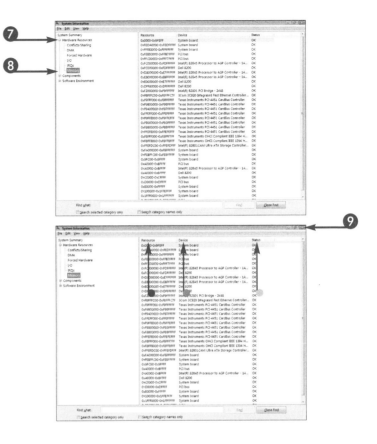

● Memory addresses appear here.

● Device names appear here.

● Memory status appears here.

9 Click the Close box to close the window.

Do I have to set up memory address settings?

▼ Usually Windows Vista handles all memory address allocations. Windows Vista allocates memory when you set up the device, and occurs each time Windows Vista starts. Devices are designed to use certain memory address ranges, so you should not have to set these manually. If you do, such as if you recognize a memory address conflict, contact the manufacturers of the devices and obtain the memory address settings for the devices. You can then use Device Manager to modify the settings.

Will the System Information tool show if my Random Access Memory (RAM) is bad?

▼ Not directly. However, if you are experiencing problems with your RAM, you may notice that some of the listings in the Status column of the System Information tool show up as Errors or Warnings. If your RAM is going bad, you probably will not be able to access too many applications, including System Information. A key diagnostic tool for your RAM runs each time your start your computer. If a problem is detected during boot, you will see a warning message that your memory may have a problem.

PART VI

Work with the Command Prompt

Y ou can run batch files, scripts, and command-line utilities using the command prompt. This is particularly useful for automating basic administrative and housekeeping tasks. It is also critical for some system support utilities that are available only as command-line tools. If you are familiar with and still recall the old MS-DOS command line, then this is essentially the latest version of the DOS prompt, and behaves the same way.

To launch the command prompt you use the Run program from the Start menu. If you use the command prompt often, you might even create a

shortcut on the desktop to the cmd.exe file. This will allow you to open the command prompt window quickly without going through the Start menu. When you run the command prompt, a text-based screen appears, showing you a prompt indicating the currently logged drive and directory. A blinking underscore indicates the location of the cursor. To run a command-line command, type the name of the command or program, followed by any parameters. If it is a program, do not type .exe or .com. To exit, you can type **exit** and press Enter when the command prompt next appears or click the Close button.

Work with the Command Prompt

① Click Start.

② Click All Programs.

Note: After you click All Programs, the Name changes to Back.

③ Click Accessories.

④ Click Run.

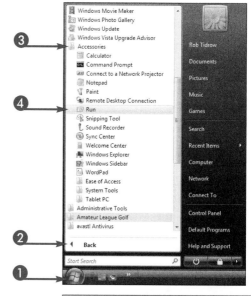

The Run dialog box appears.

⑤ Type **cmd.exe**.

⑥ Click OK.

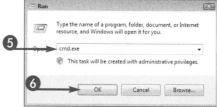

The command prompt appears in a text window with a blinking cursor.

7 Type the command or batch file name, for example, **dir /p** displays the first page of the directory listing for the current folder.

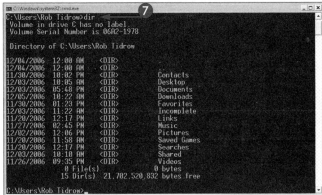

Can I enlarge the command prompt window?

▼ Yes, to do this right-click the command prompt window title bar. A menu appears. Click Properties to open the C:\ Windows\systems32\cmd.exe Properties dialog box. Click the Layout tab. In the Window Size area, you can change the Width and Height settings to increase the size of the window. For example, the default width is 80. Click inside the Width box and type a new value, such as 120. Click inside the Height box and type a new value, such as 50. Click OK to save your settings.

The command prompt window fonts are too small. How do I enlarge them?

▼ To do this, right-click the command prompt window title bar. A menu appears. Click Properties to open the C:\Windows\ systems32\cmd.exe Properties dialog box. Click the Font tab. From the Size list, click a new size for the fonts. For example, you can select a font size of 10×18 to make the fonts larger than the default ones. When you click a size, the Window Preview shows an example of the new font size. Notice too that the window size will change as well to accommodate the new font sizes. Click OK to save your settings.

Improve System Performance

Windows Vista includes tools to help you keep your system running at peak performance. As you use your computer, system performance degrades for various reasons. Installing new programs, uninstalling old ones, saving and deleting files, using the Internet, and performing other activities take a toll on your system. Serious issues include virus and spyware problems, corrupted system files, and boot problems.

To help improve your system, you need to perform regular system maintenance. Some of the actions you can perform include freeing up disk space, defragmenting your hard drive, improving graphics performance, and running ScanDisk on the hard drive.

Often these built-in utilities take care of the problem and speed up or improve system performance.

The Tools tab found on a disk's properties dialog box includes three Windows utilities: Error Checking, also known as ScanDisk; Defragmentation; and Backup. See Chapter 24 for how to use the Defragmentation tool on the Tools menu. The Backup utility is not necessarily a system performance utility, but it is invaluable when it comes to restoring files in the event of a system problem. See the section "Back Up and Restore Data," later in this chapter. You can set up Windows to run these tools automatically by using the Scheduled Tasks program.

Improve System Performance

Check for Errors on Your Disk

① To run Error Checking, or ScanDisk, on your computer, click Start.

② Click Computer.

The Computer window appears.

③ Right-click a disk you want to check.

④ Click Properties.

The Properties dialog box for the selected drive appears.

⑤ Click the Tools tab.

⑥ Click Check Now.

The Check Disk window appears.

⑦ Click both check disk options (☐ changes to ☑).

⑧ Click Start to scan the selected drive.

Note: *Error Checking can take several hours to complete depending on the size of the disk, number of errors found, and speed of your computer.*

The Checking Disk Removable Disk window appears.

⑨ When the scan is finished, click the See details arrow.

Note: *See details changes to Hide details.*

The Checking Disk window expands to show details of the scan and your disk.

⑩ Click Close to close the report window.

How can I see the performance of my processor?

▼ You can use the Windows System Performance Monitor. Click Start, click All Programs, click Accessories, and then click Run. In the Run dialog box, type **perfmon** and click OK. The Reliability and Performance Monitor opens. On the main window, you can view the processor peformance by looking at the CPU graph. Also, click the arrow on the CPU bar below the graph. A detailed account of the processes, such as programs and services, actively running appears.

Are any programs or utilities available to help me improve Windows Vista system performance?

▼ Yes, several commercial products and freeware/shareware products are available to help you optimize your computer. One of the most popular commercial programs is Norton SystemWorks 2006. You can find out more about this product at www.symantec.com. For other system optimization programs, do a search on www.google.com, or another search engine, to find information about the various utilities available for download. Some of the keywords you can use in a search include *Windows Vista utilities* and *Windows Vista system tools*.

Create New Partitions

You can divide a disk into multiple partitions, also called *volumes*, when you install Windows Vista. After you install Windows Vista, you can further optimize storage and system performance by changing disk volume sizes. With partitions, you can divide a large disk into several smaller logical disks. For example, if you have a 160GB hard drive, you could partition it into four 40GB partitions, each appearing and behaving like a separate hard drive. One partition would be labeled C, the next D, the next E, and the last F. Partitions do not have to be of equal size. One partition, say the boot partition, could have only 100GB, while another partition could have the balance of the hard disk (5605GB).

Partitioned drives let you organize your files and programs as you see fit. For example, you may have four partitions. You could store primary Windows and system files on your C drive; install programs on your D drive; store your multimedia files in your E drive; and, finally, store documents and database files on your F drive.

You can perform partitioning prior to installing Windows or as Windows Vista is installed. If you do it during installation, Windows creates just one partition.

You also can create a partition on a drive that has unallocated disk space. This space has not been set up as a partition yet. You may have unallocated space on a new drive that you installed, or on a volume that has not be configured yet.

Create New Partitions

① Click Start.

② Right-click Computer.

③ Click Manage.

The Computer Management window appears.

④ Click Disk Management to display the disk information for your computer.

● A list of all installed disks and information about each one appears. You can find out a disk's drive letter, its status, its capacity, its free space, and other important information.

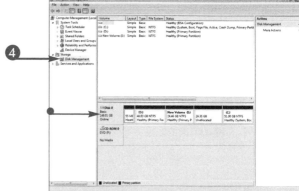

⑤ Right-click an unallocated region of a drive.

⑥ Click New Simple Volume.

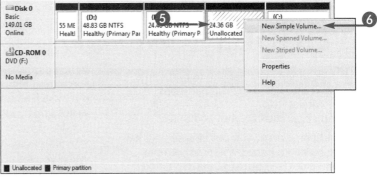

The Welcome to the New Simple Volume Wizard window appears.

⑦ Click Next.

I have Windows Vista installed but want to create a partition. How do I do that with my current drive?

▼ Unfortunately, after Windows is installed, you cannot partition the drive without losing all the drive's data, including Windows itself. This is because if you have just one partition, Windows uses it as the system and boot partition. If a disk has unallocated space on it, you can partition it. Sometimes large disks come with unallocated space from vendors if you specify that you want the disk set up this way.

How can I add partitions to my existing Windows computer?

▼ If you want to set up partitions on a computer and have only one disk, and the disk has one partition and no unallocated space, consider purchasing and adding a second hard drive to the system. You then can partition that drive into multiple partitions. The computer would then have your original hard drive formatted as the primary partition and labeled as C and a second drive with multiple partitions, such as D, E, and F. When you do purchase a second hard drive, look for the largest one for the best price. Hard drives in excess of 160GB are not uncommon.

continued

PART VI

Create New
Partitions *(Continued)*

Windows Vista enables you to partition a drive into one or several partitions. Partitions help you organize data files, programs, and system files on your computer.

When you partition a drive, you can choose whether to format the partition. If the partition is set up as a File Allocation Table (FAT) or FAT32 partition, you should choose to format it as a New Technology File System (NTFS). Formatting it as an NTFS file system takes advantage of Windows Vista's advanced file system features, such as security. It is best practice to

format a drive any time you create a new partition. Formatting removes all data from the drive — the data is removed when you partition a drive anyway — and cleans up any logical errors that may have formed on the disk. Formatting also attempts to fix physical errors on the disk.

When you set up a partition size, you specify the number of megabytes (MBs) each partition consumes. Some users like to create partitions of equal size. For example, on a 160GB drive that will have two partitions, each partition will be 80GB.

The Specify Volume Size window appears. Here you can specify the partition size you want for the disk.

8 Type a value for the partition size.

9 Click Next.

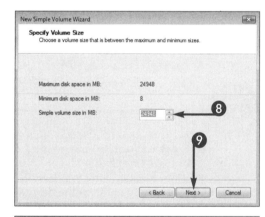

The Assign Drive Letter or Path window appears. Here you can specify the drive letter you want to name the partitioned drive.

● Click here to change the drive letter.

10 Click Next.

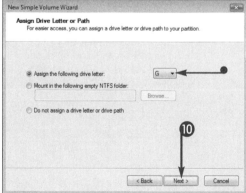

The Format Partition screen appears.

● The default format settings are usually acceptable for most drives.

⑪ Click Next.

The Completing the New Simple Volume Wizard window appears.

⑫ Click Finish to format and partition the disk.

The Disk Management window appears.

⑬ Click Yes to continue with the partitioning process.

When finished, the information for the newly partitioned drive appears in the Computer Management window.

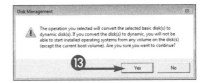

Are there any other programs that let me manage my drives, particularly setting up partitions?

▼ Yes, there are some third-party programs that let you create and manage partitions. In fact, some of them are easier to use than the built-in tools that come with Windows. Also, some disk-partitioning software enables you to manage partitions without the risk of losing data stored on the hard disk. One such software is Acronis Disk Director Suite at www.acronis.com. Another fantastic tool for partitioning drives is Symantec's PartitionMagic at www.partitionmagic.com/partitionmagic.

After I create partitions, can I install a second operating system on my computer?

▼ Yes. You must have a boot manager to manage which operating system boots when you start your computer. Windows Vista does not include a boot manager for dual-boot puposes. PartionMagic includes BootMagic to help you switch between operating systems. You also need to have the installation software for each operating system you plan to install. For example, to install Windows Vista, Windows 2003, and Linux — a Unix operating system — you must have the Windows Vista CDs for Windows Vista, a copy of Windows Server 2003 for that operating system, and a copy of the Linux CD for installing Linux.

Create Dynamic Disks

Windows Vista Professional enables you to set up disks in two different storage types — basic and dynamic. Basic storage is the default type of storage Windows Vista uses. Previous versions of Windows, such as XP, 2000, 98, and Me, also use basic storage. A basic storage disk includes basic volumes, such as primary partitions, extended partitions, and logical drives.

With dynamic disks, Windows Vista includes storage features normally found only in advanced operating systems, such as Windows NT Server, Windows 2000 Server, and Windows Server 2003. Dynamic disks

enable you to create five different disk structures not available on basic disks. These include simple, spanned, striped, mirrored, and RAID-5.

One of the main reasons for using dynamic disks is for setting up fault-tolerance duties. *Fault tolerance* is protection for your computer system against hardware problems, such as hard disk failure. When you lose your hard disk, the data on the disk is usually lost as well. For this reason, fault tolerance is used to make redundant copies of your data. With dynamic disks, you can set up fault tolerance through mirroring, RAID, and spanned drives.

Create Dynamic Disks

① In the Disk Management window, right-click the drive you want to change to a dynamic disk.

Note: To access the Disk Management window, repeat steps 1 to 4 in the section "Create New Partions."

② Click Convert to Dynamic Disk.

The Convert to Dynamic Disk dialog box appears. This dialog box shows a list of all the basic disks installed on your system that you can convert to dynamic disks.

Systems that have only one disk installed show only Disk 0 as the option available.

③ Select the disk you want to convert (☐ changes to ☑).

④ Click OK.

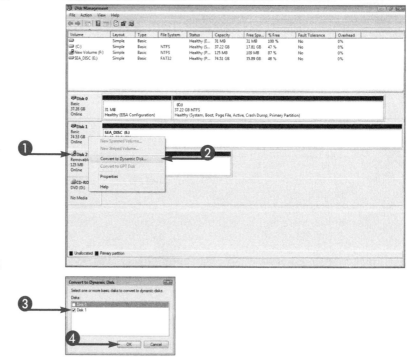

The Disks to Convert dialog box appears. This dialog box shows a list of the disks to convert and the partition information about each disk.

● To see volume information about the disks, click Details.

⑤ Click Convert.

The Disk Management window appears warning you that when you convert the disk to a dynamic disk you cannot run other operating systems besides Windows Vista from the volumes on the selected disks.

⑥ Click Yes.

Another message appears warning you that any disks with file systems will now be dismounted, which means they will temporarily be unusable until the conversion finishes.

⑦ Click Yes to convert the disk to a dynamic disk.

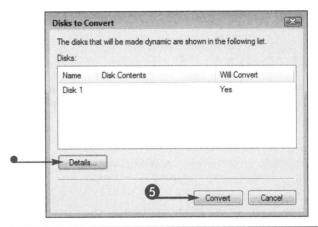

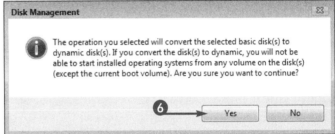

I have several folders set up as shared objects on my disk now. Can I convert the disk to dynamic and still share those folders?

▼ Yes, but there is a catch. Only systems running Windows Vista, Windows XP Professional, Windows 2000, and Windows Server 2003 can access those folders on the dynamic disk. Computers running Windows 95, 98, or Me, or non-Windows operating systems, for example Macintosh, cannot access those shared folders. If your company, organization, or home has a network in which shared folders are used, make sure all your systems are using Vista, XP, 2000 Server, or 2003 Server before converting to dynamic disks. Otherwise you cannot share your Vista folders with the other computers.

After I have a disk configured as dynamic, can I switch it back to basic?

▼ Yes, but the disk must be empty before you can switch it back to basic — copy any files on that disk to a backup disk. This means that any disk you want to convert back to basic must have a secondary drive — not the primary boot disk. Open the Computer Management window and double-click the Disk Management object under Storage. In the bottom right pane, right-click the disk you want to convert. Click Delete Volume for each volume on the disk. After you delete all the volumes on a disk, right-click the disk and click Convert to Basic Disk.

PART VI

Set Disk Quotas

O ne of the most important tasks for network administrators is managing disk space on their servers. With Windows Vista, you can use disk quotas to limit the amount of space users can consume on a disk volume. Although you can set disk quotas on stand-alone computers, you will generally set up disk quotas on volumes that are on a network share.

Disk quotas let you set an upper limit to the amount of space users can consume. This alleviates the problem of disks running out of space when a user takes up too much space on a drive.

When you set disk quotas and a user exceeds his or her quota, you can set Windows to deny extra space or simply log the event and let the user continue to save files past the quota. When you deny users space beyond the quota, you run the risk of users losing important data. If you allow users disk space even if they exceed their quota, you can review event files periodically to see which users may need more disk space allocated to them.

Set Disk Quotas

① Click Start.

② Click Computer.

The Computer window appears.

③ Right-click the drive on which you want to set quotas.

④ Click Properties from the menu that appears.

⑤ Click the Limit disk space to option (○ changes to ◉).

⑥ Type the amount of space to which to set the limit.

⑦ Click the down arrow and select the unit of measure for the amount.

⑧ To set a warning level so users know they have reached their disk quota, type the value.

⑨ Click the down arrow and select the unit of measure for the amount.

⑩ Click Apply.

The Disk Quota dialog box appears.

⑪ Click OK.

⑫ To see the statistics, click Quota Entries in the Properties dialog box.

The Quota Entries window appears.

⑬ Click Quota.

⑭ Click the Close box to close this window.

⑮ Click OK to confirm your changes in the Properties dialog box.

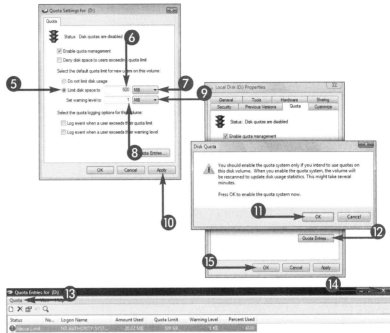

What is a disk volume?

▼ A disk volume is a disk area on which files can be stored. Every Windows computer has at least one disk volume. A physical disk, such as a hard drive, can be set up for one or multiple volumes. A volume can span more than one disk as well. Volumes are denoted by a letter, such as C. When you view your C drive using My Computer or Windows Explorer, you are looking at the disk volume of C. If you partition a drive into multiple volumes, you then have multiple drive letters.

How can I determine the amount of space a user needs?

▼ One way is to ask each user what type of work he or she performs. Use this information to allocate enough space for the user's needs. Another way is to allocate equal amounts of space to everyone, for example, 50MB, and then check these drives periodically to ensure that space is being used. if you determine that space will never be used by a certain user, reallocate that space to another one.

Back Up and Restore Data

Perhaps one of the most important jobs you can perform as a user or administrator is also one of the most overlooked jobs. This job is backing up your data. Organizations spend billions of dollars each year backing up and archiving their data in the event the data must be restored due to some kind of data loss.

You can use the Windows Backup Status and Configuration utility to create a backup of your data. Windows can run the backup as an automatic task, such as daily, or as a manual task. The Back Up Files

tool provides a way for you to select individual files to back up. For instance, you can use this option to select all the files you store in a working folder, such as your Documents folder, and then have Back Up Files back up the files every day before you shut down your computer, or if you leave your PC on all night, it can run late at night.

The other feature of Windows Vista Backup is the Complete PC Backup tool. It enables you to create a backup of your entire computer, including system settings, applications, and your files.

Back Up and Restore Data

Back Up Files

① To create a backup job, click Start.

② Click All Programs.

Note: After you click All Programs, the name changes to Back.

③ Click Accessories.

④ Click System Tools.

⑤ Click Backup Status and Configuration.

The Backup Status and Configuration window appears.

⑥ Click Set up automatic file backup.

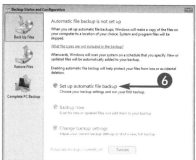

The Back Up Files Wizard appears.

⑦ Click the down arrow and select the destination drive for your backup, such as the E drive.

⑧ Click Next to continue.

The Which file types do you want to back up? screen appears.

⑨ Click to select the file types you want to back up (☐ changes to ☑).

This example shows selecting Pictures, Music, and E-mail.

⑩ Click Next to continue.

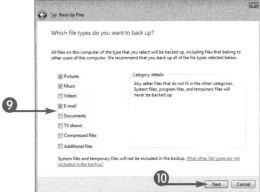

I often forget to run daily backups manually. Should I let Windows do it daily?

▼ Yes, in fact that is the preferred choice of systems administrators. Daily backups ensure the data is backed up every day so that you can restore it if your system has a problem. By doing it every day, you minimize the loss of time you would incur re-creating important files. Also by having Backup perform the daily backups automatically, you ensure that all the data you want backed up is actually backed up each time. You do not, for example, have to remember each day if you backed up your documents, graphics, or system files the day before.

I do not have any important files on my computer. Why should I back them up?

▼ Backing up is a personal choice for your own personal documents. For networks and many organizations, creating backups is a required loss-prevention and security procedure. Businesses rely on computer data for much of their daily work. The data on you computer, if you are in a company environment, probably belongs to the company. The company does not want to pay you to re-create loads of data each time the data is lost. You should back up any files you do not want to, or cannot, re-create, including databases, customer lists, accounting files, and customer correspondence.

continued

Back Up and Restore Data *(Continued)*

The Backup Status and Configuration program enables you to restore data to a different location if necessary. You might restore to a different location if you want to keep any existing data that happens to be in the backup data original location. After the data is restored to a different location, such as to a temporary folder, you can then copy any data from the restore directory back to its original location if you want it there. One of the main reasons to restore to a different location is if the data in the original location has changed since your backup set was made, and you need to retain this changed data.

For example, you may have a folder in which a customer relationship database is stored. You work in this database every day and your backup is created at midnight every night. That means if you restore your backup set after you start work one morning, all changes to the database you have made will be lost. Instead, restore to a different location and examine the data before copying to the original location. Of course, if the data in your original location is corrupt beyond repair, your best bet is to restore to the original location.

Back Up and Restore Data *(continued)*

The How often do you want to create a backup? screen appears.

⑪ Click the How often down arrow and select the frequency by which you want to back up the files.

⑫ Click the What day down arrow and select which day to run the backup.

⑬ Click the What time down arrow and select the time of day to run the backup.

⑭ Click Save settings and start backup.

● After the backup job finishes, the Backup Status and Configuration window appears.

Look in the Backup status section for the status of your backup job.

⑮ To change a backup setting, click Change backup settings.

The Back Up Files Wizard appears.

⑯ Follow the prompts to set the backup location, file types, and frequency.

⑰ Click the Close box when done.

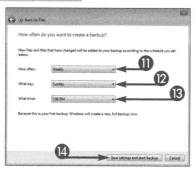

The Backup Status and
Configuration window appears.

⑱ Click Complete PC Backup.

The Windows Complete PC Backup
window appears.

⑲ Click Create a backup now.

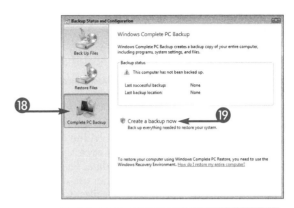

The Where do you want to save the
backup? window appears.

⑳ Select a drive where you want the
backup to be saved (○ changes
to ◉).

㉑ Click Next to continue.

**When I restore a backup file, what
happens to any data that is still on my
disk?**

▼ During restore, if you chose the Advanced
Restore method, you have the choice of
leaving existing files and just adding the
ones on the restore disk to them, replacing
existing files if they are older than the ones
on the restore disk, or replacing existing
files. If you are looking to rebuild a
computer due to a catastrophic loss or
possible virus infection, the last option is
the best. However, if you want to compare
files on the restore disk to ones still on
your system, choose the first one.

Where should I store my backup files?

▼ The best place to store backup files is in a
place where they cannot be damaged or
stolen. Many times users create daily
backups to media that they store locally,
such as in a locked cabinet or file box.
Then, once a week another backup is
made that includes all changes made
during the course of the week. This
backup, usually burned to DVD-R or CD-R,
is carried off-site and stored in a safe place.

Before taking private or confidential data
from your company, however, ask your
system administrator or manager if privacy
concerns restrict this type of activity. By
having a backup off-site, you can restore
the data in the event your on-site backup
is destroyed or stolen.

PART VI

continued

Back Up and Restore Data *(Continued)*

In the event of a disaster or data loss, you need to restore your backup files. Windows Vista enables you to restore files you backed up. This is done by using the Restore Files tool on the Backup Status and Configuration window and accessing the media on which you backed up your data. Files you back up using the Back Up Files tool can use disks, discs, or network locations to store the files. Complete PC Backups can be saved to bootable media, such as disks or removable disks, for example, CD-ROM or DVD discs.

When you run the Restore Files tool, you have the option of restoring files that were backed up on your

computer, or by using the Advanced Restore feature, you can restore files that were originally backed up from another computer. If you want to restore your computer back to a previous time, such as before a virus problem or system failure, restore the backup to its original location. This copies the backup data over any data that currently resides in the original location. On the other hand, you might choose to restore to a different location from the original if you want to examine the backup files without overwriting your current data.

Back Up and Restore Data *(continued)*

The Confirm your backup settings window appears.

㉒ Click Start backup.

The backup starts. When the backup is finished, the Backup Status and Configuration window appears.

Restore Files

① Click Restore Files.

The Restore Files part of the Backup Status and Configuration window appears.

② Click Restore files.

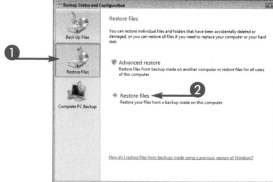

The What do you want to restore? window appears.

③ Click an option to select Files from the latest backup or Files from an older backup.

④ Click Next to continue.

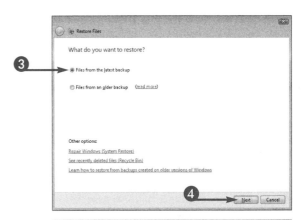

The Select the files and folders to restore window appears.

⑤ Select the files to restore.

⑥ Click Next.

Windows restores your files.

What are some of the types of files that I should back up on a regular basis?

▼ Some of the files you may want to back up on a regular schedule include important files, such as:

- Bank statements
- Digital pictures and videos
- Windows system files
- E-mail addresses
- E-mail messages
- Internet or network connection settings
- Music files
- Internet Explorer bookmarks
- Office templates and clip art
- Offline Web pages
- Personal financial files

On one of our computers, the Restore security settings option is not available during the Restore process. Why not?

▼ For this option to be available the operating system must be set up as an NTFS file system, not a FAT file system. You can restore the files to a FAT file system, but you just will not be able to restore the files with the Restore security settings. After you restore your files to the drive that has the FAT file system, consider converting the file system to the NTFS file system.

Work with Wireless Networks

I f you have a wireless network transmitter as part of your home network, or if you are using a wireless network at work or in a public location such as an airport, a convention center, or a café, you can easily locate wireless networks in your area.

You must have a wireless networking adapter either built in or installed as an adapter card or a Personal Computer Memory Card International Association (PCMCIA) card. The standard protocols for running wireless networking are Institute of Electrical and Electronics Engineers (IEEE) 802.11x protocols. The most common variants that you may encounter are 802.11b, the older but broadly available protocol,

running at speeds of 5.5 or 11 Mbps, and 802.11g, newer and backwardly compatible with 802.11b, running at speeds up to 54 Mbps. The 802.11n has recently been announced, which will combine many of the earlier specifications into one and be part of hardware devices.

If you have a wireless adapter installed in your PC but have not yet connected to your home or business wireless network, you see a wireless networking icon in the notification bar with a red X covering it indicating that your wireless adapter is up and running but not connected to a network.

Work with Wireless Networks

① Right-click the wireless networking icon.

② Click Connect to a network from the menu that appears.

The Select a network to connect to window appears.

③ Click your wireless network from the list.

④ Click Connect.

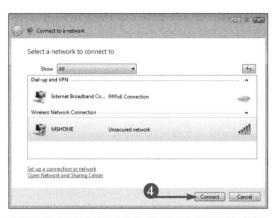

The Successfully connected to the network window appears.

⑤ Click Close.

The wireless network icon on the Notification bar shows that you are actively connected to a network.

I do not see any wireless networks listed. What should I do?

▼ First, confirm that your wireless network is up and running with another computer. If it is, check to see if you are close enough to be receiving a signal, 100% is optimal, by right-clicking the wireless networking icon. If you are receiving a weak signal, try to move closer to the transmitter. Another trick is to disconnect your wireless network adapter, if it is a PCMCIA card or USB adapter card, and then reconnect it to your computer. This forces Windows to look for the new hardware device, which in turn looks for any wireless networks in your range.

Are there ways to secure my home wireless network?

▼ Yes. You can employ a couple of different methods. One is the Wired Equivalent Privacy (WEP) method, which uses a network security key to allow users to access wireless networks. Another is Wi-Fi Protected Access (WPA), which uses the WEP key, but checks to make sure the key has not been tampered with. You also can hide your network name — service set identifier, or SSID — among other things. The techniques involved are beyond the scope of this book. Go to www.microsoft. com and search on the phrase "wireless networking security" for more information.

continued

Work with Wireless Networks *(Continued)*

After you have selected your local wireless network, you can click Connect. If you are using a home or business wireless network, it should be a security-enabled one. Otherwise, your network is open to anyone within wireless range of a transmitter. For more information on secure wireless networking, search on "wireless networking security" in Help and Support or consult your network hardware documentation. In most cases, you need to have the network key — usually a 64-bit or 128-bit WEP key — ready to access your wireless network. Enter the key and confirm to access your network. The screen displays dots instead of the characters you typed, as with a password.

If you are trying to access a more public wireless network, be aware that this is a more risky situation in terms of security. Before accessing a public network, make sure that you have your network settings configured for a Public network. This sets your Windows Firewall settings for maximum protection. To do this, right-click your wireless networking icon and click Network and Sharing Center. Click Windows Firewall, click Change Settings on the Windows Firewall window, and then click Block All Incoming Connections. Click OK. You then have additional protection against unauthorized access to your PC in a relatively unprotected environment.

Work with Wireless Networks *(continued)*

⑥ Right-click the wireless network icon to view your wireless network.

⑦ Click Network and Sharing Center.

The Network and Sharing Center window appears.

These icons indicate connection status and signal strength.

⑧ Click Manage wireless networks.

The Manage Wireless Networks window appears.

● Windows attempts to connect to these wireless networks in this order.

9 Drag a network up or down to reorder the networks.

● Windows displays an icon and the word *Move* to indicate you want to reorder the networks.

10 To delete a network, click the network to remove.

11 Click Remove.

A message appears warning you that by removing the network you no longer will have access to it.

12 Click OK.

Just how secure is wireless networking?

▼ Using the currently and commonly available hardware with 802.11b or 802.11g and WEP, wireless networking has distinct vulnerabilities. Vista supports the newer, more secure encryption protocol WPA that works with IEEE 802.11i. Hardware supporting this standard has become widely available, but you should still weigh the likelihood of unauthorized access — how close your transmitter is to public access — and the sensitivity of your data against the convenience and cost-effectiveness of a wireless solution.

My wireless adapter has separate software to access wireless networks. Which should I use?

▼ Any time a manufacturer provides software for your hardware device, defer to that software. This is especially true if the software is written specifically for Windows Vista. When you install the wireless network device and software is provided, be sure to follow the installation directions *exactly* as written. Often, users are in a hurry to plug in their devices, wait for Windows to set up the device, and then start using it. However, some manufacturers require that you first start loading software, and then plug in the network adapter.

Install and Use ClearType

You can take advantage of Microsoft's ClearType technology to make the text on your screen easier to read, especially if you are using a liquid crystal display (LCD) screen, such as those found on portable computers and flat panel monitors.

ClearType reduces the jaggedness, commonly referred to as *raster jag,* of screen fonts. By manipulating the brightness of individual subpixels in each character, ClearType makes the characters appear smoother. ClearType is effective only with color quality settings of 256 colors or higher. It works best with 24-bit or 32-bit color, High or Highest.

ClearType technology is at its most effective when used with a flat panel screen. Although it usually improves the appearance of screen fonts on traditional cathode ray tube (CRT) monitors as well, in some situations, ClearType makes the text appear slightly less well defined on this kind of monitor. Use the Standard method of smoothing screen fonts if you are using a CRT monitor and the text appears blurry to you.

ClearType comes already installed with Windows Vista. You can activate it or determine whether it has already been activated.

Install and Use ClearType

1 Right-click an empty area of your desktop.

2 Click Personalize from the menu that appears.

The Personalization window appears.

3 Click Windows Color and Appearance.

The Appearance Settings
dialog box appears.

● Note the appearance of the
  text without ClearType.

④ Click Effects.

The Effects dialog box
appears.

⑤ Click this option to choose
  the method to smooth text
  (☐ changes to ☑).

⑥ Click the down arrow and
  select ClearType.

⑦ Click OK.

● Note the improved
  appearance of the text.

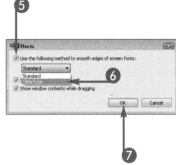

How can I make sure my display colors are set correctly for ClearType?

▼ Right-click any empty area of your
desktop. Click Personalize from the menu
that appears. Click Display Settings. In the
Display Settings dialog box, make sure the
Color setting is set to the highest one for
your card and monitor capabilities. The
greater the number of colors, the more
finely ClearType can adjust the screen
fonts. Choose the highest setting that
appears in your drop-down list, preferably
High (24-bit) or Highest (32-bit).

When I adjust my ClearType settings, can I compare samples side by side so I can pick the one that looks best?

▼ Yes. Microsoft has a ClearType tuner on
the Web. Start Internet Explorer and go to
www.microsoft.com/typography. Mouse
over ClearType in the left column and a list
of options appears. Click ClearType tuner.
Depending on your security settings, you
may be asked whether you want to install
the ActiveX control for ClearType tuner.
After the ClearType tuner is installed, you
can follow a simple four-step process to
make adjustments by comparing samples
side by side on your screen.

Configure Power Management

You can configure power settings for your portable PC from the Control Panel. Windows Vista provides a list of power schemes from which you can choose or change individual settings and assign a name to your own custom power scheme. You can also set low-battery alarms, view the amount of power remaining in your battery or batteries, and have your battery power display in the taskbar notification area.

To configure power options, display the Control Panel and click Change Battery Settings. The Select a Power Plan window appears. Select a power plan that applies

to your situation. Each plan has separate settings for AC and battery power if you have a portable PC. Each plan has settings for when Windows should shut down or hibernate; or put monitors, hard disks, and entire PCs to sleep when the system has been idle for so many minutes. The three types of plans are Balanced, Power Saver, and High Performance. The default plan for a laptop or desktop PC is Balanced.

You also can customize each plan to suit your working situation. For example, you may want to set the laptop displays not to turn off if you are giving a presentation in front of people.

---

① Click Start.

② Click Control Panel.

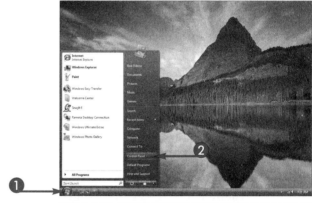

The Control Panel appears.

③ Click Change battery settings.

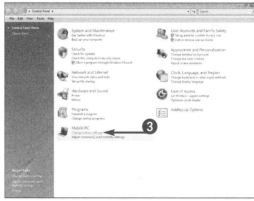

The Select a power plan window appears.

● These icons compare battery life to computer performance for each plan.

④ Click Change plan settings under a plan.

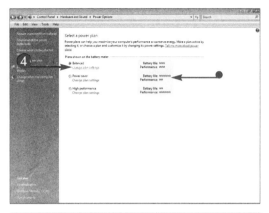

The Change settings for the plan: Balanced window appears.

⑤ Click the Turn off the display down arrow for On battery and select a time to turn off the monitor when it is not connected to AC power.

How do I keep my PC from turning off my monitor and hard disks too soon?

▼ You can either select a power plan that makes minimal or no power saving changes during idle times, such as High Performance, or you can modify a plan with very long time settings for the display and computer and save it by clicking Save Changes. If you want to keep the monitor on at all times, select Never from the drop-down list next to the Turn Off the Display setting. Do the same for the hard disk by selecting Never from the drop-down list next to the Put the Computer To Sleep setting.

How do I set options for the longest battery life?

▼ Click the Power Saver power plan from the Select a Power Plan window, and click to turn off the monitor and the computer for as little time as you feel comfortable with. For example, if you want the monitor to shut down if you leave your laptop for as short a duration as one minute, click 1 Minute from the drop-down list next to the Turn Off the Display setting. Do the same for the Put the Computer To Sleep setting.

continued

Configure Power Management *(Continued)*

Y ou can configure how Windows Vista manages power for a number of different devices and situations. For example, with the Advanced Settings dialog box, you can set Vista so that when you wake up your computer, the password screen appears. This is ideal for situations in which you may be pulled away from your office for a long period and your system goes into sleep mode. If someone besides you attempts to wake up the computer, the user will not be able to access your system without the required password. Without this feature, unauthorized users could gain access to your computer by awaking it.

Other settings you can modify include turning off the hard disk, but not the entire computer — CPU, CD/DVD drives, network adapter, and so on. This helps preserve battery life when your computer is idle or when your hard disk is not being accessed. You also can set power-saving modes for wireless network adapters, configure power button settings that you can control on your laptop keyboard, set what Windows does when you close your laptop lid, set search and indexing sleep settings, and set sleep modes when your computer shares multimedia files across a network.

Configure Power Management *(continued)*

6 Click the Put the computer to sleep down arrow for On battery and select a time to put the computer to sleep when it is not connected to AC power.

7 Click Change advanced power settings.

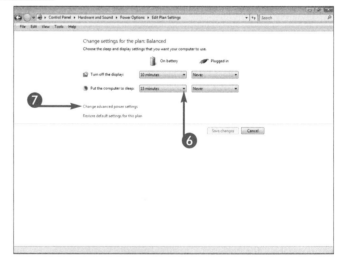

The Advanced settings tab of the Power Options dialog box appears.

This example shows how to set Vista to handle what happens when you close the laptop lid.

8 Click the plus sign (+) next to Power buttons and lid to expand the listing.

⑨ Click the plus sign (+) next to Lid close action to expand the listing.

⑩ Click the drop-down menu next to On battery.

A list of choices appears.

⑪ Click Sleep.

⑫ Click OK.

The Change settings for the plan window appears.

⑬ Click the Close box to close the window.

When the computer is running on battery power, the battery icon appears on the taskbar. You can see the percentage of power remaining if you hover the mouse over it; If it is running on AC power, a plug icon appears instead.

How do I see when my battery has fully charged if my PC is running on AC power?

▼ Click the battery icon on the Notifcation bar. This displays a small pop-up window with the status of the battery charge. A battery that is charged to 100% reads Fully Charged. When your battery is low, it reads Low and you may experience some performance problems until the battery is fully charged again. For example, low battery charge can cause the comptuer to run more slowly than normal, especially when you are performing CPU- and display-intensive tasks, such as Web browsing.

Are there other ways I can prolong battery life?

▼ In addition to the power options settings, you can dim your display — how you do this depends on your individual hardware; consult your PC manufacturer's documentation — remove any optional removable drives you are not using, and do not leave floppy disks, CD-ROMs, or DVDs in drives if they are not being used. Also, if you use your CD/DVD drive to play back music while you work, consider ripping the music to your hard drive and then removing the disc from the disc drive. If you have PCMCIA cards or USB devices that you are not using, remove them from their slots as well.

Configure the Power Button for Sleep Mode

I n previous Windows versions, you could configure standby and hibernation modes for your PC from the Control Panel. Standby mode would put your data into memory and put your computer into a low-power state without turning off the power. You could resume work quickly from this state. In hibernation mode, Windows would save your files and enable you to turn off your computer from there. For some computer users, however, hibernation mode did not work really well, and users could not get their machines out of hibernation without doing a hard reboot, sometimes losing critical data that the hibernation had not saved yet.

With Vista, Windows combines the standby and hibernation mode to give you the sleep mode. Hibernation is still available in the Advanced power settings area, but you may want to test it first before relying on it over the long haul.

The sleep power-saving mode puts your system into a standby status, saves all your data automatically to your hard drive, and, when you resume work, restores Windows back to where it was when sleep mode came on. You can set up your power button to put your computer in sleep mode when you press it.

Configure the Power Button for Sleep Mode

① Click Start.

② Click Control Panel.

The Control Panel window appears.

③ Click Change battery settings.

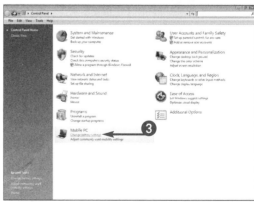

The Power Options window appears with Select a power plan showing.

④ Click Choose what the power buttons do.

The Define power buttons and turn on password protection window appears.

⑤ Click When I press the power button down arrow to see a list of choices of what Vista should do when you press the power button while on battery power.

⑥ Click Sleep from the list.

⑦ Click Save changes.

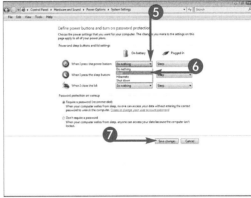

If I choose to have my laptop switch to Do nothing mode when I close the lid when I am running on battery power, could that run my battery down?

▼ Yes. You should avoid having the Do Nothing mode be the default when you close the lid or press the power button, unless you have sleep, or hibernation if that works on your laptop, enabled and have your power plan set to sleep after a brief period of idle time. See the section "Configure Power Management" for more information.

Can I switch to Hibernate mode with open applications?

▼ For the most part, yes. However, there is a practical limit. If you are using a network or Web application, although Vista attempts to restore network connections, it depends on network connectivity, and as a result, it may not preserve your state exactly. Avoid using Hibernate mode in such situations. Again, you should test Hibernate mode on your computer before relying on it for full-time deployment. Also, turn off hibernation if you plan to give a presentation with a projector using your laptop.

Set Up VPN Connections

Y ou can set up Virtual Private Networking (VPN) connections in Windows Vista that enable you to take advantage of existing Internet connections to a corporate network through a remote access server using encrypted transmissions. VPN connections enable you to work from a remote location and connect directly with the main network.

In preparation for setting up a VPN connection, you need to have all the necessary technical data from your network administrator, such as whether to use a Windows domain logon; whether to use a Point to Point Tunneling Protocol (PPTP) or Layer 2 Tunneling Protocol (L2TP) Internet Protocol Security (IPSec) VPN

connection; which user authentication to use; the IP address of the server; and so on. In most situations, the network administrator gives you very specific guidance about which options to set in order to ensure a successful connection. In some situations, you may need to obtain a different username and password from your administrator.

To set up a new VPN connection, use the Connect to a Workplace Wizard from the Network and Sharing Center. This wizard walks you through naming the VPN connection, entering your VPN connection IP address, and more.

Set Up VPN Connections

① Click Start.

② Click Network.

The Network window appears.

③ Click Network and Sharing Center.

502

The Network and Sharing Center window appears.

④ Click Set up a connection or network.

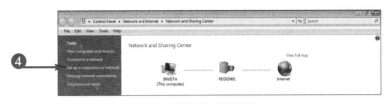

The Choose a connection option window appears.

⑤ Click Connect to a workplace.

⑥ Click Next to continue.

The How do you want to connect? window appears.

⑦ Click Use my Internet connection (VPN).

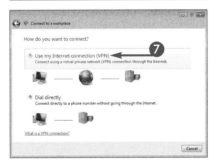

Is there another way to get started?

▼ Yes. If you have selected to have the Connect To icon appear on your Start menu, click it and then click Set up a connection or network from the Select a network to connect to window that appears. When the Choose a connection option window appears, click Connect to a workplace. This starts the wizard to set up your VPN connection. When you have finished using the wizard, you can select the connection by clicking Start, clicking Connect To, and then clicking your VPN connection.

Can I use a dial-up connection to get to a VPN connection?

▼ If you use a dial-up connection to establish your connection to the Internet, it may be possible to get to a VPN connection but it will be very slow. Talk to your network administrator about the availability and feasibility of a dial-up connection to your corporate network. Instead of using the Use my Internet connection (VPN) option in step 7, select Dial directly, type the remote access number your company uses for VPN connections in the Telephone number field, and continue filling out the VPN connection setup windows.

PART VI

continued

Set Up VPN Connections *(Continued)*

After you have initiated the VPN connection setup windows and selected VPN as your connection type, you are asked to specify a host name — microsoft.com — or IP address of the host server — four numeric groups separated by dots. Next, you are asked to give the VPN connection a name. This name is for your reference; it does not need to be a corporate Web site URL or network server name. This concludes the information necessary to do the basic setup for the connection.

When you have a named connection, you can change any settings required by your corporate VPN by selecting the connection in the Network Connections window, right-clicking the VPN connection icon, and clicking Properties. This brings up a Properties dialog box for this connection. This is where you need to follow the instructions of your network administrator to make the settings match your corporate VPN's requirements. There are five tabs: General, Options, Security, Networking, and Sharing. Most likely, any settings you will change appear in the Security tab, which contains ones such as data encryption, authentication, and sharing settings.

Set Up VPN Connections *(continued)*

After selecting Use my Internet connection (VPN), the Type the Internet address to connect to window appears.

8 Type the host name or IP address here.

9 Type a name here, for example, **Tidrow VPN Connection.**

10 Click Don't connect now; just set it up so I can connect later (☐ changes to ☑).

11 Click Next.

The Type your user name and password window appears.

12 Type your username here.

13 Type your password here.

14 Click Create.

The Connection is ready to use window appears.

15 Click Close.

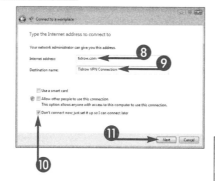

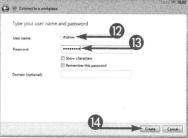

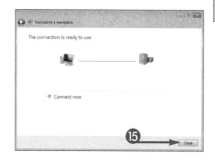

The Network and Sharing Center window reappears.

⑯ Click Connect to a network.

The Select a network to connect to window appears.

⑰ Click your VPN connection, for example, **Tidrow VPN Connection.**

⑱ Click Connect.

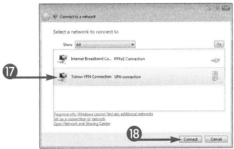

What is the minimum I need to know to get a VPN connection up and running?

▼ You need to know the host name for your corporate VPN or IP address, and authentication information — username, password, or SmartCard. However, your company may require you to have additional software installed on your local computer for security purposes. Also, some companies have created their own "kiosk" type Internet browsers that they require their users to use to access the VPN. These browsers usually have limited features to keep rogue users from accessing and damaging VPN sites.

Can I access my corporate intranet with a VPN connection?

▼ In most cases, yes. Your network administrator needs to assist you with the specifics for your intranet. Again, this may require a special Internet browser or specialized software to access the intranet. For example, your company may require that you install a VPN software client that communicates with a VPN software host on the company server. Although VPN connections are very handy for many corporate users, they can also open up security holes that malicious users can compromise for illegal activity, such as data theft, virus planting, and more.

Configure Offline File Settings

You can configure files that you work with on a network drive to be available to you when you are offline in Windows Vista. After you have modified a file offline, you can synchronize it with the one on the network drive when you next connect to the network. You can make any folder, subfolder, or file available offline, assuming you have the appropriate access rights on the network for that folder or file.

To make a file or folder available offline, go to Computer and select the network drive where the folder or files reside. Open the network drive and

locate the desired folder or file. Right-click the item and click Always Available Offline from the drop-down menu that appears. If you are making a large amount of data available offline, you see a synchronization window with a progress bar to indicate where you are in the process. When the process is complete, the icon appears with an added symbol to indicate that it is a synchronized item. You can elect to synchronize upon connection, or you can force a synchronization by right-clicking the item and then clicking Synchronize from the menu that appears.

Configure Offline File Settings

Make a Network Item Available Offline

1 Click Start.

2 Right-click Computer.

3 Click Open.

The Computer window appears.

4 Right-click the network drive.

5 Click Open from the menu that appears.

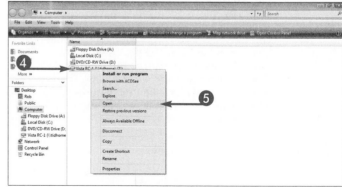

The folder for that drive appears.

6 Right-click the item you want to make available offline.

7 Click Always Available Offline.

After the synchronization processes, the Always Available Offline dialog box appears.

8 Click Close.

● The item appears with the Sync symbol to indicate that it is available offline.

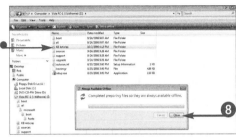

Synchronize the Offline Item with the Network Item

9 Right-click the item.

10 Click Sync from the menu that appears.

Is there any reason I should not make the whole network drive available offline?

▼ Yes. In order to make an entire mapped network drive available offline, the entire contents must also reside on your local hard drive. When the drives synchronize, every file is checked. Depending on the size and number of files, this can very time-consuming. Therefore, exercise discretion when you decide what you need to have available offline. Also, if you have multiple user accounts set up on your computer, you may not be able to make all users' folders avaiable for offline access.

Can I turn off the offline file feature?

▼ Yes. Simply right-click the item and then click Always Available Offline option again to remove the feature from the item. The icon indicating offline availability and synchronization disappears from the file or folder icon. You may want to do this if your suspect an unauthorized user is accessing files in this folder without permission and viewing them offline. This can happen in companies where contractors visit, connect to a network resource for a short period of time, download files from offline resources, and then read those documents when they are away from your company.

Use Disk Cleanup

Y ou can take advantage of Windows Vista's Disk Cleanup tool to examine a disk drive and remove old or unwanted files. This "housecleaning" process should be performed periodically and helps you avoid clutter and free up disk space. More free space gives you not only more room for new programs and data but it also allows your drive to work more efficiently and enables you to more effectively defragment your hard drive. See the section "Defragment the Hard Disk" for more information.

To launch Disk Cleanup, click Run from the Start menu, type cleanmgr, and then click OK. You can also find the Disk Cleanup tool in the System Tools folder of Accessories, which you access through the All Programs menu. Once Disk Cleanup is launched, you are asked to choose a drive to clean up. If you have one hard disk drive, it can have a volume name but usually has the drive listed as C:. Select the drive you want to clean up from the drop-down list and click OK. The Disk Cleanup tool scans your disk to determine how much space you can save and to group the files that are candidates for removal or compression into categories.

Use Disk Cleanup

1 Click Start.

2 Click All Programs.

Note: After you click All Programs, the name changes to Back.

3 Click Accessories.

4 Click Run.

The Run dialog box appears.

5 Type **cleanmgr**.

6 Click OK.

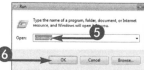

The Disk Cleanup Options dialog box appears.

7 Click Files from all users.

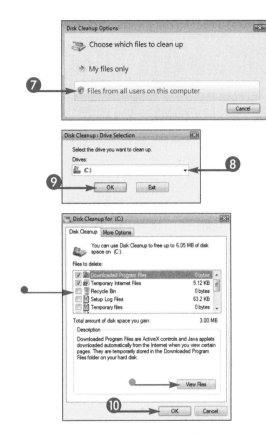

The Disk Cleanup: Drive Selection dialog box appears.

8 Click the Drives down arrow and select the drive you want to clean up.

9 Click OK.

You see a progress bar while Disk Cleanup scans your disk.

● The Disk Cleanup tool displays selected files as candidates for deletion.

● Click here to view the list of files for a selected category.

10 To delete the list of files suggested, click OK.

How confident can I be that the files selected are not important ones being deleted?

▼ Windows Vista has standardized folders for certain types of files that are necessary but inherently temporary in nature. You can confidently delete any files in categories labeled "temporary." For the Recycle Bin, it is up to you to make sure you have not recently made any accidental deletions. To double-check what is in the Recycle Bin from within the Disk Cleanup tool, select Recycle Bin and click View Files.

How can I remove programs that I no longer use?

▼ You can use the Installed Programs Control Panel applet to select and then remove programs you do not use, or more likely have forgotten you even had installed. You can use the Disk Cleanup tool to display this Control Panel applet quickly if you are already viewing the Disk Cleanup dialog box. Click the More Options tab and then click the Clean Up button. The Change or Remove a Program window appears. Here you can select a program and remove it.

PART VI

continued

Use Disk
Cleanup *(Continued)*

After clicking OK to delete temporary files, Disk Cleanup asks to you to confirm this and then proceeds with the disk clean-up operation. If you have deleted temporary files and compressed old files and still need more disk space or simply want to be more thorough, you can take advantage of some additional, discretionary clean-up procedures on the More Options tab of the Disk Cleanup dialog box. From this tab, you can remove Windows components that you do not use, other applications that you do not use, or all but the most recent system restore points.

Clicking Clean up in Windows Components takes you to the Windows Components Wizard. To add, remove, and change Windows components, see Chapter 3 for more information. Clicking Clean up in Installed Programs takes you to Installed Programs in the Control Panel. Check the Last Used On column to isolate possible candidates for removal. Click Clean up in System Restore to remove all but the last system restore point — avoid doing this if you have been having system problems.

Windows asks you to confirm the deletion.

⑪ Click Delete files to confirm the cleanup operation.

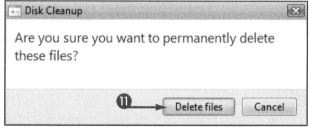

Disk Cleanup shows a progress bar to indicate how far along it is in the operation.

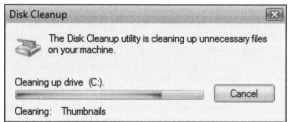

The Desktop Cleanup for dialog box appears.

⑫ Click the More Options tab.

⑬ Click Clean up to remove older system restore points, if you are not having system problems.

Windows asks you to confirm the deletion.

⑭ Click Yes to confirm removal of older system restore points.

⑮ Click OK to close the Disk Cleanup for dialog box.

If I click Clean Up in Windows Components, I notice that some boxes are already checked for removal. Can I rely on these suggestions?

▼ You should review all of them; they are only suggestions and you may intend to use some of the programs that Windows suggests. Some users think they should click all the options listed on the Disk Cleanup window. This may not be a good idea in all cases. For instance, you might use the Temporary Internet Files to help speed up Web navigations by caching downloaded pages in your browser. If you clean them with Disk Cleanup often, you will not have these cached files.

What are system restore points?

▼ The System Restore tool in Windows Vista keeps track of the system configuration at regular intervals and when you do something like make changes to system settings, update a driver, or install a new application. System Restore saves these snapshots of your system settings, called *system restore points*, so that you can "roll back" to a previous configuration if the new one makes your system unstable. You can also use the System Restore tool to create a restore point manually immediately prior to making a change such as updating a hardware driver.

Defragment the Hard Disk

You can speed up performance by periodically defragmenting your hard disk. The data stored on your hard disk is stored in blocks. If the blocks are *contiguous* as in all together, this occurs more quickly. If the blocks are not contiguous, the files are said to be fragmented. The Disk Defragmenter tool is a remedy for this situation.

Disk Defragmenter first analyzes the disk to determine whether a substantial portion of it is fragmented. If so, it recommends defragmenting. If the disk is not very fragmented, Disk Defragmenter tells you the disk does not need defragmenting, because disk

defragmentation can take a substantial amount of time — from several minutes to several hours — depending on the size and speed of the hard disk and the degree of fragmentation. If Disk Defragmenter recommends defragmenting, you can elect to view the report or immediately proceed to defragmenting.

To help keep your disks optimized on a regular basis, Windows Vista enables you to set up a schedule to run Disk Defragmenter on a schedule. For example, you can set Disk Defragmenter to run every Tuesday at 2:00 am, or the third day of each month.

Defragment the Hard Disk

① Click Start.

② Click All Programs.

Note: After you click All Programs, the name changes to Back.

③ Click Accessories.

④ Click Run.

The Run dialog box appears.

⑤ Type **dfrgui**.

⑥ Click OK.

512

The Disk Defragmenter appears.

7 Click Modify schedule to change when Disk Defragmenter runs automatically.

The Disk Defragmenter: Modify Schedule dialog box appears.

8 Click here to change how often Disk Defragmenter runs.

9 Click here to specify when Disk Defragmenter runs.

10 Click here to specify the time of day Disk Defragmenter runs.

11 Click OK.

The Disk Defragmenter window reappears.

12 Click Defragment now to run the Disk Defragmenter manually.

Note: *After you click Defragmentation now, the button changes to Cancel defragmentation.*

Disk Defragmenter will run in the background at the time designated.

13 When the tool is finished, click the Close box to close the Disk Defragmenter window.

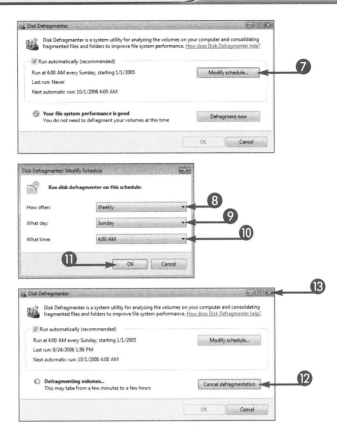

After defragmenting the disk, the Disk Defragmenter tool reports that it was unable to defragment some files. Is something wrong?

▼ Probably not; it is often the case that some files cannot be moved on the hard disk. These are usually system files that Windows determines are best left where they are. If a substantial percentage of your hard disk cannot be defragmented, view the report to determine the nature of the files. You many want to uninstall a program and then reinstall it after defragmentation to resolve the problem. In addition, if you have several large files, such as video files, that are several gigabytes in size, Disk Defragmenter may not defragment them.

How often should I defragment my hard disk?

▼ This depends on how full your hard disk is and how much data you save to disk. If you use your computer intensively, install and update programs frequently, or use large databases that you store locally on your hard drive, a good rule of thumb is once a week. Otherwise, you can get by with running Disk Defragementer once every month or so. You can also use Scheduled Tasks to set this to occur at regular intervals. For more on scheduling tasks, see Chapter 21.

PART VI

Set Windows Performance Options

Y ou can improve performance in Windows Vista by adjusting system properties that affect performance such as visual effects, processor scheduling, memory usage, and virtual memory. You must be logged in as an administrator to do this. To access these settings, right-click Computer from the Start menu and then click Properties. Click the Advanced system settings link on the System Properties windows. Click Settings in the Performance dialog box to bring up the Performance Options dialog box.

The Visual Effects tab enables you to make adjustments based on your priorities and preferences.

The pre-selected options on this tab are not very helpful: the default selection, Let Windows choose what's best for my computer, selects all visual effects, as does the Adjust for best appearance option. Going too far in the other direction, the Adjust for best performance option simply removes all the visual effects listed and makes your system look like prior Windows releases, for example, Windows Me. It makes the most sense to select Custom and clear any purely cosmetic visual effects but leave those that aid in using the interface. You can clear all effects from the beginning through Slide taskbar options, with few adverse effects.

Set Windows Performance Options

① Click Start.

② Right-click Computer.

③ Click Properties.

The System page appears.

④ Click Advanced system settings.

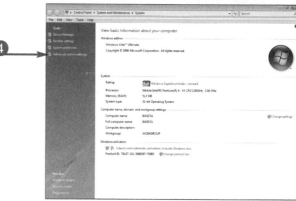

The System Properties dialog box
appears.

5 Click the Advanced tab.

6 Click Settings to change performance
settings.

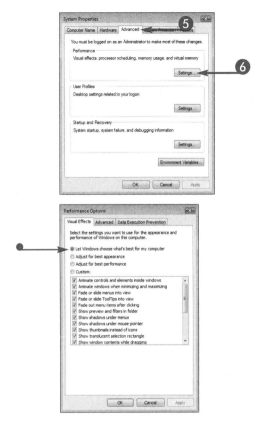

The Visual Effects tab of the
Performance Options dialog box
appears.

● The default setting enables all
Windows Vista visual effects.

**Do visual effects really make a difference
in system performance?**

▼ Yes. The amount of system resources
devoted to graphics can be high on most
standard computers. Some computers can
act sluggish just because the system is
trying to display stuff quickly on the
screen. One way to test graphics
performance is to run the perfmon tool
and compare processor activity when the
Show window contents while dragging
effect is turned on to when it is turned off.
For more on monitoring performance, see
Chapter 21.

**I find showing a shadow under my mouse
pointer helps me see the mouse. Do I
need to turn off that effect?**

▼ No. Keep whichever effects you find useful
but remember that you are making
trade-offs between visual appeal and
performance. Another trick you might try
to see mouse pointers better is to choose a
different background color, wallpaper, or
theme. For more on choosing Windows
themes, see Chapter 5. Some backgrounds
and themes make it easier than others to
pick up the mouse pointer color.

PART VI

continued

Set Windows Performance Options *(Continued)*

Y ou can make your own decisions about what effects to retain, but some suggestions are to retain those effects that aid in making the user interface readable for you and easier to use and to disable those that are essentially "window dressing." In the example that follows, screen font smoothing is retained because it makes the words more legible, and smooth-scrolling is preserved for the same reason — without it, scrolling lists flicker as they go by, making them hard to read. The last option is what gives the desktop the Vista "look and feel." If you disable this option, your screen will look like an earlier version of Windows.

Besides visual effects, you can assign prioritization of processor scheduling and memory usage. You can also adjust the paging files size for virtual memory. These settings are located on the Advanced tab of Performance Options. In most cases, you should select the Programs option for both Processor scheduling and Memory usage, and give priority to user applications. The Virtual memory setting enables you to adjust how Windows Vista behaves when it switches from random access memory (RAM) to virtual memory — which lets a large file on the hard disk be used as if it were system RAM.

Set Windows Performance Options *(continued)*

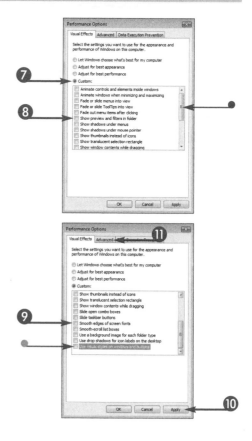

⑦ Click Custom to make custom changes (○ changes to ◉).

⑧ Click to uncheck the check boxes for cosmetic visual effects (☑ changes to ☐).

● Drag the slider to access options at the end of the list.

⑨ Continue to clear check boxes for any remaining unwanted visual effects (☑ changes to ☐).

● If you clear this option, the desktop icon label will no longer have a drop shadow. The Recycle Bin icon on your desktop, for example, is a desktop icon with a drop shadow.

⑩ Click Apply.

Disabled visual effects disappear, for example, no drop shadows with desktop icon labels.

⑪ Click the Advanced tab.

⑫ Click Programs to give programs
priority in processor scheduling
(○ changes to ◉).

⑬ Click Background services to give
programs priority in memory usage.

⑭ Click Change to change paging file size
for virtual memory.

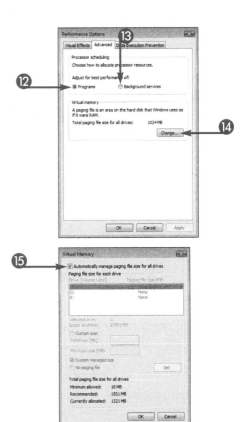

The Virtual Memory dialog box appears.

⑮ Click Automatically manage paging file
size for all drives to clear the checkbox.

Why should I select a different hard drive for the paging file?

▼ The default is the C drive that contains
your system. If you have more than one
local physical drive, however, you may get
performance gains by switching the
paging file to the other drive, assuming
your additional hard drive is as fast as your
C drive and assuming it has plenty of free
space. Do not use a removable hard drive,
such as one that connects via a Universal
Serial Bus (USB) port, in case you
accidently disconnect the hard drive; then
Windows will not be able to locate the
page file drive. Instead use a permanently
installed hard drive in your system.

Why should I change from having the system manage the size?

▼ If the system dynamically changes the
paging file size, it leads to system
slowdowns when the paging file is being
changed. You may also want to have a set
amount of hard disk space allocated for
the paging file for systems on which the
drive space is limited. However, if you
notice you keep running out of space on
your hard drive, purchase and install a
larger hard disk for your system — hard
drives in the 160GB range are reasonably
priced — than the one micromanaging
your paging file size.

PART VI

continued

Set Windows Performance Options *(Continued)*

You can set a custom size for your paging file to improve your system's performance when it uses virtual memory, moving from faster RAM to the virtual RAM of hard disk access. After selecting the drive, click Custom size. Check to see your system's current Recommended size. A good rule of thumb is to double that number and type the larger number in both the Initial and Maximum size fields. Next, click Set to change the paging file size. The new size in MB (megabytes) appears to the right of the drive letter and volume label. Click OK and a

message appears letting you know that these changes to virtual memory will not take effect until after you restart Windows.

After clicking OK to close Performance Options and again to close System Properties, a message appears asking whether you want to restart your computer. Click Yes to restart and have the changes take effect. Your new changes should help speed performance of your system. For additional ways to optimize performance, check out the Help and Support center and search for *performance.*

Set Windows Performance Options *(continued)*

⑯ Select a hard drive for the paging file.

⑰ Click Custom size to enter a custom page size (○ changes to ◉).

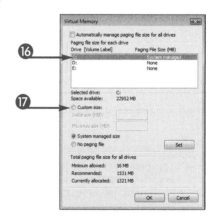

⑱ Type a new page size here, usually twice the recommended size listed below.

⑲ Type the same new page size again here, usually twice the recommended size listed below.

⑳ Click Set.

The new paging file size appears.

㉑ Click OK to close the Virtual Memory dialog box.

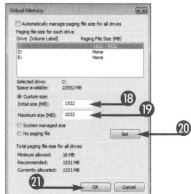

Windows reminds you that you must restart your computer for changes to take effect.

㉒ Click OK.

㉓ Click OK to close the Performance Options dialog box.

㉔ Click OK to close the System Properties dialog box.

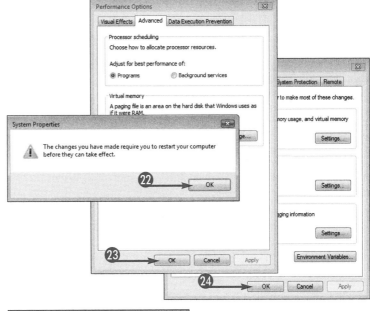

Windows says that to apply these changes you must restart your computer now.

㉕ Click Restart Now to do so.

My computer was much faster when I first got it. Why has it slowed down?

▼ Usually the reason for this is that you have gradually filled the hard disk with additional programs and data files. Many software products and hardware devices install small helper applications, often referred to as *applets,* that are loaded every time you load Windows. If you use the Windows Vista Indexing service to index your files, the system slows as your index database grows and more files are added to your system. Also, you may want to run Windows Defender daily to keep malware from slowing down your computer.

What can I do to reduce the number of extra programs?

▼ The safest way is to use the Installed Programs feature of the Control Panel to review your programs and uninstall and remove any that you do not use. See Chapter 3 for more on adding, removing, and changing Windows components. You also can use the uninstall programs that are packaged with many programs you want to remove. Usually you can find these uninstall programs on the Start menu subfolder in which the program is stored.

Common Troubleshooting Steps

Although Windows Vista went through a lengthy and widespread testing phase — more than five years in development and millions of beta testers — it is not immune to problems. When problems arise, you want to be able to fix them quickly, without losing critical data and important files. A good way to minimize downtime and data loss is to have a troubleshooting checklist you can depend on during times of crisis.

One of the first things you should do if you experience a problem is to write down all error messages that appear. The programmers of Windows and other programs have included these error messages to provide feedback to users like you and to technical support persons. Some error messages are so generic that they may be of little help to you. Others, however, are specific to the problem, and provide error code numbers to help you research and fix the problem.

Examples of how to diagnose and fix problems with your computer, as well as how to deal with common Windows Vista troubleshooting situations, will be useful.

Common Troubleshooting Steps

Diagnose Hardware Problems

1. After a hardware problem occurs, click Start.

2. Right-click Computer.

3. Click Properties from the menu that appears.

The System window appears.

4. Click Device Manager.

The Device Manager appears, with a list of all the hardware devices on your computer. Devices that are not working correctly show up with a red X or yellow exclamation point.

⑤ Double-click a device that is showing a problem.

The Properties dialog box for the device, a modem in this example, appears.

● The Device status area usually provides enough information to start diagnosing the problem.

⑥ Click the General tab.

⑦ Click Reinstall Driver.

● In this example, Reinstall Driver appears to help the user fix the problem.

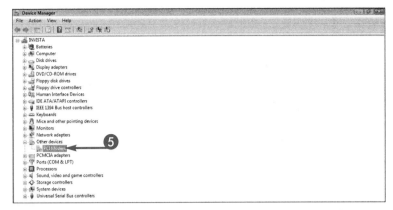

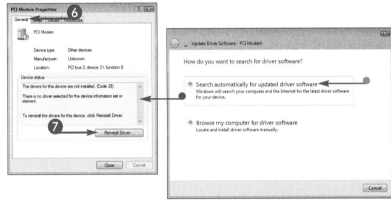

How can I document the problem in writing?

▼ You can document your troubleshooting problem in Notepad by clicking Edit and then clicking Time/Date from the drop-down menu. The current time and date will appear at the top of the document. Type a description of the problem. Then save the document to your Documents folder.

Are there any utilities provided with Windows Vista that I can use for troubleshooting problems?

▼ Yes, in fact, several tools exist. The following is a list of those utilities:

System Information

System Restore

Device Manager

Event Viewer

Windows Task Manager

Check Disk

I have access to the Internet with another computer. Which sites should I visit for troubleshooting advice?

▼ A number of Web sites, listserves, and newsgroups are available to help you during those times when Windows Vista is failing. One of the first places you should consider visiting is the Microsoft Vista Help and Support site. For more information, see the section "Find Help on a Topic." In addition, you can find a large number of support documents in the Microsoft Knowledge Base. Go to www.support.com and click Search Knowledge Base. You can read article abstracts and click the link to read the entire article. See the section "Search the Microsoft Support Knowledge Base" for more information.

PART VI

Find Help on a Topic

You can get help on a given topic from the Start menu. The Start menu has a Help and Support option that takes you to the Help and Support tool. This is a centralized location for help, technical support, and training for Windows Vista. Many computer manufacturers customize the Start menu to include their own support information about the products installed on your computer. Consequently, you may see additional manufacturer support information or a slightly different organization of the Help and Support tool information. The Help

and Support tool enables you to look for a Help topic from a list of categories, search for a topic using a text search, get online support or Remote Assistance, or perform some common tasks with help as you go.

From the Help and Support tool, you can go back and forth between topics you have recently viewed. If you cannot find what you are looking for in the list of topics, you can use the Search feature to find what you need. If the Help and Support tool lacks the troubleshooting information you need, click the Get Online Help.

---

① Click Start.

② Click Help and Support.

The Find an answer page of the Windows Help and Support window appears.

③ Click Windows Basics from the Find an answer section.

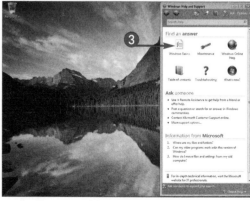

The Windows Basics screen appears.

④ Scroll down the list of help topics.

⑤ Click Getting help under the Help and support category.

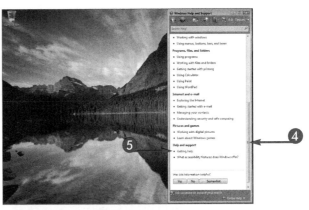

A list of tips for using Help appears in the right column.

⑥ Click a link in the In this article section.

● The section you click appears.

What if I cannot find the topic I need in the list displayed?

▼ You can type any word or phrase in the Search Help box and press Enter to search through the Help topics, or you can click the Table of Contents icon at the top of the Windows Help and Support window and then begin clicking categories to find a topic in the Help index.

How can I make the Help screen text larger to make it easier to read?

▼ Click Options on the Windows Help and Support window. From the submenu that appears, click Text Size and then click a size larger than the current setting, such as Larger or Largest.

Can I get additional topics and articles online?

▼ Yes. One of the main upgrades for Vista's Help and Support tool is the online help feature. Help and Support has the Get Online Help and Get Offline Help options. You can use the Offline Help option to have Help and Support connect to the Windows Online Help Internet site to enable you to post questions to Windows communities for help and to perform other help tasks. To change to the Get Online Help option, open the Windows Help and Support tool. At the bottom of the window, click Online Help and then click Get Online Help.

Fix a Problem with Troubleshooting Articles

If your computer is not operating quite as expected, use the Windows Vista troubleshooting articles to help you fix Windows. Windows Vista's troubleshooting articles work to locate the problem by process of elimination, asking you along the way if your problem has been solved, and giving you the chance to try the next item or skip it and try something else.

Sometimes articles can perform the necessary diagnostic procedures on your computer via software and inform you directly how to resolve the problem. Depending on the nature and severity of the problem,

you may want to have a pen and paper ready to write down specific technical information, especially if you are not able to use a printer to make hard copies of this type of information. In addition, it is a good idea to have your Windows Vista disks and any hardware installation disks at the ready.

You also can use the interactive features of Windows Help and Support to find out solutions to fixing problems. Click the Windows Communities link under the Ask Someone section to join online forums for posting and reading messages about Windows problems.

Fix a Problem with Troubleshooting Articles

1 In the Windows Help and Support window, click Troubleshooting.

Note: *To access the Help and Support window, click Start and then click Help and Support.*

The Troubleshooting in Windows help page appears.

Note: *The list of troubleshooters' entries may be in a different place in your list of entries from the one shown here.*

2 Click the name of the troubleshooting article you want to read.

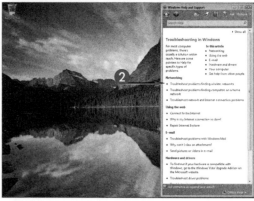

The screen with the troubleshooting article appears.

③ Read the article to learn how to diagnose and solve the Windows problem.

④ Click a link in the article.

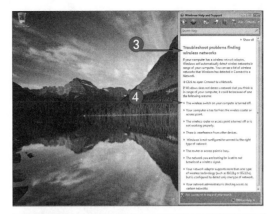

● More information about the problem and solutions to it appear.

Note: *You may need to write down settings or instructions during the course of a troubleshooting session. The articles let you know if this is necessary.*

Continue to follow the guided articles and procedures until you resolve your problem.

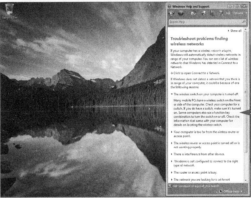

I do not know exactly what the problem is, so I do not know which article to pick. Where do I start?

▼ On the starting page of the Help and Support tool, click Windows Communities on the Find an answer page. Find a community that is similar to the problem you are experiencing and post a question to the community. See the next section, "Get Support Online from Microsoft," for more online help details.

The troubleshooting article says I may have an outdated driver for my hardware device. What do I do?

▼ Most hardware manufacturers have free, downloadable updates to their drivers to support the latest Microsoft system updates. Check the manufacturer's technical support page on the Web to see if such an update is available. Or click the Update your drivers link under the Information from Microsoft category on the Find an answer help page.

What if my problems require me to restart Windows Vista during a troubleshooting session?

▼ If possible, launch the troubleshooting article from a second computer and answer the questions for the first one. If you have access to only a single computer, the troubleshooter tells you to print out or write down where you are in the troubleshooter before it requires you to restart. Once Windows Vista restarts, retrace your steps to get to where you left off in the troubleshooting article.

Get Support Online from Microsoft

nother way to help solve your Windows Vista problems is to get help from Microsoft's online support options. Microsoft provides such extensive online support that it can be overwhelming. This also means the information you need may be deeply buried. It is a good idea to familiarize yourself with how online support is organized, and the various tools it offers, so that you can find the information efficiently when you need it.

You can get your online support in whichever way best suits your needs and preferences. You can read how-to articles that have been grouped in categories,

post questions to a Windows community, such as an electronic bulletin board, or ask a technical support professional direct questions through the Microsoft Online Help and Support Web site. You can get help via e-mail, chat, telephone, or Remote Assistance where the technician takes control of your desktop and works through the solution with you as if he or she were there. Articles and downloads are free, as are most types of upgrade and installation support. You may be charged for some types of additional online and telephone support, but you are notified in advance in such cases.

Get Support Online from Microsoft

Find a Solution

1 In the Windows Help and Support window, click Windows Online Help and Support.

Note: To access the Help and Support window, click Start and then click Help and Support.

The Windows Vista Help and Support page appears.

2 Click a topic that closely matches your system's problem.

The Microsoft Help and Support page for that topic appears. This example shows the page for getting help for music problems.

③ Click a link for a solution to your problem.

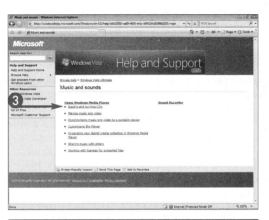

The page for the solution you selected appears. Read and follow the instructions in the solution page.

If I have a friend or colleague whom I know can help me with my problem, can they help me online?

▼ Yes, if your friend or colleague uses Windows Vista and you are both connected to the Internet, you can take advantage of Remote Assistance to use online chat, have him view your screen, or with your permission take over your desktop. Firewalls and protected corporate networks can sometimes make this feature require some additional work on your part. See the instructions for the Remote Assistance feature for more details. See Chapter 18, "Working with Networking Services," for more information on using Remote Assistance.

What if I have questions that are not on these Web pages?

▼ You can find an enormous amount of information by using search tools found on the Web. For example, go to www.google.com and enter a search string of the problem. If you are searching for a problem ripping music in Windows Media Player 11, you would use a search similar to "Media Player 11" AND "rip". Press Enter to see the results. More times than not, you will find the answer you need from somone on the Internet.

continued

Get Support Online from Microsoft *(Continued)*

When you have reached Microsoft Vista's Help and Support home page, you can select different categories of Vista and find help for your problem. Checking online support is also the best way to get the latest information about updates and service packs. Periodically check the Help and Support home page at Microsoft to keep yourself up-to-date on Windows Vista.

The Help and Support home page for Windows Vista also has a section called Expert Advice that provides articles on timely issues, such as searching, security, and other items. The best way to make sure you have

the most current security updates is to have Automatic Updates turned on using the Security Center. See Chapter 8 for more details. The Help and Support home page also has links to related communities, where you can discuss issues with other users in a moderated forum.

If the help you need is more specialized, such as if you are an information technology worker, you can also access the Microsoft Vista: Resources for IT Professionals or Windows Vista Developer Center pages. These pages have a number of links to in-depth articles about Windows Vista and related technologies.

Get Support Online from Microsoft *(continued)*

Find Help for Windows Version

① For help on a specific Windows version, click Browse Help.

② Click the version of Windows you have.

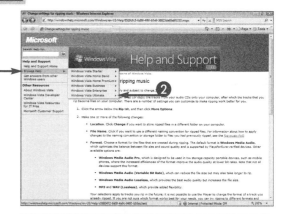

A submenu appears that includes help topics for that version.

③ Click a category.

A page appears that has links to articles about the topic you chose. This example shows Security and privacy help.

④ Click a link to an article.

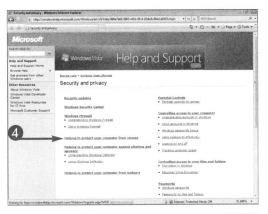

A list of topics appears in the Web browser window.

Can I get information about other Microsoft products?

▼ Yes. To get information about other Microsoft products, such as Microsoft Office Word, navigate to the Microsoft home page by clicking the Microsoft logo at the top-left side of the page and then clicking Support under the Resources heading. This takes you to the Microsoft Help and Support home page. You also can type in **http://support.microsoft.com** to get here. After you are here, click a product from the left side of the page. If you cannot find your product in this list, click Select a Product at the top of the page to show the Select a Product Solution Center page. It includes links to all the supported Microsoft products.

How do I search for articles?

▼ To search for articles on the Windows Vista Help and Support site, click to get to the Help and Support site. The Search Help For box appears in the upper left-hand side of the window. This box is on all the Help and Support pages, not just the home page for Help and Support. To use it, type a search keyword or phrase and click Go. A list of links related to your keyword appears. You can further refine your search to a version of Vista by clicking the drop-down arrow next to Edition and clicking your product version, such as Ultimate.

Search the Microsoft Support Knowledge Base

I f the help you need is more specialized, you can get help efficiently for your problem by searching the Microsoft Support Knowledge Base (KB). This is an extensive, indexed, frequently updated database of support articles from Microsoft. When you have a problem that you suspect is less common, such as issues with your particular hardware or software configuration, this is a good place to start to try to find a solution. KB articles often have practical workarounds as temporary solutions to help customers before updates and fixes are available. They also have detailed instructions for helping you recover from

hardware failures and data loss. You can access the Microsoft Support Knowledge Base from the Help and Support home page.

The Advanced Search feature has several useful options to help you refine your search in an intelligent and efficient way. You can efficiently limit the scope of the search to just one product, such as Windows Vista. If you select a product, you then have the option to perform a Filtered Search to look for only information about your selected product, or a Weighted Search that is weighted toward your product but also searches for related topics.

Search the Microsoft Support Knowledge Base

① Open Internet Explorer.

② Type **http://support.microsoft.com** in the Address Bar.

③ Click the Refresh button or press Enter.

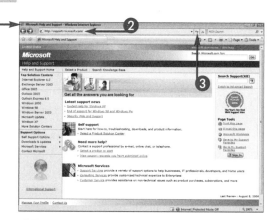

The Microsoft Help and Support Web page appears.

④ Click Search Knowledge Base.

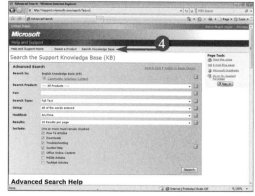

The Advanced Search screen for Search the Support Knowledge Base (KB) appears.

● You can go to a simplified search screen by clicking the Switch to Basic Search link.

⑤ Click the Search Product field down arrow.

⑥ Select a product from the product list, for example, Windows Update.

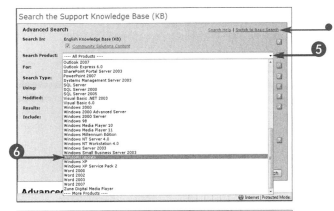

● The product you selected appears.

⑦ Type keywords you want to search for in the KB.

⑧ Click the Search Type down arrow and select Full Text for the most searches.

⑨ Click the Using down arrow and select All of the words entered to search all the text in step **7**.

⑩ Click the Modified down arrow if you want to filter your search based on how recently the article was added or modified.

⑪ Click Search.

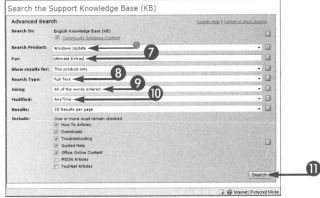

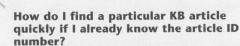

How do I find a particular KB article quickly if I already know the article ID number?

▼ Select Article ID from the Search Type drop-down list and type the article ID six-digit number in the For field. Click Search to start the search. Often you can find the Knowledge Base article ID from other sources, such as an online article, a posting in a Windows Community or other newsgroup, or a Microsoft support person. The reason IDs are used in these cases is so that if the article title changes, users can still find the article using the ID, which will not change.

I want to narrow my search to just printer problems with Windows Vista. How do I do that?

▼ Type **Windows Vista AND printer problem** in the For field. Select Boolean — text contains AND/OR — in the Using drop-down list. Click Search to begin the search. The Boolean text — AND and OR — helps refine your search to locate articles that include your entire text string. If you had typed Windows Vista OR printer problem, KB would have returned all Vista articles, and all articles with *printer problem* in them. That would be a lengthy list of articles!

continued

Search the Microsoft Support Knowledge Base *(Continued)*

When you have launched your search, you can select articles from the Search Results. Articles are listed with the closest match first. Scroll through the articles, reading the article title and summary to ascertain whether it is what you are looking for. The article's ID is listed in parentheses after the title. Click the title that appears underlined and in blue at the top of the article to view the article. Do not worry about losing your place if it turns out not to be the article you need; you can simply click Back to return to the Search Results page.

When you view the KB article, there is a section at the beginning of each article called "On this Page" with links that help you navigate to the part of the article that interests you. If the article addresses a specific problem, there are headings such as Symptoms, Cause, and Resolution, or Status if there is as of yet no resolution. If the article is purely informational and not problem solving, it has Summary and More Information. To print an article, click Print.

Search the Microsoft Support Knowledge Base *(continued)*

- You can click Back if you are not happy with the results and want to refine your search.

⑫ Scroll through the list of articles to find the one you think best suits your needs.

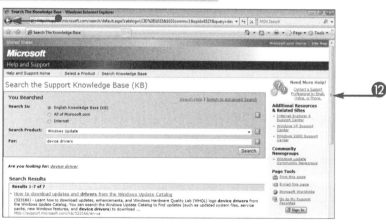

⑬ Click the title to view the article.

You can also right-click the link and click Open in New Tab to view the article in a new tab and to leave your search results in a tab.

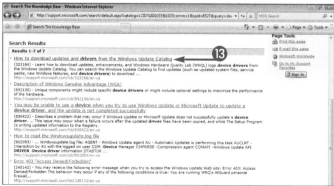

⑭ Click a link in the On This Page section to navigate through the article quickly.

● This is a handy reference number Microsoft and IT support technicians use. You can also check this area to see how recent the information is, or to see if there has been an update or correction to the article.

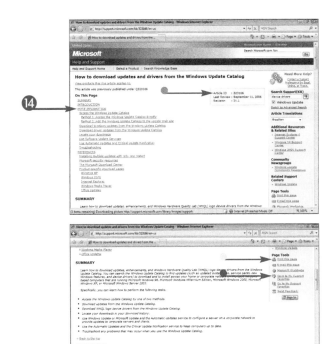

● The link you clicked takes you to the appropriate section of the article.

● You can click here to print the article.

● You can click here to add this KB article to your Support Favorites list.

What if I want to send this information to someone in e-mail?	What if I find too few or no KB articles to choose from?	What if I did not find what I needed in the KB article?
▼ Scroll to the right column of the page and find the Page Tools section. Click E-mail this page. Your default e-mail program as set up in the Default Programs Control Panel appears with the KB article name in the Subject field and a URL link to the page. Address the e-mail, add message text as necessary, and click Send. Ensure the URL for the support document is still correct before sending the message.	▼ You can click the Back button and refine your search. To broaden your search, make sure Weighted Search is selected as the Product Filter option. Take out any words that are not relevant.	▼ Scroll to the right and choose from one of the additional help categories: Contact a Support Professional by Email, Online, or Phone; Additonal Resources & Related Sites; Community Newsgroups; or Related Support Centers.

PART VI

Start Windows in Safe Mode

Windows Vista enables you to start in Safe Mode. One way to fix Windows Vista is to start it in Safe Mode because this mode uses only the basic drivers and software to get Windows running. You may want to use Safe Mode if you suspect that a specialized driver, such as one for a high-end graphics card, or application is causing problems. You can also use Safe Mode to find and destroy spyware files.

When you run Windows in Safe Mode, not all features are functional. One main component that is not functional is printing. Although printing is a critical

feature of Windows, Microsoft decided to keep it out of Safe Mode because so many errors are caused by the printing subsystem. If you want to print something, get Windows working correctly and boot into Normal Windows instead of Safe Mode.

Another feature that is not always functional is networking. You can start Safe Mode with or without networking support. You may need networking support to access critical shared folders while you conduct troubleshooting tasks. On the other hand, you may want to disable networking if you think Windows networking support is causing problems with your system.

Start Windows in Safe Mode

① If Windows is still running, shut it down.

② Restart your computer.

③ After the basic input/output system (BIOS) information, press F8.

Note: Let your computer run a few seconds before you press F8. You may need to press F8 a few times for the next screen to appear.

The Advanced Boot Options window appears.

④ Use your keyboard up arrow to move to the Safe Mode option.

⑤ Press Enter.

Windows boots up into Safe Mode.

Note: If prompted, log on to Safe Mode using your username and password.

● The What is safe mode? help article appears informing you that Windows is now in Safe Mode.

Note: The graphics are not the same as your normal Windows display settings, because Safe Mode uses the default standard VGA setting.

⑥ Perform any troubleshooting tasks you need to perform.

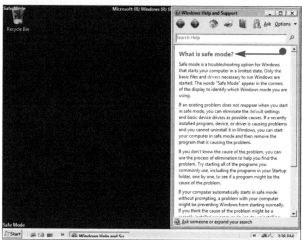

- For example, you can uninstall a program that may be affecting your computer adversely.

- As another example, you can reinstall a hardware device that is causing a problem.

Note: *Follow the steps in the section "Common Troubleshooting Steps" to access the Device Manager.*

- Devices that are not working correctly show up with a red X or yellow exclamation point.

Double-click a device that is showing a problem.

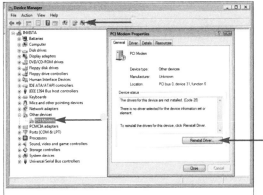

When I started Windows today, it said that it was running in Safe Mode. I did not specifically tell it to run in Safe Mode, so why is it running like this?

▼ For a couple of reasons. The main reason for Safe Mode to start after a previous shutdown is that a problem occurred during the last shutdown. You may not have noticed any problem the last time you shut it down because the problem may not have presented an error message. If your computer starts in Safe Mode, sometimes you can correct the problem by shutting down and restarting Windows. If you boot into Windows normally, then your problem was corrected.

I am in Safe Mode. Can I start Windows in Repair mode from here?

▼ You cannot start Windows in Repair mode from the Windows Advanced Options Menu. You must have your original Windows Vista CD to boot to Repair mode. See the section "Repair Windows" for more information.

Can I run anti-spyware programs from Safe Mode?

▼ Yes, and it is always a good idea to do so in the first place. In Safe Mode, fewer system and non-system programs run during startup; therefore, spyware tools, such as Lavasoft's Ad-Aware, can locate and remove more spyware programs that may be running on your computer.

Restore Windows

Windows Vista includes a feature that lets you restore Windows to a previous date. This feature is called System Restore. System Restore is handy if you accidentally make an incorrect change in your system Registry, a virus or spyware has invaded your system, or Windows just starts acting strangely.

You can restore your computer to a previous date, turning back all changes that have been made to the computer since then. The only thing that does not change is your data files, such as word processing documents, spreadsheets, photos, and the like. They are not deleted or lost during the restore process. Programs, hardware settings, device configurations, and Windows changes are all put back to the date you select.

System Restore can be one of your first troubleshooting utilities to help correct Windows problems if Safe Mode does not help. Although System Restore is not perfect, it is very helpful. One thing to keep in mind with System Restore, however, is that you must have a Restore Point — a checkpoint of your system — to go back to. If you ever turn off System Restore, all your old Restore Points are lost for good.

Restore Windows

① Click Start.

② Click All Programs.

Note: After you click All Programs, the name changes to Back.

③ Click Accessories.

④ Click System Tools.

⑤ Click System Restore.

The System Restore window appears.

⑥ Click Recommended restore (○ changes to ◉) to restore your computer to the latest restore point.

⑦ Click Next to continue.

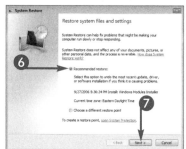

The Choose a restore point window appears.

A list showing available restore points on your system appears. Each restore point shows the date and time, the type of restore, and a description.

8 Click a restore point.

9 Click Next.

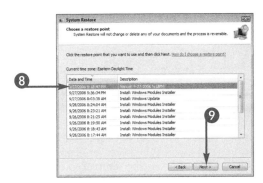
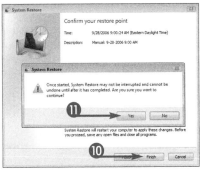

The Confirm your restore point window appears.

10 Click Finish.

A System Restore message appears asking if you are sure that you want to proceed with the restore process.

11 Click Yes.

Windows appears to freeze for a moment and then begins the restore process. Do not turn off your computer!

After the restore point is restored, Windows shuts down and restarts.

12 Log on to Windows.

Windows may continue the restore process. After it restarts, the System Restore screen appears.

13 Click Close when the System Restore process is complete.

I deleted a personal file and emptied the Recycle Bin. Can I use System Restore to get my file back?

▼ No. System Restore is not capable of restoring data files. As soon as you clear your Recycle Bin, your files are gone. If you have deleted an important file, think about implementing a backup procedure — unrelated to System Restore — to ensure critical data files are backed up so that you can restore them later if you encounter a similar situation. System Restore does not deal with data files because of security. Imagine that you delete sensitive files from your computer. You leave the company. The next person who uses your computer could, if System Restore restored data files, access those old files.

Should I create my own Restore Points?

▼ Yes. Any time you make changes to Windows or your computer, such as add new hardware, update new programs, or change Windows in a major way, create a restore point. To do this, click Start, click All Programs, click Accessories, click System Tools, and then click System Restore. When the System Restore window opens, click the Open System Protection link. The System Properties window appears. Click Create and type a name for your restore point, such as the current date or description of the changes you just made. Click Create. Windows Vista creates the restore point.

Repair
Windows

Sometimes Windows does not start or run correctly even if you have done a System Restore, or you may not be able to boot into Windows, in Safe Mode or Normal. During these times, your next line of action is to repair Windows. To do this, you need to use the setup DVD that came with Windows. If you do not have it, purchase or borrow one.

When you repair Windows, you simply recopy the original Windows files back to their default location. Sometimes this corrects problems you are experiencing if the original files have become corrupted or deleted.

One of the most interesting parts of the repair process occurs when you first start it. One option you will find is to repair Windows at the Recovery Console. You would think this would be the option to select. It is not.

Instead, you use the Recovery Console if you want to use command prompt utilities to work out problems. The one you may want to try is the `chkdsk /r` command. This runs Check Disk on your hard disk to find and repair — at least attempt to repair — problems with the hard drive.

Repair Windows

① Insert the Windows DVD into the DVD drive.

② Restart your computer.

As your computer starts, a message appears telling you to press any key to boot to the DVD.

③ Press a key to boot to the DVD.

You have only a few seconds to make this choice, so do it quickly.

● Windows prepares the setup screen.

A Windows Vista screen appears with options for setting up languages, time and currency formats, and keyboard and input methods.

④ Click Next.

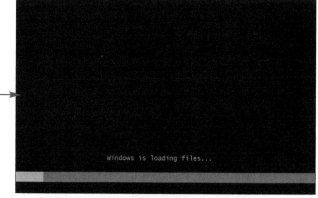

The Windows Vista Install now screen appears.

⑤ Click Repair your computer.

The System Recovery Options window appears.

⑥ Click Microsoft Windows Vista.

⑦ Click Next.

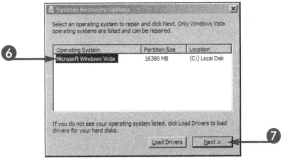

I have not deleted any files in my Windows folder. How can they be deleted?

▼ Viruses, spyware, also known as *adware* or *malware*, and even some legitimate programs can delete files. Viruses and spyware are created for one use — to cause problems on users' computers. If a virus can delete Windows system files, it will. In the case of legitimate programs, Windows system files can be deleted if the original programmer of the application is not careful in how he or she names and stores files. Other times you may install software not intended for Windows Vista, such as programs written for Windows 3.1, that may cause problems with Windows files.

Can I use my friend's copy of Windows to repair my version?

▼ Yes, but you cannot legally use that copy to reinstall Windows on your computer. In fact, because of Windows' activation requirement, you will not be able to activate that copy of Windows because your friend has already done so. However, to repair Windows, you can use a copy. Keep this in mind: If this copy is an Original Equipment Manufacturer (OEM) copy — it will say so on the DVD label — and it includes restore information for your friend's computer, do not restore your computer with that DVD. You may lose all your data or cause other problems to occur on your system.

continued

Repair
Windows *(Continued)*

When you run the Windows Vista recovery tool, you can choose to perform a number of different tasks. For repairing Windows, choose the Startup Repair tool. If you need to restore Windows using a System Restore setting and you cannot start Windows properly, use the System Restore option from the Choose a Recovery Tool screen.

In the event you have to restore Windows from a Complete PC backup you created previously, use the Windows Complete PC Restore option. See Chapter 22 for more information on creating Complete PC backups.

To check your computer's memory for errors, click the Windows Memory Diagnostic Tool from the Recovery Tools screen. This tool examines the random access memory (RAM) hardware installed on your computer and reports any errors it finds. This is handy if you determine your hard drive works properly but your system continues to behave erratically. Sometimes the problem can be a result of bad RAM that needs to be replaced.

Finally, the Recovery Tools screen provides an option to enable you to start your computer to the command prompt. You can then enter commands for diagnosing and repairing your system.

Repair Windows *(continued)*

The Choose a recovery tool window appears.

⑧ Click Startup Repair.

Windows searches for system problems. This may take some time, so be patient.

When problems are found, Windows repairs them automatically. The Restart your computer to complete the repairs window appears when it has finished repairing them.

⑨ Click Finish.

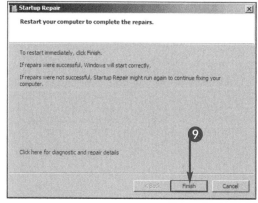

A window appears with details about the diagnosis and repairs.

⑩ Click Close.

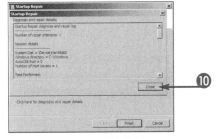

Windows shuts down and restarts.

Note: Your programs all remain intact after the repair is finished.

When I start my computer, I do not have access to a DVD. What should I do?

▼ Your DVD device must boot before your hard drive does, or you will not see the option for starting the computer with DVD support. You must change this in your computer's BIOS settings. Sometimes the option says CD support if your device is a CD/DVD combo device. To access the BIOS settings, boot your computer and press the keyboard combination to start your computer's system setup feature. Usually this means pressing Del, F1, or a similar key. Find the boot order option and change it so your DVD, or CD, boots first. Save the settings and then reboot the computer.

How long should the Repair Windows tool take?

▼ It depends on several factors, including the overall speed of your computer. Generally computers with faster processors, a large amount of RAM, and faster hard drives will not take as long as older computers. Also, if Windows locates a large number of errors, your system may need a lot of time to repair them. The best thing to do is to let Repair work and do something else until it finishes. Make sure, however, that no one shuts down your computer during the repair process.

Reinstall Windows

Y ou have tried restoring and repairing Windows. You have even called a technical support person who wanted to charge $80 an hour to walk you through the same processes you just performed. You now need to consider reinstalling Windows.

What is involved with reinstalling Windows? It depends on your approach. You can reinstall Windows to the exact same spot it was originally. If you do this, you must reformat your hard drive and lose all your data, program files, device drivers, and so on. Or, you can reinstall Windows into a different directory, such

as to one called VISTA02, and retain all your data files and any device driver folders already on your system. The downsides, however, are that you still need to reinstall all your programs into the new directory, and that you will have a previous copy of Windows on your system. Also, keep in mind you need at least 15GB of free hard disk space when installing a second copy of Windows on your computer.

You can delete the previous copy of Windows, however, when you get your computer back up and running. This approach is preferable because you will have your data files still on the computer.

Reinstall Windows

① Insert the Windows Vista DVD into to your DVD drive.

② Restart your computer.

A message appears telling you to press any key to boot to the DVD.

③ Press a key to boot to the DVD.

You have only a few seconds to make this choice, so do it quickly.

A Windows Vista screen appears with options for setting up languages, time and currency formats, and keyboard and input methods.

④ Click Next to continue.

The Windows Vista Install now screen appears.

5 Click Install now.

The Type your product key for activation screen appears.

6 Type your Windows Vista activation code in the Product key box.

7 Click Next to continue.

The license terms screen appears.

8 Click I accept the license terms (☐ changes to ☑).

9 Click Next to continue.

I get an error message at boot time that says Unmountable Boot Drive. What should I do?

▼ Use the Windows Vista DVD and boot to the Recovery Console. Click the Repair option. If prompted, specify the operating system you want to repair and enter the administrator password if requested. Type **chkdsk /r** at the command prompt to locate and repair any bad hard disk sectors. Restart the computer.

If this does not work, you can try using some third-party programs designed for recovering data from corrupt hard drives and repairing bad boot disks. Two excellent choices include GetBackData at www.runtime.org and Partition Table Doctor at www.ptdd.com.

You mention device drivers as a reason to install Windows to a new directory. What is the big deal about drivers?

▼ Many times when computer manufacturers prepare your computer in the factory, they make a folder called Drivers, INF, or a similar name. The device drivers in this folder are designed to work with the hardware devices — DVD drives, sound cards, network adapters, graphics cards — installed in your computer. If you lose this folder, you may have a difficult time locating all the device drivers for your computer. Even if you contact the manufacturer, it may or may not still have the drivers for your exact computer.

continued

PART VI

Reinstall
Windows *(Continued)*

The Windows Reinstall option enables you to set up an existing hard drive or set up a new one. When you set up to a new one, you must format the hard drive to accept Windows, your programs, and your files. It is easiest to do this during the reinstall process. Instead of choosing a hard drive that already exists, click New on the Where do you want to install Windows screen. You then set the amount of disk space to allocate for the hard drive and click Apply.

Next, click the Format command on the Where do you want to install Windows screen. Click OK when the warning about losing all your data appears. Windows formats the drive. Depending on the size of the drive and speed of your computer, the time it takes to format the drive will vary. For large drives, for example, more than 100GB, you may have to wait for more than an hour until the format finishes. When the formatting is finished, click Next to continue setting up Windows on this drive.

Reinstall Windows *(continued)*

The Which type of installation do you want? screen appears.

⑩ Click Custom (advanced).

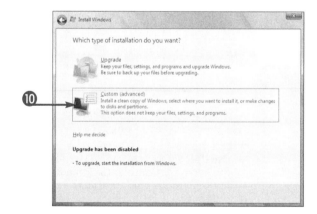

The Where do you want to install Windows? screen appears.

⑪ Click the hard drive on which to install Windows Vista.

⑫ Click Next to continue.

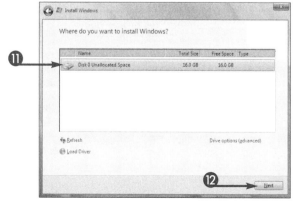

The Installing Windows screen appears. It shows the process of the installation.

As Windows installs, it will shut down and restart a few times. Keep the DVD in the DVD drive during this time.

You are prompted for configuration information, such as regional settings, time and date settings, and network information.

After Windows reinstalls, it boots to the log on screen, if a user password was set up, or to the Windows desktop.

At this point, you need to reinstall all your applications using the Add/Remove Programs icon in the Control Panel. Make sure your hardware devices are working. Test your sound card, modem, and so on. Then customize the Windows environment to your liking.

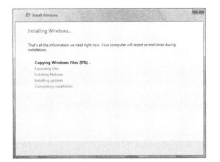

My computer cannot read from my DVD during the installation process. What can I do?

▼ One solution is to contact Microsoft or the place from which you purchased your copy of Windows Vista and ask for a replacement DVD. Sometimes you can get a replacement for a fraction of the cost if you registered your copy of Vista initially. Another solution is to attempt to gain access to your hard drive via Safe Mode or another method and copy the contents from the DVD to your hard drive. This can take some time because the DVD contains several gigabytes of data. Next attempt to start the installation from the hard drive in Safe Mode.

After I reinstall Windows, I cannot find my pictures that were there. Where are they?

▼ I hope you made a backup copies of these files before you reinstalled Windows. In fact, you need to have made a backup *before* your system went bad. When you reinstall Windows to get your system working again, you replace your old hard drive settings and files with new ones. Any data files on your system before the reinstall — including your photographs — are now gone. If you do have them on a backup, restore them to your system using the Backup Status and Configuration tool. See Chapter 22 for more details.

View System Health Reports

One way to keep Windows Vista running properly is to evaluate its health from time to time. You can do this by using the new System Diagnostics tool in Windows Vista. You can use the System Diagnostics tool to generate a report of your computer's hardware resources, processes, response time, and configuration details. The System Diagnostics tool is part of the Reliability and Performance Monitoring tool discussed in Chapter 21.

The System Diagnostics tool runs several checks on your system. You can get reports on the software configuration, hardware configuration, CPU, network, disks, and memory. The tool shows you system and application errors, the results of basic system checks, and details of resource utilization.

You should run the System Diagnostics tool periodically to get an idea of how well your computer is performing. One of the first things you might consider doing after you install Windows Vista is to run the System Diagnostics tool to get a baseline of your system. You can then use this baseline to gauge system performance against future System Diagnostics tests after you have used Windows Vista for several weeks or months.

View System Health Reports

① Click Start.

② Click Control Panel.

The Control Panel appears.

③ Click System and Maintenance.

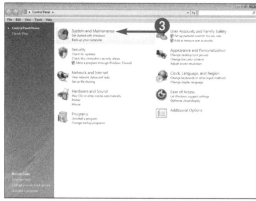

The System and Maintenance window
appears.

④ Click Performance Information and
Tools.

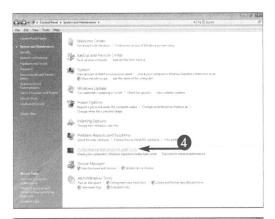

The Rate and improve your
computer's performance window
appears.

⑤ Click Advanced tools.

MASTER IT

**Can I run other programs while the
System Diagnostics tool runs?**

▼ Yes, in fact you may want to run several
programs as the System Diagnostics tool
collects data for the various System
Diagnostics reports. This way you put
Windows Vista to work as it's being
evaluated. You will get a truer baseline by
running programs and processes than you
normally would. For example, if you
normally have Microsoft Office Outlook
2007, Internet Explorer 7, and Windows
Photo Gallery open as you work, run them
when you start System Diagnostics.

**If the System Diagnostics tool finds
errors, do I have to correct them now?**

▼ No, but you should look at the errors and
warnings that the System Diagnostics tool
finds and consider fixing them soon. Some
errors or warnings result from an outdated
device driver, such as one for a sound card
or flash drive. Other errors or warnings
may be more serious, such as the Security
Center reporting a possible malware
intrusion on your computer. You should at
least make a note of these problems in a
document, or save the report to a file that
you can reference later when you have
time to fix the problems.

PART VI

continued

View System Health Reports *(Continued)*

If you are having problems with Windows Vista, the Warning section within the System Diagnostics reports may help you solve them. The Warning section includes two reports: the Error report and the Warning report. The Error report shows serious problems with an installed program, such as an application found by Windows Defender that may be malware. The Warning report shows potential problems that Windows Vista alerts you to that may need to be corrected at some time. In most cases, a warning does not cause Windows to stop working, but fixing the problem may avert a problem in the future.

When you run the System Diagnostics tool to view a report of your system's health and performance, give yourself some time to run it and analyze the reports. The System Diagnostics tool collects system data for 60 seconds, and then takes several minutes to generate all the data needed to compile the reports.

The System Diagnostics Reports window has nine main sections. The System Diagnostics Report section is the top section, followed by the Diagnostics Results section. These sections are expanded fully when the System Diagnostics tool finishes collecting data and compiling its reports. To run the System Diagnostics tool, you must log on with administrator privileges.

View System Health Reports *(continued)*

The Use these tools to get additional performance information window appears.

6 Click Generate a system health report.

The Reliability and Performance Monitor window appears with System Diagnostics displaying.

● The System Diagnostics tool collects data for 60 seconds.

The System Diagnostics Report displays.

7 Click an error to read more information about it.

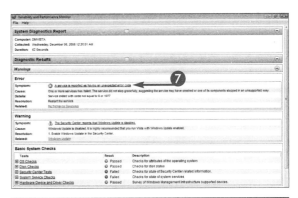

● The section of the report describing the error appears.

8 Click the Report icon in the Hardware Configuration section.

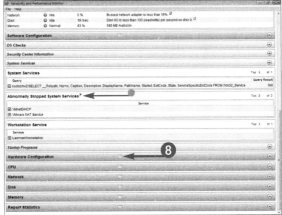

Some of the data in the reports have information such as HKLM\SOFTWARE\. What does this mean?

▼ When you see a path like that, such as HKLM, HKCU, and so on, you are looking at keys in the Windows Registry. The *Windows Registry* is the centralized database of settings and configuration data for Windows Vista. It has settings for almost everything that goes on in Windows. For example, when you install an application in Windows Vista, files are copied to your hard drive, but configuration data is stored in the Windows Registry. This data can include the size and placement of program windows, colors, and even sounds that play for a program.

Can I change Windows Registry settings if the System Diagnostics tool reports an error for a Registry key?

▼ Yes, but you have to be extremely careful when editing the Registry. You should first make a backup of the Registry files in case you change something in the Registry that makes Windows fail to work properly. In fact, a corrupt Registry file can cause Windows to not boot at all. To modify the Registry, you use the Registry Editor. Click Start, click All Programs, click Accessories, and then click Run. Type **regedit** and press Enter. To export a backup of your Registry, click File, and then click Export. Type in a name, click All under the Export range area, and then click Save.

continued

View System Health
Reports *(Continued)*

Along with the System Diagnostics Report section and the Diagnostics Results section, the System Diagnostics tool includes information in seven other sections. These seven sections display below the top two sections, but they are collapsed. You must expand them to see the details of the reports. To expand a section, click the title bar for that section or click the down arrow on the right side of the section. If the section is collapsed, click it once to expand it. If the section is expanded, click it and it collapses.

After you expand a section, you may need to expand subsections to see more details on a topic. For example, the Software Configuration Report section shows items such as operating system checks, system services details, and system services that have been abnormally stopped, such as through an application or hardware error. To see Security Center Information, you must expand that subsection.

Another way to navigate the reports is to click the Report icon on each section. This displays a submenu of all the sections and subsections of the reports. Click a link to the section or subsection you want to view, and the System Diagnostics tool takes you to that area.

A menu appears.

9 Click Computer Information to display the Computer Information data.

9

- The Report Statistics section appears with the Computer Information data viewable.

10 Click File.

The File menu appears.

⑪ Click Print.

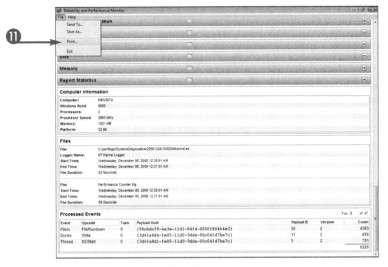

The Print dialog box appears.

⑫ Click Print to send a copy of the report to a printer.

Windows Vista prints a copy of the report.

Can I send a copy of the System Diagnostics report to my help desk person?

▼ Yes, but you must have an e-mail program, such as Windows Mail, configured on your computer. After you run the System Diagnostics tool to create your system's report, click the File menu. From the File menu, click Send To. A message window from your e-mail application appears, with a copy of the report attached as a hypertext markup language (HTML) file. Fill in a recipient's e-mail address in the To box and type a message in the message area. The generic subject "Emailing: report" is added to the Subject box. Click Send to send the message with attached report.

In the Error subsection of the Diagnostics Results section, I see a link called Performance Diagnostics. What is it for?

▼ Connect to the Internet and then click that link to see a Windows Vista Help and Support page that lists help articles for diagnosing performance issues. For example, a link to the article called "Ways to improve your computer's performance" displays an article that teaches you about different methods for improving Windows Vista's performance. The System Diagnostics report may also include other links to other helpful support articles and sites.

Save System Diagnostics Reports

After you run the System Diagnostics tool to gather data and compile system reports, you can save the reports to your hard drive or another location. This is handy if you want to keep a record of all your System Diagnostics reports to compare them later. Also, if you are responsible for gathering information about your system and reporting it to an information technology (IT) worker or systems administrator, the System Diagnostics tool is a great tool for gathering most of the critical information about your system. By saving the reports in a file, you can save them to a network server or intranet site, where IT workers or administrators can retrieve them for review.

When you save a System Diagnostics report to file, Windows Vista saves the information to an HTML file. It is a Web page that you can then view using Internet Explorer 7.

By default, Windows Vista saves the System Diagnostics report file to your Documents folder. You can save it there or select a different location from the Save As dialog box. Each report consumes about 3MB of space.

① Run a System Diagnostics report using the System Diagnostics tool.

The System Diagnostics report appears.

② Click File.

The File menu appears.

③ Click Save As.

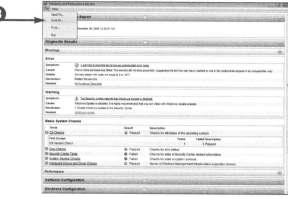

The Save As dialog box appears.

④ Type a name for the file in the File name box.

⑤ Click Save to save the file.

Windows Vista saves the System Diagnostics report as a file to your Documents folder.

The System Diagnostics report window reappears.

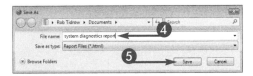

Can I view these reports in other applications?

▼ You can view the report in any application that supports HTML files. Of course, this includes Web browsers. However, many word processors, including Microsoft Office Word 2007, spreadsheets such as Microsoft Office Excel 2007, and other programs can display HTML files. If you try to import a System Diagnostics report file into one of these programs, you may not see all the data or it may not appear in the correct format. If this is the case, open the System Diagnostics report file in Internet Explorer 7.

The IT person in my office asked me to see which port my Internet traffic is using. Can I use the System Diagnostics report to find this?

▼ Yes, the System Diagnostics tool provides an easy way to find out about your computer's Internet traffic, whether it's inbound or outbound. Traffic is basically the data packets that get sent to and from the Internet using ports. To find out which port this traffic is using, click the Network section to expand it. Next, click the TCP section to expand it. In the TCP Outbound Traffic and TCP Inbound tables, look for the Port columns.

continued

continued

continued

continued

continued

INDEX

continued

You can master all kinds of topics visually, including these.

All designed for visual learners—just like you!

Read Less–Learn More®

Visual

Macromedia Dreamweaver 8 and Flash 8

ISBN-10: 0-471-77618-1
ISBN-13: 978-0-471-77618-5

Microsoft Windows Vista

ISBN-10: 0-470-04577-9
ISBN-13: 978-0-470-04577-0

3ds Max 8

ISBN-10: 0-7645-7992-4
ISBN-13: 978-0-7645-7992-9

For a complete listing of *Master VISUALLY*® titles and other Visual books, go to wiley.com/go/visual

Visual
An Imprint of WILEY
Now you know.